16738

7/94

Illness & Loss

THE LINKAGE OF
THEORY AND PRACTICE

WITHDRAWN

Clinical Sociological Perspectives on Illness & Loss

THE LINKAGE OF THEORY AND PRACTICE

Editors

Elizabeth J. Clark, PhD, CCS

Jan M. Fritz, PhD, CCS

Patricia P. Rieker, PhD

Associate Editors

Dr. Austin H. Kutscher

Robert A. Bendiksen, PhD, CCS

The Charles Press, Publishers
Philadelphia

The Charles Press, Publishers
Post Office Box 15715
Philadelphia, Pennsylvania 19103

Library of Congress Cataloging-in-Publication Data

Clinical sociological perspectives on illness and loss: the linkage of theory and practice/editors, Elizabeth J. Clark . . . [et al.].
    p.   cm.
  Includes bibliographical references.
  ISBN 0-914783-42-4. — ISBN 0-914783-41-6 (pbk.)
    1. Terminally ill—Psychology.   2. Sick—Psychology.   3. Death—Psychological aspects.
  4. Social medicine.   5. Loss (Psychology)
  I. Clark, Elizabeth J., 1944–
    [DNLM: 1. Attitude to Death.   2. Attitude to Health.
  3. Philosophy, Medical.   4. Sociology, Medical.   W 85 C641]
  R726.8.C57   1990
  155.9'37—dc20
  DNLM/DLC   90-1529
  for Library of Congress   CIP

Chapter 3, Changing the definition of the situation: Toward a theory of sociological intervention, was adapted from the *Clinical Sociology Review,* 1984 (2):51–63 by permission of the Sociological Practice Association.

Chapter 9, Thanatometer: A scale for the measurement of awareness and acceptance of death, was adapted from the *South African Journal of Sociology* (1986) 17(3):71–74 with permission.

Chapter 11, From the ivory tower to the hospital ward: A role analysis of the clinical ethicist, includes the ethics consultation form from Lutheran Hospital-LaCrosse, reprinted with permission.

Chapter 15, Ethical standards of sociological practitioners, is copyrighted by the Sociological Practice Association and reprinted with permission.

Chapter 23, Intervention for cancer patients: A clinical sociology approach to program planning, was adapted from the *Journal of Applied Sociology* (1984)1(1):83–96 by permission of the Society for Applied Sociology.

Contents

Editors

Robert A. Bendiksen, PhD, CCS, Professor of Sociology, University of Wisconsin, LaCrosse, WI.

Elizabeth J. Clark, PhD, CCS, Associate Professor, Department of Health Professions, Montclair State College, Upper Montclair, NJ.

Jan M. Fritz, PhD, CCS, Science Associate, Division of Cancer Prevention and Control, National Cancer Institute, Silver Spring, MD.

Dr. Austin H. Kutscher, President, The Foundation of Thanatology; Professor of Dentistry (in Psychiatry), Department of Psychiatry, College of Physicians and Surgeons, Columbia University, NY.

Patricia P. Rieker, PhD, Director of Psychosocial Research, Dana Farber Cancer Institute; Assistant Professor, Harvard Medical School, Boston, MA.

Contributors

Panos D. Bardis, PhD, Department of Sociology, The University of Toledo, Ohio.

James W. Begun, PhD, Associate Professor, Department of Health Administration, Virginia Commonwealth University, Richmond, VA.

Juanne N. Clarke, PhD, Professor of Sociology, Wilfrid Laurier University, Waterloo, Canada.

Norman A. Dolch, PhD, Professor of Sociology, Louisiana State University, Shreveport, LA.

Gerry R. Cox, PhD, Professor of Sociology, Fort Hays State University, Hays, KS.

Jack Ferguson, PhD, Professor of Sociology, Windsor University, and Associate Medical Staff, Harper University, Detroit, MI.

Tamara Ferguson, PhD, CCS, Adjunct Professor of Sociology in Psychiatry, Wayne State University School of Medicine, and Research Associate, Lafayette Clinic, Detroit, MI.

Suzanne Fleming, PhD, Division of Cancer Epidemiology, New Jersey Department of Health, Trenton, NJ.

Ronald J. Fundis, M.Phil, Professor of Sociology, Fort Hays State University, Hays, KS.

Elizabeth Gear, MA, Medical Department, Conoco, Inc., Houston, TX.

David F. Gordon, PhD, Assistant Professor of Sociology, SUNY Geneseo, Geneseo, NY.

Bernard J. Hammes, PhD, Director of Medical Humanities, Gundersen Medical Foundation, LTD., LaCrosse, WI.

L. Allen Haney, PhD, CCS, Professor of Sociology, University of Houston, Houston, TX.

Masako Ishii-Kuntz, PhD, Assistant Professor of Sociology, University of California, Riverside, CA.

Christopher Jay Johnson, PhD, Executive Director, Institute of Gerontology and Alzheimers Resource Center, Northeast Louisiana State University, Monroe, LA.

George Kabele, PhD, Professor, Postgraduate Medical and Pharmaceutical Institute Center for Preventive and Social Pediatrics Prague, Czechoslovakia.

Devorah Kalekin-Fishman, PhD, School of Education, University of Haifa, Haifa, Israel.

Avigdor Klingman, PhD, School of Education, University of Haifa, Haifa, Israel.

Nancy G. Kutner, PhD, Associate Professor, Department of Rehabilitation Medicine, Emory University School of Medicine, Atlanta, GA.

Elliot D. Luby, MD, Professor of Psychiatry and Law, Wayne State University School of Medicine, and Chief of Psychiatry, Harper Hospital, Detroit, MI.

Laura E. Nathan, PhD, Associate Professor of Sociology, Mills College, Oakland, CA.

Russell W. Roberts, MD, Private Practice, Shreveport, LA.

Dorothy B. Rosenberg, PhD, Department of Sociology and Anthropology, West Virginia University, Morgantown, WV.

Don Sabo, PhD, Professor of Sociology, D'Youville College, Buffalo, NY.

Luella D. Sibley, MSW, Private Practice, Shreveport, LA,

Roger A. Straus, PhD, National Analysts, Philadelphia, PA.

Acknowledgments

The editors wish to acknowledge the support and encouragement of the American Institute of Life-Threatening Illness and Loss, a division of The Foundation of Thanatology, in the preparation of this volume. All royalties from the sale of this book are assigned to the Foundation of Thanatology, a tax exempt, not for profit, public scientific and educational foundation.

Thanatology, a new subspecialty of medicine, is involved in scientific and humanistic inquiries and the application of the knowledge derived therefrom to the subjects of the psychological aspects of dying; reactions to loss, death, and grief; and recovery from bereavement.

The Foundation of Thanatology is dedicated to advancing the cause of enlightened health care for terminally ill patients and their family members. The Foundation's orientation is a positive one based on the philosophy of fostering a more mature acceptance and understanding of death and the problems of grief and the more effective and humane management and treatment of the dying patient and bereaved family members.

The publication of this book was supported in part by a grant from the Lucius N. Littauer Foundation.

PART I

Theory into Practice

This volume is the result of a joint effort of the Sociological Practice Association (founded in 1978 as the Clinical Sociology Association) and the Foundation of Thanatology.

Although the professional association for clinical sociologists has been in existence just over a decade, clinical sociology has been part of American sociology since the beginning of the field in the late 1800s. Clinical sociology refers to the application of a sociological perspective to the analysis and design of intervention for positive social change at any level of social organization.

Since its inception in 1968, the Foundation of Thanatology has been a leading advocate for the chronically and incurably ill, and for the bereaved. Its goals are the fostering of positive approaches to illness and recovery from loss and grief. It conducts educational, research, and practice efforts for the health care community and the general public.

This book is the first blending of the fields of clinical sociology and thanatology. Each has much to contribute to the other, and combined, they may lead us to an even greater awareness of the needs and problems of those who are ill, dying, or bereaved, and to a better understanding of how we may effectively address those needs.

1

Overview of Sociology's Contribution to Intervention in Life-Threatening Illness, Dying, Loss and Grief

Elizabeth J. Clark

The linkage of sociology and thanatology has had a relatively short history. Despite the fact that Durkheim wrote *Suicide* in 1897, as recently as 30 years ago the "sociology of death" was identified as a "neglected area of research" (Faunce and Fulton, 1958). Since sociology is concerned with social phenomena, there has been question as to whether death can properly be considered a sociological phenomenon. Vernon (1970: 3) contends that:

1. Death has many social dimensions;
2. Dying is a social process;
3. Death and dying are woven into all social systems; and
4. Social conditions may hinder or contribute to death.

In 1975 Pine noted the growing body of literature on the study of death from a sociological perspective, and described several major approaches. One approach entailed sociological studies concerned with the process of dying which focused on the social problems that dying patients face. Another approach focused on professionals whose work brings them into contact with death—physicians, nurses, clergy, and funeral directors. A third approach addressed the impact of death on society and emphasized reactions to the occurrence of death.

Fulton's groundbreaking work on *Death and Identity* in 1965, revised in 1976, used a sociological perspective to cover such major areas as theoretical discussions of death, attitudes and responses toward death, reactions to death, and ceremony, social organization and society. Also in the late seventies, textbooks on medical sociology began to include chapters on death and dying (see for example Cockerham, 1978).

Several major sociological concepts have had an important impact on thanatology and have contributed to the way we currently view life-threatening illness, death and dying, and loss and grief. Interaction, a key sociological concept, is one. Another is the "definition of the situation"—"If men define situations as real, they are real in their consequences" (Thomas and Thomas, 1928: 572). Others are the concept of deviance, and labeling or societal reaction theory.

To highlight the role that sociology has played in the development of the field of thanatology, some specific examples of the application of sociological concepts are given below. Topics such as illness as social deviance, the sick role, social role expectations for the terminally ill, social death, the social process of dying, and the social organization of dying and death are briefly reviewed.

ILLNESS AS SOCIAL DEVIANCE

The medical view of illness is deviance from the biological norms of health and well-being, and involves the presence of a pathogenic mechanism. The sociological view is that illness is a deviant social state brought about by disruption of normal behavior through disease (Cockerham, 1978). A distinction can be made, then, between disease, a medical entity defined in biological and physiological terms, and illness, a social entity defined in terms of social functioning (Suchman, 1965).

The sociological view of illness initially was formulated by Talcott Parsons (1951) in his concept of the sick role. The basis for the sociological view of illness lies in the sociological definition of deviance as any act or behavior that violates the social norms of a given social system.

Obviously, from the point of view of a social system, illness signifies disruption and failure to enact those social roles—familial, occupational, and other roles—on which the system rests. To bring the ill person from the sick role to previous levels of social functioning, therefore, is as desirable to society as it is to the individual.

The specific aspects of Parson's concept of the sick role can be divided into four categories:

1. The sick person is exempt from his or her "normal" social roles;
2. The sick person is not responsible for her or his condition;
3. The sick person has an obligation to try to get well;
4. The sick person should seek technically competent help and cooperate with the physician.

There have been numerous critics of Parson's model (see for example, West, 1989; Wolinsky, 1980). One frequent criticism is that the concept of the sick role does not readily extend to the patient with a chronic illness that cannot be cured, or to the terminally ill patient.

SOCIAL ROLE EXPECTATIONS FOR THE TERMINALLY ILL

The role of the dying patient is quite different from the sick role. Whereas Parson's sick role describes the behaviors a sick person should adopt in accordance with the normative demands of the temporary situation, the dying person's illness does not fit the pattern of a temporary condition allowing for eventual return to wellness (DeSpelder and Strickland, 1982). In our society, the social role expectations for the dying are not well defined. There are no clear behavioral prescriptions for appropriately bringing one's life to a close. It is likely that this lack of norms increases the suffering of the dying individual and results in some degree of alienation.

Once an individual is labeled as terminally ill or dying, there may be significant and negative consequences. For example, health care professionals may begin using avoidance techniques to distance themselves from the dying patient. In one study (Bowers, et al., 1964), it was found that nurses take longer to answer the bedside calls of terminally ill patients than to answer the calls of those who are less seriously ill. Health care professionals also may make a judgment about the patient's "social loss"—based on factors such as age, education, race, occupation, family status, social class, talent, beauty, and accomplishments (Glaser and Strauss, 1984). "Low social-loss" patients may receive very minimal routine care.

SOCIAL DEATH

Families and friends also may begin treating the person differently once it is determined that recovery is not possible. They may engage in anticipatory grief, which, if carried to extremes, can have a harmful effect on the patient.

Anticipatory grief refers to grieving that occurs prior to the actual loss (Lindemann, 1944). Many deaths that occur have been expected, and it is during this period of expectation that the potential survivor begins to experience some of the various responses to grief (Worden, 1982). This may serve a positive function for the family, but it can have negative consequences for the person who is dying.

Sudnow (1967: 74) describes the social death of a patient in a hospital setting as that point "at which socially relevant attributes of the patient begin permanently to cease to be operative as conditions for treating him, and when he is, essentially, regarded as dead." Kalish (1966) refers to symbolic or social death, and notes that once an individual is considered socially dead, the surviving family members can attend to other matters with more efficiency and with a reduction of affective involvement. He divides social death into two parts— when the individual defines himself or herself as dead, as in "as good as dead"; and when he or she is defined as dead by others. Kalish concludes that, most likely, the acceptance of such definitions by significant others results in a self-fulfilling prophecy and hastens the actual biological death of the patient.

THE SOCIAL PROCESS OF DYING

Dying is a social (interactive) process that involves numerous individuals with individual value systems and past experiences. Like individuals, societies have attitudes toward death which are reflected in normative practices.

While death has been a constant throughout history, there have been some notable shifts in the meanings of death (from the sacred to the secular), in the demographics of death (from younger to older age groups), and in the setting of death (from the home to institutions). Until this century, the social role of the dying person was more or less fixed by custom, but rapid social and techno-logical advances have largely eliminated the traditional role of dying (DeSpelder and Strickland, 1982).

Two of the most notable studies describing the modern day process of dying are those of Kübler-Ross, a psychiatrist, and Glaser and Strauss, sociologists. Kübler-Ross' (1969) pioneering work in educating hospital personnel about the dying has led to an increased understanding of the special needs of dying pa-tients. Kübler-Ross delineated five stages through which a dying patient may pass during the dying process: denial and isolation, anger, bargaining, depres-sion, and acceptance.

Although Kübler-Ross acknowledges that some persons may not experience all five stages, and that there may be some repetition of stages, the basic idea of her model is that there is a "typical" sequence. Because of this, her descrip-tive stages tend to be viewed as prescriptive, and health care professionals frequently interpret the dying patient's behavior in terms of these stages and work toward making them a reality. In this way, what the model supposes may become a self-fulfilling prophecy (Kamerman, 1988).

Charmaz (1980), in sociology perhaps the most effective critic about Kübler-Ross' work, maintains that Kübler-Ross' stages may be the consequence of institutional demands and staff needs, rather than the universal pattern of the experience of dying. For example, bringing a patient to the acceptance stage may make patient management easier and bring a sense of orderliness to the dying process.

Glaser and Strauss (1965) look at the dying process from rather than a psychological, perspective. They examined the int between dying patients and their families and health care st participant observations and personal interviews in several hospitals, Glaser and Strauss developed a typology of awareness contexts for dying. These awareness contexts all were derived from observing the social settings of, and the interpersonal communications about, death. The researchers noted that physicians were reluctant to disclose information to patients about dying and that nurses and other staff frequently followed the doctor's pattern. Interaction could be divided into four awareness contexts:

1. *Closed awareness*—the patient does not recognize that death is impending, although the staff knows, and family and friends may know.
2. *Suspected awareness*—the patient suspects that he or she is dying but has not been directly told by those who know.
3. *Mutual pretense*—everyone, including the patient, recognizes the fatal diagnosis, but all act as though it were not the case.
4. *Open awareness*—staff, family, and patient openly acknowledge and discuss the patient's impending death.

Patients may move from one awareness context to another (from suspected to open, for example) or may maintain one awareness context with family (perhaps mutual pretense) and another with staff (perhaps open). It should be noted that an open awareness context does not necessarily make dying or death easier to accept, but the awareness context is a crucial element in determining the interaction among patient, family members, and staff. An open awareness context will allow the patient to seek support, and may help to decrease normlessness and alienation.

THE SOCIAL ORGANIZATION OF DYING

The vast majority of Americans now die in institutional settings. It is estimated that as many as 90 percent of urban deaths, and 80 percent of all deaths occur in hospitals or nursing homes (DeSpelder and Strickland, 1982). Death has been displaced from the home, which had been the traditional site, to institutions that can provide specialized technological care. This displacement has contributed to the diminution of traditional death rituals. Death has become less visible in the community and more bureaucratized. Death in the hospital is not controlled by the dying person or the family, but by the physician, hospital staff, and others, who may not only define the circumstance of death, but also determine when death actually occurs (Cockerham, 1978).

As noted by Kamerman (1988), hospital patients are subject to two sets of forces: (1) hospitals are organizations and may have organizational goals separate from, and sometimes in conflict with, treatment goals; and (2) hospitals are bureaucratically organized and have characteristics common to bureaucracies.

The classic study on the social organization of death was conducted by Sudnow (1967). By utilizing participant observation in two large hospitals, he was able to describe how death actually is handled in an everyday setting. One principle of bureaucracy is the ordering of regularly occurring, and even extraordinary, events into predictable and routine procedures. The personnel in the hospitals Sudnow observed encountered death so frequently that their behaviors and tasks at the time of death became routinized. Deaths were viewed with detached regard—as ordinary workday events. These findings highlight the trend toward the modern depersonalization of death.

THE SOCIAL ORGANIZATION OF DEATH

Death, like dying, has become bureaucratized and is barely visible in the community. Blauner (1966) notes that modern society largely has succeeded in containing mortality and its social disruptiveness. He further contends that American culture is faced with a "crisis of death" because the modern demographic and structural conditions do not fit our traditional concepts of appropriate death, and no new concepts have arisen to take their place.

Mourning rituals are also in a state of flux. The time alloted for mourning has been truncated, and, unlike earlier in the century, we now lack clear social definitions of what constitutes appropriate mourning behavior. Fulton describes the "deritualization of mourning" (1976: 341), and claims that ritual for the dead is now seen as empty and formalistic, an end in itself, instead of augmenting social unity or serving sacred purposes.

Since Lindemann's classic study in 1944 of the symptomatology and management of acute grief, a large body of knowledge has accumulated. We now recognize that the type of death is a determinant of the grief reaction (Vachon, 1981), and that losses from suicide, fetal death, stillbirth, violent crime and natural disaster create particular problems for the survivors. We also are seeing an increase in complicated mourning or abnormal grief reactions. Worden (1982) emphasizes the role of social factors in complicated or abnormal grief. Lazare (1979) identified three social conditions which may contribute to complicated grief reactions. These are: (1) when the loss is socially unspeakable (such as suicide or death from a violent crime); (2) when the loss is socially neglected (such as in abortion or stillbirth); and (3) when there is an absence of a social support network (which is often the case for the elderly).

SOCIOLOGICAL INTERVENTION IN THANATOLOGY

Much work remains to be done in trying to understand the social aspects of death-related topics. More importantly, sociologists need to move beyond research and theory-building to the development and application of intervention and prevention strategies.

This volume on clinical sociology is an attempt to further these efforts. It is divided into five major sections. Section I addresses the translation of sociological theory into practice. The four chapters contained in this section encompass the history of "using sociology" in clinical settings (Fritz, "The Uses of Sociology in Clinical Settings"), of developing an applicable theory of sociological intervention (Straus, "Changing the Definition of the Situation: Toward a Theory of Sociological Intervention"), integrating sociological concepts and theories into clinical training and practice (Rieker and Begun, "Linking Sociology to Clinical Practice"), and of teaching students how to think sociologically about dying and death and how to conduct research in these areas (Cox and Fundis, "Teaching the Sociology of Dying and Death").

The other four sections—Sociological Explanations of Illness and Death Attitudes, Clinical Ethics, Special Populations and Special Problems, and Organization and Structure as Sociological Variables—each contain their own introductions.

REFERENCES

Blauner, R. 1966. Death and social structure. *Psychiatry* 29: 378–94.

Bowers, M., et al. 1964. *Counseling the Dying*. New York: Thomas Nelson.

Charmaz, C. 1980. *The Social Reality of Death: Death in Contemporary America*. Reading, MA: Addison-Wesley.

Cockerham, W. 1978. *Medical Sociology*. Englewood Cliffs, NJ: Prentice Hall.

DeSpelder, L. and A. Strickland. 1982. *The Last Dance: Encountering Death and Dying*. Palo Alto, CA: Mayfield.

Faunce, W. and R. Fulton. 1958. The sociology of death: A neglected area of research. *Social Forces* 36: 205–209.

Fulton, R., ed. 1976. *Death and Identity* (revised edition). Bowie, MD: Charles Press.

——— 1965. *Death and Identity*. New York: John Wiley.

Glaser, B. and A. Strauss. 1965. *Awareness of Dying*. Chicago, IL: Aldine.

——— 1964. The social loss of dying patients. *American Journal of Nursing* 64(6): 119–21.

Kalish, R. 1966. Social distance and the dying. *Community Mental Health Journal* II: 152–55.

Kamerman, J. 1988. *Death in the Midst of Life*. Englewood Cliffs, NJ: Prentice Hall.

Kübler-Ross, E. 1969. *On Death and Dying*. New York: Macmillan.

Lazare, A. 1979. Understanding grief. In A. Lazare, ed. *Outpatient Psychiatry: Diagnosis and Treatment*. Baltimore, MD: Williams and Wilkins, 498–512.

Lindemann, E. 1944. Symptomatology and management of acute grief. *American Journal of Psychiatry* 101: 141–149.

Parsons, T. 1951. *The Social System*. New York: The Free Press.

Pine, V. 1975. *Caretaker of the Dead*. New York: John Wiley.

Suchman, E. 1965. Social patterns of illness and medical care. *Journal of Health and Human Behavior* 6: 2–16.

Sudnow, D. 1967. *Passing On: The Social Organization of Death*. Englewood Cliffs, NJ: Prentice Hall.

Thomas, W. and D. Thomas. 1928. *The Child in America: Behavior Problems and Programs*. New York: Knopf.

Vachon, M. 1981. Type of death as a determinant in acute grief. In: O. Margolis et al., eds. *Acute Grief: Counseling the Bereaved*. New York: Columbia University Press.

Vernon, G. 1970. *Sociology of Death: An Analysis of Death-Related Behavior*. New York: Ronald Press Company.

West, C. 1989. Talcott Parsons' "Sick Role" and its critiques. In P. Brown, ed. Perspectives on Medical Sociology. Belmont, CA: Wadsworth Publishing Company, 145–152.

Wolinsky, F. 1980. *The Sociology of Health: Principles, Professions, and Issues*. Boston, MA: Little, Brown.

Worden, J. W. 1982. *Grief Counseling and Grief Therapy*. New York: Springer Publishing.

2

The Uses of Sociology in Clinical Settings

Jan M. Fritz

Sociology, the study of social relations and the causes and consequences of human behavior, emerged in the United States in the 1890s and early 1900s.[1] From the beginning, the discipline has been characterized by diversity.

There is at present general agreement that the field is a science, but there is little consensus on many other basic considerations. Some sociologists do only case studies, while others religiously use quantitative analysis. Some think the highest objective is discovery based on scientific detachment, while others insist science should not be divorced from empathetic humanism. There are also differences of opinion about which topics are most important (e.g., sociological practice, social institutions, theoretical development, the life course, peace studies or political economy) and the influence of funding sources on research topics and findings.

This diversity has made the field hard to explain to non-sociologists. In addition, the lack of agreement on theoretical frameworks, value orientations, methodological approaches, and important topics has led frequently to intra-discipline power plays and intolerance of minority viewpoints.

Yet, this diversity also has been a source of strength, producing the dynamism that results from shifts in focus from one topic or approach to another. This diversity also holds an important promise—one that tens of thousands of sociology students have memorized as the "sociological imagination."[2] This imagination allows individuals to step beyond their own circumstances, beyond personal troubles, and to view their lives in a cross-cultural, historical perspective. It also encourages individuals to move toward clinical sociology by envisioning and creating a world that deals with its social problems.

This chapter focuses on the emergence and promise of clinical sociology, one of the areas of sociological practice.[3] In 1966 Alfred McClung Lee (1966:330), a past president of the American Sociological Association and a co-founder of the Sociological Practice Association, identified three ways in which social scientists could be "clinical:"

(1) through critical discussions with practical observers of spontaneous social behavior in problematic situations, (2) through scientific utilization of available clinical data, and (3) through participation directly in clinical situations.

All of these approaches—but particularly the first and third—are emphasized in the contemporary definition of clinical sociology.

Clinical sociology is viewed here as the creation of new systems as well as the intervention in existing systems for purposes of assessment and/or change. Clinical sociologists are humanistic scientists who are multi-disciplinary in approach. They engage in planned social change efforts by focusing on one system level (e.g., interpersonal, small group, organization, community, international), but they integrate levels of focus in their work using a sociological frame of reference.

THE ROOTS OF AMERICAN CLINICAL SOCIOLOGY

The origins of the field date back at least five centuries to the work in North Africa of Arab historian and statesperson Abu Zaid Abdalrahman ibn Muhammad ibn Khaldun Wali-ad-Din al-Hadrami, best known as Ibn Khaldun (1332–1406). He founded "the science of human social organization," the basis for what is now called sociology (Baali, 1988:xi, 107). In his *Muqaddimah,* Ibn Khaldun provided numerous clinical observations based on his work experiences, which included seal bearer, secretary of state, ambassador, negotiator and judge. In the latter role, he was seen as a reformer who practiced with "strict honesty and great integrity" (Baali, 1988:1–3; Fritz, 1989a:73).

Ibn Khaldun was the first to use a scientific approach to the study of social life in combination with intervention. But he and many other individuals, now designated as early sociologists, were not called sociologists during their lifetimes. Identifying the earliest clinical sociologists is difficult because many did not use that label to describe themselves. Nonetheless, a review of the work of early scientist-practitioners shows clearly those who were precursors of the field and those who were clinicians.

Among those in Europe who would be included, at the very least, as precursors of contemporary clinical sociology were the classical sociologists Auguste Comte, Emile Durkheim and Karl Marx.[4] Among those whose work has been identified directly as clinical sociology is Beatrice Webb (1858–1943). Webb, a co-founder of the Fabian Society who helped to establish the London School of Economics, had a strong influence on British social policy (Fritz, 1989a:76).

THE HISTORY OF AMERICAN CLINICAL SOCIOLOGY, PART I

The first American sociologists were practitioners and professors—and some combined these roles. But chroniclers of the field have said that in the first third of the twentieth century, the male sociologists at the University of Chicago were the most important force in the development of American sociology. Although these sociologists had a variety of interests and perspectives, they were frequently referred to as "The Chicago School." That label was given to them as early as 1930 (Bernard, 1930:133), but apparently was not used by the Chicago sociologists of the 1920s to describe themselves (Cavan, 1983:408).

"The Chicago School" is a label with limitations. If it were replaced by "The Chicago Network" (Fritz, 1985) or "The Chicago Circle" (Thomas, 1983:390),[5] the new label would call attention not only to the men in the sociology department, but to the women sociologists who held a variety of positions at the university (Deegan, 1987, 1988; Fritz, 1989a). Moreover, it would give due recognition to the involvement and impact of Chicago practitioners, including the women of Hull House, a prominent social settlement house. A label such as "The Chicago Network" also would direct researchers to look at the influence of these early sociologists on practitioners and practice settings as well as on sociology professors and university sociology programs.

The work of the early sociologists in Chicago was directed, in different ways, at the resolution of pressing social problems. Some of the first members of the University of Chicago's sociology department, Charles Henderson and Albion Small, would be included in this group, along with Marion Talbot, an administrator and professor at the University of Chicago, and Jane Addams, the head of Hull House (Fritz, 1989a).

There were, of course, differences of opinion on how to get involved in the issues facing the community (Deegan, 1988:37–39). For instance, some at the university saw the settlement houses and the city as a "sociological laboratory" (White, 1929a: 24–25; Park, 1929; Burgess, 1929:47), a place where university professors might test their ideas. There was great utility to this work, but some questioned whether it might be undertaken primarily to meet the scientific interests of the professors and their students.

Others were concerned about referring to the community and settlement houses as "sociological laboratories." To them, even the use of that term seemed to indicate a lack of respect for the work of the organizations. In the view of some, settlement houses, for instance, were established to meet community needs; scientific assistance could be useful, but it should follow the community interests, not be the driving force for these interests.

This example illustrates the tension that so frequently exists when an individual or program tries to meet both scientific and community needs. While it is possible to meet both objectives, the struggle to do so can overwhelm the community interests or dilute the scientific possibilities. An interventionist has to be aware of the dilemma, respect the community's right to set an agenda and be accountable for proposing particular research and intervention strategies.

University sociologists were very interested in working in "laboratory settings" in the mid-1920s. While some talked of doing this research in the city or neighborhood, sociologist Ernest W. Burgess (1929:47) pointed out that this work was already in progress "on a small scale . . . with institutes of child research."

Burgess (1886–1966), a graduate of the University of Chicago and a faculty member from 1919–1951, is considered one of the second generation of sociologists who taught there. During his career he was president of the American Sociological Association, the National Conference of Family Relations, and the Gerontology Society. Burgess was active in civic affairs in Chicago, supervised sociological work in clinics, was on the advisory board of a child guidance center (The South Side Child Guidance Center, 1930) and taught the first courses in clinical sociology.

Burgess' courses in clinical sociology were offered at the University of Chicago from 1928 through 1933 (Fritz, 1989b). The courses focused on pathological cases and the analysis of personalities. They also discussed the roles sociologists, psychologists, and psychiatrists held in child guidance clinics.[6]

Students enrolled in Burgess' 1928 and 1929 clinical sociology classes were the clinical sociologists at two community child guidance clinics.[7] Among their tasks were (Cottrell, 1929:1):

intensive treatment work, such as attempting treatment of the home situation, placement of the child in foster home, vocational adjustment, adjustment in school, cooperation with settlement in recreational adjustment. . . .

The South Side Child Guidance Center also indicated an interest in being a "sort of training laboratory for students interested in the field of Clinical Sociology." One of the clinical sociologists, Leonard Cottrell (1929:3), stated in his annual report that 16 students had received assistance in case analysis during that year. He thought that full student involvement for "carefully selected students . . . may be thought of as the clinic's most valuable function so far as the Department of Sociology is concerned."

Other students in Burgess' classes were affiliated with the Institute for Juvenile Research.[8] This organization "correlated sociological investigation with the case findings of the clinics" (Stevenson and Smith, 1934:153).

The work in the child guidance clinics fit with Burgess' teaching and research interests at the time. The work progressed because the child guidance centers requested assistance and the project received financial support. The University of Chicago's Local Community Research Committee provided grant money for this project from 1927 to 1929. This support was matched by local funds from the Chicago Woman's Club, the South Side Child Guidance Center, and the Lower North Child Guidance Center (White, 1929b:35–39).

Although the name "child guidance clinic" was not used until 1922, the idea

had been put into practice as early as 1909 by William Healy,[9] the founder of
the Chicago Juvenile Psychopathic Institute (Stevenson and Smith, 1934:15).
In 1934 physician George Stevenson, then director of the Division on Community Clinics for the National Committee for Mental Hygiene, and Geddes Smith
(1934:2) identified the functions of child guidance clinics:

> They study and treat patients; they seek to interest other community agencies in the
> prevention of behavior and personality disorders in children and in promising meth-
> ods of dealing with them when they occur; and they attempt to reveal to the commu-
> nity, through the first-hand study of individual children, the unmet needs of groups
> of children. Some clinics also undertake the systematic analysis of case material in
> the hope of contributing to a more exact knowledge of child behavior, and some
> provide training for students . . .

Sociologists at Tulane University in Louisiana also were involved in child
guidance work. Louis Wirth (1897–1952) was a full-time faculty member there
and he was director of the New Orleans Child Guidance Clinic. In the spring
of 1930, he was scheduled to teach what was the nation's second course in
clinical sociology. Because Wirth accepted a fellowship to work in Europe that
year, the course was taught by another faculty member. The course was described in the university catalog (*Tulane University Bulletins,* 1928–29) as a
"clinical demonstration of behavior problems and practice in social therapy
through staff conferences and field work in a child guidance center."

In 1931 when Wirth returned to the United States, he joined the faculty at
the University of Chicago and published "Clinical Sociology," an article about
the contributions a sociologist can make in child development clinics. The following year, he taught a course in clinical sociology.

While clinical sociology was part of the Chicago tradition from at least 1928,
a discussion of the subfield first surfaced in print in New Haven. Milton C.
Winternitz (1885–1959), a physician, and Dean of Yale University Medical
School from 1920 to 1935, thought of medicine as a social science. In the
earliest known publication discussing clinical sociology (Winternitz, 1930), he
wrote of his intention to form a "clinical sociology section." He wanted each
medical student to have a chance to analyze cases based on a medical specialty
as well as a specialty in clinical sociology.

Winternitz vigorously sought funding for his proposal from the Julius Rosenwald Fund through Michael M. Davis, director of the Fund's medical services.
Davis had studied sociology at Columbia University,[10] and been the director of
the Boston Dispensary as well as the director of New York City's Committee
on Dispensary Development, before joining the Rosenwald Fund.

While Winternitz (1931a, 1931b) noted the success of a course in the medical
school's section on public health that was "modeled directly after the outlined
plan for clinical sociology," he couldn't obtain the funds needed to put the

department in place (Fritz, 1989c). He never lost interest in the program, and even mentioned it in his final report as dean in 1936.

THE HISTORY OF AMERICAN CLINICAL SOCIOLOGY

Between World War II and the mid-1970s, sociology was characterized by its empirical approaches, theoretical developments, and academic employment. Periodically there was some interest in applied sociology, but clinical sociology essentially went unnoticed. The histories of sociology didn't include information about clinical sociology, and consequently, most sociologists didn't know it existed. Also, the development of clinical sociology was slow during this period because clinical sociologists themselves were often unaware of others with similar interests.

The first formal definition of clinical sociology, written by Alfred McClung Lee, appeared in H.P. Fairchild's *Dictionary of Sociology* in 1944. That same year Edward McDonagh published "An Approach to Clinical Sociology" in *Sociology and Social Research.*

McDonagh thought he had come up with the idea of a clinical sociology independently; he may have been influenced by his dissertation work on the group health movement, in which he noted that "group health associations favored the centralization of physicians and medical equipment in a clinical setting and purported the advantages of pooling ideas and health providers—in opposition to solo practitioners." McDonagh's article stressed the value of working in "clinical" groups and discussed the kinds of community problems that might be tackled by a clinical research group (Fritz, 1986:11–12).

In 1946 George Edmund Haynes' "Clinical Methods in Interracial and Intercultural Relations" was published. Haynes, the first black recipient of a Ph.D. from Columbia University, was a co-founder of the National Urban League (1910) and the first black to hold a sub-cabinet post in the U.S. government. In 1946 Haynes was Executive Secretary of the Department of Race Relations at the Federal Council of Churches. His article discussed the department's urban clinics, which dealt with interracial tension and conflict.

Publications mentioning clinical sociology began to appear at least every few years (Fritz, 1989b). Among them were publications by Alvin Gouldner (1956), Warren Dunham (1964) and Julia Mayo (1966). Gouldner also taught a course entitled "The Foundations of Clinical Sociology" at Antioch College in the mid-1950s. The course was taught at the highest undergraduate level and students were expected to have successfully completed the department's course in social pathology. The course was described in the following way in the *Antioch College Bulletin* (1953:123):

A sociological counterpart to clinical psychology, with the group as the unit of diagnosis and therapy. Emphasis on developing skills useful in the diagnosis and therapy of group tensions. Principles of functional analysis, group dynamics, and organizational and small group analysis examined and applied to case histories. Representative research in the area assessed.

THE UTILITY OF CLINICAL SOCIOLOGY

The Sociological Practice Association (SPA) was founded in 1978 as the Clinical Sociology Association. During the last decade, those who established the SPA have used their collective skills in organizational development and, despite limited resources, have begun to change the landscape of American sociology. Even the most conservative sociology organizations now include information about clinical sociology in their newsletters, although these organizations still have not developed plans to integrate clinicians.

The term "clinical sociology" was first used in the United States by well-known university professors who were receiving, or anticipated receiving, funding for clinical work.[11] These sociologists often used the term "clinical sociology" in a limited way, referring only to sociological work within actual clinics.

The term "clinical sociology" was used in a variety of ways from the late 1930s to the mid-1970s. But in the 1970s and 1980s the most frequent definition was the broadest one. It referred to intervention on various levels (e.g., individual, group, organization, local community, national, international) and in various settings such as clinics, courts, schools, neighborhoods, and board rooms. That usage is historically accurate because some early advocates recognized the broad use of the term,[12] and a review of the variety of intervention activities undertaken by The Chicago Network shows that a broad definition has a basis in fact.

While the field can be defined narrowly or broadly, much of the actual work of clinical sociologists has been, and is, in health care settings. The contributions of sociologists in these settings differ, depending on each individual practitioner's training (B.A., M.A., Ph.D. or C.C.S., certified clinical sociologist),[13] length and type of experience, and areas of competence. In general, we might expect the following contributions from a certified practitioner:

Theoretical analysis. The clinical sociologists has had extensive training in theory. The result is a working knowledge of the range of major theories— beyond sociological—affecting her or his area of specialization, and the ability to translate theories into practice. The clinical sociologist is expected to periodically reflect on her or his own theoretical approach, and the possible effects of this theoretical approach on the work undertaken. The clinical sociologist also is expected to provide a theoretical perspective, when the situation warrants, for clients, colleagues, and employers.

Social systems perspective.   A sociologist's training emphasizes understanding of (1) the social system—a configuration of positions, roles and norms—as a dynamic force and (2) the effects of membership in overlapping systems. The clinical sociologist is expected to be knowledgeable about systems, to move between theory and practice in working with systems, and to assist individuals and groups in assessing and possibly changing systems.

Levels of analysis.   The clinical sociologist is expected to concentrate on a level of analysis (e.g., individual, small group, local community, international) when undertaking an intervention project. But the translation of social theory, concepts, and methods into sociological practice requires an ability not only to recognize various levels, but to move between levels for analysis and intervention (Freedman, 1984).

Methodological sophistication.   A sociologist receives extensive training in research methods. The clinical sociologist is expected to know the comparative strengths and weaknesses of qualitative and quantitative methods in practice settings. A clinical sociologist also is expected to recommend appropriate methods by taking into account objectives, ethical considerations, and available resources.

Intervention skills.   A clinical sociologist will have interdisciplinary training and substantial intervention experience in her or his specialty area. The certified practitioner would go beyond simply pointing out a few of the difficulties in a situation. The practitioner would provide an analysis,[14] suggest alternative ways of humanistically dealing with a situation and, when possible, actually initiate or assist in the intervention. In any intervention, the clinical sociologist is bound by a code of ethics, and is expected to identify and address ethical issues that may arise.

Specialized body of knowledge.   Each clinical sociologist has a frame of reference which emphasizes social factors (e.g., socio-economic conditions, ethnicity, gender), and at least one or two areas of special competence, such as health promotion, gerontology, community organization, and social policy. A clinical sociologist is expected to work in areas where she or he has particular expertise, and to advise those involved before undertaking work that goes beyond his or her special areas of knowledge or intervention.

The six major contributions mentioned above are very important, but the list could be considerably longer, depending on a practitioner's skills and the requirements of the task at hand. Clients, colleagues, and employers should understand that clinical sociologists are not the only professionals with these skills. Practitioners in various fields may be competent in these areas, although a certified clinical sociologist's training may have broader emphasis on theory, research methods, and systems analysis than the training in other fields.

Clinical sociologists have made valuable contributions in health settings for over 60 years. If this trend is to continue, sociological practitioners must have ongoing networking possibilities, as well as increased training and employment opportunities.[15] At the same time, there must be growing recognition of the contributions of clinical sociologists, and better collaboration among the disciplines involved in health care.[16]

NOTES

1. There is no exact date for the establishment of the discipline. One or more of the following often are used to set an approximate date: *The American Journal of Sociology* was launched at the University of Chicago in 1895, sociology courses appeared in academic institutions in the 1890s, and the American Sociological Society (now the American Sociological Association) was established in 1905.

2. C. Wright Mills (1959) introduced the idea of the sociological imagination in the following way:

Nowadays men often feel that their private lives are a series of traps . . . They do not possess the quality of mind essential to grasp the interplay of man and society, of biography and history, of self and world . . . The history that now affects every man is world history. Within this scene and this period, in the course of a single generation, one-sixth of mankind is transformed from all that is feudal and backward into all that is modern, advanced and fearful . . . What they need . . . may be called the sociological imagination.

The sociological imagination enables its possessor to understand . . . what is going on in the world (and) what is happening in themselves as minute points of the intersections of biography and history within society . . . By its use men whose mentalities have swept only a series of limited orbits often come to feel as if suddenly awakened in a house with which they had only supposed themselves to be familiar . . .

It is now the social scientist's foremost political and intellectual task—for here the two coincide—to make clear the elements of contemporary uneasiness and indifference . . . I believe the social sciences are becoming the common denominator of our cultural period, and the sociological imagination our most needed quality of mind.

Mills wrote his powerful, poetic book in the late 1950s. It is unfortunate that he chose to use the word "men" instead of "people" in his widely-distributed statement about a liberating force.

3. The practical sociology of the 1900s is now referred to as sociological practice (Fritz and Clark, 1989). This label includes two areas, clinical sociology and applied sociology. Clinical sociology refers primarily to intervention, while applied sociology refers to research specifically designed to help in resolving problems faced by organizations such as businesses or government agencies.

4. Comte believed the scientific study of societies would provide the basis for social action. Durkheim and Marx provided a clinical perspective—a model or framework—for the analysis of social dilemmas (Fritz, 1989a:73).

5. Deegan (1988:3) plans to write a volume which will describe the " 'female' Chicago School of Sociology." The alternative names—Chicago Network or Chicago Circle—would more adequately cover the practice and academic bases from which the women operated.

6. Louis Wirth was director of the Child Behavior Clinic at Tulane University (Smith and White, 1929:265 and *Tulane Scraps*, 1929), and Harvey Zorbaugh was in charge of the Social Behavior Clinic at New York University. Both men held academic appointments in sociology at their respec-

tive universities and, at some point, provided research assistance to the University of Chicago's Local Community Research Committee (Smith and White, 1929:258–65).

7. Clarence E. Glick (1989), now an 83-year-old sociologist from Hawaii, began graduate study at the University of Chicago in the spring of 1927. Burgess arranged for Glick to be the clinical sociologist at the Lower North Side Child Guidance Center. Another class member, Leonard S. Cottrell (1899–1985), was for two years a "Clinical Sociologist for the Institute of Juvenile Research," and acted as such with the South Side Child Guidance Clinic. Cottrell also was a probation officer for the Juvenile Court for two years and a research sociologist for the Institute for Juvenile Research for one year (Cornell University Archives File on Leonard S. Cottrell, biographical statement for promotion, n.d.).

8. According to a document in the Burgess Collection at the University of Chicago (Laboratory for Criminological Research, n.d.),

> (The Institute for Justice) is the oldest center for child study in the United States having been founded in 1909 under the name The Juvenile Psychopathic Institute, with Dr. William Healy as director. Under the administration of Dr. Hermann M. Adler, 1917–29, it was transferred from county to state auspices and has expanded its work in many directions . . . In Chicago it maintains a branch at the Juvenile Detention Home and has affiliated with it the Lower North Side Child Guidance Center and the South Side Child Guidance Center. Besides maintaining a service program, it conducts a large research program. The case records of children examined is now increasing at the rate of 1000 a year.

9. According to Ruth Shonle Cavan (1983:413), a graduate student at the University of Chicago from 1922 through 1926, "In his course on delinquency, Burgess depended on a series of cases of delinquent boys published by a psychiatrist, William Healy."

10. Davis wrote his dissertation, *Gabriel Tarde, An Essay in Sociological Theory,* in 1906.

11. Winternitz vigorously sought funding from the Rosenwald Fund for a department of clinical sociology (Fritz, 1989c), and Burgess' work in clinical sociology had funding from a university research group, a local women's organization and child guidance groups. Tulane University sought funding for its child guidance center from the Commonwealth Fund and the Community Chest (*Tulane Scraps,* 1929; Wyckoff, 1925, 1928).

12. For example, Dean Milton Winternitz (1932:50–51), of the Yale Medical School, said the following in his 1930–31 annual report to the president of Yale:

> The field of clinical sociology does not seem by any means to be confined to medicine. Within the year it has become more and more evident that a similar development may well be the means of bringing about aid so sorely needed to change the basis of court action in relation to crime . . .
>
> Not only in medicine and in law, but probably in many other fields of activity, the broad preparation of the clinical sociologist is essential . . .

13. The Sociological Practice Association (SPA) has certified experienced clinical sociologists since 1984. To gain the title "certified clinical sociologist," an individual must submit an acceptable portfolio which includes documentation about training and experience. The applicant must have had training in a related discipline, written theoretical and ethical statements, and provided specified kinds of references. If the certification committee finds the applicant's portfolio acceptable, the applicant is invited to give a demonstration before peers and a reviewing panel. The reviewing panel meets with the applicant after the demonstration, and then rates the applicant and makes a recommendation regarding certification to the SPA Certification Committee.

14. Roger Straus (1984:52,54) has said that sociological intervention may be characterized in the following way:

> (1) directed at the operational definition of the situation, in such a way as to (2) take into account the multiple, interacting layers of social participation framing human problems and predicaments and their resolution.

Straus also provides the following taxonomy of sociological intervention:

Level of Participation	Target of Intervention
Persons	Conduct
Groups	Role Structure
Organizations	Institutions
Worlds	Culture

15. Some initiatives—such as state licensure, job classification and third-party payment author-ity—may set standards for health care, but they also may be exclusionary. Because of the costs involved in tackling current and proposed restrictive policies, professional organizations that are relatively small and have few resources are not able to assure members that they can protect their right to practice.

16. Collaboration here means that each of the disciplines involved in health care has the possibility of taking the lead in situations requiring research, administration and/or intervention. Too often one field may dominate, and "collaboration" means working together, but only under the direction of someone from the dominant field.

REFERENCES

Antioch College Bulletin. 1953. Foundations of clinical sociology. Course description.

Baali, F. 1988. *Society, State and Urbanism: Ibn Khaldun's Sociological Thought.* Albany, NY: State University of New York Press.

Bernard, L.L. 1930. Schools of sociology. *Southwestern Political and Social Science Quarterly* 11(September):117–34.

Burgess, E. W. 1929. Basic social data. In T.V. Smith and L.D. White, eds. *Chicago, An Experiment in Social Science Research.* Chicago: University of Chicago Press, 47–66.

Cavan, R. S. 1983. The Chicago school of sociology, 1918–1933. *Urban Life* 11/4(January):407–20.

Cornell University Archives File on Leonard S. Cottrell. (n.d.) Leonard S. Cottrell, biographical statement for promotion. Leonard S. Cottrell file, 1935–85. Cornell University, Department of Manuscripts and Archives.

Cottrell, L. S. 1929. Report of the Sociologist of the South Side Child Guidance Center for the period from January 1, 1928 to June 1, 1929. Ernest Burgess Papers. Box 13, Folder 4. Department of Special Collections, The Regenstein Library, The University of Chicago.

Davis, M. M. 1906. Gabriel Tarde, An Essay in Sociological Theory. PhD dissertation. Columbia University, NY.

Deegan, M. J. 1987. An American dream: The historical connections between women, humanism, and sociology, 1890–1920. *Humanity & Society* 11/3(August):353–65.

———1988. *Jane Addams and the Men of the Chicago School, 1892–1918.* New Brunswick, NJ: Transaction, Inc.

Dunham, H. W. 1964. Anomie and mental disorder. In Marshall B. Clinard, ed. *Anomie and Deviant Behavior.* New York: Free Press of Glencoe, 128–57.

Freedman, J. 1984. Integration of levels of focus: Is this what makes clinical sociology unique? Clinical Sociology Association Presidential Address. San Antonio, Texas. August.

Fritz, J. M. 1985. Making tracks: The history of clinical sociology. In J.M. Fritz, *The Clinical Sociology Handbook.* New York: Garland, 3–25.

———1986. The history of clinical sociology: The initial contributions of Edward McDonagh and Marie Kargman. *Clinical Sociology Review* IV:11–13.

———1989a. The history of clinical sociology. *Sociological Practice* VII:72–95.

———1989b. The emergence of American clinical sociology. Manuscript.

———1989c. Dean Winternitz, clinical sociology and the Julius Rosenwald Fund. *Clinical Sociology Review* VII.

Fritz, J. and E. Clark, eds. 1989. Sociological Practice: The Development of Clinical and Applied Sociology. VII. East Lansing, MI: Michigan State University Press.

Glick, C. E. 1989. Telephone interview. January 19.

Gouldner, A. 1956. Explorations in applied social science. *Social Problems* III/3(January):169–81. Reprinted pp. 5–22 in A. Gouldner and S.M. Miller, eds. *Applied Sociology*. New York: Free Press, 1965.

Haynes, G. E. 1946. Clinical methods in interracial and intercultural relations. *The Journal of Educational Sociology* 19/5 (January). Reprinted in the 1988 issue of the *Clinical Sociology Review* VI:51–58.

Ibn Khaldun, Abd al-R. 1967. *The Muqaddimah: An Introduction to History*. Translated by Franz Rosenthal. Three volumes. Princeton, NJ: Princeton University Press.

Laboratory for Criminological Research. (n.d.). Mimeographed document describing proposed laboratory facilities for criminological research. Ernest Burgess Collection. Box 2, Folder 12. The Department of Special Collections, The Regenstein Library, The University of Chicago.

Lee, A. McC. 1944. Sociology, clinical. In H.P. Fairchild, ed. *Dictionary of Sociology*. New York: Philosophical Library, 303.

———1966. *Mutivalent* Man. New York: George Braziller.

Local Community Research. 1927. Local Community Research, Report to the President of the University of Chicago. February 1. Ernest Burgess Collection. Box 13, Folder 1. The Department of Special Collections, the Regenstein Library, The University of Chicago.

Mayo, J. 1966. What is the 'social' in social psychiatry? *Archives of General Psychiatry* 14:449–55.

McDonagh, E. C. 1944. An approach to clinical sociology. *Sociology and Social Research* 27/5 (May-June):376–83. Reprinted in the 1986 *Clinical Sociology Review* Volume IV.

Mills, C. W. 1959. *The Sociological Imagination*. New York: Grove Press.

Park, R. E. 1929. The city as a social laboratory. In T.V . Smith and L.D. White, eds. *Chicago, An Experiment in Social Science Research*. Chicago: University of Chicago Press, 1–19.

Schwendinger, H. and J. Schwendinger. 1974. *The Sociologists of the Chair: A Radical Analysis of the Formative Years of North American Sociology (1883–1922)*. New York: Basic Books.

Smith, D. 1988. *The Chicago School: A Liberal Critique of Capitalism*. New York: St. Martin's Press.

Smith, T.V. and L. D. White, eds. 1929. *Chicago, An Experiment in Social Science Research*. Chicago: University of Chicago Press.

South Side Child Guidance Center, The. 1930. Annual Report. Chicago. Ernest Burgess Collection. Box 21, Folder 9. Department of Special Collections, The Joseph Regenstein Library, The University of Chicago.

Stevenson, G. S. and G. Smith. 1934. *Child Guidance Clinics: A Quarter Century of Development*. New York: The Commonwealth Fund.

Straus, R. A. 1984. Changing the definition of the situation: Toward a theory of sociological intervention. *Clinical Sociology Review* 2:51–63. Reprinted in the 1989 issue of Sociological Practice VII:123–35.

Thomas, J. 1983. Chicago sociology: An introduction. *Urban Life* 11/4(January):387–95.

Tulane Scraps. 1929. Head of Tulane child guidance clinic arrives. September 18. Newspaper article in the *Tulane Scraps,* a scrapbook. Volume 17. Archives, Tulane University Library.

Tulane University Bulletins. 1928-29. Clinical Sociology course description.

White, L. D. 1929a. The local community research committee and the social science research building. In T.V. Smith and Leonard D. White, eds. *Chicago, An Experiment in Social Science Research.* Chicago: University of Chicago Press, 20–32.

——1929b. Co-operation with civic and social agencies. In T.V. Smith and Leonard D. White, eds. *Chicago, An Experiment in Social Science Research.* Chicago: University of Chicago Press, 33–46.

Winternitz, M. C. 1930. Clinical sociology section to be formed. In Report of the School of Medicine. Reports to the president of Yale University, 1928-29. Bulletin of Yale University, New Haven, 92–94.

——1931a. Report of the School of Medicine. Reports to the president of Yale University, 1929-30. Bulletin of Yale University. New Haven.

——1931b. Notes on clinical sociology. Yale University Archives. School of Medicine, Records of Dean. YRG-27-A-5-9. Box 112, Folder 2604.

——1932. Clinical sociology. Pp. 50–51 in Report of the dean of the School of Medicine, 1930-31. Bulletin of Yale University. New Haven.

——1936. Report of the dean of the School of Medicine to the university president, 1934–35. Bulletin of Yale University. New Haven.

Wirth, L. 1931. Clinical sociology. *American Journal of Sociology* 37:49–66.

Wyckoff, G. P. 1925. Letter to Tulane University president, A.B. Dinwiddle. July 16. G.P. Wyckoff file. Archives, Tulane University Library.

——1928. Letter to Tulane University president, A.B. Dinwiddle. July 30. Louis Wirth file. Archives, Tulane University Library.

3

Changing the Definition of the Situation: Toward a Theory of Sociological Intervention

Roger A. Straus

Sociology, unlike medicine or psychology, has never sought to maintain the strong disciplinary boundaries typical of "a specialty." Rather, in its historical posture of a generalizing social science encompassing the subject areas of the other social/behavioral disciplines, sociology has freely disseminated to others its findings, concepts, and methods while maintaining only a marginal interest in "applied" work. Consequently, while our subterranean tradition of clinical sociology reemerged around 1978, we have found it difficult to specify exactly the special contribution or expertise of the sociological practitioner.

To limit the domain of clinical sociology to what self-identified clinical sociologists do or have done would, if anything, be counterproductive, as Lee (1973) and others have argued. As one who has been intimately concerned with the problem of defining our field for some years now, I believe we are ready to move beyond presentation of the variety of roles enacted by clinical sociologists (cf. Straus 1979a) to tease out the underlying logic of approach characterizing the specifically *sociological intervention.*

In this chapter, then, I shall state my findings that, on the basis of analyzing the published and unpublished literature of the field, the sociological intervention may be characterized as (1) directed at the operational definition of the situation, in such a way as to (2) take into account the multiple, interacting layers of social participation framing human problems and predicaments and their resolution.

Contemporary practitioners of clinical sociology almost universally character-

23

ize themselves as *humanists* in Lee's sense of the term (1973). While extrinsic to my general definition, this value orientation is useful when differentiating clinical sociological practice from more conventional "applied social science" (Lee 1978). Our interventions are aimed at empowering clients, instead of simply adjusting them to the "realities of life." Rather than adopt the expert's role of prescribing a better or more appropriate reality for the client, we strive to minimize interference with the client's worlds and values; rather than serve the needs of "the system," we attempt to serve the needs of the human beings comprising the social unit or system in question (Straus 1982).

OPERATIONAL DEFINITION OF THE SITUATION

Translation of social theory, concept, and method into practice necessitates both theoretical eclecticism and some reworking of our usual formulations. Thomas's "definition of the situation" (1931) is usually understood phenomenologically to mean that whatever a person or group believes or accepts to be so is real in its consequences. While it is important to deal with socially constructed realities at this intrapersonal level, since they form the basis upon which conduct will be constructed by human actors (Blumer 1969), redefinition of internalized meanings and cognitive maps is mainly a concern of sociological counselors working with individuals and primary groups (Straus 1982). Most sociological interventions are more concerned with the manifestation of these "realities" in patterns of conduct and joint conduct being enacted by the individuals, groups, and/or systems under scrutiny.

Thomas's statement of the principle was somewhat ambiguous about the nature of the definition of the situation, but was clear about the dialectical relationship between the individual's definition and the definition of the situation *presented* by others. These concepts are neatly summarized in Sarbin's (1976) characterization of the dramaturgical perspective holding that

> actors not only respond to situations, but also mold and create them. . . . The interactions of participants define the situation. The units of interest are not individuals, not organisms, not assemblages of traits, but *interacting persons* in identifiable contexts.

It is the pattern of these interactions that corresponds to the operational definition of the situation and that is the target of sociological intervention.

LEVELS OF SOCIAL CONTEXT

Both the original statement of definition of the situation and its dramaturgical operationalization are clear about the situated nature of conduct. They are not so clear about the complex and many-tiered nature of social ecologies and about how human behavior is situationally organized with respect to a subject's concrete location within that *total* social context. However, clinical sociologists are sensitive to the implications of how "social systems" at every level influence ongoing action. This sensitivity is then translated into practical actions designed to mitigate negative interlevel influences and use these dynamics strategically to guide and stabilize positive change. As Freedman and Rosenfeld have put it (1983), the clinical sociologist uses a paradigm of "the integration of levels of focus" incorporating both "macro" and "micro" viewpoints. Thus, the characteristic sociological intervention combines multiple foci: "the group member, the groups to which the person belongs or desires to belong or not belong, organizations, committees, subcultures, culture, and society."

In this chapter it is necessary to adopt a typology of the various levels of social context; clearly, how one slices the social continuum represents a pragmatic choice relative to one's purpose. For example, Parsons (1951) selected a scheme appropriate to his theory of social action, while Lofland (1976) utilized an entirely different model of "human systems." As my purpose here is to describe sociological intervention generically, we will look at just four "quantum levels" of social participation: persons, groups, organizations, and worlds.

The first two of these correspond to general usage. *Persons* are social actors defining themselves in conduct; for our purposes, they *are* their acts. The routinized patterns of conduct colloquially referred to as "one's act" are framed by (that is, organized in terms of) the culture of the worlds in which persons participate and the roles they play in the various groups in which they are involved.

Each level of social structure is viewed as the emergent pattern of routinized conduct representing a dialectical synthesis between the next "higher" and "lower" levels. *Groups,* then, would be conceptualized as persons with more or less routinized social relations or *roles.* The actual role structure of the group operationally defines that group. As groups necessarily establish at least tacit patterns of relationship with other groups, they inevitably become tied into any number of formal or informal organizations.

A special usage of *organizations* is employed here; this level of organized, identifiable intergroup relations is most often referred to as a "social system" (Znaniecki 1934). However, since any interacting set of persons can be considered to form a "social system," and their relations can be analyzed in terms of systems theory (von Bertalanffy 1968), it seems best to employ another term for this structural level. *Organizations,* then, may range up through wider and wider scales of intergroup relations from "formal organizations," corporations, and associations to communities and governments. The operational definition of organizations consists of their *institutions,* meaning the routinized patterns of social relations often simply referred to as their "organization."

The highest level of social context in this typology is the *social world.* This usage is adapted and expanded from Lofland's definition: "Complexly interrelated sets of encounters, roles, groups, and organizations seen by participants as forming a larger whole are often and properly thought of as 'worlds,' as in the phrases 'the business world,' 'the academic world,' 'the sports world' '' (1976:29). In the sense employed here, a world is operationally defined by its culture, primarily the nonmaterial culture of norms, values, folkways, mores, language, and technology differentiating its participants from members of other social worlds. Those who share a subculture by definition share a world; larger-scale worlds might include the entire society, the civilization of which it is a part, and, possibly, Spaceship Earth itself.

THE SOCIOLOGICAL INTERVENTION

If we identify the operational definition with the target of intervention, this scheme generates the following taxonomy of sociological intervention:

Level of Participation	Target of Intervention
Persons	Conduct
Groups	Role Structure
Organizations	Institutions
Worlds	Culture

The intervention itself will, in one way or another, involve a strategy of redefining the situation. At the personal level, for example, sociological counseling might involve reconstruction of the client's assumptive realities and social-behavioral tactics specifically designed to change his or her conduct in everyday life (Straus 1979b). Unlike more conventional "psychological" or "psychosocial" counseling, only minimal attention would be placed upon intrapsychic constructs such as defense mechanisms or personality traits. On the other hand, integration of levels of focus leads the sociologist to approach a person's difficulties at this personal level as *social problems* intimately tied to cultural and subcultural factors, located in history and society, reference groups, family dynamics, and the social construction of reality. Straus (1979b) has shown how, for example, obesity can be managed through a specifically sociological intervention.

MODES OF INTERVENTION

Interventions may be organized in terms of three different modes: the direct, indirect, and cooperative. These represent different strategies for attacking a problem. In real life, interventions generally combine one or more modes, but it remains valuable to consider them as ideal types when thinking about and planning change projects.

By "direct mode" I refer to the commonsensical approach of attacking a problem head-on. One might assess a troubled organization, devise a strategy of intervention, and then guide management in implementing the suggested changes. Since this requires the change agent to take the role of expert or "doctor," it tends to conflict with humanist values and is therefore more typical of the social engineering approach than sociological intervention. On the other hand, while the direct mode can provoke resistance and socialize clients to rely upon external authority and "expert" guidance, it remains an invaluable tool in the sociologist's kitbag. In fact, it is often expedient or even necessary to take an initially authoritarian role prior to weaning the client to a position of self-management (Straus 1977).

Indirect interventions enable one to avoid problems of resistance and dependency by employing tactics of indirection and/or indirect attack. The former was pioneered by noted hypnotherapist Milton V. Erickson (1980), who developed the strategy of "indirect suggestion." The approach has been popularized in consulting circles as "neurolinguistic programming" and has been adapted to social science based interventions by those affiliated with the Mental Research Institute in Palo Alto (Watzlawick, Weakland, and Fisch 1967). In family therapy, for example, indirect tactics might involve getting family members to cooperate with the identified problem behavior of a child, so as to get the parents to stop doing whatever they have been "doing about it," thus blocking perpetuation of an operational definition that aggravates or maintains the family system's problem (Fisch, Weakland, and Segal 1982).

Indirect attack is more typical of sociological intervention as practiced by clinical sociologists; the problem is resolved by directing redefinition efforts at higher or lower levels of social participation rather at the level at which the identified problem lies. Cheek and Baker (1977) found that subject resistance and ethical problems associated with resocialization programs for prison inmates could be avoided by organizing "self-control training" programs for inmates. This created the latent function of reducing recidivism—the identified problem— which occurs at the organizational level of the criminal justice system.

Cooperative intervention tends to be favored in principle by clinical sociologists. In this mode the client's active participation in the change process becomes the key feature of the intervention (Lippitt and Lippitt 1978). Those who will be affected by the intervention are helped to participate in, or even take primary responsibility for, making decisions about and implementing the redefinition process; the role of the sociologist becomes, more than anything else, that of a facilitator (Glass 1981).

The cooperative mode may also be employed in social research to increase the study's clinical value (Leitko and Peterson 1982). Jaques's "social analysis" techniques (1982) might typify the "pure" cooperative intervention. However, in many cases (as when the situation is highly politicized and marked by considerable power differentials) the facilitator role may prove too cumbersome or simply impractical. A pure cooperative approach also may not fit the sociologist's personal strengths or style; in such cases, a mixed-mode approach will be followed.

In practice, the principle of eclecticism extends beyond theory to mode. Cases of actual sociological intervention generally display considerable theoretical eclecticism, an admixture of modal strategies, and elements of indirect approach designed to take advantage of the integration of levels of focus. In any case, the change agent can only benefit from clarifying the modes of intervention being employed.

THE PERSONAL LEVEL

I will now flesh out these principles by discussing a variety of sociological interventions that show how these practices relate to the taxonomy. Direct intervention at the personal level, while the logical beginning point, is the most difficult to differentiate from the conventional practices of psychotherapy and counseling, but subtle—and highly significant—differences can be seen.

Even though most practitioners working at this level are associated with the microsociological paradigm of the Chicago School, they focus on the person as a member of society and not just as "an individual" with private problems. They employ a social perspective in analysis and design of intervention that focuses on (1) the client's actual conduct in everyday life; (2) the internalized sociocultural realities that frame and organize that conduct; and (3) the relationship between these realities, the person's conduct, and his or her situation in terms of the various levels of social context (Powers 1979a, b; Straus 1979b). Sociological interventions, whether direct or indirect, may often take clearly social forms, as in directing clients to appropriate community support networks to reinforce their definitions of the situation, or to peer self-help groups to help them reconstruct their realities outside a therapy framework (Glassner and Freedman 1979; Straus 1982).

Indirect approaches more clearly illustrate the special features of a sociological approach at this level. Coombs (1980) describes a drug and alcohol abuse prevention program offering a dramatic alternative to conventional asocial models which seek to scare youths away from experimentation or treat identified users on the presumption that only sick, deviant, or deficient personalities become abusers. His approach is aimed at individuals who are in a marginal position and are likely to adopt substance-abusing identities—generally those of junior-high-school age. Coombs intervenes by working with the family groups of identified marginal youth so as to enhance family solidarity, keep the family as the youth's primary reference group (rather than drug-abusing peers), and remedy deficits in family skills such as communication, doing things together, or working as a group. Thus, the goal of defining the subject's conduct in a prosocial direction is accomplished indirectly, through what Coombs calls "family strengthening." In this kind of program, the indirect attack becomes the sociologist's primary tactic. Minimal attention is given to substance abuse itself or to correcting antisocial behavior; these are dealt with through indirect intervention at the group level.

THE GROUP LEVEL

Interventions at the group level are primarily directed at role structure, taking into account such factors as authority relationships, consensus regarding roles and their boundaries, degree of involvement in roles, role strain or conflict, informal versus formal realities, and the degree to which the operational definition of the group facilitates or hinders attainment of its collective purposes (see Capelle 1979). A nonsocial approach at this level can certainly be found in the practice of many marital therapists or business consultants, but such an approach becomes difficult to justify given the manifestly systemic nature of the social group, in which the whole is conspicuously more than the sum of its individual parts.

A direct sociological intervention might be exemplified by William Foote Whyte's solution to a restaurant chain's problems of inefficiency, worker dissatisfaction, and high turnover. He found that there were problems in the role structure of these restaurants. Waitresses, that is, women, were placed in a position of giving orders to the higher-status cooks, who were men: those of relatively lower status were giving orders to their nominal superiors, a problem compounded by a violation of gender roles then current in American culture. Whyte's solution was to resolve role strain by a simple mechanical expedient: employment of rotating metal bands with clips on them—known as "spindles"— which allowed waitresses to post their orders in systematic fashion without having to convey them verbally to the male cooks. The changes incurred by this intervention were so dramatic that something of the sort has become standard throughout the industry. Note how this intervention related the role structure of the group to the broader norms governing conduct in the general society.

Cooperative intervention at this level is illustrated by Kleymeyer's organization of the "Program for Humanization of Health Care in the University Hospital" at Cali, Colombia (1979). The sociologist was initially recruited as part of a quantitatively oriented research team investigating the causes of the disuse of outpatient services. He trained some of their native interviewers to conduct field observations of service delivery in their spare time. Evaluating their reports, he found that the public considered the services dehumanizing, anxiety provoking, and alienating. He was then invited by the hospital's leadership to devise strategies to mitigate this situation.

Recognizing the potential problems for an outsider in trying to impose change from above, Kleymeyer chose to adopt the role of costrategist, instigator, and facilitator of change. He allowed the politically savvy head of human relations for the hospital to do the actual moving and shaking. In selecting, designing, evaluating, and fine tuning innovations, he drew upon key hospital personnel, client interviews, professionals on the scene, and workers' forums that had been developed early in the change project, so that intervention was permitted to take a locally generated and self-directed course. These innovations included courses in human relations and first aid for hospital staff, workers' forums, creation of an in-house position of "patients' representative," material incentives for humane and competent treatment, and other changes involving training personnel in necessary role skills, redefining existing roles, or developing new patterns of social relations. By this strategy, Kleymeyer sought to establish a permanent, self-perpetuating, participatory institutional structure that would outlive his contractually limited tenure in the hospital setting.

THE ORGANIZATIONAL LEVEL

Strategies at the organizational level represent, for the most part, an elaboration of group-level tactics. However, redefinition is primarily aimed at the institutionalized patterns of relations *between* groups rather than role relations within the group.

Direct tactics, although often too straightforward, can be effective. For example, Trist (1981) describes an intervention in the Norwegian shipping industry. Onboard facilities were redesigned to promote a sense of community among the various crew and officer groups who must live together under isolated conditions twenty-four hours a day over extended periods of time. Redefinition of the shipboard environment to facilitate this new pattern of social relations included creating common recreation rooms and dining halls where all ranks and ratings could mingle (normally each group ate and socialized independently in status-graded facilities); integrating deck and engine room crew; and reducing status differentials between officers and crew.

An example of an indirect approach has been described by Freedman and Rosenfeld (1983), who were invited by the New Jersey Division of Mental Health and Hospitals to assist in the implementation of mandated changes aimed at humanization of services and expediting the release of clients to their local communities. Their initial assignment involved implementing a new standardized record-keeping system for the six state hospitals. It soon became obvious, however, that there was no real agreement, even among leadership, as to precisely what was desired or how to go about doing it. Furthermore, true implementation of the new policies would require significant redefinition of roles, relations between various groups within the hospital system, and even meanings of basic terms such as *case management* or *team approach.*

To forestall conflict, and yet implement these major redefinitions, they devised an indirect strategy centered on the introduction of a new form. As is usual in such organizations, a training program was instituted concerning the use of this form. In this case, however, both the design of the form itself and that of the training program were deliberately organized to have the latent function of redefining roles, institutions, and the culture of this system. Thus, an ostensibly limited and innocuous innovation—a new record-keeping technology—was used as an indirect strategy for organization-scale change.

Cooperative strategies at this level have long been a staple of sociological practice (Shostak 1966; Jaques 1982). However, this kind of approach has only recently been extended to areas such as the management of social impacts from government or industrial development projects. "Social Impact Management" (Preister and Kent 1984), for example, brings members of communities to be affected by large-scale projects into the process of negotiating and working out a mutually acceptable plan to deal with issues and manage potential impacts that will be agreeable to or actually benefit those affected by the proposed development. Special care is taken to identify and involve community networks and to mitigate impacts at all levels of the local context so as to maintain the integrity of community life and organization.

THE WORLD LEVEL

At the highest scale we are considering, that of social worlds, sociological interventions can take even more complex forms. For Lee (1979), the direct approach at this most macrosocial level is identified with humanistically framed, change-oriented research; he views the sociological clinician as seeking to understand through firsthand materials how socially organized situations actually function and how they can be influenced; he then suggests practical strategies for modifying or coping with problematic social realities, trends, and developments. His work has included the study of propaganda in our society with the goal of sensitizing the broad public to the problem, and generating the consciousness necessary to defend them from this kind of manipulation. Significantly, his major work on the subject was published in 1952, during the rise of the cold war mentality and rapid expansion of the advertising profession. Clearly his intent was to generate cultural defenses against the manipulation of society by elites.

California's "Friends Can Be Good Medicine" campaign is a good example of a world-scale intervention combining both indirect and cooperative modes.

By devoting a small fraction of its annual mental health budget to this preventive intervention, the state hoped to combat rising demands upon its physical and mental health systems. Its strategy was based on the copious recent literature documenting the inverse relationship between involvement in primary groups and the rates of incidence of mental and physical health problems (see Hunter 1982 for a summary of the literature). Its plan was to bring about a change in culture by raising the general consciousness regarding the direct personal benefits of developing and maintaining social support networks (Hunter 1982). This strategy therefore incorporated both indirect and direct approaches.

Delivery utilized a cooperative approach. The consulting firm hired for the campaign developed printed training and information materials, audiovisual training films, and a series of radio and television spots stressing the message that "friends can be good medicine." Ten paid coordinators then recruited volunteer regional coordinators (I was one) from county agencies and networks. After a trainers' workshop, these volunteers then recruited and trained community-level leaders from education, churches, business, government, and other local networks to deliver workshops and set up local events during the month of June 1982. The entire state was to be saturated by community-based, consciousness-raising events supported by a media blitz—all at minimal cost to the state. This was the first statewide mental health prevention program.

This campaign, designed exclusively by psychologists and "applied behavioral scientists," illustrates some of the pitfalls stemming from exclusion of sociologists from organizing and implementing sociological intervention. In this case, the "cultural approach" historically associated with clinical sociology (Wirth 1931) would have had dramatic impact. Instead, the beautifully designed and printed workbooks stressed the interests of "hip," humanistic psychologists—alternative life styles, consciousness-raising groups, and new games. They were also written so as to require a high level of literacy and intellectual orientation. In effect, they might have been designed to be rejected by rural, working-class, and poor people; businessmen; and conservatives: most of the population, in fact. The materials also evidenced no awareness on the part of their producers of the long-term macrosocial changes underlying the disruption of traditional support networks and primary group structures, leaving the impression that alienation from significant others was a purely individual matter, entirely correctable by personal action.

BETWEEN-LEVELS INTERVENTION

It is important to point out that the model presented here can also be used to typify interventions targeted at interpersonal, intergroup, interorganization, and interworld problems. In essence, between-level interventions operate at the next level upscale. An interpersonal problem would be treated as a blockage, misalignment, or other difficulty at the group level. In solving such a problem, one helps those concerned to work out joint definitions of the situation by clarifying their respective roles and statuses. Intervention might involve improving communications, resolving contradictions in participants' definitions of the situation, or creating entirely new, mutually acceptable definitions, including recognition of their de facto status as a group. Except that our model typifies interworld collectivities simply as higher-scale social worlds, the same logic is followed at the higher levels of between-levels intervention.

CONCLUSION

It has been my concern in this chapter to tease out the generic logic and structure of sociological interventions. By presenting this within a taxonomic framework, I have sought to sensitize the practitioner to the special features of the sociological approach and also to move a discussion of the substance of clinical sociology up to a more concrete and hence manageable level.

Implicit in the foregoing is the premise that many or most problems encountered in social life, from the personal to the societal levels, can best be understood and dealt with as *social problems*. They cry out for sociological intervention, which is defined here as reconstructing the operational definition of the situation with reference to the multiple, interacting layers of social context framing any particular case.

Clinical sociology is not identical with sociological intervention, for both sociologists and nonsociologists can and do engage in this form of work. However, it becomes apparent that the clinical sociologist is best qualified to practice sociological intervention because the approach lies squarely in the domain carved out by sociological training, sociological tradition, and the special sensitivities inculcated only by immersion in a specifically sociological perspective.

NOTES

1. Those specializing in sociological counseling or therapy at the personal level might wish to discriminate a still more micro-scale intervention: the *intrapersonal*. Here, the client's phenomenological definitions of the situation as manifested in cognitive, psychomotor, or psychosomatic self-interactions become the target for change (Straus 1983). However, these are still analyzed within the context of a social problem framed by culture and group participation and managed similarly to intervention at the molar "personal" level.

REFERENCES

Blumer, H. 1969. *Symbolic Interaction: Perspective and Method.* Englewood Cliffs, NJ: Prentice-Hall.

Capelle, R. G. 1979. *Changing Human Systems.* Toronto: International Human Systems Institute.

Cheek, F. E., and J. C. Baker 1977. Self-control training for inmates. *Psychological Reports* 41:559-68.

Coombs, R. H. 1980. Family strengthening to redirect drug-prone youth. Presentation at the Pacific Sociological Association meetings, Anaheim, California.

Erickson, M. V. 1980. *The Collected Papers of Milton Erickson,* Edited By E. Rossi. New York: Irvington.

Fisch, R., J.H. Weakland, and L. Segal. 1982. *The Tactics of Change.* San Francisco: Jossey-Bass.

Freedman, J.A., and P. Rosenfeld. 1983. Clinical sociology: The system as client. Paper presented at the joint meetings of the Eastern Sociological Society and Clinical Sociology Association, Baltimore, Maryland.

Glass, J. 1981. Facilitating change in human systems. Paper presented at the Southern Sociological Society meetings, Louisville, Kentucky.

Glassner, B. and J. A. Freedman. 1979. *Clinical Sociology.* New York: Longman.

Hunter, L. 1982. Friends can be good medicine: Resource guide. Sacramento: California State Dept. of Mental Health, Mental Health Promotion Branch.

Jaques, E. 1982. The method of social analysis in social change and social research. *Clinical Sociology Review* 1:50–58.

Kleymeyer, C. D. 1979. Putting field methods to work. *American Behavioral Scientist* 22(4):589–608.

Lee, A. McC. 1952. *How to Understand Propaganda.* New York: Rinehart.

——1973. *Toward Humanist Sociology.* Englewood Cliffs, NJ: Prentice-Hall.

——1978. *Sociology for Whom?* New York: Oxford University Press.

——1979. The services of clinical sociology. *American Behavioral Scientist* 22(4):487–512.

Leitko, T. and S. Peterson. 1982. Social exchange in research: Toward a 'New Deal.' *Journal of Applied Behavioral Science* 18(4):447–62.

Lippitt, R. and G. Lippitt 1978. *The Consulting Process in Action.* La Jolla, CA: University Associates.

Lofland, J. 1976. *Doing Social Life.* New York: Wiley-Interscience.

Parsons, T. 1951. *The Social System.* Glencoe, IL: The Free Press.

Powers, S. 1979a. The role of clinical sociologist in a multispecialty health facility. *American Behavioral Scientist* 22(4):543–56.

——1979b. Clinical sociological treatment of a chronic slasher. *Case Analysis* 1(3):169–79.

Preister, K. and J. Kent. 1984. Clinical sociology and social impact: from assessment to management. *Clinical Sociology Review* 2.

Sarbin, T. 1976. Hypnosis: The dramaturgical perspective. Paper presented at the meetings of The Society for Clinical and Experimental Hypnosis.

Shostak, A. D. (ed.) 1966. *Case Studies in Social Problems and Directed Social Change.* Homewood, IL: The Dorsey Press.

Straus, R. A. 1977. The life change process. Unpublished PhD thesis, University of California-Davis.

——1979a Clinical sociology. Edited by Straus. Special issue of *American Behavioral Scientist* 22 no. 4.

——1979b Doing clinical sociology in behavioral counseling: A model weight management program. *Case Analysis* 1(3):181–201.

——1982 Clinical sociology on the one-to-one level: A social behavioral approach to counseling. *Clinical Sociology Review* 1:59–74.

——1983 The potential of symbolic interactionism: Thinking, feeling, imagining, and holistic social psychology. Unpublished paper.

Thomas, W. I. 1931. *The Unadjusted Girl.* Boston: Little, Brown.

Trist, E. 1981. The evaluation of socio-technical systems. Occasional Working Paper No. Z, Ontario Quality of Working Life Center. Toronto: Ministry of Labor.

Watzlawick, P., J. H. Weakland, and R. Fisch. 1967. *Change: Principles of Problem Formation and Problem Resolution.* New York: Norton.

Wirth, L. 1931. Clinical sociology. *American Journal of Sociology* 37: 49–660. Reprinted in *Clinical Sociology Review.* 1:7–22.

von Bertalanffy, L. 1968. *General Systems Theory.* New York: George Braziller.

Znaniecki, F. 1934. *The Method of Sociology.* New York: Farrar and Rinehart.

4

Linking Sociology to Clinical Practice

Patricia P. Rieker and James W. Begun

Medical sociologists have consistently exhibited concern for the application of sociological knowledge to health and health care delivery problems. Because of the large number of medical sociologists employed in applied settings, and the growing interest in direct intervention in individual cases based on sociological analysis, "clinical sociology," emphasis on the application of medical sociology is increasing. This emphasis is reflected in a recent spate of textbooks and articles detailing the contributions of sociology and the other social sciences to improving the diagnosis and treatment of health problems (Todd, 1989; Fisher, 1988; Rieker and Carmen, 1984; Fitzpatrick et al, 1984; Johnson et al., 1982; Eisenberg and Kleinman, 1981; Mishler et al., 1981; Brenner et al., 1980; Hingson et al., 1981; Counte and Christman, 1981; Glassner, 1981; Shuval, 1981). Ruderman (1981:928) notes that medical sociologists "have remained outside of the substance of medicine. They deal neither with the patient's illness nor with the physician's knowledge. As a result, medical sociology . . . remains sociology *outside* of medicine."

We argue that sociologists have failed to devote enough attention to the process of applying knowledge from medical sociology to clinical practice and education. Literature such as that cited above chronicles the many developments in sociological knowledge which are relevant to improving health care. The necessary final step in making sociological knowledge accessible to health practitioners, however, is seldom taken. This step involves distinguishing a sociological (or, more generally, a "social") perspective of the illness process from perspectives traditionally taught to and accepted by health providers. The final step also involves applying the social perspective to actual cases, so that *clinicians* can concretely *experience* the *translation of sociological knowledge into clinical practice.*

In this chapter we describe one way of presenting and using sociological

36

knowledge in clinical settings. We attempt to show how sociologists can communicate knowledge about the etiology of illness which is treated in clinical settings, and how such knowledge can help direct the provider of care to more appropriate interventions. We hope that the framework will be useful to other medical sociologists faced with the need to communicate or apply sociological concepts and findings in order to improve the quality of health services delivery at the patient-clinician level.

LEVELS OF EXPLANATION OF HEALTH AND ILLNESS[1]

For analytic purposes, we can formally distinguish three complementary methods of explaining the onset and course of illness. The first level of explanation, familiar to all, is a *biological* one—disease is explained as an abnormality in the individual's biological processes. Similarly, the *psychological* level of explanation explains certain diseases as disruptions in the individual's emotional and psychodynamic processes. Both of these levels of explanation focus on individual health and pathology independent of the social structure, as direct causal linkages of biological and psychological factors to disease are demonstrated to exist *within* the individual patient.

The third mode of explanation, the *social* level, contrasts sharply with the first two. A social explanation is concerned with the impact of social structure on individual behavior. In this view, most abstractly, social structure consists of the organization of a set of social positions, with "social positions" referring to the role expectations faced by all individuals by virtue of their placement in society. The illness process is intricately influenced by the social positions which an individual holds and by other elements of the social structure, such as the law, economy, polity, and cultural values.

All three levels of explanation are necessary for a comprehensive understanding of health and illness. It is axiomatic in contemporary medical thinking that health and illness are multi-determined (e.g., Engel, 1982; Weiner, 1978). The etiology of illness, the process of treatment, and the health care outcome are alike in not being explicable by a single model of interpretation or a single level of analysis. There is ready agreement that in any episode of illness, from onset to conclusion (and of course in the increasingly prevalent chronic conditions there *is* no decisive "conclusion," save death), biological, psychological, and social factors are all implicated.

While the contributions of biological and psychological factors to the illness process are well appreciated, the influence of social factors is not. Our characteristic habits of mind urge us to seek single causes and simple, direct logics of cause-and-effect. These relationships are easier to demonstrate at the biological and psychological levels, where links with the disease are often explicit and observable. The association between *social* factors and illness is less explicit and requires more demonstration and justification; this is indicated by the familiar criticism that sociological knowledge is not relevant to clinical practice.

SOCIAL STRUCTURE AND THE ILLNESS PROCESS

What follows is a simple model for linking the individual's illness process to social structure, and simultaneously to the knowledge generated by sociology that is relevant to clinical care. The model provides a framework for understanding how elements of the social context influence the illness process. Relevance is achieved by organizing the model around the *illness process*, which is the center of the clinician's activity. The social context of illness includes consideration of all the factors outside of the individual which influence illness (see Figure 1).

In the social model, the illness process is defined by four overlapping stages. The first phase in the illness process is conceptualized as the "Onset" stage. The major contribution of social factors to explaining the onset of illness has important implications for *preventing* illness and promoting health, which after all should be the ultimate goal of health care delivery systems. After the onset of illness, individuals respond in different ways, making "Response" the second stage in the illness process. An individual's socially conditioned response may or may not lead to interaction with some type of clinician. Because we are concerned particularly with those circumstances when this does occur, the third stage in the illness process is the "Interaction" between patient and clinician. The interaction eventually leads to some kind of "Outcome," which defines the final stage in an illness sequence or leads to the onset of another sequence.

Each stage of the illness process is influenced by structural factors, such as social institutions, cultural values, technology, and, more directly, the social positions of patient and clinician. The social positions of patients and clinicians are defined by age, sex, ethnicity, occupation, education, social class, religion, family situation, and geographic location.

An individual's social position can shape the onset of illness, response to illness, interaction with clinicians, and, depending on the nature of the illness, the outcome of the interaction. For example, some individuals may not perceive the organic onset of disease as illness. Pain may simply be denied or ignored. Signs of illness may not be interpreted as symptoms. If illness is acknowledged, an individual may or may not adopt a sick role. Financial problems might not "allow" an individual to admit that he or she is sick.

When an individual does acknowledge ill health symptoms, he or she generally contacts a clinician. At this stage, relative social positions shape the attitudes, behavior, and role performance of the clinician in interaction with the patient. Social positions may affect the clinician's feelings about the patient, perception of the illness, and decision about what type of treatment is most

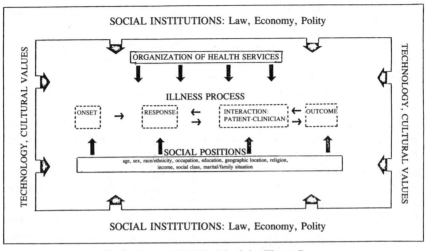

Figure 1. A Social Model of the Illness Process

appropriate. (For an in-depth analysis of gender effects on clinical encounters see Todd, 1988.)

As indicated above, illness proceeds within and is influenced by structural factors such as social institutions, technology, and cultural values. Social institutions that affect the illness process include the law, the polity, and the economy. These general, macro-level influences determine how a society develops mechanisms and distributes resources for coping with illness and disease. For example, cultural values incorporated into sex-role socialization can be used to help explain the differential morbidity and mortality rates of males and females. National and state laws, such as those governing Medicare and Medicaid, affect the utilization behavior of patients and the treatment patterns of providers.

The social model of illness is an oversimplification of a complex process, but it provides a perspective for understanding the interrelatedness of social institutions, cultural values, technology, social positions of patients and clinicians, health, and illness.

IMPLICATIONS OF THE SOCIAL MODEL OF THE ILLNESS PROCESS FOR CLINICAL PRACTICE

The social explanation of behavior places illness in a wider social context, alerting the clinician to look beyond the patient's biology and psychology for information. Even when armed with relatively accurate information about the biological, psychological, and social factors influencing an illness episode, however, the clinician faces a dilemma: how to weigh the relative contributions of these sets of factors in the course of illness in a given case, and how to apply that information most effectively in treatment. The intellectual and organizational aspects of this dilemma are largely unexplored and unappreciated by sociologists, yet they are perhaps the most compelling practical issues confronting clinicians who believe that multiple layers of causation exist for most illness.

There are circumstances, such as with medical trauma and acute symptom relief, when the answer to the "how-to-intervene" dilemma is obvious. In addition to treating acute symptoms, however, the clinician must often address issues of restoration of health, recurrence, and long-term care. During this process, when the clinician must still make many decisions about how and where to intervene, the answers are less obvious. We believe that the more information the clinician obtains about the patient's definition of the situation and the social context of the illness, the more efficacious and humane subsequent decisions will be. Knowledge of the patient's social context aids the clinician in developing empathy, making the appropriate diagnoses, prescribing a realistic treatment regimen, and predicting the psychosocial outcomes of the illness episode.

In the remainder of this chapter, we will describe three cases of actual clinical experiences of patients and health care providers which illustrate the use of a broad, social model to interpret individual cases in clinical practice or education. The analyses following the cases are written as though the audience is involved in clinical practice or education.

The following case-example illustrates how information about social context challenges the boundaries of the role of the clinician and results in more effective health care delivery.

CASE #1: Secondary Exposure to Lead Poisoning

After a routine examination for the Early and Periodic Screening, Disease and Treatment (EPSDT) program at a local health department, lab test results showed that a 20-month-old, white, healthy male had an elevated PhB (whole blood lead). Despite the fact that the child was asymptomatic, the public health nurse telephoned the child's home to discuss the lab test results with his mother. The child's grandmother answered the telephone and explained that the child's mother was in the hospital being treated for lead poisoning. The father was not living at home. The nurse then asked the grandmother to bring the other children in the family to the health department; those children were also found to have above-normal lead levels.

Clearly, something in the family's physical environment was contributing to lead poisoning. The public health nurse continued the investigation and decided to interview the child's mother in the hospital. During the conversation she learned that the mother was employed at a plant that manufactured lead-acid storage batteries. After some probing, the nurse found out that the mother's work required much hand labor, and, consequently, that she was in continuous contact with the lead oxide coating of battery plates. No uniform or garment covers were provided by the company, and the mother wore her work clothing home. The mother was unaware of any potential health risks arising from her occupation. Obviously, however, the mother's clothing was transmitting lead oxide particles to her home and children.

The medical director of the health department, a physician, became involved. He notified the battery plant of the apparent problem, and the plant offered full cooperation to the health department in checking other workers' children. In all, 55 children were examined and 13 were referred to a nearby university hospital for evaluation by specialists. Four of the 13 were hospitalized, and plans were made to follow all 55 children for some time " to see that they don't get into trouble."

While the battery plant implemented numerous changes in ventilation, uniform laundering, plant housekeeping, and employee blood tests, soon after the incident several families filed multi-million dollar law suits against the company for failing to provide safe working conditions.

Dissecting the Social Context

The hazardous work situation described above is not an unusual one. Today, there is a much greater awareness on the part of both employers and workers of the effect of the quality of work life, particularly in settings involving exposure to toxic substances, on illness. In the past, this important link was often ignored by workers and clinicians. In the case of pediatrics, for example, Dolcourt et al. (1978:565) wrote that "Occupational histories are seldom obtained in the routine practice of pediatrics, and then may not include maternal occupation." This problem was recognized in 1979 in a major recommendation of the American Public Health Association, which began as follows:

The American Public Health Association,

Noting that all physicians and other health workers have a potential role in the detection of occupationally induced illness; and

Observing that physicians and other health personnel have often had little training in taking occupational health history; and

Observing that diagnosis of occupationally induced illness is often delayed by lack of adequate occupational history; and

Pointing out that recognition of occupational agents of disease may be promoted with the use of a systematically and efficiently organized ongoing study of associa- tion of diseases and symptoms with features of the job environment . . . .

The statement continued with recommendations for the development and implementation of national guidelines for the taking of occupational histories, including past and present job assignments (APHA, 1979:305).

One lesson of this case is clear: Clinicians need to be aware of one social position—occupation—of all patients and members of the patients' families. This element of the social context is being recognized as a crucial precipitant of more and more diseases, including many cancers, brown lung (byssinosis), and black lung. As more mothers work outside the home, secondary childhood exposure to industrial toxins can be expected to pose greater health risks. The influence of occupation on illness can be experienced psychologically, as in feelings of stress generated by extreme job pressure, before it has a direct physical effect. In the case above, the physical effect of occupation is more direct and obvious, as the work setting of the patient's mother clearly transmitted the direct cause of disease (lead oxide).

More generally, the social model of the illness process directs the clinician to elements of the social context which may be relevant to the onset of illness. Data collection in the form of history taking is systematized, and the clinician is prompted to consider all possible clues as to the etiology of the illness.

Having obtained relevant information and having instituted medical treatment of the immediate physical symptoms, the clinician in the case above is faced with another critical decision: *What are the limits to the clinician's role?* Does the clinician have a responsibility beyond the individual patient? In the above case, as in most cases, the decision was complicated by the involvement of multiple clinicians in the treatment process—a public health nurse, a health department physician, and university-based medical specialists. While in this case the involvement of health department clinicians made the decision to contact the employer a relatively straightforward one, it is not clear that most privately practicing physicians would have pressed the investigation beyond the individual patient. The assumption of a greater responsibility for the health of the plant's workers and their families required a greater time commitment on the part of the clinicians. In many cases, as in this one, clinicians also may become involved as witnesses in law suits between patients and employers.

The social model provides a perspective for understanding the macro- and micro-influences on the clinicians' reactions in this case. At the macro-level, the influence of social institutions, technology, and cultural values on the reaction of the clinicians can be distinguished. For example, new scientific knowledge about the effects of toxic agents on physical health and the technology to detect those effects has led to discovery of the widespread existence of occupational health problems and has made possible the cost-effective screening of large numbers of individuals. Government has expanded its role in protecting workers in their job settings, evidenced most clearly by the development and enforcement of job safety standards in the 1970s by the Occupational Safety and Health Administration and the Environmental Protection Agency. This represents a shift from individual to societal responsibility for the exposure to certain health risks. In this country, the improving condition of the economy in the late 1970s and early 1980s was instrumental in promoting this shift in responsibility.

The social positions of the clinician and patient are also prominent in an understanding of the various responses to the lead poisoning situation. The occupation and educational background of one of the clinicians was particularly significant, as the public health nurse was trained to look for occupational sources of illness. The physicians involved in the case were relatively young and newly trained, and had a commitment to a broader and more activist model of the role of the physician. That the problem arose in a small business in a small community facilitated the quick, voluntary cooperation of the battery plant with the health department. The fact that the patient's mother in this case was a single parent with low prospects for job mobility probably raised the likelihood of the clinicians and patients seeking a cooperative solution with the company. Most of the company's employees wanted to maintain their jobs. Both employers and employees are hurt when redress of occupational health hazards requires closing down a business.

The social model of illness applies equally to physical and emotional ill-health. The lack of understanding of the distinctive features of the social explanation of behavior is as common among mental health care providers as among other clinicians. For example, only recently have psychiatrists begun to systematically examine how social factors shape the development, and sometimes the destruction, of a patient's social identity and psychological well-being (Rieker and Carmen, 1984). Clearly, clinicians still do not fully accept or understand the interplay between social and psychological processes and physical illness. Case examples 2 and 3 demonstrate the applicability of the social model to psychiatric treatment.[2]

CASE #2: Consequences of Family Violence

Ms. Snow is a 26-year-old woman who had been taking sedatives as a sleeping aid. She was admitted to a local, small community hospital complaining of headache, nausea, vomiting, and fever. Various cultures, including blood and urine, were negative for any bacterial organisms. During this admission, a drug history of the uses of Placidyl and Darvocet was obtained, although Ms. Snow fully denied this. She was then referred to an inpatient psychiatric center at a large teaching hospital for treatment for withdrawal from hypnotic sedatives.

On admission to the psychiatric center, there was no evidence of psychosis or other major psychiatric diagnosis. Following completion of the withdrawal procedures, the patient was interviewed extensively and it was discovered that she had a long history of physical abuse by her family prior to her marriage, and more recently, by her husband. The patient came from a rather chaotic family situation where both parents had a long history of alcohol abuse.

Early in the course of hospitalization, the patient's husband appeared at the hospital and made numerous threats to damage the patient, staff, and property. He was angry that his wife had been hospitalized. After probing the extent of the violence within her marriage, it became obvious that Ms. Snow had a history of depressive symptoms, such as poor appetite, loss of energy, insomnia, feelings of worthlessness, inappropriate guilt, and thoughts of suicide. The clinicians concluded that family violence had served to reinforce and exacerbate her underlying depressive disorder, and that the use of sedative hypnotics was an attempt at self-medication, which resulted in the temporary drug use that led to her hospitalization. Shortly after being hospitalized, it was determined that Ms. Snow was also suffering from hyperthyroidism.

The patient's hospital course was interesting in that she responded readily to support and external validation that her marital situation was contributing to her depressive symptoms. Episodes of contact with her husband elicited fear, confusion, increased anxiety, difficulty sleeping, and difficulty concentrating. During treatment the patient gradually developed more self-esteem and became more and more self-reliant. Investigating various alternatives at the time of discharge, she decided to seek the aid of a Women's Shelter in a nearby community. At the time of discharge, the feeling was one of optimism with regard to her potential recovery, if supportive systems could be found. The decision was made not to place this patient on antidepressant medication, as her hyperthyroidism could readily have predisposed her to an underlying depressive disorder, and until that was under control, it was felt that antidepressants would be inappropriate.

Dissecting the Social Context

This case illustrates the interplay between physical symptoms, the underlying psychological processes, and the social arena in which the personal dynamics are played out. Take for example the initial decision by the local community doctor to refer the patient to more specialized psychiatric facilities for treatment. Without the details of the situation, we can speculate that the local doctor's decision to refer the patient for drug-addiction withdrawal was an appropriate response to the acute symptoms, although it is clear that the patient's treatment needs were more complex. Once the acute symptoms were no longer problematic, the clinicians at the psychiatric center undertook a more comprehensive evaluation of the psychological and social sources of the patient's condition. During this evaluation they uncovered not only the fact that the patient was currently a victim of wife abuse, but also that she had a history of family violence and depression-related symptoms. Realizing the contribution of the violence to the patient's current depression and apparent drug-addiction, the clinicians were able to validate that the marital situation was one of the factors contributing to her multiple symptoms and to encourage the patient to confront that issue directly. By the time the patient was released from the hospital, enough evidence had accumulated to convince the clinicians that the violence in the marital situation needed to be eliminated before beginning drug therapy. As a result, the clinicians reinforced her decision to seek assistance from a shelter for abused women after exploring the alternatives.

Using a women's shelter as an adjunct form of treatment that provides a therapeutic environment is an option which derives from research clarifying the extent and consequences of family violence (Rieker and Carmen, 1984). This new knowledge has been accompanied by legislation supporting the development of shelters and legal mechanisms protecting the victim. These developments have also influenced the training of clinicians to seek information about violence and to recognize the physical and psychological attributes to victimization (Hilberman, 1980).

Social changes affecting the marital roles of men and women also enter into the next case, in which a middle-aged male is forced into retirement due to a disability.

CASE #3: Response to Physical Disability

Mr. Carr is a 52-year-old man who became disabled with chronic lower back pain that made him unable to work. Before this disability, he had been a chief detective in a community police force. Following his unemployment, he became increasingly depressed, feeling that he was useless because he was not able to work. Prior to being admitted to a psychiatric inpatient unit, he began drinking excessively and had become suicidal.

While in the hospital, Mr. Carr expressed concern about losing control and was particularly worried about his irritability, especially with his ten-year-old son. He made it clear that he felt that he was nothing if he could not be a "hardworking man," and that staying home and doing things like housework and cooking, while his wife worked, was unmanly. He did perform these tasks but kept them hidden from public view. The role shift that his disability had necessitated generated considerable tension in the marriage. Although his wife was enjoying some of the increased freedom and the new job that she had taken, she also shared some of her husband's feelings that he was not as much of a man if he was not bringing in money.

Mr. Carr came from a family where his father was a very hard worker who had died at the age of sixty-five, one month after his retirement. His mother was a traditional housewife who had not worked outside the home. The patient identified strongly with his father's work habits and frame of mind. Both he and his wife had remarked shortly before his father's death that it would be disastrous for him ever to retire.

After extensive evaluation, the clinicians felt that unless Mr. Carr's rigid sex role assumptions were challenged, his depression would continue. As part of the treatment plan, they deliberately challenged his notion that his masculinity could only be defined by external achievements and his money-making potential. It became clear that he and his wife were locked into a power struggle over many things, most notably liquor, and that Mr. Carr was unable to compromise appropriately because he had already lost so much control over his life that any compromise was seen as further emasculating him. Three weeks into the hospitalization, the clinical team noted that Mr. Carr was not being constructively confronted about his behavior; they then realized that they were responding to his feelings of impotence by feeling themselves that confronting this would challenge his manhood.

Mr. Carr was passive in many ways. This pattern was, in part, a defense against his rage about what had happened to him and was also one of the ways he tried to control his pain. Since he could not determine which specific thing aggravated his pain, he tried to do nothing. He had an extremely difficult time getting angry and even when provoked on the ward would find many ways to deny his anger.

Eventually, Mr. Carr was confronted with the need to grieve the loss of his job, to which it was likely he would never be able to return. He had managed up to this point to cling to vague hopes that somehow things would turn around. During the course of his hospitalization he did considerable grieving around this issue, and on a weekend pass went over to his boss' house and turned in his badge. He was upset at this meeting, as was his boss, but Mr. Carr felt good about the step he had taken to move on. He also began to recognize that he had what he called a "communication problem'' with his wife. This consisted of not revealing any of his feelings to her, including sadness and anger.

In family therapy considerable effort was devoted to this problem, as well as to the issue of the role changes within the marriage. It became obvious that Mrs. Carr also had had considerable difficulty accepting her husband's disability and that the grief would, in fact, have to be experienced by both of them in order for it to have a supportive effect. In group therapy, Mr. Carr did get some support for his work around the house. When he asked other men his age what they would think about his doing the housework if they came over to his house, they rather matter-of-factly stated that "they would just think he was doing the housework.'' In occupational therapy Mr. Carr began to develop new skills that included copper tooling and building electronic devices. He was taught some relaxation techniques by a recreational therapist and a medical student that seemed to help with his lower back pain. He began to think of ways to enjoy his leisure time, rather than seeing it as a constant reminder of how useless he was.

Dissecting the Social Context

This case highlights the influence of social variable—sex-role values and expectations—on the patient's response to his physical disability and the meaning he attached to it. The patient's narrow and rigid conception of masculinity meant that loss of the ability to work and to provide for his family resulted in feelings of worthlessness, unexpressed anger, and eventual depression. His inability to work outside the home necessitated a shift in family roles which the patient found further humiliating and unacceptable. The clinicians' focus on the part that the rigid sex-role expectations played in the patient's incapacitating depression made it possible for the patient to begin coping with the reality of the changes in his marital situation. The discovery that his wife shared these rigid expectations was a crucial feature in the effectiveness of the family therapy. Unlike the situation in Case #2, maintenance of the marital relationship was a feasible focus of treatment because of the stability and strength of the emotional ties.

The new knowledge generated by the attention focused on the detrimental effects of restricted sex roles for both men and women directs clinicians to identify the fundamental part that such conceptions can play in the etiology of physical and emotional problems (Rieker and Carmen, 1984). Changes in values about sex-role expectations in the wider social context make it possible for men and women to alter their behavior and attitudes without negative consequences for their family and social situation.

CONCLUSIONS

Taken together, the cases presented in this chapter demonstrate the difficulty in actual clinical practice of separating the biological, psychological and social components of the illness experience. Usually, no one level of causation is sufficient by itself to give a full understanding of the onset, response, treatment, and outcome of illness. In all of the cases, social forces (e.g., competitive cultural values, occupational setting, marital situation, and sex role expectations) contributed to an understanding of why the illness process proceeded as it did.

For the clinician, the complexity of the decision about how best to treat a patient derives from the interweaving of the factors responsible for the illness. In the cases described, the patients benefited from the fact that clinicians understood the social components of illness and chose to address them in treatment. We have argued that a social perspective must be differentiated from biological and psychological perspectives, and that such a perspective must be applied at the level of the individual patient-case, if medical sociology is to be fully linked to the clinical practices of health providers. It is probable that knowing the exact contours of the social model is less important than the intellectual task of differentiating it from other disciplines and applying the social perspective to clinical cases. While there is no formula that will resolve clinicians' dilemmas about illness etiology and treatment, a thorough understanding of the role of social factors in the illness process will help individual clinicians and therapeutic teams make more enlightened decisions.

Movement toward more widespread use of sociology in health science education curriculums and clinical practices will require more extensive efforts by sociologists to understand the difficulties of applying sociological knowledge to the individual cases seen by clinicians. We suggest that further sociological research investigate the clinical decision-making process in terms of which types of information are defined as relevant by clinicians in individual cases, and whether, as we believe, recognition of the social level of analysis by clinicians actually results in improved outcomes for patients. Finally, the applicability of a social model of the illness process clearly will vary by clinical specialty and subspecialty, presumably, for example, being more useful to the family practice physician than the surgeon or radiologist, and development of models for specialty-specific application is required.

NOTES

1. Much of the material in this section and the next section ("Social Structure and the Illness Process") is presented in more detail in earlier work (Begun and Rieker, 1980; Rieker and Begun, 1980). It is summarized here to provide necessary background to the analysis of case material later in the chapter.
2. The names used in cases 2 and 3 are fictitious.

REFERENCES

American Public Health Association (APHA) 1979. *American Journal of Public Health* 69:305.
Begun, J. W. and P. P. Rieker. 1980. Social science in medicine: The question of relevance. *Journal of Medical Education* 55 (March): 181–85.

Brenner, M. H, A. Mooney and T.J. Nagy, eds. 1980. *Assessing the Contributions of the Social Sciences to Health.* Boulder, CO: Westview Press.

Counte, M.A. and L.P. Christman. 1981. *Interpersonal Behavior and Health Care.* Boulder, CO: Westview Press.

Dolcourt, J. L., H.J. Hamrick, L.A. O'Tuama, et al. 1978. Increased lead burden in children of battery workers: Asymptomatic exposure resulting from contaminated work clothing. *Pediatrics* 62:563–66.

Eisenberg, L. and A. Kleinman, eds. 1981. *The Relevance of Social Science for Medicine.* Dordrecht, Holland: D. Reidel.

Engel, G. L. 1982. The biopsychosocial model and medical education. *New England Journal of Medicine* 306 (April 1) 802–805.

Fisher, S. 1988. *In the Patients' Best Interest.* New Brunswick, NJ: Rutgers University Press.

Fisher, S. and A. Todd, eds. 1983. *The Social Organization of Doctor-Patient Communication.* Washington, DC: The Center for Applied Linguistics.

Fitzpatrick, R. J. Hinton, S. Newman, G. Scambler, and J. Thompson. 1984. *The Experience of Illness.* London: Tavistock Publications

Glassner, B. 1981. Clinical applications of sociology in health care. *Journal of Applied Behavioral Science* 17 (July-August-September): 330–46.

Hilberman, E. 1980. Overview: The wife-beater's wife reconsidered. *American Journal of Psychiatry* 137: 1336–47.

Hingson, R., et al. 1981. *In Sickness and in Health: Social Dimensions of Medical Care.* St. Louis, MO: Mosby.

Johnson, A. W., O. Grusky, and B. H. Raven. 1982. *Contemporary Health Services: Social Science Perspectives.* Boston, MA: Auburn House.

Mishler, E. G., L.R. Amarasingham, S.T. Hauser, et al., eds. 1981. *Social Contexts of Health, Illness and Patient Care.* Cambridge: Cambridge University Press.

Petersdorf, R. G. and A. R. Feinstein. 1981. An informal appraisal of the current status of medical sociology. *Journal of the American Medical Association* (March 6): 943–50.

Rieker, P. P. and J. W. Begun. 1980. Translating social science concepts into medical education: A model and a curriculum. *Social Science and Medicine* 14A (December): 607–12.

Rieker, P. P. and E. (Hilberman) Carmen, eds. 1984. *The Gender Gap in Psychotherapy: Social Realities and Psychological Processes.* New York: Plenum Press.

Ruderman, F. A. 1981. What is medical sociology? *Journal of the American Medical Association* (March 6): 927– 29.

Shuval, J. T. 1981. The contribution of psychological and social phenomena to an understanding of the aetiology of disease and illness. *Social Science and Medicine* 15A (May): 337–42.

Todd, A. D. 1989. *Intimate Adversaries: Cultural Conflict between Doctors and Women Patients.* Philadelphia: University of Pennsylvania Press.

Weiner, H. 1978. The illusion of simplicity: The medical model revisited. *American Journal of Psychiatry* 135 (July, Supplement): 27–33.

5

Teaching the Sociology
of Dying and Death

Gerry R. Cox and Ronald J. Fundis

Historically, people have responded to dying and death in ways predictable to their culture. The understanding of norms, values, beliefs, creeds, and social structures has provided insights not only into the process of dying and death, but also into the nature of human organizations and social interactions in crisis situations. The recognition of the value of the study of the dying process has led to the development of the sociology of death and dying as an important substantive area within the general field of sociology.

As an academic discipline, sociology provides the framework to study the social institutions, social processes, and social behaviors involved in the dying process. Human behavior in connection with the dying process is no less important than human behavior in a bureaucracy, street gang, or blended family. By applying theoretical analysis and appropriate research methods to the study of the process, sociology is able to provide a scientific analysis of the dying process. The sociology of death and dying should provide insights into the social aspects of dying and death, the social functions of institutions involved in the process of dying and death, and the social behavior of those involved in this process.

TWO AREAS OF STUDY

The sociology of death and dying has two separate but closely interrelated areas: (1) The sociology *in* dying and death; and (2) the sociology *of* dying and death.

Sociology in dying and death can be characterized as applied research and analysis. The focus would be on the collaboration with health care personnel, clergy, hospice workers, and others involved in the dying or bereavement process. The work of the sociologist in dying and death focuses on the direct application of sociological knowledge to patient or survivor care. Some of the tasks for the sociologist in dying and death would include: identifying the factors that influence the social attitudes involved in the dying process; specifying the variables that affect the grieving process; determining the influence of socioeconomic status, racial and ethnic background, education, and occupation on the dying and death process; understanding the roles of health care personnel in the dying and death process; evaluating effective and ineffective bereavement approaches for clergy and other care providers; and so forth. Sociologists with these capabilities often work in medical schools, nursing schools, hospice programs, public health organizations, mortuary science/funeral director schools, seminaries, and government agencies.

The sociology of death and dying has a different emphasis. It approaches the process of dying and death as a form of human behavior. The emphasis is on the social processes that occur in the dying and death process and how these processes contribute to the understanding of sociology and of social life in general. There are few unique or special theories that belong exclusively to the sociology of death and dying. The sociology of death and dying uses the theories of general sociology to study social processes, rather than creating its own theories, since it shares the same goals as all other areas of sociology, and thus may be characterized as the research and analysis of the processes of dying and death from a sociological perspective. Although some sociologists of death and dying are employed in the same institutions as sociologists in death and dying, the majority work as professors in sociology departments of universities and colleges.

TEACHING DEATH AND DYING

The sociology of dying and death as a sociology course can focus on traditional sociological topics applied to dying and death (see Appendix A for possible content areas of a Sociology of Death and Dying course). Since people of all ages die, dying and death are life-cycle concerns. People at different stages of the life cycle face their own deaths and manage the deaths of others according to the stage that they are experiencing. A three-year-old child dies not fully understanding what dying is all about, while an eighty-year-old person will approach his or her impending death with much more knowledge and awareness.

The study of comparative and cross cultural materials can add to the understanding of one's own cultural practices. Demographic materials can produce understanding of mortality and morbidity rates by culture, ethnicity, race, and other variables. Discussion of the carrying capacity of a given ecosystem can develop. The course that emerges could be thematic, and mostly descriptive, or more theoretically and methodologically sophisticated. The course could be designed to meet general education requirements, since the study of dying and death is concerned with questions that are rooted at the center of human experience. The class would not be an indoctrination in any one point of view, but rather an introduction to diverse points of view. It would not offer a step-by-step manual for dying and death, but the class would focus on enduring ideas, values, and issues. It could offer a framework within which to make ethical decisions and think through questions of human conduct and character, thus enabling students to deal more rationally and reasonably with the decisions that each person faces each day.

Sociology of death and dying courses offer sociologists the opportunity to teach sociology using a topic that students find interesting and challenging. Interest and enthusiasm for sociology itself should be one of the major goals and major results of teaching the sociology of death and dying.

AN OVERVIEW FOR THE NOVICE

Not too many years ago, dying and death were very much a natural part of the total family experience. When more than one generation of the same family lived in the same house, the dying processes took place in the family circle, as did death itself. Children, as well as adults, were thus able to view the process of dying, death, and grief as natural parts of the total life cycle. Because of the changes in family structure, family members today do not undergo as much exposure to death. Dying and death typically have been removed from the family experience.

As a result, modern individuals, who pride themselves on mastery over their physical and social environments, have blurred their own visions of death because they seldom witness either death or the dying process. In the modern world, death is an abnormality and is removed from the individual level; therefore, it is more difficult to manage. How is a person today to cope with his or her own dying when the deaths that he or she experiences are infrequent, highly impersonal, and viewed as abnormal?

Death increasingly has become institutionalized, mechanized, and dehumanized. Children, in most instances, have been excluded from death altogether. Out of concern for their children, parents and others try to shield them from death and the dying process. Often children are not a part of the funeral activities and are misinformed about the details of the death. This lack of experience leads to fear and misunderstanding. An understanding of death must be based on assumptions about the meaning of human existence. Even an initial conception of death depends upon our views about the nature of our being. For instance, a definition of death as a change in the state of being to an afterlife is quite different from a definition of death that focuses on the end of bodily processes and being. In either case, an idea about human life and the union of persons into community is presupposed. An understanding of death is not possible without these assumptions.

Moreover, explanations of death are based on the larger considerations of human essence, on the ideal of what may be achieved in our human existence. No matter how much the explanations of death and dying might claim to be free of values, they contain some notions about human possibilities. Whether questions are raised about the treatment of a corpse, the criteria physicians must use to decide when death takes place before transplanting organs, or the means for providing for one's family after death, ideas about the meaning of human existence are expressed.

Death is a multifaceted topic. Death can be approached from medical, religious, philosophical, psychological, anthropological, and sociological viewpoints. All of these perspectives, some more developed than others, offer their own theories of death and dying. Societies, and the theories that have been developed to explain them, involve ways of structuring fact and truth. Their procedures may be as simple as a faith in immortality through having children, or as complex as an elaborate scheme which includes a world design and a purpose for every action that has ever occurred in this world, including death.

USE OF THEORY IN DEATH AND DYING

The field of sociology often has been criticized for having too much concern for theory. This is, perhaps, due to a misunderstanding of what theory really is. Most students are accustomed to thinking that theory is boring and not very useful, while actually, the opposite is true. Theory is the way in which we attempt to make sense out of the world. It allows us to explain phenomena as they occur and to predict future behavior. It allows us to see vague happenings more clearly and to make sense out of seemingly disparate events. Theories are made to be tested. The rejection process of the scientific method allows us to reduce the number of possible explanations for phenomenon by at least one. The theories that survive the rejection process provide the "best" answer to the research question. Theories are never proven to be true; they simply are not rejected (see Dubin, 1978; Gibbs, 1972; or Chafetz, 1978). The major theories and research strategies of sociology can be applied to the teaching of death and dying.

In addition to considerations of existence and essence, any explanation of death also takes a position in regard to the social order. Structural functionalists, for example, given their particular ideas about human existence and essence, support established arrangements for handling the dead and explaining death, while conflict theorists seek to undermine the established arrangements for handling the dead and develop alternative explanations for the death process itself. No understanding of death can proceed without a recognition of the existing order and how it is related to the ideals or operating paradigms of that society.

The three major theoretical paradigms of sociology are structural-functional-ism, conflict, and symbolic interactionism (Macionis, 1989). For years, structural- functionalism has dominated sociological theorizing (Macionis, 1989). This theory focuses on order. How are the various parts of a society held together? A society is an integrated, dynamic whole. Each type of death will have a different impact on the stability of the social system. The death of a President such as John F. Kennedy is more traumatic to the society than the drowning of a retired worker in an automobile accident. Death from disasters, murders, terrorism, and other violent circumstances causes more disruption than the quiet social death of those who are aged, homeless, or institutionalized. The structure of the society provides values, norms, and attitudes toward dying and those who die. What is taught by our institutions, mass media, movies, and other socializing agents helps to shape these values and attitudes. When deaths occur, the structural-functionalist examines how order is restored. All societies have institutionalized structures to restore order and social equilibrium. An examina-tion of the funeral industry, grieving customs, and religious traditions would be typical studies of such institutionalized structures (See Blauner, 1966; Black, 1961; Denisoff, 1974; Turner, 1979; Johnson, 1981; Merton, 1968). For the structural-functionalist, social change is something which essentially comes from outside the social system and disrupts that system.

And yet, since social life does not seem to be orderly and tranquil, conflict theory focuses on the disorder or conflict within the system. Conflict theorists view society as a system of competing elements based on division of labor and social order. The individual and groups within the system are continually en-gaged in a competitive struggle for existence. The social system is inherently unequal, as typified by differential medical care, death rates by social class, and life expectancy (Shneidman, 1980). Examinations of occupational risk, attitudes toward the elderly, and victimization would be typical studies of con-flict theorists. An individual's chances in life are viewed as a product of the system, not of the individual. The focus of conflict theory is on power and inequality (McLellan, 1977; Perdue, 1986; Coser, 1956; or Wallace, 1986). The relevance of this perspective to a death and dying course is obvious.

Symbolic interactionism is a major sociological theory at the micro level (Macionis, 1989). This theory suggests that people behave toward objects, in-cluding other people, according to meanings and perceptions developed through social interaction. People adapt to social situations according to their perceptions of reality and attach their own social meanings to social situations. Their subjec-tive interpretations are learned from others. People are constantly interpreting their own behavior, as well as that of others, in terms of learned and shared meanings, values, and perceptions. Each cultural group develops rituals, feel-ings, and perceptions of what death is and how to manage it when it occurs.

From caskets to halos, people have created thousands of death symbols. Individuals interact with each another using rituals and symbols to manage death (see Stryker, 1980; Turner, 1986; Perdue, 1986; Kinloch, 1977).

Not all theories focus on order or change in the social system. Role theory places the emphasis on the roles people play. Those with "roleless" roles, such as the elderly, the homeless, and migrant workers, are often treated as though they are less important to society than those with other roles. They are given medical care last, if at all. Their funerals are little noted nor long remembered by society. In almost all areas of death and dying, an individual's role has a great impact on death management practices. Age and gender roles are worthy of note here. And what role should the survivors play? How long should one grieve? What is the role of the funeral director when one dies? What are the roles of medical personnel around the dying? Role theory provides a framework to understand the expectations and constraints on individuals in the dying and death process (see Wilson, 1983; Turner, 1986).

Disengagement theory, which has been used primarily with the elderly, also applies to other age groups during the dying process. The dying person and the survivors may practice mutual withdrawal during the dying process. Those who disengage may lose their will to live. Poverty and other social conditions may contribute to the process of disengagement during the dying process. Used as a theory in the sociology of dying and death, disengagement theory is still in the initial stages of development (Cumming and Henry, 1961; Cottrell, 1974; or Smith, 1985).

Another theory in the initial stages of development is socioenvironmental theory. This theory focuses on the impact of the social and physical environment on people's behavior. Like the earlier "Chicago School" (see Shaw and McKay, 1972; Park, 1955), the socioenvironmental approach directs its efforts at explaining the impact of factors such as ghettos, immigration, race relations, urbanization, and street gangs (Macionis, 1989). The impact of life style, social life, and social class on medical care, causes of death, and social support are concerns of the socioenvironmental approach. Such studies are becoming more numerous (see Park, 1967; Kinloch, 1977; or Perdue, 1986).

Exchange theory attempts to analyze how individuals interact on the basis of what each stands to gain or lose (Macionis, 1989). The patterns of death management practices in most societies consistently show that a network of friends and family provides regular support to dying individuals and their survivors. They, in turn, are expected to provide the same support to others in their time of need. Reciprocity is the basic principle of exchange theory. People who gain a lot from others are under pressure to give a lot. An imbalance is viewed as an injustice. Children often give their parents grand funerals because of the fortunes they inherited from their parents. Children may receive enhanced social support from others because they gave their parents a grand funeral. Those who give more than they get may feel offended or dissatisfied. Parents invest in love, dreams for the future, and even money for their children. Is it any wonder that they feel cheated when their child dies? The application of exchange theory to death related events can be very useful (see Johnson, 1981; Turner, 1986; Perdue, 1986).

RESEARCH IN DEATH AND DYING

The contemporary approach of the social sciences, and more particularly of sociology, to death-related research is comparable to the taboo-laden Victorian attitudes toward sex. Most death-related research has developed only in the last twenty years or so. How is it possible that a topic as universal as death can be so deeply disturbing and taboo as a subject for research? Perhaps it is because people today think that to die is to be annihilated. Today dying is seen as a lonely experience, taking place in the dehumanized environment of hospitals and institutions, and thus is more feared than it was in the past when dying took place at home. The meaning of death has become almost universally negative (Weisman, 1972). This does not mean that people do not write about death. In 1965, when the book *Death and Identity* was published, the bibliography, going back to 1845, included 400 items, while less than a decade later, in 1973, Robert Fulton was able to produce a comprehensive bibliography of over 2600 items, an excellent listing of sources relevant to sociologists (Fulton, 1973). Unfortunately, most of this vast literature was written by people in disciplines other than sociology, and much of it was not based upon empirical methods.

To understand the empirical world, sociologists use research to explain and predict human behavior. Standardized techniques or methods are used by sociologists to gather information. Scientific knowledge is thus acquired through the application of these research principles. The scientific method is a never-ending process of seeking knowledge. It combines empiricism, which always treats correspondence with the real world as the final test of its theories, with rationalism, which seeks to organize sense observations into a logical framework for understanding some segment of the world.

The usefulness of the scientific method in sociology is an open question. Like any approach, it has both its supporters and its opponents. The positivists (Comte, 1974; Durkheim, 1964; Collins, 1989) believe that sociology became an academic discipline when it adopted the scientific method of research. Others think that the intrusion of science will lead sociology to a tragic end and argue for a more humanistic emphasis (Shneidman, 1980). Seemingly, many of those who choose to write about death have followed the latter approach.

Sociologists do basic research and applied research. Basic research is designed to add to the stock of human knowledge. It develops without regard to whether or not it has practical application. This type of knowledge has an intrinsic value. Studies of near-death experiences, cross-cultural funeral customs, practices of death management of the ancients, or types of disposal of human remains might be examples of such research . While such studies may lead to some practical application, the focus is on the knowledge generated, not the application. Basic research tends to be discipline oriented and is aimed primarily at other professionals in the discipline, while applied research is designed to address practical problems.

There are several types of data-gathering strategies for research. Some of these include evaluation research, policy-based research, field research, social experiments, social monitoring, survey research, and secondary analysis of existing data.

Evaluation research is a common type of applied research. Essentially, it is an attempt to determine the degree of success of a particular program or practice. One might study a hospice program or a group like Compassionate Friends to determine the areas where change might be needed and where the greatest success might take place. Services provided by funeral directors also could be studied using evaluation research (Cox and Fundis, 1985).

Policy-based research is an attempt to assess the impact of policies that are implemented or not implemented. Studies of the impact of the Federal Trade Commission's regulation of the funeral industry (De Spelder and Strickland, 1987) would be an example of policy-based research. Studies of abortion and euthanasia would be heuristic issues for policy research.

Field research is essentially concerned with observing individuals and groups in the field, that is, in their own special settings. Basic research also can use this approach. Data-gathering techniques might include participant observation, interviewing, and other structured observation techniques. One may study events such as the impact of a teenage suicide on a rural school district, the adjustment of a community to the murder of a youth, the death of a President (such as Kennedy's assassination), and public mourning practices.

One type of social experiment is an attempt to assess the impact of policies and programs, and to anticipate their problems and promises if implemented on a large scale. A group planning to begin a hospice program, for example, might try to work with one or two families to assess their resources and their ability to start a more formalized and ambitious program. Similar studies could be done on interagency cooperation regarding the terminally ill or on the handling of grief among survivors.

Social monitoring is essentially noting trends or social indicators of changes in society. Patterns of mortality or changing death management practices would be potential topics for study, as would be the proliferation of academic courses on death issues and practices (Cox and Fundis, 1986).

Survey research is perhaps the most widely used method in sociology. A survey is an attempt to use a sample to make statements about the larger population. The setting of the research design—the sample, questionnaire or interview schedules, data preparation, and so forth—is critical to the success or failure of the research. This approach permits access to many people. Attitudinal research is typically based on surveys. A recent example would be Bardis' Thanatometer (1986), which is a scale for the measurement of awareness and acceptance of death.

Secondary analysis, or the analysis of existing records, involves attempts to make sense of the "facts" they present. Durkheim's classic study of suicide is an excellent example of this type of research (1951). The Bureau of the Census and the United Nations are sources for documents that provide massive amounts of data that could be analyzed to enhance a death and dying course or enrich an empirical article.

The list of methods described above is not intended to be exhaustive or complete. Any standard research text would offer a broader description of research methods. The intent here is simply illustrative. (See Appendix B for possible research topics for Sociology of Death and Dying courses.)

CONCLUSIONS

While death-related courses, research, and writings have mushroomed in the last few years, there are still major theoretical and empirical gaps in what has been produced. In short, death-related research and education is still an uneven and relatively unexplored field of study in many ways.

Courses in the sociology of death and dying are often interdisciplinary in nature. Units on death and dying are very common in philosophy, ethics, bioethics, psychology, education, nursing and medicine, as well as in sociology. Much of the emphasis in death and dying courses is descriptive in content. Some sociologists are encouraging the use of a more sophisticated level of theory and method in teaching death and dying in order to provide the intellectual excitement that sociology can bring to the topic (see Cox and Fundis, 1986). Sociologists will thus be able to look forward to interesting and useful contributions from their teaching and research in the sociology of death and dying. (See Appendix C for a selected bibliography of scholarly resources.)

REFERENCES

Bardis, P. D. 1986. Thanatometer: A scale for the measurement of awareness and acceptance of death. *South African Journal of Sociology* 17 (3):71–74.

Black, M. 1961. *The Social Theories of Talcott Parsons*. Englewood Cliffs, NJ: Prentice-Hall.

Blauner, R. 1966. Death and the social structure. *Psychiatry* 29:378–94.

Chafetz, J. S. 1978. *A Primer on the Construction and Testing of Theories in Sociology*. Itasca, IL: F.E. Peacock.

Collins, R. 1989. Sociology: Proscience or antiscience? *American Sociological Review* 54(1):124–39.

Comte, A. 1974. *The Positive Philosophy*. New York: AMS Press.

Coser, L. 1956. *The Functions of Social Conflict*. New York: Free Press.

Cottrell, F. 1974. *Aging and the Aged*. Dubuque, Iowa: William C. Brown.

Cox, G. R. and R. J. Fundis. 1985. Death management practices: Funeral directors revisited. *University Forum* 35:9–15.

Cox, G. R. and R. J. Fundis, eds. 1986. *Resources, Instructional Materials and Syllabi for Courses on the Sociology of Death and Dying*. Washington, DC: American Sociological Association.

Cumming, E. and W. E. Henry. 1961. *Growing Old: The Process of Disengagement*. New York: Basic Books.

Denisoff, R. S., O. Callahan, and M. M. Levine, eds. 1974. *Theories and Paradigms in Comtemporary Sociology*. Itasca, IL: F.E. Peacock.

DeSpelder, L.A. and A.L. Strickland 1987. *The Last Dance: Encountering Death and Dying*. Palo Alto, CA: Mayfield.

Dubin, R. 1978. *Theory Building*. New York: Free Press.

Durkheim, E. 1951. *Suicide: A Study in Sociology*. Translated by J. A. Spaulding and G. Simpson. New York: Free Press.

Durkheim, E. 1964. *The Rules of Sociological Method*. New York: Free Press.

Fulton, R. 1973. *A Bibliography on Death, Grief and Bereavement (1845–1973)*. Minneapolis: University of Minnesota.

Fulton, R. 1973. *Death and Identity*. New York: Wiley and Sons.

Gibbs, J. 1972. *Sociological Theory Construction*. Hinsdale, IL: Dryden.

Johnson, D. P. 1981. *Sociological Theory: Classical Founders and Contemporary Perspectives*. New York: Wiley.

Kinloch, G. 1977. *Sociological Theory: Its Development and Major Paradigms*. New York: McGraw-Hill.

Macionis, J. J. 1989. *Sociology*. Englewood Cliffs, NJ: Prentice- Hall.

McLellan, D. 1977. *Karl Marx: Selected Writings*. Oxford: Oxford University Press.

Merton, R. K. 1968. *Social Theory and Social Structure*. New York: Free Press.

Park, R. E. 1967. *On Social Control and Collective Behavior*. Chicago: University of Chicago Press.

Park, R. E. 1955. *Society*. New York: Free Press.

Perdue, W. C. 1986. *Sociological Theory*. Palo Alto, CA: Mayfield.

Poloma, M. 1979. *Contemporary Sociological Theory*. New York: Macmillan.

Shaw, C. R. and H. D. McKay. 1972. *Juvenile Delinquency and Urban Areas*. Chicago: University of Chicago Press.

Shneidman, E. A., ed. 1980. *Death: Current Perspectives*. Palo Alto, CA: Mayfield.

Smith, W. J. 1985. *Dying in the Human Life Cycle: Psychological, Biomedical, and Social Perspectives*. New York: Holt, Rinehart and Winston.

Stryker, S. 1980. *Symbolic Interactionism*. Menlo Park, CA: Benjamin/Cummings.

Turner, J. H. 1986. *The Structure of Sociological Theory*. Chicago: Dorsey.

Turner, J. H. and A. Maryonski. 1979. *Functionalism*. Menlo Park, CA: Benjamin/Cummings.

Wallace, R. A. and A. Wolf. 1986. *Contemporary Sociological Theory: Continuing the Classical Tradition*. Englewood Cliffs, NJ: Prentice-Hall.

Weisman, A. D. 1972. *On Dying and Denying*. Pasadena, CA: Behavioral Publications.

Wilson, J. 1983. *Social Theory*. Englewood Cliffs, NJ: Prentice Hall.

Appendix A
Possible Content Areas for Sociology of Death and Dying.

Sociology of Death and Dying
Attitudes Toward Death
Literature and Death
Cross- cultural Perspectives on Death
Defining Death, Life, and Ethics
Medicine, Treatment, and Ethics
Legal Aspects of Death
Philosophy and Death
Sudden Infant Death Syndrome
Children's Attitudes Toward Death
Teaching Children About Death
The Dying Child
Medical Profession and Death
Hospice
Treating the Terminally Ill
Grief and the Child
Grief Management
Risking Death
Violent Death
War Death
Stress: Smoking, Drugs and Death
Suicide
Suicide Prevention
Funerals: Cross-cultural Approaches
Near-Death Experiences
The Future of Death

Appendix B
Possible Research Topics for Sociology of Death and Dying

I. Terminally Ill and the Process of Dying
    1. Stages of Dying
    2. Problems of the Terminally Ill
    3. Coping with Death and the Terminally Ill
    4. Terminally Ill and Institutions
    5. Therapy for the Terminally Ill
    6. What Should the Terminally Ill be Told
    7. Training for Dealing with the Terminally Ill
    8. Behavior of Medical Personnel Toward the Terminally Ill
    9. Alienation and Rejection of the Surviving by the Terminally Ill
    10. Reconciliation and Closeness to the Surviving by the Terminally Ill
    11. What the Dying Can Teach the Living
    12. Personal Involvement with the Dying
    13. Effects of Working with the Dying
    14. Professional Distance: Is it Necessary?
    15. Prolonging the Life of the Terminally Ill: Pros and Cons
    16. Ethics of Allowing the Terminally Ill to Die
    17. Comparison of the Young Terminally Ill with the Elderly Terminally Ill
    18. Relations with the Family of the Terminally Ill
    19. Religion and the Terminally Ill
    20. Pastoral Care of the Terminally Ill

II. Children and Death
    1. Children's Attitudes Toward Death
    2. Children's Literature and Death
    3. Children and Funerals
    4. The Child and Death
    5. Grief and Children
    6. Terminally Ill and Children

III. Funeral Practices and Customs
    1. Open Casket Funerals: Pros and Cons
    2. Changing Role of the Funeral Director
    3. Changing Funeral Practices
    4. Changing Funeral Practices in Other Cultures
    5. Cremation

6. Social and Psychological Values of the Funeral
7. Cemetery Practices
8. An Analysis of the Training of Funeral Personnel
9. Monuments or Markers—A Study on Social Stratification
10. Death Counseling for Funeral Directors
11. Funeral Costs
12. Body Present?
13. Public versus Private Funerals
14. Wakes, Shivahs, and Visitations
15. Flowers or other Memorials
16. To View or Not to View the Body
17. Function of a Funeral
18. Values of a Funeral
19. Death as a Rite de Passage
20. Attitudes Toward the Funeral Director
21. Attitudes Toward the Funeral Service Profession
22. Attitudes Toward the Funeral Service
23. Funeral Sermons—Content Analysis
24. Cross-cultural Rituals for the Dead
25. Comparative Funeral Rites
26. Thanatology

IV.   Social Cultural Aspects of Death
1. Government Involvement in Death (Funeral, State, whatever)
2. Mythological Views of Death
3. Local Funeral Practices
4. Mortality Patterns of Selected Groups
5. Death and Humor
6. Death in Literature
7. Death in Education
8. Death in Television and Movies
9. Death and Modern Technology
10. Primitive Views on Death
11. Death as Viewed by a Particular Religion
12. Grief and Mourning Patterns of Selected Groups
13. Reincarnation
14. Euthanasia
15. Anti-systhenasia
16. Death Symbols
17. Institutionalized Dying
18. Capital Punishment

19. Abortion Issues, Transplants, etc.
20. Death and the Bible (Koran, etc.)
21. Legal Death
22. Medical and Biological Definitions of Death
23. Historical Perspectives on Death
24. Sociological, Anthropological, Philosophical, or Religious Views of Death
25. Traditional Solutions to Problems of Defining Death
26. Spiritualism
27. Stages of Grief
28. Grief as Therapy
29. Dynamics of Grief and Grieving
30. Adaptation to Loss
31. Non-Adaptation to Loss
32. Institutions and Grief
33. Anticipatory versus Reactive Grief

V.   Attitudes Toward Death
1. Denial of Death
2. Awareness of Death
3. Romanticism of Death
4. Acceptance of Death
5. Fear of Being Dead—End of Existence
6. Fear of Loss of Bodily Awareness and Functions
7. Fear of Being Mutilated
8. Fear of Dying—Pain, Method, etc.
9. Fear of Dying from a Specific Illness
10. Fear of Death—No Longer Able to Care for Survivors
11. Origins of Attitudes Toward Death
12. Death and Age
13. Death as a Taboo
14. Asian (Mexican, etc.) Attitudes Toward Death
15. Sexual Differences in Relating to Death
16. Occupational Differences in Relating to Death
17. Religious (etc.) Differences in Relating to Death
18. Avoidance of Death as a Topic in Society
19. Avoidance of Death as a Topic for the Individual

VI. Mortality Studies and Suicide
1. Demographic Trends and Death
2. Frequency of Types of Deaths
3. Personal and Social Characteristics of Death

4. Socioeconomic Characteristics of Death
5. Suicide Intervention Practices
6. Suicide Prevention Centers
7. Suicide Notes, etc.
8. Attitudes Toward Suicide
9. Historical (Religious, Philosophical, etc.) Views of Suicide
10. Suicide in Literature (movies, TV, etc.)
11. Theories of Suicide

Appendix C
Selected Bibliography of Scholarly Sources for Teaching Death and Dying

Aiken, L. R. 1985. *Dying, Death, and Bereavement*. Boston: Allyn and Bacon.

Aries, P. 1974. *Western Attitudes Toward Death: From the Middle Ages to the Present*. Baltimore, MD: Johns Hopkins University Press.

Backer, B. A., N. Hannon, and N. A. Russell. 1982. *Death and Dying: Individuals and Institutions*. New York: John Wiley.

Bardis, P. D. 1981. *History of Thanatology: Philosophical, Religious, Psychological, and Sociological Ideas Concerning Death from Primitive Times to the Present*. Toledo, OH: University Press of America.

Bender, D. 1974. *Problems of Death*. Anoka, MN: Greenhaven Press.

Berger, P. L. 1967. *The Sacred Canopy*. New York: Doubleday.

Brim, O., et. al. 1970. *The Dying Patient*. New York: Russell Sage Foundation.

Brown, N. O. 1959. *Life Against Death*. New York: Vintage Books.

Cavan, R. S. 1928. *Suicide*. Chicago: University of Chicago Press.

Coron, J. 1973. *Suicide*. New York: Charles Scribner's, Sons.

Despelder, L.A. and A.L. Strickland. 1983. *The Last Dance: Encountering Death and Dying*. Palo Alto, CA: Mayfield.

Douglas, J. 1967. *The Social Meanings of Suicide*. Princeton, NJ: Princeton University Press.

Dumont, R. and D. Foss. 1972. *The American View of Death: Acceptance or Denial*. Cambridge, MA: Schenkman Publishing Company.

Durkheim, E. 1973. *The Elementary Forms of the Religious Life*. New York: Free Press.

Durkheim, E. 1973. *On Morality and Society*. Chicago: University of Chicago Press.

Durkheim, E. 1951. *Suicide*. New York: Free Press.

Easson, W. 1970. *The Dying Child*. St. Louis, MO: Thomas.

Farber, M. L. 1968. *Theory of Suicide*. New York: Funk and Wagnalls.

Feifel, H., ed. 1959. *The Meaning of Death*. New York: McGraw-Hill.

Ferretii, V.S. and D.L. Scott. 1977. *Death in Literature*. New York: McGraw-Hill.

Folta, J. and E. Deck, eds. 1966. *A Sociological Framework for Patient Care*. New York: John Wiley and Sons.

Fulton, R., et. al., eds. 1978. *Death and Dying: Challenge and Change*. Reading, MA: Addison-Wesley.

Fulton, R. 1973. *Death, Grief and Bereavement: 1845-1973*. Minneapolis: University of Minnesota.

Fulton, R. 1965. *Death and Identity*. New York: John Wiley.

Gibbs, J.P., ed. 1968. *Suicide*. New York: Harper and Row.

Glaser, B. and A.L. Strauss. 1968. *Time for Dying*. New York: Aldine.

Glaser, B. and A.L. Strauss. 1965. *Awareness of Dying*. New York: Aldine.

Gordon, D. C. 1972. *Overcoming the Fear of Death*. Baltimore, MD: Penguin Books.

Gorer, G. 1969. *Death, Grief, and Mourning*. Garden City, NY: Doubleday.

Green, B.R. and D. Irish. 1971. *Death Education: Preparation for Living*. Cambridge, MA: Schenkman Publishing Company.

Grollman, E. A. 1971. *Explaining Death to Children*. Boston: Beacon Press.

Grollman, E. A. 1970. *Talking About Death*. Boston: Beacon Press.

Hardt, D. V. 1979. *Death: The Final Frontier*. Englewood Cliffs, NJ: Prentice-Hall.

Harmer, R. M. 1963. *The High Cost of Dying*. New York: Crowell-Collier Press.

Hinton, J. 1967. *Dying*. Baltimore, MD: Penguin Books.

Irion, P. E. 1970. *The Funeral: Vestige or Value?* Nashville, TN: Abingdon Press.

Jackson, E. M. 1965. Telling A Child About Death. New York: Channel Press.

Jackson, E. M. 1957. *Understanding Grief*. New York: Abington Press.

Jackson, E. M. 1970. *When Someone Dies*. Nashville, TN: Abingdon Press.

Kalish, R. A. 1981. *Death, Grief, and Caring Relationships*. Monterey, CA: Brooks/Cole.

Kastenbaum, R. J. 1981. *Death, Society, and Human Experience*. St. Louis, MO: Mosby.

Kestenbaum, V., ed. 1982. *The Humanity of the Ill*. Knoxville: University of Tennessee Press.

Koff, T. H. 1980. *Hospice: A Caring Community*. Cambridge, MA: Winthrop.

Kübler-Ross, E. 1985. *On Children and Death*. New York: Collier.

Kübler-Ross, E. 1978. *To Live Until We Say Goodbye*. Englewood Cliffs, NJ: Prentice-Hall.

Kübler-Ross, E. 1975. *Death: The Final Stage of Growth*. Englewood Cliffs, NJ: Prentice- Hall.

Kübler-Ross, E. 1974. *Questions and Answers on Death and Dying*. New York: MacMillan.

Kübler-Ross, E. 1969. *On Death and Dying*. New York: MacMillan.

Leming, M. R. and G. E. Dickinson. 1985. *Understanding Dying, Death, and Bereavement*. New York: Holt, Rinehart and Winston.

Lifton, R. J. and E. Olson. 1974. *Living and Dying*. New York: Praeger.

Linzer, N. 1977. *Understanding Bereavement and Grief.* New York: Yeshiva University Press.

Lundahl, C., R. 1982. *A Collection of Near-Death Research Readings.* Chicago: Nelson-Hall.

Mack, A., ed. 1972. *Death in American Experience.* New York: Schocken Books.

Mills, L.O., ed. 1969. *Perspectives on Death.* New York: Abingdon Press.

Mitford, J. 1963. *The American Way of Death.* Greenwich, CN: Fawcett.

Morgan, E. 1984. *Dealing Creatively with Death: A Manual of Death Education and Simple Burial.* Burnsville, NC: Celo.

Nagy, M. H. 1965. *The Meaning of Death.* New York: McGraw-Hill.

Nisbet, R. A. 1965. *Emile Durkheim.* Englewood Cliffs, NJ: Prentice- Hall.

O'Neill, J. 1985. *Five Bodies: the Human Shape of Modern Society.* New York: Cornell University Press.

Parkes, C. M. 1973. *Bereavement.* New York: International University Press.

Pattison, E. M. 1977. *The Experience of Dying.* Englewood Cliffs, NJ: Prentice- Hall.

Pearson, L. 1969. *Death and Dying.* Cleveland, OH: Case Western Reserve University Press.

Pine, V. R. 1975. *Caretaker of the Dead: The American Funeral Director.* New York: John Wiley.

Roslansky, J. D. 1973. *The End of Life.* Amsterdam: North Holland Publishing Company.

Schmitt, R. L., R. Gorshe, and S. Lindberg. 1979. Dying as a status passage and the organizational career: A strategy for researching organizational environments, In N. K. Denzin, ed., *Studies in Symbolic Interaction: A Research Annual*, Vol. 2 (419–56). Greenwich, CN: JAI Press.

Schultz, R. 1978. *The Psychology of Death, Dying, and Bereavement.* Reading, MA: Addison-Wesley.

Scott, N. A., Jr. 1967. *The Modern Vision of Death.* Richmond, VA: John Knox Press.

Shneidman, E. S. 1980. *Death: Current Perspectives.* Palo Alto, CA: Mayfield.

Shneidman, E. S. 1974. *Deaths of Man.* Baltimore, MD: Penguin Books.

Stephenson, J. S. 1985. *Death, Grief, and Mourning: Individual and Social Realities.* New York: Free Press.

Stillion, J. M. 1985. *Death and the Sexes: An Examination of Differential Longevity, Attitudes, Behaviors, and Coping Skills.* Washington, DC: Hemisphere.

Sudnow, D. 1967. *Passing On: The Social Organization of Dying.* Englewood Cliffs, NJ: Prentice- Hall.

Toynbee, A., et. al. 1969. *Man's Concern with Death*. New York: McGraw-Hill.

Vernon, G. M. 1973. *Death Meanings*. Salt Lake City, UT: Association for the Study of Religion.

Vernon, G. M. 1980. *The Sociology of Death*. New York: Ronald Press.

Weir, R. F. 1980. *Death in Literature*. New York: Columbia University Press.

Wilcox, S. G. and M. Sutton. 1981. *Understanding Death and Dying: An Interdisciplinary Approach*. Sherman Oaks, Calif.: Alfred.

PART II
Sociological Explanations of Attitudes Towards Illness and Death

Attitudes are orientations individuals express that indicate beliefs, feelings, and behaviors. Most health care providers and educators would agree that the responses to illness and death are multidetermined. What they may fail to appreciate is the extent to which responses to loss and change are the result of underlying values and existing social arrangements. With this in mind, the four chapters in this section examine sociological explanations of attitudes towards illness and death.

Sabo's article, "Men, Death Anxiety, and Denial: Critical Feminist Interpretations of Adjustment to Mastectomy," provides insight into the way gender attitudes and values, and other relational factors, determine a man's response to his partner's mastectomy. Going beyond conventional sex-role theory, Sabo explores the complex social and psychological dynamics set into motion by a couple's confrontation with a life threatening illness. While it may be adaptive for men to initially deny that the life threatening disease and mutilating treatment have altered the emotional core of *both* husband and wife, Sabo argues that over the course of time, continued denial has adverse political and social consequences for the couple.

"The Causes of Cancer: Women Talking," shows that after a cancer diagnosis, all patients try to find an explanation for the disease's onset and meaning. In Clarke's study of 50 women with cancer, the search for meaning took the form of making attributions about the "cause" of the illness such as God's will, difficult family relationships, or stress. Adopting an attribution which makes sense of the traumatic event produces a feeling of control over the cancer experience. Clarke describes how this feeling, in turn, enables patients to begin the task of rebuilding the diminished self-esteem and self-efficacy needed to cope with the distressing aspects of an uncertain future.

In her article, "The Death Certificate as a Reflection of Attitudes," Rosenberg illustrates how the death certificate can be used to teach students not only

69

about society's norms and values about death, but also about their own feelings on that subject. With sensitivity and humor, she demonstrates how the death certificate, when viewed as a sociological document, can become an interactive teaching tool with both analytic and emotional dimensions.

In the article, "Thanatometer. A Scale for the Measurement of Awareness and Acceptance of Death," Bardis discusses the development and empirical testing of a quantitative instrument, the Thanatometer, that assesses knowledge of, and feelings about, death. Results from initial tests of the instrument indicated that respondents' race, religion, and community size were associated with various attitudes about death and dying.

In "A Social System Perspective on Cadaver Organ Transplantation," Kutner analyzes why, relative to other countries, the United States has such a low success rate in procuring donor organs. Among the many reasons, some of the most prominent include religious beliefs, superstition, avoidance of death issues, fear of AIDS, unsympathetic treatment from hospital staff, and lack of awareness about procedures. She also points out how the process of organ transplantation has been dehumanized by competition among hospitals and disagreement about policies. Several factors that help to comfort families of donors and to make the process less traumatic involve maintaining the individuality of the donor, follow-up services for families, and trained staff who can address the problems sympathetically.

Much sociological research has been conducted on the definition of illness, adopting the sick role, and on stages of the illness experience (see for example, Mechanic, 1968; Twaddle, 1969; Parsons, 1975; Suchman, 1965). The articles discussed above extend this research and provide concrete examples of how sociological concepts and analyses can be used to understand that subjective reactions to illness and death are shaped by the interrelatedness of our personal characteristics, our deeply embedded patterns of socialization, and by general socio-cultural and socio-political contexts.

REFERENCES

Mechanic, D. 1968. *Medical Sociology: A Selective Review.* New York: Free Press.

Parsons, T. 1975. The sick role and the role of the physician revisited. *Milbank Memorial Fund Quarterly* 53: 257–78.

Suchman, E. 1965. Stages of illness and medical care. *Journal of Health and Human Behavior* 6: 114–28.

Twaddle, A. 1969. Health decisions and sick role variations: An explorative. *Journal of Health and Social Behavior* 10: 105–14.

6

Men, Death Anxiety, and Denial: Critical Feminist Interpretations of Adjustment to Mastectomy

Don Sabo

"You throw a rock into a pond. There are rippling effects. Cancer is that rock."

—A 42-year-old wife and mastectomy patient.

Researchers are increasingly taking into account how gender influences emotional and cognitive reactions to illness and death. The growing salience of gender in understanding the human response to death is part of the "changing picture" in thanatology and psychosocial oncology which flows from the emerging dialogue between the women's movement and the death education movement (Stillion, 1985).

To date, the consideration of gender has relied almost exclusively on mainstream sex role theory which assumes that differential patterns of gender socialization cause differences in the behavior and psychological makeup of women and men. This theory owes its intellectual heritage to *liberal* feminism and generally focuses on issues of individual rights and equality of opportunity. Sex differences in psychosocial adjustment to illness or death, therefore, are said to derive from gender socialization.

Critical feminist perspectives have yet to become part of the ongoing dialogue between psychosocial oncologists, thanatologists, and feminist theorists. The concepts of "power" and "conflict" are central to critical feminist theory. In contrast to liberal feminism, the focus is on power differences between spouses rather than sex differences, that is, relational process rather than roles. As Hall puts it, "Gender is a socially and historically constructed set of power relations" (1989:6). Critical feminists regard marriage, for example, as an institution that

71

historically has served the social, sexual, psychological, and political interests of men more so than women. Relationships between the sexes in marriage both reflect and reinforce the structured inequality favoring males, and the cultural devaluation of women and femininity which exist within the larger political economy.

This chapter uses critical feminist theory to expand current thinking about how gender shapes men's anxieties and adjustments to mastectomy. It very consciously attempts to nudge current thinking beyond mainline role theory which assumes a false symmetry between wife and husband and ignores the existence of power inequities between women and men (Messner and Sabo, forthcoming). Clinical insights and interpretations are based on interviews with women and men faced with adjustment to mastectomy.

REVIEW OF THE LITERATURE

Researchers have found that females admit death anxiety more readily than do males. Though evidence for sex differences in concerns about death during infancy and childhood is not conclusive, during adolescence and young adulthood males *do* appear less likely than females to admit anxiety and fears about death. This overall pattern of male denial and female expressiveness concerning death and dying persists for adults between 25 and 65 (Berman and Hayes, 1973; Templer, Russ and Franks, 1971). According to some researchers, men's fears concerning death and illness are exacerbated by psychosocial factors tied to the mid-life transition during the forties. The male "mid-life crisis" is depicted as a life-phase in which some males reevaluate life goals and face existential issues surrounding mortality and physical vulnerability (Farrell and Rosenberg, 1981; Levinson, 1974; Gould, 1972; Vaillant and McArthur, 1972). Though concerns about death among those 65 and older generally tend to decrease, Stillion's (1985) review of the available research found that men still tend to be less expressive about death than women.

The literature on psychosocial adjustment to mastectomy also reveals a propensity for denial among males. Husbands experience varying degrees of psychological difficulty after their wives' mastectomies. In response, many affect airs of confidence and calm to assuage their wives' concerns. This brave front probably helps husbands to cope with their own feelings of powerlessness, insecurity, and anxiety caused by the cancer, the breast loss, and the threat to their wives' lives (Grandstaff, 1976). Clinical observers argue that the brave front or "protective guardian role" that male partners set up not only forms a barrier against introspection about their own individual feelings and reactions to the mastectomy, but also often leads to misunderstanding between spouses and a vicious cycle of mutual denial within the marriage. Feelings and perceptions of key issues become blurred, and communication between spouses becomes tenuous. Unexpressed emotions and denial of the problem, moreover, are perceived by the mastectomy patient as rejection. This, in turn, stimulates more withdrawal, blocks communication, and promotes further feelings of rejection (Bard and Sutherland, 1955; Metze, 1978; Sabo, 1986).

THEORY

According to mainline sex role theory, men's affinity for denial is owed to differential gender socialization. Stillion's (1985) theory of sex roles and death attitudes is representative of the socialization approach. She basically argues that different gender stereotypes or "sex-typed messages" for males and females exist within sexist culture which serve as guideposts for gender socialization. For example, males are expected to be stoic, independent, powerful, and macho, while females are supposed to be emotionally expressive, dependent, fragile, and ultrafeminine. Patterns of socialization and gender identity development generally conform to these cultural mandates and, consequently, help shape individual attitudes about death. Males learn to suppress fears about death and dying, to regard asking for help and self-disclosure as expressions of feminine dependence, and to affect an outward air of stoic self-control. Females, in contrast, learn that displays of concern about death or depending on others for help are appropriately feminine and permissible.

Critical feminists would point out, however, that gender socialization theory ignores the fact that patterns of male gender socialization *express and reproduce* men's institutional domination of women. This means that within male-dominated institutions and cultures, men learn to function psychologically in ways that maintain their authority and psychosocial priorities rather than women's.

Chodorow's (1978) work helps uncover connections between male dominance structures and male psychology. When comparing "female" and "male" psychology, she holds that women's social orientation is personal and men's is positional. Girls learn to attune to and accept the needs of others, while boys, in contrast, become much more individuated. There is much truth in her scheme. However, critical feminists would ground these psychological distinctions in social structure and sexist ideology: one reason why boys learn to separate themselves from others and evaluate themselves and others according to status is because they are striving to fit into male-dominated, hierarchically organized institutions such as marriage, sports, government and business. Hence, male "psychology" or gender identity derives from and revolves around status and power differences between the sexes and among men.

Stated directly, critical feminists recognize that gender identity "develops and persists as a social, economic, and political category" (Andersen, 1988:320). Many of the psychological traits attached to masculinity in our patriarchal culture, such as aggressiveness, ambition, success-striving, virility, toughness, and competitiveness are really about men's preoccupation with power over others and attempts to impose their definition of reality on others.

Critical feminist theory provides a useful tool for understanding aspects of men's reactions and adjustments to illness and death. It not only takes gender into account, but recognizes that structured inequalities and power differences between the sexes transform emotion and perception, and influence men's behavioral adjustments to disease and death.

METHOD

Convenience samples of 52 husbands and wives were interviewed by the researcher over a three year period. The 38 husbands of mastectomy patients were recruited via a newspaper article in a large northeastern urban area or by a mail canvass of community professionals in the same area. All 38 men participated in an extensive, semi-structured, 2-hour interview dealing with their wives' reactions to mastectomy. The interview topics included the marital problems encountered, how the mastectomy had changed the marital relationship, the wife's and husband's chief concerns and fears, sexual adjustment, the degree to which the wife could rely on the husband for emotional support, and whom the subject approached for support. A core of 6 men also participated in an ongoing, multisession men's discussion group with two facilitators which met for over 2 years. After 6 months of meetings, the 6-man discussion group created an American Cancer Society pilot program, the Reach To Recovery Men's Support Network, which was designed to provide male partners of mastectomy patients with a supportive forum to raise common concerns and ask questions about breast cancer and adjustment to mastectomy. The support group meetings provided the researcher with further opportunity to make clinical observations and, in addition, to recruit additional interviewees.

Speaking engagements and a mail canvass of professional contacts were used to recruit 14 married female subjects who had undergone a mastectomy within the last three years. The researcher emphasized that he was chiefly interested in what wives had to say about *their husband's* reactions and adjustments to the mastectomy. Willing participants were instructed to telephone the researcher to learn more about the nature of the study and, if desired, to make arrangements for a later telephone interview. This procedure allowed respondents to remain anonymous if desired; telephone conversations were conducted on a first-name basis only. Semi-structured, in-depth interviews with the 14 wives focused on the same general areas of personal and marital adjustment; however, the main emphasis was on their perceptions of how their husbands reacted and adjusted to the mastectomy.

MEN'S DENIAL AFTER MASECTOMY

The psychological impact of mastectomy on husbands was often severe. Anxiety reactions, depression, feelings of inadequacy concerning their ability to help their spouses through the crisis, hypochondriacal preoccupations, and concerns about intimacy were common. The interviews and clinical observations of the support group sessions, however, revealed that denial was the most central response of men to their wives' mastectomies. As the interviews with husbands and wives progressed, it became clear that, in varying degrees, men used denial to minimize their own concerns about illness and mortality, to cope with the responsibilities of caring for their wives, and to negotiate a definition of the marital situation which reflected the husband's psychosocial concerns and made the wife's concerns secondary.

The interviews showed that, like marriage itself, denial had a history. It had a beginning point within the individual, then took on various interpersonal functions, and ultimately, became rooted in the taken-for-granted world of the marital relationship. Furthermore, husbands' adoption of denial as a coping mechanism usually followed a general pattern. As couples made the psychosocial trek from diagnosis and hospitalization, returning home and rethinking a marriage fractured by illness and the threat of death, and making long-term adjustment, the husbands' denial passed through similar stages. The net effect for many couples was the maintenance of a pre-mastectomy marital status quo which did not recognize much of the impact of breast cancer and mastectomy.

Diagnosis and Hospitalization: Contrary to gender stereotypes that men are unfeeling, the husbands' initial emotional reactions were quite intense. The diagnosis and surgery triggered disbelief, alarm, and painful feelings of isolation. Like their spouses, men's chief concerns revolved around the threat of mortality and breast loss. The husband's major fear was that his wife might die. One man compared his emotional state at this time to "being hit across the gut by a two-by-four." Others, alone in offices, bathrooms, or automobiles, cried "like babies." One 35 year old woman recalled the moment when her husband told her the doctor had called with "bad news," "He was sitting there gazing at me with some weird kind of admiration and started crying uncontrollably."

Husbands shared their spouses' chief anxieties concerning breast loss and the threat of mortality. However, whereas wives underwent mastectomy with at least minimal social and emotional support (e.g., relatives, women friends, nurses), husbands experienced the diagnosis, surgery, and hospitalization essentially alone. Many a husband felt pushed aside to a waiting room position as events unfolded around his wife's bedside. Some had a chance to talk over sensitive issues with women friends and relatives; only 3 found other men to talk to openly. The statement below captures most husbands' confusion and isolation:

> I'd go to work and be in a daze. I didn't know what to do. I wanted to do something, but didn't know where to begin. I didn't know what the next person was thinking. I didn't know what my wife was thinking. Should I cry with her or be strong? Should I talk or should I shut up? Should I take her in my arms or would this make her feel worse than she already did? I felt extremely isolated. No one knew, or really even cared to know, what I was going through.

Husbands also worried about their ability to help their spouses through the experience of cancer and surgery. The husband silently questioned whether he could meet the responsibilities of supporting, loving, and reassuring his spouse that she and the marriage would survive. Husbands readily understood that their wives must cope with considerable emotional stress and build a new self-image fragmented by illness and disfigurement. Yet the men only vaguely realized that their own emotional makeup and self-concept also was being affected by the surgery and the resultant changes in their marital lives.

As the period of hospitalization progressed, the men pushed awareness of their feelings into the background and placed their wives' feelings in the foreground. They all reported discussing their wives' concerns about breast loss and dying, but almost none talked about their own concerns. The most typical response was to assert, flatly and ardently, that the breast loss "made absolutely no difference at all" to them and that their "feelings and attraction had not changed at all." Similarly, the men declared that they were "completely confident" that the doctors "had got it all" and that the "cancer would never return."

Interviews revealed that this show of certitude initially was designed by the husband for his wife's benefit. Husbands secretly worried that "something had gone wrong with the surgery," "my wife would die," or "she was riddled with cancer." Hence, the husband's denial during hospitalization was more of a public performance than an unconscious defense mechanism. Some wives reported "seeing through" their husbands' protective optimism and regarded it chiefly as support and loving concern. Ten of the 14 wives, however, wished that their husbands would have been more open about their "true" thoughts and feelings. A 44-year-old mother of two stated,

> Before I had the surgery, he was very supportive. Afterwards we had good talks but they were mostly about me. He never really did talk about himself and I know he was just as scared as I was.

In summary, the seeds of the husbands' denial appeared to be sewn during the diagnosis/hospitalization period. Husbands quickly moved from initial confusion and inner loss of control to affecting an outward air of bravado and emotional control. While husbands justified their "act" on the grounds that it was what their spouses needed, there is evidence that spouses actually desired more forthright communication and emotional openness from husbands.

The Protective Guardian Posture: As the initial shock of diagnosis and surgery faded, the men increasingly defined their primary role as that of protective guardians of their wives' physical and emotional well-being. In order to take on the role of protective guardians, husbands further developed the capacity to deny their feelings—not just publicly, but privately as well. On a conscious level, this denial was designed to allay the wives' fears of sexual rejection, disfigurement, and further illness. Indeed, during the months immediately following surgery, the facade of optimism probably was necessary in that the physical and emotional needs of the patient were most pressing. At a deeper emotional level, however, putting on a "brave front" helped husbands to unconsciously deny their worst fears. For example, a "just-turned-40" husband talked about the first time he and his spouse "made love" after her mastectomy.

> She had wanted to talk about sex with me but I felt funny about this. I told her that it (the scar) wouldn't bother me sexually. When we made love for the first time, she burst into tears and cried and cried. I think she couldn't believe that it wouldn't make a difference to me. I didn't talk a whole lot about it but just acted on it. I made love in the same way I had done before, and the actions spoke louder than any words could.

Observations of the men's support group made it clear that most husbands had little or no insight into the fact that their own feelings about masculinity, death and illness, and being a husband and lover had been changed by the mastectomy. Initial group meetings showed that, for men, post-mastectomy emotional and marital adjustment was believed to revolve solely around wives. Femininity had been challenged by cancer and disfigurement—not masculinity. However, as the group continued to meet, it was evident that behind their declarations to wives that the cancer would never return, or that its return was only a remote possibility, there remained many personal misgivings. The men expressed fears of losing their wives, and at least periodically experienced anxiety about their own death as well. "Sometimes I'm terrified," one participant confided. "I try not to let her know but I'm sure she's aware of it." Another said, "For me, the one thing that is difficult to live with that has become part of my life is being fearful of death. It's a scary thought that has stemmed from being reminded of my own mortality because of the mastectomy." It seems that a direct confrontation with the realities of cancer can chink even the thickest masculine armor.

DENIAL AS INTERPERSONAL AGENDA

In the context of the husband-wife relationship, men used the protective guardian role as an interpersonal device or unconscious strategy which enabled them to curtail or block communication about issues such as breast loss, fears of losing a spouse, concerns about mortality. They especially avoided dealing with how they themselves felt about these issues. While some women pleaded with their husbands to talk about what was on their minds, others reported having to resort to nagging or haranguing. Still others staged dramatic confrontations designed to evoke earnest responses. One woman entered her husband's shower and "forced him to look" at her. "What are you thinking?" she demanded. "I feel sorry for you," was the only reply. Another woman challenged her mate with the question, "How does it feel to know that you'll never go to bed with a woman with two breasts again?" After he replied, "It doesn't mean anything to me," she produced copies of *Penthouse* magazine which he had kept hidden from her.

Mainline sex role theorists see men's silences and women's proddings for more intimate communication as consistent with traditional gender socialization. The sex differences in psychosocial adjustment to mastectomy also might be explained as extensions of the "husband role," which revolves around "instrumental/adaptive functions", and the "wife role," which revolves around "expressive/integrative functions" (see Parsons, 1951). In contrast, critical feminist theorists remind us that the husbands denial is more than a psychological process or role orientation. It is also a manifestation of a power struggle to redefine the conjugal agenda in the wake of a life-threatening illness and, moreover, to deal with intimacy issues within the husband-wife relationship.

Reconstructing the Conjugal Status Quo: When the wife returned home from the hospital, the husband seemed to sigh with deep relief. Her homecoming was viewed as a sign that the marriage was "returning to normal." As wives gradually (although for some, almost immediately) resumed old tasks (e.g., childcare, cooking, cleaning, working outside the home), husbands expressed relief that things were returning to "the way they used to be." Men resumed full work involvement or, if retired, former activities. On the surface, the husband felt less confused and saw himself as "getting back on [his] feet."

Wives indicated that their experience with cancer fundamentally had changed their self-concepts and the ways they thought about life. Breast cancer had been an existential crisis which had triggered a reassessment of life, including marriage. They talked about the urge "do things differently" or "explore new directions." Though their hopes were high for complete recovery, they expressed their appreciation for each day and resolved to live life to the fullest.

The longings for self-evaluation and life-change that so many of the women expressed contrasted with the men's yearnings to return to the pattern of conjugal relations that existed before the intrusion of cancer. The men's energies seemed to be caught up in denying the past to make for a livable present; the women's energies seemed more grounded in present visions of the future. Indeed, these orientations represent two conflicting agendas for marital adjustment. By frustrating women's impulses to change themselves and their relationships, men's denial postures can be interpreted as a psychosocial mechanism which re-establishes the pre-mastectomy interpersonal "status quo."

Caretaking Versus Intimacy: The interviews revealed that wives lobbied for increased intimacy with their husbands in a variety of ways. At some level, moreover, husbands got the message. The wives' needs to more fully process the psychosocial impact of mastectomy on the marriage pressured the husbands to increase their soul-searching and self-disclosure. The changes in role demands immediately following the mastectomy also pressured husbands to increase conjugal intimacy. Many husbands, especially those middle-aged and older, saw the husband role primarily as that of provider and protector, and relied upon their wives to maintain the emotional end of the relationship. The medical and affective demands accompanying the mastectomy, however, shifted the burden of expressing emotional support and psychologically integrating the family from wife to husband. As one man stated,

> Before the operation, Joan did most of the work around the house. When she was hospitalized, and during the following weeks and months of radiation and chemotherapy, however, I had to do much more parenting, cooking, talking seriously with the kids, and above all, comforting and staying close to my wife.

Most of the husbands interviewed experienced the new role demands and increased interpersonal pressures to be more intimate as personally threatening and incompatible with their former images of themselves as husbands and providers. Being the strong one in the relationship did not translate as being in touch with one's feelings and emotional openness. Indeed, as male denial progressively took shape within the post-mastectomy relationship, there seemed to be an overall flight from intimacy toward caretaking, and, in the process, the husband's caretaking became a defense against intimacy.

Caretaking is not the same as intimacy (Messner, 1985). As Rubin (1983:90) observed, "Intimacy is some kind of reciprocal expression of feeling and thought, not out of fear or dependent need, but out of a wish to know another's inner life and to be able to share one's own." In the months after the surgery, domestic life began to take familiar patterns and the husband became more deeply immersed in the protective-guardian role. The husband defined his primary mission as "taking care of my wife"; i.e., to help her through the post-surgical healing process, chemotherapy sessions, and physician visits; to support and reassure her that she and the marriage would survive the illness; to make sure that her "femininity" and feelings of attractiveness were not destroyed by the breast loss. Even the few husbands who disclosed that they had "stopped loving" their wives before their mastectomies prioritized the role of caretaker. As one middle-aged executive revealed, "There had been nothing between us for a long time, a very long time, but I still felt I owed her something for all the years.'' Hence, love was not necessarily a prerequisite for caretaking. Indeed, the interviews suggested that, for many husbands, the caretaker role actually became a vehicle for husbands to further retreat into denial-- denial that the cancer had altered the marital relationship and, further, denial of wives' increased needs for a sharing that went beyond caretaking.

THE BITTER FRUITS OF DENIAL

Denial is seldom a solution to a problem. At best, it postpones addressing a personal or interpersonal issue. At worst, it complicates the situation and debilitates the individual. Men's denial and flight from intimacy in the wake of mastectomy took a toll.

Anxieties about Death and Illness: Denial often intensified a husband's anxieties. As time passed, maintaining a calm, confident, ''on stage'' posture with his wife became more difficult. Inner life became more stressful. Most husbands reported increased moodiness, loss of energy, and gnawing fears about their own health and death. Clearly, the energy put into denying feelings and maintaining the masculine posture of the protective guardian is not without psychic costs.

Men's denial of their own emotional needs created unique psychological difficulties which took the forms of brooding, withdrawal, depression, and preoccupations with aging. One wife noticed, for example, ''He's much more uptight about health and afraid that every little sniffle or pain he gets means something serious is wrong.'' Indeed, most of the men reported developing fears and misgivings about their health and death, yet they reported rarely discussing these concerns with their spouses. After breast cancer struck, death and dying became a real possibility. For many husbands, it was a first reckoning with mortality and vulnerability to serious illness. One middle-aged husband disclosed that his wife's breast cancer signalled that he ''was no longer invincible.'' A 56-year-old said that the mastectomy made him realize that his ''marriage was no longer growing but dying.'' A 40-year-old lawyer explained that,

> Everything was going fine in our marriage and then the illness changed things. Often when I look at my wife, I think of death; her death, my death, just plain death. I hate it. I don't think about my marriage in the same way.

Anger and Resentment: The pattern of denial originates in order to allay a wife's fears of rejection and recurrence. However, with the passage of time, the maintenance of a calm, confident, ''on stage'' posture with his wife becomes a progressively trickier role for the husband to play. Moreover, it seems unlikely that wives actually found their husbands' performances totally believable, thus opening a door to distrust and, perhaps, resentment. As one man put it,

> My wife asked me how I deal with worrying whether she'd get cancer again. I told her that I put it out of my mind, that I just have to push it out. She thought that

this was terrible because it means that I wasn't supporting her, and that I don't love her. Then she gets angry.

It was apparent that the anger of many wives stemmed in part from their frustration with their husbands' denial. When wives were asked, "What advice would you give men to help them better understand mastectomy?" these responses were typical:

- Be honest and try not to hide any feelings.
- Before the surgery my husband was trying to be positive, strong, and supportive. Once the crisis was over, he kept wearing the mask. I'd tell men to let the strong man act go.
- Be themselves. Be honest. Don't try to be the brick wall or the strong one. It sounds corny, hold hands and go through it together. Don't lie—to your wife or to yourself.
- Be a person first and save a lot of the man-stuff for later.

For most husbands, anger stirred beneath the surface. Some men's anger was directed at physicians or, more generally, the impersonal aspects of the diagnosis and treatment process. Others suppressed their anger at what was regarded as "life's unfairness." Finally, several men felt constrained to hide any open expression of anger or frustration for their wives. They worried that their wives might misinterpret any such emotional reactions as directed at them. As one support group participant stated:

When I come home from work after a bad day, I don't want my wife to see me angry because she'll blame herself for it. So I go out and mow the lawn or work on the car. You guys think back to the first time you got angry after the operation. Your wife probably thought it was because of the mastectomy. Right?! Right?!

Two wives reported that their husbands were "always angry" and on the edge of violence. One woman in her mid-forties confided:

He had always had a temper before the mastectomy, but now it seems like he's ready to explode all the time. He's never hit me but he rants and raves and screams at me when he snaps.

Another reported that her husband had become impotent "because of the mastectomy." He avoided virtually all physical contact and would watch TV or go on "long walks" so that he could climb into bed after she was asleep. She confronted him and demanded that they "really talk" about his feelings, the impotence, and the fact that their marriage was crumbling. "I guess I pushed him too hard," she reported, "He shook me and yelled, 'I wish that you were dead' ".

Male anger is often a response to perceived powerlessness or, put another way, lack of control over one's self and others. In varying degrees, a man's anger may be a simmering reminder that his efforts to establish an interpersonal agenda of denial may not be working.

Long-range Adjustment on Male Terms: Most of the men interviewed, it appeared, had not come to grips with the emotional and interpersonal effects of mastectomy on themselves and their wives. For these men, to varying degrees, denial had become a way of life; the illusions of safety and sameness had taken root.

A marital relationship built upon mutual denial may mitigate against self-expression, interpersonal flexibility, and psychological growth. Denial acts as too strong a filter for the nuances and ambiguities of marital interaction to pass through and receive clarification. In short, it may be that a man's acting out the denial role, with or without the complicity of his spouse, may disallow or complicate the development of a new marital relationship in the wake of a mastectomy.

CONCLUDING REMARKS

Denial is the central emotional response of a man to his spouse's mastectomy. Denial can be a valuable defense mechanism in the early stages of the mastectomy crisis and, for this reason, should not be quickly judged either pro or con on feminist grounds. Early psychological denial, however, may soon take on a pattern of fervent and conscious desire for the post-mastectomy relationship to return to the old, pre-mastectomy status quo. One obvious problem with this perception and longing, however, is that it belies the facts. The breast is gone. Cancer has struck a physical and psychological blow. Misgivings about recurrence and mortality are real—especially for women. The emotional core of *both* wife and husband has been altered and, fundamentally, the marital relationship has changed.

A husband's denial after his wife's mastectomy has many functions. It staves off his fears about death and dying, facilitates his caretaking of his recovering wife, and enables him to cope psychologically in a manner which is generally consistent with his upbringing and gender psychology. Within a critical feminist framework, however, denial also has social and political contours and consequences. Generally, a man's denial tends to bring back or conserve the old, pre-mastectomy relationship and, in effect, mitigates against a woman's urgings for interpersonal and marital change. The denial posture also represents an extension of, rather than a departure from, traditional male psychology which revolves around dominance-striving, status aggrandizement, self-control, emotional inexpressivity, and the devaluation of women and femininity (Connell, 1986; Sabo, 1980). The overall result is the reproduction of male-dominance within marriage and its attendant values and interpersonal practices.

It must be recognized that one limitation of feminist theory is what Connell

(1986) calls its "categoricalism." That is to say that it often treats "all men" as if they were alike. The interviewer in this study soon discovered that not all men and not all marriages were alike. There were varying degrees of denial, just as there were different levels of patriarchal authority in the marital relationship. Some couples, especially younger ones, were attempting to develop a more egalitarian relationship. The forces of advanced industrial capitalism are transforming, perhaps even eroding, the patriarchal dimensions of conjugal life. Yet patriarchal values and male dominance remain prominent; struggles between the sexes are ensuing in all institutions, including marriage. Sociologists and clinicians, therefore, should stress gender in their analyses of men's responses to illness and death. (For example, see Joiner and Fisher, 1981). In addition, their theories should recognize that men's psychological posturings and struggles with spouses to define and conduct the marital relationship are intricately related to larger social and political issues in sexual politics. Traditional men and patriarchal marriages are not born, they are made, and the complex social-psychological dynamics involved in men's adjustments to mastectomy are essential elements within this process.

As should be obvious from the limited and extremely pragmatic approach of this study, conclusions need to be voiced conservatively. The aim of the inquiry was not to create an empirical foundation for generalization, but rather to foster insight into the myriad conjugal factors which ultimately shape a man's response to his partner's mastectomy.

REFERENCES

Andersen, M. 1988. *Thinking about Women: Sociological Perspectives on Sex and Gender.* New York: Macmillan.

Bard, M. and C. Sutherland. 1955. Psychological impact of cancer and its treatment. *Cancer* 8:656–77.

Berman, A. L. and J. E. Hays. Relation between death anxiety, belief in afterlife and locus of control. *Journal of Consulting and Clinical Psychology* 41:318.

Chodorow, N. 1978. *The Reproduction of Motherhood.* Berkeley, CA: University of California Press.

Connell, R. W. 1986. *Gender and Power.* Stanford, CA: Stanford University Press.

Farrell, M. P. and S. D. Rosenberg. 1981. *Men at Midlife.* Boston: Auburn House.

Gould, R. L. 1972. The phases of adult life : A study in developmental psychology. *American Journal of Psychiatry* 129:521–31.

Grandstaff, N. W. 1976. The impact of breast cancer on the family. In J. M. Vaeth, ed. *Breast Cancer—Its Impacts on the Patient, Family, and Community.* New York: S. Karger, 146–56.

Hall, A. 1989. How should we theorize gender? In M. Messner and D. Sabo, eds. *Men, Sport and the Gender Order: Critical Feminist Perspectives.* Champaign, IL: Human Kinetics Press.

Joiner, J. G. and J. Z. Fisher 1981. Psychological adjustment to mastectomy. In E. Howell and M. Bayes, eds. *Women and Mental Health.* New York: Basic Books, 411–18.

Levinson, D. J., C. M. Darrow, E. G. Klein, M. H. Levinson, and B. McKee 1974. The psychosocial development of men in early adulthood and the midlife transition. In D. F. Ricks, A.

Thomas and M. Rof, eds., *Life History Research in Psychopathology*, Vol. 3. Minneapolis: University of Minnesota Press.

Messner, M. 1985. The changing meaning of male identity in the lifecourse of the athlete. *Arena Review* 9 (2):31–59.

Metze, E. 1978. Couples and Mastectomy. In P. C. Brand and P. A. van Keep, eds. *Breast Cancer—Psychosocial Aspects of Early Detection and Treatment*. Baltimore, MD: University Park Press, 25–31.

Parsons, T. 1951. *The Social System*. New York: The Free Press.

Rubin, L. B. 1983. *Intimate Strangers*. New York: Harper and Row.

——1976. *Worlds of Pain: Life in the Working-Class Family*. New York: Basic Books.

Sabo, D. F., J. Brown and C. Smith, 1986. The male role and mastectomy: Support groups and men's adjustment. *Journal of Psychosocial Oncology* 3 (2):19–31.

Sabo, D. F. 1985. Sport, patriarchy and male identity: New questions about men and sport. *Arena Review* 9 (2):1–30.

——1980. Conjugal equality and male sexuality: Sex role identity and sexual behavior. A dissertation in the Department of Sociology, State University of NY at Buffalo.

Stillion, J. M. 1985. *Death and the Sexes: An Examination of Differential Longevity, Attitudes, Behaviors, and Coping Skills*. New York: Hemisphere Publishing Corporation.

Templer, D., C. F. Russ and C. M. Franks, 1971. Resemblance of parent-child death anxiety as a function of age and sex of child. *Developmental Psychology* 4:108.

Vaillant, G. E. and C. C. McArthur, Natural history of male psychological health: The adult life cycle form eighteen to fifty. *Seminars in Psychiatry* 4:415-27.

7

The Causes of Cancer
Women Talking

Juanne N. Clarke

Coming to terms with a significant change in one's pattern of ongoing activity is an important challenge in adult life. Sudden and unexpected disability or serious illness in oneself or in one's significant other, or death in another, have been shown repeatedly to create changes for the individual in areas such as self-esteem, identity, key interpersonal relationships, life-styles, and everyday patterns of action. In short, much of the taken-for-granted reality of a person suddenly confronted with a life-threatening event is thrown into confusion and subject to innumerable questions.

Whenever the ongoingness of everyday life is disrupted, whether the disruption is major or minor, human beings, being meaning-making creatures, try to understand the interruptions. They attempt to understand the cause or causes of the interruptive event, examining why it has happened, not in an abstract and theoretical way, but in a personal way. Not only is the prime cause sought, but it tends to be seen as having actually been predictable. Retrospective control (Cowie, 1976) is the psychological term for the process which Marshall (1980) refers to as the life review process or the legitimation of biography.

Cancer is an event which is known to have a tremendous impact on the identity (Peters-Golden, 1982; Clarke, 1985), and on the significant relationships of people with the diagnosis (Dunkel-Schetter and Wortman, 1982; Wortman and Dunkel-Schetter, 1979). It has been the most feared disease in North America for a significant period of time. It is a disease with profound stigmata attached to it (Sontag, 1977; Peters-Golden, 1982). The stigma is not limited to discrete, biophysical processes or anatomical parts. It is so profound that it affects the whole person. Once diagnosed with cancer, one relates to oneself as a new being, betrayed by the body one had taken for granted for so long. No longer can the individual make the assumption, long unconsidered and undiscussed, that the body can be treated as the basis for self-action. Malignant growth can occur at any time and often begins and spreads outside of the awareness of the individual. Both because of its incidence as the second most frequent cause of death and serious morbidity, and because of its powerful, negative, stigmatized social meaning, cancer's impact on people is an important subject of investigation.

A good deal of research suggests that the personal adjustment of an individual to a life-threatening illness such as cancer is dependent on her or his ability to make sense of the threatening experience, to find a personal meaning in it and through understanding of this meaning or message to gain a sense of control over the recurrence of the event, and retrospective cognitive control over the occurrence of the previous event (see Bury, 1982 and Taylor, 1983). Only when the individual has dealt with the issues of meaning and mastery is it possible for her or him to reestablish a positive self-image out of the broken image which was caused by the threatening event.

The meaning given to the threatening event is also a crucial component of interpersonal relationships, whether with friends, relatives, or health care providers. As Kleinman (1980) has noted, one important component of any illness, as well as recovery from the illness, is the set of beliefs that patients, as well as doctors and significant others, have about the condition. Relevant to any set of beliefs about illness are ideas about cause, probable course, and typical strategies for cure including their benefits and side-effects. The meanings people give events have a variety of consequences that are known to affect mood states (Stoeckle and Barsky, 1980), successful diagnosis and treatment (Kleinman, et al., 1978; Zola, 1966), compliance (Becker, 1974), and health-promoting behaviour (King, 1953). Good outcomes also depend on the extent to which physicians understand the patient's point of view regarding the meaning and cause of the disease, and accept the correctness of the patient's point of view as a description of the patient's reality.

The purpose of this chapter is to describe the meanings of the cancer diagnosis, based on data gathered in an interview study of 50 women who had received a cancer diagnosis. The data focus on the kinds of explanations that women offered for their disease. Each of the women, interviewed in an open-ended manner, discussed the cause of her disease at great length. After speaking of the shock and horror of first learning of the cancer diagnosis, they all asked questions such as Why me? Why now? Why this type of cancer? They asked, "Who am I now that I have cancer?" "In what ways am I the same person as I was before I had cancer?" In trying to answer such questions the women gave explanations and causes which made sense to them.

There is a positivistic tradition in the study of the meaning of disease which focuses specifically on beliefs about cause. Three studies which have examined beliefs about the causes of cancer provide contradictory data about lay etiological theories. Blaxter (1983) asked 46 middle-aged, working class women what they felt to be the causes of illness. They responded with lists of numerous discrete causes of a variety of illnesses such as heredity, stress, strain, and poverty. However, they tended not to speculate about the causes of cancer or even to mention the disease by name. When pressed, they replied that the causes of cancer seemed to be random or mysterious.

In a similar study, Pill and Stott (1982), interviewed "upper" working class, and younger middle-aged women from Wales. Again, women mentioned infections and germs as the most common causes of illness, followed by life-style, heredity, and stress. Almost half the women responded with concepts of cause that involved individual responsibility. That these women, young, and of a slightly higher social class, were more likely to be better educated and to own homes than the women in Blaxter's (1983) sample, may account, in part, for their greater sense of control over life than was expressed by Blaxter's working-class respondents.

Another investigation of beliefs about illness causation focused specifically on beliefs about cancer held by matched groups of cancer and non-cancer patients (Linn, et al., 1982). The primary finding was that cancer patients held more equivocal and complex beliefs about the causes of cancer than the other patients. Moreover, cancer patients were more likely to list causes outside of their own control. When asked to rank causes of the disease they mentioned God's will and inheritance among the top four. The non-cancer patients mentioned neither of these among their top four causes of the disease. "The person without cancer can afford to be more dogmatic about causes and likely to think in stereotypes. The closer he comes to dealing with the disease, the less clear-cut and more complex the explanations become" (Linn, et al., 1982:838).

While these three studies are related to an understanding of the meanings of cancer, they are not adequate as sources for a number of reasons. The primary limitation of all three studies is that the respondents were asked specific questions about cause by the researchers, who thus directed the sorts of responses they wanted. This has the advantage of comparability of data from respondent to respondent, but may suffer from answers that are of greater relevance to the researcher than to the respondent. An additional problem with two of the studies is that they asked respondents to speculate about the causes of disease in an abstract way. Such neutral understanding of the causes of cancer in general, may have little or no relationship either to the specific understanding of cause, or more general meaning when the cancer is one's own. In addition, neither Blaxter (1983), nor Pill and Scott (1982), talked to respondents who had a specific disease and were asked to comment on its personal meaning.

Socio-psychological literature also deals with "meaning," although it is defined as cause in a positivistic and definitive manner. In this context retrospective control refers to the reestablishment of a sense of control through taking personal responsibility for having previously caused a negative outcome. A number of studies of attribution have examined the relative impact on adjustment of blaming the self, or blaming an external force (e.g., God, fate, another person, genes). Bulman and Wortman (1977) studied a small group of quadraplegics and paraplegics and found that those individuals who took responsibility for their paralysis rather than blaming it on others made more successful adaptations. Meyer and Taylor (1982) found that for victims of rape, however, self-blame was negatively associated with coping. The acceptance of blame was beneficial to coping only when it could be used by the person to gain mastery or control. The acceptance of self-blame was detrimental when it was inappropriate (to the individual) as a strategy for reestablishment of mastery. In other work, (Taylor, Lichtman and Wood, 1982), self-blame was associated either positively or negatively with coping and adjustment.

As interesting as this work is, it must be criticized for the same limitations as the previous studies. The research is very specifically positivistic and suffers from the limitations of positivism (see Clarke, 1983). The purpose of this paper is to describe, in rich and intimate detail and in the language of the respondents, the meanings of cancer in the lives of a sample of women in southwestern Ontario.

METHODS

This chapter fits within a feminist paradigm both theoretically and methodologically. It is feminist in theory because it redresses the lack of focus on the lived experience of women by examining the meaning of cancer for a sample of women. Its specific goal is to describe the world views and the experiences of women who have received a cancer diagnosis, from their own perspectives and in their own words.[1] Because the purpose of the research was to provide insight into the self-understandings and meanings of cancer among women who have or had cancer, rather than to test hypotheses for generalization to a broader population, the sampling method used was a non-probability strategy. There is an important place for such samples in social science because they allow accessibility to respondents for whom a complete population list is unavailable.

To gather women into the sample, whose final size was 50, I started by interviewing one woman, a friend of a friend who had cancer. After this and subsequent interviews, I was given names of other women who had agreed to talk with me. The process of data collection involved visiting each woman for a period of several hours and listening to her tell her story about the impact of the cancer diagnosis on her life. I was told by many women, on the telephone as I made the appointment for the interview, that they really couldn't talk about themselves without direction and I had better come prepared with a questionnaire. To serve their expressed needs I wrote an open-ended interview schedule of some 15 pages with approximately 50 questions. However, at no time was it necessary for me to use this. I began every interview with an open-ended question such as "Could you tell me about the impact of cancer on your life?" In every case the woman was able to talk at length about herself, her family, her friends, and how she felt the cancer diagnosis fit within the whole context of her ongoing life. Empowered to describe their experiences by the presence of a researcher who listened intently and with interest, each woman expressed pride in herself because she had been able to describe and analyze her own life experiences. At the end of each interview, I was thanked by each woman for listening. The tapes of the interviews were transcribed and returned to each woman. Several women sent back further comments on, and clarifications of, the material in the transcriptions they received. At the end of each interview I asked each woman if she knew of anyone else who had had cancer and who might be willing to talk to me. I asked each woman to contact the individuals to ask their permission before giving me their names. Each person gave me at least one name. Many called with the names of several other women who were willing to be interviewed. As the sample was demographically and geographically dispersed (in terms of such variables as age, marital, family, and work status, and rural or urban location), I am confident that it is a reflection of more than a homogeneous group of women. During the process of asking others if they would agree to an interview, several women began to talk to one another about their experiences with the interview, and with cancer, and a form of consciousness-raising ensued. Some women became involved in local self-help groups for people who had had a cancer diagnosis. Thus the praxis of self-awareness, consciousness-raising, and collective action, aspects of a feminist methodology, evolved as a result of the research process.

FINDINGS

When asked to describe their lives in the context of having received the cancer diagnosis, women considered the personal meaning of the disease. Once they had come to terms with the reality of the diagnosis, and the necessary treatments, women began to ask themselves questions about the personal relevance or message of the disease. Why me? Why now? Why this type of cancer? Who am I now that I have cancer? What did I do to deserve this disease? What did I do to cause this disease? What can I do to prevent it from recurring or to help make myself better?

The answers that women gave to such questions cannot be easily categorized in the terms thought of in the research previously described. Whether or not they blamed themselves or blamed others, for instance, would be a reductionist description and explanation of the gestalt of the comments. Such explanations as provided by brief references to genes, heredity, pollution, and stress would decontextualize and render simplistic the detail and depth of the self-analysis in the context of the search for meaning.

Instead, the search for meaning and cause must be seen as a integral part of the value structure and world view of each woman. It is important to note that these perceptions need not bear any resemblance to the medical descriptions of cause or prognosis. Women who had been religious considered the disease to be, in one way or another, a message from God. More secular women, who were struggling with their ties to their nuclear families, whether of origin (mothers, fathers, sisters, brothers) or procreation (husbands, children), thought of the failings in their family lives as the cause of their cancer. Some looked to particular strains and stresses from being overworked and feeling burdened. Others focused their explanations on what was taken to be a common and much-discussed cause of illness in the media at the time—stress. These women explained the disease in terms of an ongoing stress exacerbated by a particularly traumatic physical or personal event.

The next section of this chapter discusses, on a case-by-case basis, examples of women who saw one of these issues as the cause of her illness. For Betty, cancer had a religious meaning. For Georgie, the disease was linked to her family relationships. Carol's cancer was a message to her about the stress in her life.

Betty's explanation concerned her relationships with God and her church. She had been raised within the United (Methodist) Church by reasonably devout parents. As a child she had been active in Sunday School, and later she was a member of the youth club at the church. In fact, she was president of the youth club and won certificates for perfect attendance at Sunday School. The church was a significant source of her social relationships, and a basis for her self-identity and values as she was growing up. When she went away to nursing school she became friendly with a number of girls who had no interest in "churchy" things and who held agnostic beliefs. She ended her affiliation with the church.

After she graduated from nursing school she met and married a former Roman Catholic who had left his church in anger over what he believed were repressive views on sexuality and birth control. Betty and her husband had three children, all of whom were raised outside church affiliation. When she was diagnosed with cancer she had been married about 20 years and her oldest child was 17 years old.

For Betty, coming to terms with her diagnosis involved coming to terms with her relationships with God and her church. As far as she was concerned, the illness was a spiritual message. It was God's way of reminding her of her sinful ways. As she said:

> "I know that I must take this diagnosis seriously. I know that I am not going to die, at least not yet, and I feel that this is warning from God of my responsibility to Him. I have neglected my spiritual self and I have failed to provide that opportunity for my kids. Before it's too late I intend to fix that. I have been meeting with the minister of the United Church, my church. He has been giving me (Bible) verses to think about. I have gone on a retreat sponsored by the church. I am praying regularly and reading the scriptures every day now."

Betty believed that her disease was a sign of her lack of religious faith. For Betty, the cure, not only for this particular disease, but for the rest of her life and the prevention of recurrence, required the reawakening of her spiritual self.

Georgie felt that her illness resulted from the pain she had experienced as a child in her nuclear family but had not resolved. Georgie was the eldest, of three girls and two boys, in a family in which her mother stayed home to care for the children and her father travelled on business. As Georgie was growing up she frequently was embarrassed by and worried about her mother, who often had too much to drink. She said that she wouldn't know, on a daily basis, as she returned from school, what her mother would be like. Sometimes her mom seemed fine, busy with her housework and her reading, and content. At other times, she would be drunk and angry. When she was angry she would shout and belittle the kids. Because Georgie was the eldest she felt that she should protect the younger ones. While she was able to protect them from physical violence, she was not able to prevent their mother's verbal abuse. On the weekends, when her father was home, her mother didn't drink, and her father couldn't believe the stories Georgie told him about how her mother behaved during the week. Georgie had grown up resenting both of her parents, and before her diagnosis had coped with this by living in a distant city, some two days drive from her parents. But she attributed her cancer to her unresolved anger and bitterness towards her parents.

> "I guess I always knew that it would come back to haunt me. I could never figure out how to trust my parents so I left them to their own devices. I have lived my life and they theirs. Now, however, with this diagnosis and with the threat of death that it has meant I need to come to terms finally with my mom and dad. I still haven't figured out how to do that but I am trying. I have called and written more in the last year (since diagnosis) than in all the fifteen previous years. They are writing back. I still have to go to see them and I am going to as soon as I finish my last chemo."

For Georgie, cure involved a resolution of her "unfinished business," her unresolved childhood hurt.

Carol's experience will be used to illustrate the explanation of stress for illness. For Carol, an immediately prior set of events was taken to be the cause of her cancer. In this case, while she did describe her family background, it was by way of portraying the idyllic past which had preceded her dreadful married life. Carol had been married for ten years. They were unable to have children and her husband had been unwilling to go through the process of adoption. Although she had always had paid employment, Carol had never had money of her own. At the beginning of the marriage their joint income had gone to the down payment and mortgage payments on their house, as well as housekeeping expenses. Later, Carol's husband claimed the money for things that he wanted, such as the latest model car every year, a motorboat, and a camper trailer, and he purchased them without Carol's consent. She did not agree to these purchases, nor did she want the items bought by her husband, but Carol felt that she had no choice but to put her salary toward these expenditures to mollify, if not please, her husband. Her own clothes were handmade. Her holidays were planned by her husband. She had virtually no money for her own discretionary spending. When Carol received her cancer diagnosis she realized how much she resented the marital arrangement into which she and her husband had fallen. To Carol, her cancer diagnosis was a message that she had to do something about her unhappy situation:

> "Now, I don't know how I could have gone along with it for so long. You know, there was a time when I asked my husband for money for pantyhose and he said, 'No, we don't have enough.' I wonder how I could have been so dumb. But things are different now. I am insisting on my own money. I took a trip to the Caribbean with my sister-in-law this spring. He didn't like it but he didn't try to stop me. I am hopeful that we can change."

Carol felt that her cancer was linked to her marital unhappiness, and that the cure for her cancer, as well as her return to health in a larger sense, meant that there had to be major changes in her marital relationship.

CONCLUSION AND DISCUSSION

One of the first questions people often ask when confronted with a serious illness is "Why?"[2] These women who were diagnosed with cancer were no exception. They asked and sought answers to such questions as "Why me?" "Why now?" "Why this type of cancer?" People move through their lives searching for meaning in everyday and in extraordinary events. We are meaning-making creatures. Meanings that make sense will be sought whenever people are confronted with new situations and new expectations. A crucial aspect of meaning-seeking occurs in the confrontation with death, "the fundamental anxiety." As Marshall (1980) says, when our lives seem to be drawing to a close, or when sudden, unexpected events occur, people's thoughts turn to their life stories. We write and rewrite our autobiographies. We want them to show not necessarily a story of success, happiness, fame or the like, but one that "makes sense," is meaningful (Marshall, 1980).

In an overarching schema, socio-psychologist Taylor (1985) offers a theory of cognitive adaptation that enhances adjustment to threatening events. She states that when a person experiences a life-threatening event, the adjustment process revolves around three issues: (1) the search for meaning; (2) the motivation to achieve mastery over the event and to rationalize it in the context of one's life in a more general sense; and (3) the attempt to improve self-esteem. The search for meaning involves the search for answers to questions such as "Why me?" "Why now?" Only when the person has answered these questions in a way that provides self-satisfaction can he or she move on to seek mastery or control. Efforts at mastery involve attempts to control the event, to put it in the context of the life so that it not only makes sense (is meaningful), but so that it was also, in a sense, predictable as an outcome of previous life experience. In addition, a sense of mastery depends on the development of the belief that one can manage whatever the future brings. Because threatening experiences often diminish self-esteem, processes which seek to enhance this aspect of the self must be initiated to ensure adequate adjustment.

Each woman in this sample clearly sought meaning for "her" cancer in the context of her total life experience and her values. All of the women answered the question "Why me?" in a way that was highly personal. "Why me?" is not considered a question relevant only to the body or to physical pathogens. It is of existential significance. Regardless of the particular medical or biological explanation given, the subjects in this study looked beyond it. Each woman tried to place the diagnosis in her life as a somewhat, if only retrospectively, predictable event. They sought the meanings and messages of cancer in their lives as people who have made a whole series of life decisions.

A cybernetic, or system-based, model of analysis is one that moves beyond the individual and his or her behavior and looks at the systems within which the individuals lives. This perspective examines not only the views of the individual, but how the views and beliefs of the individual affect others in the network of interaction, and, in turn, how the beliefs of others act on the beliefs of the initial subject of study. It is within this context that it is crucial for medical and nursing personnel, counselors, and the significant others of cancer patients to listen to and understand the beliefs of those patients. Just as cancer patients themselves must come to terms with the meaning of the diagnosis, so, too, must significant others begin to acknowledge the cancer's significance for them. Only with such acknowledgement can honest con   place. That such communication can be of great benefit documentation.

NOTES

1. Throughout this article, I use the awkward phrase, "the wor diagnosis," instead of any of the more common phrases "cance even "person with cancer." This has been done for the following

(1) To emphasize that the person "with cancer" is also a person who has for most of her life not had cancer, an individual with a whole history, round-of-life and probable future without cancer;

(2) To emphasize that a person "with cancer" is a patient when, and only when, explicitly under the care of a doctor;

(3) To emphasize that the person "with cancer" has or has had a disease but is not a "victim" ("a living being offered as a sacrifice in a religious rite or a person cheated, foiled or injured;" [Merriam-Webster Dictionary])

(4) To clarify that cancer the disease, and the experience with cancer are separable phenomena; and finally

(5) To emphasize that the experience of cancer is not the attribute of an individual but the outcome of a relationship between society and that individual.

2. Why Not Me?

As we've discovered, the first response to the cancer diagnosis was often "Why me?" and "Why this type of cancer?" The next response was often "Why not me?" Jen said:

Of course, I asked, "Why me?" I think it was through reading. I could not read a book at first. For about six weeks. And I'm an avid reader, until I read a book about a contemplative nun. . . . About a business woman, and all her struggles, her widowhood and how she finally became a nun. And I guess the struggles she was going through were similar enough to the struggles I was going through and so I moved to the "Why not me?" stage.

Susan, too, talked of the "Why not me?" stage as following the "Why me?" stage:

At first I was so full of myself, and of the latest stuff on the cancer personality—you know, the perfectionist—and on cancer and stress that I just thought I've brought this on myself. Then I looked around me and started realizing that everyone has some infirmity and this was mine for now.

REFERENCES

Becker, M.H. 1974. The health belief model and personal health behaviour. *Health Education Monography* 2:323.

Blaxter, M. 1983. Diagnosis as category and process. *Social Science and Medicine* 12:9–17.

Blumer, H. 1969. *Symbolic Interactionism: Perspective and Method.* Englewood Cliffs, NJ: Prentice Hall.

Bulman, R.J. and C.B. Wortman. 1977. Attributes of blame and coping in the 'Real World'. Severe accident victims react to their lot. *Journal of Personality and Social Psychology* 35:351–63.

Bury, M. 1982. Chronic illness as biographical disruption. *Sociology of Health and Illness* 1 (No. 2 July):167–81.

Clarke, J. 1981. A multiple-paradigm approach to the sociology of medicine: The work of the physician as an institution, ideology and activity of social control. *Sociology of Health and Illness* 3 (No. 1 March):89–103.

———1983. Sexism, feminism, and medicalism: A decade review of the literature on gender and illness. *Sociology of Health and Illness* 5, 1:62–82.

———1985. *It's Cancer: The Personal Experiences of Women Who have Received a Cancer Diagnosis.* Toronto: IPI Publishing Limited.

———1985. Cancer meanings in the media: Implications for clinicians. Paper presented at the American Sociological Association in Washington, August 1985.

Cowie, W. 1976. The cardiac patient's perception of his heart attack. *Social Science and Medicine* V. 10:87–96.

Davis, F. 1983. Deviance, disavowel: The management of strained interaction by the visibly handicapped. In H.S. Becker, ed. *The Other Side.* Toronto : Collin-MacMillan, 119–37.

Davis, F. 1963. *Passage Through Crises: Polio Victims and Their Families.* Indianapolis, IN: Bobbs-Merrill.

Dunkel-Schetter, C. and C.B. Wortman. 1982. Interpersonal dynamics of cancer: Problems in social relationships and their impact on the patient. In H.S.E. Friedman and R. DeMatteo, eds. *Interpersonal Issues in Health Care.* New York:Academic Press.

Globe and Mail. 1977. April 22, Toronto, Ontario, Canada.

——1981. Jan. 27, Toronto, Ontario, Canada.

Helman, C.G. 1985. Communication in primary care: The role of patient and practitioner explanatory models. *Social Science and Medicine* 20(9):923–31.

King, J. 1953. Health beliefs in the consultation. In Pendleton and J. Hassler, eds. *Doctor-Patient Communication.* London: Academic Press.

Kleinman, A. 1980. *Patients and Healers in the Context of Culture.* Berkeley: University of California Press.

Kleinman, A., L. Eisenberg and B. Good. 1978. Culture, illness and care: Clinical lessons from anthropologic and cross cultural research. *Annals Internal Medicine* 88:251.

Kushner, R. 1975. *Breast Cancer: A Personal History and Investigative Report.* New York: Harcourt, Brace and Jovanovich.

"The Legacy of Terry Fox." 1983. *Quest.* September, Vl. 34, pp. 34, 34sv. 40, 42, 43.

Linn, M. W., B. S. Linn, and S. R. Stein. 1982. Beliefs about causes of cancer in cancer patients. *Social Science and Medicine* 16:835–39.

Marshall, V. 1980. *Last Chapters: A Sociology of Aging and Dying.* Monterey, CA: Brooks/Cole Publishing Co.

Meyer, B. and S.E. Taylor. 1982. *Adjustment to Rape.* Manuscript submitted for publication.

Ohlendorf, P. 1983. Promising attack on cancer. *Maclean's* October 31:30–36.

Peters-Golden, H. 1982. Breast cancer: Varied perceptions of social support in illness experience. *Social Science and Medicine* 16:483–91.

Pill, R. and N.C.H. Stott. Concepts of illness causation and responsibility: Some preliminary data from a sample of working-class mothers. *Social Science and Medicine* 12: 11–22.

Rollin, B. 1976. *First You Cry.* New York: J.B. Lipincott Company.

Rubin, L.B. 1976. *Worlds of Pain: Life in the Working Class Family.* New York: Basic Books.

Schutz, A. 1971. *Collected Papers.* Vol. 3. The Hague: Martinus Nijhoff.

Sontag, S. 1977. *Illness as a Metaphor.* New York: Random House.

Stoekle, J.D. and A.J. Barsky. 1980. Attributions: Uses of social science knowledge in the 'doctoring' of primary care. In L. Eisenberg and A.D. Kleinman, eds. *The Relevance of Social Science for Medicine.* Rendel: Dordrecht.

Struder, K.E. and D. E. Chukin. 1980. *The Cancer Mission: Social Context of Biomedical Research.* Beverley Hills, CA: Sage Publications.

Sudnow, D. 1967. *Passing On: The Social Organization of Dying.* Englewood Cliffs, NJ: Prentice-Hall.

Taylor, S. E. 1983. Adjustment to threatening events: A theory of cognitive adaptation. *American Psychologist* Nov. 1983:1161–73.

Wortman, C.B. and C. Dunkel-Schetter. 1979. Interpersonal relationships and cancer: A theoretical analysis. *Journal of Social Issues* 35:120–55.

Zola, I.K. 1966. Culture and symptoms—an analysis of patients presenting complaints. *American Sociological Review* 31:615.

8

The Death Certificate as a Reflection of Attitudes

Dorothy B. Rosenberg

A major goal of death and dying courses is to increase students' understanding of the complex phenomena and issues involved in the final stage of life. For undergraduate students, the courses deal with ideas and experiences that they see as being either remote and abstract, or immediate and painfully real. In either case, the a death and dying course brings them into contact with mortality. The challenge is to engage students in ways that make them aware of their own beliefs and attitudes, and at the same time direct them beyond their personal experiences; and to begin to do this very early in the course so that they can appreciate the relevance and complexity of the materials they are studying.

The death certificate is an instrument that can be used to enhance students' awareness of society's norms and values, as well as their own feelings. This chapter examines the death certificate as a public document, describes its use in the classroom and students' responses over an eight year period, and indicates how it can be integrated into discussions of major topics and issues that are central to death and dying courses.

THE DEATH CERTIFICATE AS A PUBLIC DOCUMENT

For centuries in Europe and during the first years of colonization in the New World, the only official records of births and deaths were kept by local clergy. At birth each soul was entered into the books and was subject to the demands of the faith and the state; another entry was made at death releasing the soul to join its maker (Kastenbaum, 1986). As early as 1639 the Massachusetts Colony and the Plymouth Colony passed laws requiring that births and deaths be recorded. The information that was recorded was made available at local and county levels (Hanlon, 1964). This was also true of the records that were kept in the other colonies. It was not until the Constitution of the United States was

96

adopted and the first census taken that regional information about births and deaths was compiled and became more widely available. Data about births and deaths were gathered by taking a census of these events along with the decennial census of the population. This procedure proved to be unsatisfactory, according to the 1880 report on mortality and vital statistics (Rosenau, 1965). The need for dependable data led to the establishment of registration areas by the Bureau of the Census, the first of which was organized in 1900. This initial registration area, which contained approximately 40 percent of the United States population at the time, included the New England States, Indiana, Michigan, New Jersey, New York, and the District of Columbia. By 1933 all of the states had satisfactory state laws regarding the registration of births and deaths and had achieved a minimum of 90 percent completeness in reporting (Hanlon, 1964).

Although deaths had been reported and recorded at the local level since the early years of the colonies, it was not until the late 18th century that death certificates signed by physicians were considered important. They emerged as a byproduct of the medical interests and concerns regarding the definitive determination of death. From about the 1760s in Europe, and beginning in 1780 in the United States with the formation of the Philadelphia Humane Society, there were organized efforts by many of the leading physicians of the time to refine the criteria for the determination of death (Thompson, 1963), and to resuscitate individuals who were in a state of apparent death or "suspended animation" due to drowning, asphyxiation, or being struck by lightning. The concerns of the early humane societies and of the medicolegalists of the 1800s were prompted by fears of premature burial (Hendin, 1974). During this period physicians appeared to be reluctant to verify death and were rarely called upon to do so, leaving the responsibility to undertakers and others who had no training in human anatomy (Aries, 1982). The current requirement that a death certificate be signed by a physician was initiated by the early humane societies (Hendin, 1974), and was included in the requirements for membership eligibility in registration areas in 1900.

Since 1900, vital statistics have been collected in the United States through a decentralized cooperative system, with responsibility for registration and reporting currently vested in 57 registration areas. These include each of the 50 states, New York City, the District of Columbia, Puerto Rico, the Virgin Islands, American Samoa, Guam and the Trust Territory of the Pacific Islands.

The National Center for Health Statistics, the federal agency responsible for ensuring uniformity in reporting, makes periodic revisions and recommends their adoption by the registration areas. The Standard Certificate of Death has remained essentially unchanged since 1949. A revision, recommended for adoption in 1989, contains only four changes: printing detailed instructions for reporting the cause of death on the face and back of the certificate; providing space for a second physician's signature, if the certifying physician is not the attending physician, so that the body can be released to the funeral director and the medical details can be completed later; identifying the decedent's ethnic, particularly Hispanic, ancestry in order to examine ethnic mortality patterns, particularly in the Hispanic community; and reporting the decedent's educational level to be used as an indicator of socioeconomic status (Freedman, et al., 1988).

In current practice, the physician is responsible for certifying the medical facts concerning death while the funeral director is responsible for actually filing the death certificate with the registrar of vital statistics. In addition to being a requirement for the disposition of the remains, the death certificate is a source of protection for individuals and information for society. It protects the rights of survivors, by establishing the fact and date of death for claiming such benefits as life insurance and pensions, and for settling the estate of the deceased. The death certificate also provides information regarding sex, race, age, occupation, etc., along with the medical facts that aid in statistical analysis to determine the incidence of specific causes of death, plan for the control of communicable diseases, investigate the nature of fatal accidents, establish the need for health programs and measure the effectiveness of health services (Rosenau, 1965).

THE DEATH CERTIFICATE IN THE CLASSROOM

My Death and Dying class meets one evening a week, for two hours and forty minutes. Each week we deal with a different topic, or set of issues, beginning in the first week with the definition and determination of death. In the first class session, I ask the students to identify themselves by filling out a form, putting their own names on the first line and giving the information about themselves that is asked for, making up the answers where it is necessary. As soon as I start passing out the forms someone invariably blurts out: "Good grief, it's a death certificate!" It is a copy of the Physician's Certificate of Death for West Virginia, with identifying information removed, (see Figure 1).

I suggest that the students discuss the form and talk to the people sitting near them about how they are filling it out. After ten to fifteen minutes I collect their death certificates, pointing out that they have just had a unique, although hypothetical, experience; in reality, none of us will fill out our own death certificate. Much of the rest of the session is devoted to a brief review of the history of death certification, the process and people involved in filing the death certificate, and the utility of the death certificate for the individual and society.

Several weeks later when the readings and lecture materials deal with attitudes toward death, I analyze the class's attitudes as reflected in the information they provided on their death certificates, and I compare their responses with those

DIVISION OF VITAL STATISTICS
PHYSICIAN'S CERTIFICATE OF DEATH

LOCAL FILE NUMBER   STATE FILE NUMBER

DECEDENT — NAME FIRST	MIDDLE	LAST	SEX	DATE OF DEATH (Mo., Day, Yr.)
1.			2.	3.

RACE (e.g. White, Black, American Indian, etc.) (Specify)	AGE — Last Birthday (Yrs.)	UNDER 1 YEAR MOS. / DAYS	UNDER 1 DAY HOURS / MINS.	DATE OF BIRTH (Mo., Day, Yr.)	COUNTY OF DEATH
4.	5a.	5b. / 5c.		6.	7a.

DECEDENT
If death occurred in institution, see handbook regarding completion of residence items

CITY, TOWN OR LOCATION OF DEATH	HOSPITAL OR OTHER INSTITUTION — Name (If not in either, give street and number)	IF HOSP. OR INST. Indicate DOA, OP/Emer. Rm., Inpatient (Specify)
7b.	7c.	7d.

STATE OF BIRTH (If not in U.S.A., name country)	CITIZEN OF WHAT COUNTRY	MARRIED, NEVER MARRIED, WIDOWED, DIVORCED (Specify)	SURVIVING SPOUSE (If wife, give maiden name)	WAS DECEDENT EVER IN U.S. ARMED FORCES? (Specify Yes or No)
8.	9.	10.	11.	12.

SOCIAL SECURITY NUMBER	USUAL OCCUPATION (Give kind of work done during most of working life, even if retired)	KIND OF BUSINESS OR INDUSTRY
13.	14a.	14b.

RESIDENCE — STATE	COUNTY	CITY, TOWN OR LOCATION	STREET AND NUMBER	INSIDE CITY LIMITS (Specify Yes or No)
15a.	15b.	15c.	15d.	15e.

PARENTS

FATHER — NAME FIRST MIDDLE LAST	MOTHER — MAIDEN NAME FIRST MIDDLE LAST
16.	17.

INFORMANT — NAME (Type or print)	MAILING ADDRESS STREET OR R.F.D. NO.	CITY OR TOWN STATE ZIP
18a.	18b.	

DISPOSITION

BURIAL, CREMATION, REMOVAL, OTHER (Specify)	CEMETERY OR CREMATORY — NAME	LOCATION CITY OR TOWN STATE
19a.	19b.	19c.

FUNERAL SERVICE LICENSEE Or Person Acting As Such (Signature)	NAME OF FACILITY	ADDRESS OF FACILITY
20a.	20b.	20c.

CERTIFIER — *To be Completed by CERTIFYING PHYSICIAN Only*

To the best of my knowledge, death occurred at the time, date and place and due to the cause(s) stated. 21a. (Signature)	DATE SIGNED (Mo., Day, Yr.) 21b.	HOUR OF DEATH 21c. M

NAME OF ATTENDING PHYSICIAN IF OTHER THAN CERTIFIER (Type or Print) 21d.

NAME AND ADDRESS OF CERTIFIER (Type or Print) 21e.

REGISTRAR	DATE RECEIVED BY REGISTRAR (Mo., Day, Yr.)
22a. (Signature)	22b.

CONDITIONS IF ANY WHICH GAVE RISE TO IMMEDIATE CAUSE STATING THE UNDERLYING CAUSE LAST

CAUSE OF DEATH

PART I	IMMEDIATE CAUSE (a)	(ENTER ONLY ONE CAUSE PER LINE FOR (a), (b), AND (c).)	Interval between onset and death
	DUE TO, OR AS A CONSEQUENCE OF: (b)		Interval between onset and death
	DUE TO, OR AS A CONSEQUENCE OF: (c)		Interval between onset and death

PART II	OTHER SIGNIFICANT CONDITIONS — Conditions contributing to death but not related to cause given in PART I (a)	AUTOPSY (Specify Yes or No) 24.	WAS CASE REFERRED TO MEDICAL EXAMINER OR CORONER (Specify Yes or No) 25.

ACCIDENT (Specify Yes or No) 26a.	DATE OF INJURY (Mo., Day, Yr.) 26b.	HOUR OF INJURY 26c. M	DESCRIBE HOW INJURY OCCURRED 26d.

IF YES, NOTIFY MED EXAMINER

INJURY AT WORK (Specify Yes or No) 26e.	PLACE OF INJURY — At home, farm, street, factory, office building, etc. (Specify) 26f.	LOCATION STREET OR R.F.D. NO. CITY OR TOWN STATE 26g.

Figure 1.

of previous classes and with relevant items from the *Psychology Today* readership survey (Schneidman 1970, 1971). As we discuss various topics and issues throughout the course, I include information about norms and values, as well as the implications of the students' attitudes as reflected by their responses to the items on the death certificate.

THE STUDENT-RESPONDENTS

Even though many students respond to the exercise with sarcasm and humor, the analysis that follows shows how the death certificate can be used in linking students' views about their own deaths with attitudes and practices in our society.

Over the eight years that I have been collecting death certificates, 555 students have provided information that meets the criteria for inclusion in this analysis by stating current age or date of birth, date of death and cause of death. They represent more than 90 percent of the students attending class on the first evening in each of the fall semesters that I have taught Death and Dying.

Only two pieces of the information being examined are based on fact: the sex and the age of the respondents. Females outnumber males three to two. Traditional students (17 to 22 years of age) outnumber the non-traditional students (23 to 68 years of age), seven to three, males and traditional students are over-represented among the 46 students (7.6 percent) who did not respond to one or more of the criteria items.

All other information is pure fiction, the invented circumstances of the students' lives at the time of death. While their death certificates need not be taken seriously, they do seem to reflect the students' attitudes toward, and expectations for, both life and death.

INFORMATION AND ATTITUDES

The information needed to complete a death certificate is divided into four categories: identification of the decedent, including age, sex, marital status, date and place of death, parents' names, etc.; disposition of the remains; certification of death by the physician; and enumeration of the causes of death, including whether it was by accident or injury, whether the case was referred to a medical examiner and whether an autopsy was performed. This analysis is based on some of the biographical "facts," the cause of death, and the type of body disposal.

When Death Occurs

The timing of death can be considered in two ways, either as the age at death or as the amount of time left before death. Students were about equally divided between those dying under the age of 50 and those dying later. Nearly a third died before their 25th birthday while almost 40 percent survived beyond the age of 75. The traditional students tended to die young, before their 23rd birthdays, while those over 40 expected to survive past 75. The differences in the amount of time left between the traditional students and the non-traditional ones was insignificant; the date of death was either within the current year or more than 40 years in the future. Few of the students indicated that they had 80 or more years remaining. Females tended to have the greater longevity, however the proportion of males who claimed to live longer than the 112 years exceeded that of females by over two to one ratio. The majority of the non-traditional students were under 30 years of age, which may explain the lack of significant differences in the amount of time left between the traditional and non-traditional students.

About three out of ten students listed the date of death as the date they filled out the death certificate or before. The 163 who died right after the first class died suddenly in vehicular accidents on their way home, from shock after seeing the course outline, or from heat stroke the year the air conditioner in the classroom was broken at the beginning of fall semester. Of the 12 students who said they had already died, none indicated that this had been a real experience, and no deaths of my students were reported during the semester. One's own death is so difficult to contemplate that the findings could have two possible explanations: if I say I am already dead or that I will die today I don't have to take it seriously; or if I say that I will die when I am very old (over 85), then death is so remote that I really don't have to think about it.

Marital Status

At the time of death, some 45 percent of the students were married, about 41 percent had never married, 8 percent were widowed and less than 6 percent were divorced. Those who died before age 30 tended to have never been married, while more than six out of ten of those who died at age 30 or older were married at the time of death and about 11 percent were widowed. Men tended to be single; women tended to be widowed or divorced. Three quarters of the women who were married were survived by their husbands. Considering that the life expectancies for males are lower than for females by almost eight years, and that husbands tend to be older than their wives in our society, the female students' expectations seem unrealistically high. More than four-fifths of the men who were married were survived by their wives, a more realistic finding considering both the age differences between the sexes and the higher rates of remarriage among males, especially in the later years.

The issue is not that the findings might differ from census data or that they might be unrealistic (the findings are fictitious), but that the student-respondents, both men and women, seem to think that they will die first, leaving their spouses to cope with the grief, suffer the pain, handle the unfinished business and reconstruct their lives. This raises a question about the nature of love and whether altruism is a component of the love that is assumed to be shared by married couples. This is an issue not to be settled, but perhaps to be considered.

Place of Death

Two-thirds of the respondents died in hospitals, just over 20 percent as patients, and nearly 45 percent were either dead on arrival (DOA) or died in emergency rooms. About 20 percent died in their own homes, 10 percent died out of doors, and 5 percent died in other places, such as classrooms, offices, motels, and friends' houses.

Although these findings are fictitious, they are consistent with reality, as most deaths currently occur in hospital settings. There is a tendency for males to die out of doors or as DOAs or emergency room patients while the females tend to die at home. It may be that the place of death is a function of the cause of death. The hospital is considered to be the appropriate place for treating diseases, accidents, and injuries, and is also the place where death is pronounced even when it occurs elsewhere.

Cause of Death

In the past 65 years, over 100 publications have documented discrepancies as great as nearly 50 percent between clinical and autopsy diagnoses of cause of death (Carter, 1985), and have questioned the validity of the information on death certificates on which mortality statistics are based. Differences between clinical and autopsy findings may reflect the real difficulties in arriving at accurate diagnoses of complex disease processes. These discrepancies also may be the result of the certifying physicians' lack of information about lifestyle factors or underlying conditions, or the physicians' reluctance to list stigmatizing causes of death, such as sexually transmitted diseases, alcohol-related conditions, and suicides.

Schneidman (1980) points out that listing the cause of death on a death certificate does not automatically imply the mode of death—natural, accidental, suicidal or homicidal (NASH). For example, death due to loss of blood from a gun shot wound does not tell us whether the deceased was shot accidentally while cleaning the gun, purposely shot him or herself as a suicidal gesture, or was a victim of a homicidal act by someone else. There are no provisions on the death certificate for specifying death by legal execution, death in war or by military incursion, or death by police action. Although the NASH classification scheme is recommended by the National Center for Health Statistics, it is not used uniformly in all registration areas. For example, the West Virginia certificate, which is similar to those used by several other states, asks whether or not the death was accidental and requests details about injuries, but it does not specifically identify deaths due to homicide or suicide. In the context of the current efforts to refine the criteria for the determination of death, the death certificate does not indicate whether brain death or somatic death is being certified, and making this distinction is not among the most recent revisions (Freedman, et al., 1988).

In trying to classify the 555 student-respondents' deaths according to the NASH scheme, just over half could be considered natural and more than one quarter were accidental. Suicides and homicides account for about four percent and six percent, respectively. The remaining 11.5 percent include three males and two females who died in war, eleven deaths that could not be classified, and 47 deaths from "studentitis," a general category of deaths among college students that are due to the shock of graduating or not graduating, studying too much or too little, the pressures of non-academic life, and the like.

The reported deaths also can be examined by grouping them according to whether they were due to "inside causes" or "outside forces." "Inside causes" such as heart or circulatory problems, old age or natural causes, other acute or chronic conditions, and stress or exhaustion were responsible for some 57 percent of the deaths, while "outside forces" such as vehicle and non-vehicle accidents, drugs, poisons, and killings accounted for about 43 percent. Deaths from "outside forces" tend to occur earlier in life than "inside causes," which are most often listed by those who died after age 40. There is an exception to this pattern: three quarters of the 43 deaths from stress and exhaustion, which are considered to be "inside causes," were classified as "studentitis," an extra NASH category, and occurred among the younger students.

The five leading causes of death listed by the student-respondents were: vehicular and non-vehicular accidents, 28 percent; heart attacks, 23.6 percent; natural causes or old age, 17.4 percent; suicides or killings, 10.6 percent; all other acute or chronic conditions listed, 7 percent. According to the U.S. Bureau of the Census (1985), the six leading causes of death in 1979 were: diseases of the heart; malignancies; cerebrovascular diseases; accidents and adverse effects; pulmonary diseases; and suicides, homicides and legal interventions. Although the order differs, three of the five causes listed most frequently by the students were among the six leading causes of death in the United States.

The 39 acute or chronic conditions that were listed include 20 cases of cancer, 10 of stroke, 3 of pneumonia, 2 in childbirth, and single cases of Parkinson's disease, Hodgkin's disease, kidney failure and AIDS. The combination of the leading causes of death and places of death suggests the hope that death will come quickly and, if not unexpectedly, then as painlessly as possible. This seems to confirm Aries (1985) contention that death is avoided, ignored, and denied in contemporary society.

Each year one or more students list suicide as the cause of death, in all 20 have done so. In the session devoted to attitudes toward death I summarize the students' attitudes as reflected in their death certificates. This analysis is tongue-in-cheek and the students respond by laughing at the strange modes and unique circumstances of their deaths. Amid the levity I stop joking to note that suicide also was listed. I suggest that if this a serious consideration it could be helpful if the individual would get in touch with one of the health services or social agencies on campus or in the community. On several occasions students have commented that I handled the issue sensitively, and others have told me that they were only joking. I have not had to face the problems associated with a class member committing suicide, but there is always that risk, and a Death and Dying student did commit suicide the year before I started teaching the course.

As might be expected, some students use the death certificate as an opportunity for creativity. Every year one or two male students are shot by irate husbands, and almost every year a female student dies of a broken heart. There are relatively frequent occurences of parachutes not opening, people falling out of trees and buildings, off flag poles and pogo sticks, and from mountain tops. They also fall off bridges, sometimes wearing cement overshoes, and they are caught in avalanches and tidal waves. Some students are hit on the head with balls of various kinds, or bottles, or stones from pyramids. Others are run over by stampeeding elephants, rampaging sheep, angry turtles, enraged Republicans, pillaging pygmies and beer wagons. Airplanes crash killing pilots, passengers, and the people whose houses they crash into. There are several cases of spontaneous combustion, and one woman froze to death on a beach in the Bahamas. Some deaths are caused by too much sex and others by too little, and in one case, a 96 year old died of heart failure in prison while "serving time for running the AARP prostitution service."

Post-Mortem Investigations

Autopsies were performed or there was referral to a medical examiner or coroner in about 30 percent of the deaths. Medical examiners are physicians, usually forensic pathologists, who are appointed officials, while coroners, who may or may not be physicians, are usually elected to office. They perform similar functions in that they investigate deaths when the cause is unknown, not satisfactorily explained, accidental, suicidal or homicidal. If there is sufficient doubt regarding the cause of death, the legal official can order an autopsy to be performed (Aiken, 1985).

There is a tendency among those who die young to be referred to a medical examiner or coroner and for autopsies to be performed. It also is among the younger group that the deaths from "outside forces" tend to occur, and these include the deaths that fall under the jurisdiction of an official investigator. In about 28 percent of the 122 cases referred to medical examiners or coroners, autopsies were not performed.

If a death is not under legal investigation, an autopsy can be performed only with the permission of the next of kin. Of the 125 autopsies performed, just over 30 percent did not involve official investigations. Viewed another way, of the 433 whose deaths were not investigated, just under 12 percent of the next of kin gave permission for autopsies. This compares favorably with a contemporary national estimate of less than 14 percent (Carter, 1985).

In addition to resolving legal questions, autopsies are important quality control mechanisms. They are used to test the accuracy of clinical diagnoses, identify or confirm the basis of disease and the cause of death, monitor the interpretation of diagnostic tests, study the efficacy and toxicity of therapeutic agents, detect conditions that may have been obscured by a more prominent disease, monitor the influence of environmental factors on physiological pro-cesses, and educate medical students and practicing physicians (Geller, 1983).

In 1950, nearly half of all patients who died in hospitals were autopsied; by 1978, the proportion had dropped to about 1 out of 5 (Dying, 1978), and this trend continues. Explanations for the decline include cost, which is an expense borne by the hospital; the absence of pressure to perform autopsies since they are no longer required for hospital accreditation; physicians' orientation toward the living and their fears, in an age of malpractice suits, of what an autopsy might reveal about their skills and judgement; technologically sophisticated diagnostic instruments that make the invasive procedure unnecessary; reluctance of physicians to seek permission for autopsies at the time of death; reluctance of families to give their consent because the patient ''has suffered enough,'' the physician has not pursued the matter, or they have been discouraged by funeral directors, for whom autopsies are on an obstacle, since they hinder embalming and delay the work of preparing the body (Geller, 1983).

Disposition of the Remains

The first function of the death certificate is to permit disposal of the body. A Burial-Transit Permit replaces the Cause of Death section on one of the four copies of the certificate. When the other sections are completely filled out and signed by the attending physician and the funeral service licensee, this authorization allows the body to be buried, transported to a crematory, or removed to another facility. The person in charge of the actual disposal must complete the authorization form verifying the body disposal and file it with the state registrar of vital statistics.

Nationally, approximately 85 percent of the dispositions are burials, ten per-cent are cremations and five percent are by entombment in mausoleums, but these national averages are subject to wide regional variation (Leming and Dickinson, 1985). For example, in West Virginia the rate of cremation is less than one percent (Gocke, 1981).

Just over half of the student-respondents selected burial, approximately 37 percent selected cremation, about six percent made anatomical or organ dona-tions, nearly two percent were buried at sea, and just under four percent used other means. Current age seemed to make little difference, except that there was a tendency for the traditional students, the 17 to 22 year olds, to prefer burial or to make anatomical or organ donations, while the older students tended toward cremation or other means of disposal. It was the females who were more inclined toward donations or burial, while the males selected burial at sea or other means; the males and females did not differ in their selection of cremation. Those who were married and widowed tended to prefer burial, while the sin-gles—never married and divorced—expressed a preference for cremation and other means. The choice of an autopsy did not increase the likelihood of organ or anatomical donations. In all, only eight people donated organs before being buried or cremated, and 24 left their bodies to science.

Those who died from "inside causes" (heart or circulatory problems, old age or natural causes, acute or chronic conditions) tended to be buried while those whose deaths were the result of "outside forces" (vehicle or non-vehicle accidents, drugs or alcohol, killings) tended to be cremated. Those who died from stress or exhaustion (a part of the studentitis syndrome) tended to be disposed of in ways similar to those who died from the creative causes: almost half were cremated; and they account for 40 percent of the 20 who were disposed of by "other means." The "other means" range from stuffing or bronzing and being put on display, to the body was stolen or lost or blew up. They also include other possibilities such as cryonic suspension, fertilizer, use in automobile crash tests, hung upside down in a cave, and left on the curb in a trash bag.

THE DEATH CERTIFICATE AND THE DEATH AND DYING COURSE

At first glance the death certificate may appear to be a routine document that warrants little attention, but I have found it to be a valuable teaching tool. It is a useful device for engaging students from the first day of class on, and a rich source of information and ideas.

Imagining their own deaths—as the students must in order to fill out a death certificate—can help them begin to think about their own mortality and that of their loved ones. And if the students exchange comments and wisecracks while they are doing this exercise, they may become acquainted with others with whom they can talk about the course materials. Presenting an analysis of the students' death certificates as part of a discussion about attitudes toward death can break the ice and help the students begin to accept and deal with their anxieties about the course.

Individual items on the death certificate suggest questions for discussion throughout the course, for example: Is death an event or a process? The death certificate treats it as an event that occurs at a given hour on a given day. Is altruism a component of love? I found that more than three quarters of those who said they were married were survived by their spouses. Why do people indicate that their own deaths are imminent? Over a third of my students said that they died within the next five years. If given their choice, why do people seem to prefer to die unexpectedly? Almost six out of ten listed accidents, heart attacks or killings. Why are people reluctant to be organ donors? Less than two percent of my students would donate organs prior to burial or cremation. Are we a death denying society? The death certificate, as a legal document, may represent the routinization and bureaucratization of death in order to avoid having to deal with it, or the document as it has evolved may be evidence that our society accepts death and is able to deal with it.

The death certificate symbolizes the completion of several different processes. For the deceased, the living and the dying are over; for society, the death has been verified and certified; for family members, roles in relation to the deceased are empty. The death certificate also marks the beginning of several different processes. It legitimates the open expression of grief through customary mourning practices. It places family members in the temporary role of the bereaved. It begins the cycle of formal ceremonies that transfer the deceased from the world of the living to the world of the dead. It allows the deceased's property to be conveyed to its new owners.

As Schneidman (1980:148–149) points out, the death certificate "gives operational meaning to death . . . (and) in fact, defines its current dimensions." When considered in this light, information from and about this document can be woven into many of the topics considered in Death and Dying courses.

REFERENCES

Aiken, L. R. 1985. *Dying, Death and Bereavement.* Newton, MA: Allyn and Bacon, 134–35.

Aries, P. 1985. Death inside out. In S. G. Wilcox and M. Sutton, eds. *Understanding Death and Dying.* Palo Alto, CA: Mayfield, 39–60.

———1982. *The Hour of our Death.* New York: Vintage Books, 397–406.

Carter, J. R. 1985. The problematic death certificate. *New England Journal of Medicine* 313(20):1285–86.

"Dying Autopsy." 1978. *Time.* September 18, pp. 90–91.

Freedman, M.A., G.A. Gay, J.E. Brockert, P.W. Potrzebowski, and C.J. Rothwell. 1988. The 1989 revisions of the U.S. standard certificates of live birth and death and the U.S. standard report of fetal death. *American Journal of Public Health* 78(2):168–72.

Geller, S. A. 1983. Autopsy. *Scientific American* (March): 124–36.

Gocke, T. 1981. The Funeral Director and the American Funeral. Presentation for Death and Dying class, West Virginia University, Morgantown, W.V. (November).

Hanlon, J. J. 1964. *Principles of Public Health Administration.* 4th ed. St. Louis, MO: C. V. Mosby, 370–72.

Hendin, D. 1974. *Death as a Fact of Life.* New York: Warner Paperback Library, 15–42.

Kastenbaum, R. J. 1986. *Death, Society, and Human Experience.* 3rd ed. Columbus, OH: Charles E. Merrill, 169–73.

Leming, M. R. and G. E. Dickinson. 1985. *Understanding Dying, Death, and Bereavement.* New York: Holt, Rinehart and Winston, 305–16.

Rosenau, M. J. 1965. In P. E. Sartwell, ed. *Maxcy-Rosenau Preventative Medicine and Public Health.* 9th ed. New York: Appleton-Century-Crofts, 51–52.

Schneidman, E. S. 1980. The Death Certificate. In E. S. Schneidman, ed. *Death: Current Perspectives.* 2nd ed. Palo Alto, CA: Mayfield, 148–56.

———1971. You and death. *Psychology Today* June: 43–45; 74–80.

———1970. A psychology today questionnaire: You and death. *Psychology Today* August: 67–72.

Thomson, E. 1963. The role of physicians in the humane societies of the eighteenth century. *Bulletin of the History of Medicine* January-February: 43–51.

U. S. Bureau of the Census. 1985. Death Rates, 1960 to 1979, and Deaths, 1970 to 1979, from Selected Causes. In S. G. Wilcox and M. Sutton, eds. *Understanding Death and Dying*. Palo Alto, CA: Mayfield, 410–11.

9

Thanatometer:
A scale for the measurement
of awareness and acceptance
# of death

Panos D. Bardis

'Who knows that 'tis not life which we call death, And death our life on earth?'

—Euripides, *Phrixus*, Fragment 11.

This article is part of a major project dealing with various aspects of thanatology (science of death—Greek *thanatos,* death, and *logos,* science), the history thereof,[1] and measurement of attitudes toward death (Thanatometer: Greek *thanatos* and *metron,* measure).

The Thanatometer has resulted from an attempt to deal with an emotional issue, death, more objectively. For distortions based on one's own values contribute neither to scientific knowledge nor to the solution of individual and social problems. As Eileen Barker (1984:36) has correctly stated: 'while engaged in the exercise of describing and explaining phenomena, it is my belief that social scientists are useful only in so far as they communicate information which corresponds to the object of their study rather than colouring, distorting, confusing or over-simplifying an already messy and complicated reality with the addition of their personal beliefs and values. The ''purer'' the information, the more helpful it will be in enabling us all (as citizens) to implement our values.'

A quantitative instrument such as the Thanatometer, then, may be employed in numerous ways. For instance, Thanatometer scores, treated as dependent variables, may be compared with countless independent variables, such as age, gender, occupation, education, religiosity, and parental education and occupation. The findings could be valuable in teaching, research, counselling, and other professional activities.

The Thanatometer, which measures the degree of one's awareness and acceptance of death, was constructed by means of the Likert scaling technique (Likert, 1932:11–53). The main steps in its construction are described below.

SURVEY OF OPINIONS

In accordance with the Likert technique, the first step was to secure hundreds of opinion statements concerning death. The sources of such items were as follows:

(a) Students, professors, and others in the United States of America.
(b) Various international scientific conferences in the West and in the Orient.
(c) Personal interviews in Greece, Italy, Austria, West Germany, France, and England.
(d) Publications dealing with attitudes toward death.[2]

CRITERION OF INTERNAL CONSISTENCY

The statements thus secured were edited and typed together as a preliminary Thanatometer. The necessary instructions were also added.

Copies of the resulting instrument were distributed among 100 persons in the American Midwest who constituted a highly heterogeneous group.

The subjects who made the 10 highest and 10 lowest scores were then selected for the 'criterion of internal consistency.' Their responses thus gave the 20 most differentiating items, which constitute the final Thanatometer (see Appendix).

Some of the poor, that is, non-differentiating, statements were as follows:

(a) A highly emotional reaction to a family member's death is quite normal.
(b) Mock wakes and other such humorous activities dealing with death are acceptable.
(c) Mourning should be accepted as something normal for at least one year after a family member's death.
(d) We must accept death without any anxiety.
(e) Humorous 'cadaver parties' in college to restore voting rights for the dead are all right.
(f) The mass media should not present death sensationally.
(g) We must place less emphasis on the mortician's cosmetic restoration of corpses.

SCORING

A 5-point subscale (0–4, or 'Strongly disagree' to 'Strongly agree'), with the highest value representing the highest awareness and acceptance of death, is employed for reacting to each of the 20 items of the final scale. One's score on the entire Thanatometer is equal to the sum total of these 20 numerical responses.

It is obvious, then, that the theoretical range of Thanatometer scores is 0 (ideal-typical, or complete, non-awareness and non-acceptance of death) to 80 (ideal-typical, or complete, awareness and acceptance of death).

VALIDITY

The validity[3] of the Thanatometer was tested as follows:

The Thanatometer and race

Thanatologists and other scholars have stated that blacks tend to accept death more readily than whites (Kalish & Reynolds, 1976; Charmaz, 1980:286). Accordingly, the author gave copies of the Thanatometer to two heterogeneous groups of blacks and whites consisting of 30 members each. The arithmetic means of the Thanatometer scores were 59,72 for the blacks and 48,36 for the whites. The difference between these values gave a t of 4,07 ($df = 58$; $p < 0,001$).

The Thanatometer and familism

Familism has been defined as 'strong in-group feelings, emphasis on family goals, common property, mutual support, and the desire to pursue the perpetuation of the family' (Bardis, 1983:128). Various investigators have found that death awareness and familism tend to be directly proportional (Kalish & Reynolds, 1976; Charmaz, 1980:284–285). Indeed, when the author distributed copies of the Thanatometer and the Bardis Familism Scale (Bardis, 1978:127–156) among 30 subjects, the resulting coefficient of correlation was 0,74 ($df = 28$; $p < 0,001$).[4]

Similarly, studies suggest that extended familism and death awareness are also directly proportional (Lifton, 1968). On the basis of this knowledge, the author distributed copies of the Thanatometer and the Bardis Extended Familism Scale (Bardis, 1959: 340–341) among 30 other persons.[5] The obtained coefficient of correlation was 0,69 ($df = 28$; $p < 0.001$).

The Thanatometer and urban-rural residence

Countless investigations have indicated that people in small towns think of death rather frequently, while death awareness and acceptance among urban residents are somewhat limited.[6] In view of such findings, the author distributed copies of the Thanatometer among 30 persons coming from communities with a population of less than 5000. The obtained scores were compared with those of 30 other subjects coming from cities that had a population of at least 5000. The arithmetic mean of the first group was 62,08, while that of the urban residents was 51,42. The t for the difference between these two statistics was 3,26 (df = 58; $p < 0,005$).

The Thanatometer and religion

A thanatologist has said the following concerning death and religion: 'My con-clusion is that religious faith of itself does little to affect man's peace near death. Worry warts are worry warts no matter their theology. It is not the substance or content of a man's creed that brings peace. It is the *firmness* and the quality of his act of believing. Firm believers, true believers, will find more peace on their deathbeds than all others, whatever the religious or secular label we place on their creed. *The believer, not the belief, brings peace.*' (Kavanaugh, 1972:14). Analogous conclusions have been drawn by other scholars who sug-gest that religiosity tends to reinforce one's awareness and acceptance of death (Lessa, W. & Vogt, E., 1965:141–146).[7] The author, therefore, distributed copies of the Thanatometer, as well as of the Bardis Religion Scale (Bardis, 1961: 120–123)[8] among 30 persons representing various religious faiths. The resulting coefficient of correlation was 0,81 ($df = 28$; $p < 0,001$).

RELIABILITY

The reliability of the Thanatometer was ascertained by means of three tests:

(a) *Split-half.* A split-half reliability test involving 30 subjects resulted in a raw reliability coefficient of 0,87. The Spearman-Brown prophecy formula gave a cor-rected reliability coefficient of 0,93 ($df = 28$; $p < 0,001$).

(b) *Odd-even.* Another group of 30 respondents supplied odd-even values that led to a raw reliability coefficient of 0,83. The corrected reliability coefficient was 0,91 ($df = 28$; $p < 0,001$).

(c) *Test—retest.* Finally, 30 more persons responded to the Thanatometer twice. The reliability coefficient based on their 60 scores was 0,76 ($df = 28$; $p < 0,001$).

SUMMARY AND CONCLUSION

It has been asserted that modern man does not think of death often enough, although middle-aged persons tend to do so.[9] But death awareness and accep-tance must be measured as objectively as possible so that we may ascertain the consequences of such feelings, attitudes, and knowledge more accurately, as well as adopt measures that lead to desirable goals in this sphere.

For this reason, the author has employed the Likert scaling technique and constructed a Thanatometer, namely, a scale for the measurement of awareness and acceptance of death. The validity and reliability of the instrument were tested several times and found to be quite satisfactory.

The Thanatometer may be employed by various professionals in numerous ways, for example, in the areas of teaching, research, and counselling.

NOTES

1. In conjunction with additional research on irenology. See Panos D. Bardis, Irenometer: A Scale for the Measurement of Attitudes Toward Peace. *South African Journal of Sociology* 1984, 15:122–23.
2. Robert Blauner (1978:92–97); Philippe Ariès (1974); Jacques Choron (1963); T. Boase (1972); Philippe Ariès (1981); E. Pattison (1978:145–146); P. Koestenbaum (1976); Robert Kastenbaum and Ruth Aisenberg (1972:81–108); Michael Simpson (1979:163); Therese Rando (1984:29–30, 199–201); Robert Kavanaugh (1972:22–27); Elisabeth Kübler-Ross (1969:5–6); Kathy Charmaz 1980:77–78, 83–98, 152–154, 284–286); Gerald Gruman (1977:28–49, 74–90); James Carse (1980:219–252); Michael Leming and George Dickinson (1985:139–169, 237–239); Colbert Rhodes and Clyde Vedder (1983:53–70); David Stannard (1977:31–71). Concerning death attitudes in art, see Fred Cutter (1983); Emily Vermeule (1979). For changing death attitudes, see Lynne DeSpelder and Albert Strickland (1983:5–32). Regarding death attitudes in the media, see John Huffman (1981:36, 21–22). For attitudes toward burial and funeral customs, see Donna Kurtz and John Boardman (1971); Bertram Puckle (1926).
3. For detailed discussions regarding the statistical tests and techniques employed in the present study, see the following sources: *Validity:* Henry Garrett (1966:354–361). *The t test:* Herbert Arkin and Raymond Colton (1962:121). *Correlation coefficient:* William Beyer (Ed.). (1968:389–396). *Reliability:* Hubert Blalock (1979:12–13). *Spearman-Brown prophecy formula:* Garrett (1966:339–340, 342–345).
4. See Panos D. Bardis (1978:127–156). Copies of the scale are available upon request from the author.
5. See Panos D. Bardis (1959:21, 340–341). The Extended Familism Scale includes only items that refer to relatives beyond the nuclear family. Copies are available upon request from the author.
6. Lifton (1968); Rando (1984:5); Stannard (1977); Philip Slater (1974); Cecilia Roberts (1977); William Douglas (1969).
7. W. Lessa and E. Vogt (editors) (1965:141–146); Glenn Vernon (1970:33); Leming and Dickinson (1985:161–162); H. Feifel (1971:4); John Hinton (1972); Lifton (1968); Anne Munley (1983:233–248); R. Lifton (1973:3–15).
8. Panos D. Bardis (1961:120–123). Copies of this scale are available upon request from the author.
9. DeSpelder and Strickland (1983:27); Kathleen Bryer (1979:255–261); Barney Glaser and Anselm Strauss (1965).

REFERENCES

Ariès, P. 1974. *Western Attitudes Toward Death.* Baltimore: Johns Hopkins University Press.
———1981. *The Hour of Our Death.* New York: Knopf.
Arkin, H. and R. Colton. 1962. *Tables for Statisticians.* New York: Barnes and Noble.
Bardis, P. 1959. A familism scale. *Marriage and Family Living* 21:340–41.
———1961. A religion scale. *Social Science* 36:120–23.
———1978. *Studies in Marriage and the Family.* 2nd enlarged edition. Lexington, MA: Xerox.
———1981. *History of Thanatology: Philosophical, Religious, Psychological, and Sociological Ideas Concerning Death from Primitive Times to the Present.* Washington: University Press of America.
———1983. *Global Marriage and Family Customs.* Lexington, MA: Ginn.
———1984. Irenometer: A scale for the measurement of attitudes toward peace. *South African Journal of Sociology* 15(1):122–23.
Barker, E. 1984. *The Making of a Moonie: Choice or Brainwashing?* Oxford: Blackwell.

Beyer, W., ed. 1968. *Handbook of Tables for Probability and Statistics.* 2nd edition. Cleveland, Ohio: Chemical Rubber.

Blalock, H. 1979. *Social Statistics.* 2nd edition. New York: McGraw-Hill.

Blauner, R. 1978. Death and social structure. In Fulton, R., et al. *Death and Dying.* Reading, MA: Addison-Wesley.

Boase, T. 1972. *Death in the Middle Ages.* New York: McGraw-Hill.

Bryer, K. 1979. The Amish way of death. *American Psychologist* 34:255–61.

Carse, J. 1980. *Death and Existence.* New York: Wiley.

Charmaz, K. 1980. *The Social Reality of Death.* Reading, MA: Addison-Wesley.

Choron, J. 1963. *Death and Western Thought.* New York: Macmillan.

Cutter, F. 1983. *Art and the Wish to Die.* Chicago: Nelson- Hall.

De Spelder, L. and A. Strickland. 1983. *The Last Dance.* Palo Alto, CA: Mayfield.

Douglas, W. 1969. *Death in Murélaga.* Seattle: University of Washington Press.

Feifel, H. 1971. The meaning of death in American society. In B. Green and D. Irish, eds. *Death Education.* Cambridge, MA: Schenkman.

Garrett, H. 1966. *Statistics in Psychology and Education.* London: Longmans, Green.

Glaser, B. and A. Strauss. 1965. *Awareness of Dying.* Chicago: Aldine.

Gruman, G. 1977. *A History of Ideas about the Prolongation of Life.* New York: Arno.

Hinton, J. 1972. *Dying.* Baltimore: Penguin.

Huffman, J. 1981. Putting grief in perspective. *News Photographer* 36:21–22.

Kalish, R. and D. Reynolds. 1976. *Death and Ethnicity.* Los Angeles: University of Southern California Press.

Kastenbaum, R. and R. Aisenberg. 1972. *The Psychology of Death.* New York: Springer.

Kavanaugh, R. 1972. *Facing Death.* Baltimore: Penguin.

Koestenbaum, P. 1976. *Is there an Answer to Death?* Englewood Cliffs, NJ: Prentice-Hall.

Kübler-Ross, E. 1969. *On Death and Dying.* New York: Macmillan.

Kurtz, D. and J. Boardman. 1971. *Greek Burial Customs.* Ithaca, NY: Cornell University Press.

Leming, M. and G. Dickinson. 1985. *Understanding Dying, Death and Bereavement.* New York: Holt, Rinehart and Winston.

Lessa, W. and E. Vogt, eds. 1965. *Reader in Comparative Religion.* New York: Harper and Row.

Likert, R. 1932. *A Technique for the Measurement of Attitudes.* New York: Archives of psychology. No. 140.

Lifton, R. 1968. *Death in Life.* New York: Random House.

———1973. The sense of immortality. *American Journal of Psychoanalysis* 33:3–15.

Munley, A. 1983. *The Hospice Alternative.* New York: Basic Books.

Pattison, E. 1978. The living-dying process. In Garfield, C., ed. *Psychosocial Care of the Dying Patient.* New York: McGraw-Hill.

Puckle, B. 1926. *Funeral Customs.* London: Laurie.

Rando, T. 1984. *Grief, Dying and Death.* Champaign, IL: Research Press.

Rhodes, C. and C. Vedder. 1983. *An Introduction to Thanatology.* Springfield, IL: Thomas.

Roberts, C. 1977. *Doctor and Patient in the Teaching Hospital.* Lexington, MA: Heath.

Simpson, M. 1979. *Dying, Death and Grief.* New York: Plenum.

Slater, P. 1974. *Earthwalk.* Garden City, NY: Doubleday.

Stannard, D. 1977. *The Puritan way of Death.* New York: Oxford University Press.

Vermeule, E. 1979. *Aspects of Death in Early Greek Art and Poetry.* Berkeley, CA: University of California Press.

Vernon, G. 1970. *Sociology of Death.* New York: Ronald.

Appendix

Thanatometer

Below is a list of issues concerning death. Please read *all* statements very *carefully* and respond to *all* of them on the basis of *your own true* beliefs, *without* consulting any other persons. Do this by reading each statement and then writing, in the space provided at its left, *only one* of the following numbers: 0,1,2,3,4. The meaning of each of these figures is:

0 = Strongly disagree.
1 = Disagree.
2 = Undecided.
3 = Agree.
4 = Strongly agree.

(For research purposes, you must consider *all* statements *as they are,* without modifying any of them in any way.)

1. The terminally ill should be informed openly of their approaching death.
2. The family should visit a dead member's grave often.
3. Death is not an ugly and forbidding thing.
4. When a person dies, the hospital should not medicate the surviving family members in order to keep their emotional disruption to a minimum.
5. All of us should know as much as possible about death.
6. Hospice care for the terminally ill, in a homelike environment, and visits by family and friends are a good idea.
7. We must talk about death openly, honestly, frequently.
8. We need longer and more elaborate funerals.
9. Facing death openly makes life more meaningful.
10. It is better to say 'he died,' 'funeral director,' and 'burial' than 'he passed away,' 'undertaker,' and 'interment.'
11. We must not fear death.
12. Art should not avoid death themes.
13. When a person dies, relatives, friends, and neighbours should comfort the grieving family in every possible way.
14. It is all right for a child to touch a dead relative during the funeral.
15. During the funeral and burial, the family, relatives, friends, and neighbours should participate actively, instead of hiring cemetery crews and other strangers.
16. Literature should present death realistically.
17. It is all right to take children to funerals.
18. Every school should include at least one course on death.
19. People should be allowed to die at home rather than in the hospital.
20. Signs of mourning (black clothes, black armbands, etc.) should be acceptable.

[Score equals sum total of 20 numerical responses. Theoretical range: 0 (ideal-typical rejection of death) to 80 (ideal-typical acceptance).]

10

A Social System Perspective on Cadaver Organ Transplantation

Nancy G. Kutner

Organ transplantation, a miracle of modern medicine, offers a chance to extend life, and a chance to improve quality of life, for individuals afflicted with end-stage, terminal organ diseases. Moreover, when a cadaver organ is transplanted into a living human being, the organ, and symbolically, the donor gain extended life as well. Clearly, organ transplantation challenges traditional perspectives on the inevitability and meaning of death.

Families and individuals make the final decisions about whether to be participants in organ transplantation, and the technology would be useless if no one were willing to participate. The wishes and actions of families and individuals, organ donors and organ recipients, constitute the interpersonal framework within which organ transplantation is carried out. As a social system, organ transplantation also reflects the influence of broad social and institutional forces, especially public opinion, religious and ethical principles and concerns, economic supports and constraints, and the resources available to individuals and organizations who want to influence the way the system operates. All of these macro level forces can in turn significantly impact families' and individuals' motivation to be involved in organ transplantation.

This chapter identifies some of the major issues characterizing organ transplantation in the United States in the 1980s. The discussion focuses specifically on use of cadaver donors. Organ and tissue transplants utilizing living donors (e.g. kidney transplants, bone marrow transplants) involve a special set of issues (see Simmons, Klein, and Simmons 1977; Burley and Stiller 1985; Levy, Hou, and Bush 1986; Kaye 1987; Spital 1987); they do not, however, require us to simultaneously talk about death. The painful reality of cadaver organ transplantation is that the joy associated with being able to sustain life in one individual

116

is counter-balanced by the emotions that naturally accompany the fact of loss of life in another individual.

This analysis of the organ transplant social system begins with macro level considerations, the societal framework within which transplant policy is shaped, then moves to a micro level perspective focusing on the experience of organ transplantation for donor families and transplant candidates.

ORGAN PROCUREMENT AND DISTRIBUTION IN THE UNITED STATES

As of 1988, a man living in the United States had survived eighteen years with a transplanted heart. Many kidney transplant recipients still have the same functioning kidney after ten or more years. Organ transplantation clearly has the potential to significantly extend longevity in persons threatened with death because of deterioration in a vital organ.[1] Thus, "there can be no decision not to transplant" (Nightingale 1985:142). As Plough (1986:39) has cogently observed:

> If there is a tenet that forms the bedrock of clinical theory in . . . biomedical science in general, it is the value of increased survival. The ability of a treatment to significantly extend a patient's life where no treatment would surely result in immediate death is almost in itself an operational standard for clinical effectiveness . . . If a technology extends life, use it!

Cadaver donors are the source of most of the organs made available for transplantation in the United States. Even with kidney transplantation, in which living relative and non-relative donation are possible, because people can survive quite well with one healthy kidney, about 80% of the transplants performed in our country use cadaver organs. However, the need for organs far exceeds the available supply, and the question of how to achieve higher donation rates has become a prominent issue. Because the issue may only become real to people when they are in the midst of shock and grief at the time of a loved one's death, and because coming to terms with death is bound up with deep-seated religious and philosophic convictions, the "best" way to encourage organ donation is not easily determined. Family members who do agree to donation are understandably interested in what happens next: How is the recipient selected? Is there good stewardship of this precious resource? Public perception of how the organ distribution system actually works can significantly impact willingness to donate. There is a growing recognition of the importance of this feedback loop.

> . . . any issue that raises questions in the public mind is ultimately *bad* for organ procurement (Hull 1988:15).

Public Opinion Regarding Cadaver Organ Donation

Cadaver organ donation, an act that can only take place at the time of someone's death, is much easier to endorse in the abstract than as a reality that touches one's own family or oneself. Although about 90 percent of Americans over-whelmingly say that they support continued development of transplantation pro-grams, 40–50 percent would be reluctant to donate a relative's organs and about 80 percent do not carry an organ donor card (U.S. News 1986). When organ transplantation is thought of as a life-saving technology in the arsenal of modern medicine, public endorsement is strong. However, when asked to consider actu-ally being an organ donor, the people become more hesitant.

Educational campaigns aimed at increasing support for organ donation face a variety of sources of resistance. In addition to general reluctance to face issues of death and dying, and religious or cultural beliefs that make people uncomfortable with the thought of organ donation, willingness to donate may be negatively affected by concerns about possible AIDS exposure and by nega-tive media influences. In the novel and movie titled *Coma*, people were made aware of the possibility for setting up a warehouse of potential human donors, and Gallup polls have indicated that people fear that if they carry a signed donor card they will be viewed as potential donors first, rather than as lives to be saved if at all possible, in an emergency situation.

According to the U.S. Centers for Disease Control, the nationwide retrieval rate for cadaver organs is no more than 16.5 percent effective (Rapaport and Cortesini 1985). In the mid-1980s, legislation was passed in over 43 states requiring hospital personnel to ask next of kin about organ donation after a treating physician determined that brain death had occurred and that medical interventions should cease. This policy is known as "required [professional] request" or "routine inquiry." Initial reports indicated that the policy was producing increases as large as l00 percent in organ and tissue donations (U.S. News 1986; Izenson 1987). As of October, 1987, every U.S. hospital, as a condition of participating in Medicare and Medicaid programs, was required to have written protocols to assure that families are made aware of their option to donate. Hospitals also were required to notify a federally certified organ procurement agency about the potential donation. However, over the following nine months, the number of donations did not increase significantly and even seemed to level off or decline in some areas of the country. Many observers suggested that this national required request law may have backfired because of lack of training or lack of commitment on the part of hospital staff, resulting in requests to donate that were made at inappropriate times or in inappropriate ways. It is understandable that people do not appreciate being asked about possible donation when a patient is entering the hospital for an elective proce-dure and a life-threatening situation has not been identified. Even when the patient's condition is deemed hopeless, family members need sufficient time to deal with the shock of impending death before they can comprehend a request for organ donation. It also is understandable that people may not see a reason to consider organ donation if the hospital representative presents the inquiry as "something the government makes us do" and adds that "you certainly do not have to consider this."

Countries that have a policy of "presumed consent" are much more successful than is the United States in securing an adequate supply of cadaver organs. With a presumed consent policy, organs can be legally removed from a brain-dead individual unless that person carries a refusal card or an objection is raised by a family member. Participants have the responsibility of "opting out" under such a system; in the United States participants must "opt into" the transplant system. Public opinion in the United States does not support the concept of presumed consent (Manninen and Evans 1985) with its emphasis on taking, rather than giving, organs. The concept is viewed as contrary to upholding freedom of choice and individual rights, unless, of course, the focus is on the rights of "those whose lives hang on the outcome of our individual choices" (Caplan 1988:31).

Religious and Ethical Concerns

> The possibilities in transplantation . . . are a bit overwhelming. The best of men is a bit intimidated with the godlike tools that have fallen into his hands. God has not spoken about how we should act in each particular. The responsibility falls upon discerning men to try and try again to find the best ways of coming to terms with the new options that are open to us . . . (Sherman 1973:xvii)

Religious convictions deter members of some religious and cultural groups from participating in transplantation, either as donors or as recipients. In addition to Orthodox Jews, this seems to be especially true for blacks with fundamentalist religious beliefs, many of whom reside in the South, and for persons of Hispanic background. Black persons have been found in several studies to be less interested in receiving a kidney transplant than are whites, and organ donation is less often discussed in black families (Callender 1987; Kutner 1987). Religious or superstitious fears often are mentioned by black kidney patients, e.g. "The Bible speaks against transplants"; "I'm against any foreign object placed in the body"; "I have funny feelings about walking around with someone else's kidney when I don't even know what kind of person the donor was." Interviews with Hispanic patients have uncovered that some patients believe that doctors obtain cadaver organs by robbing graves and that if one receives a dead person's organ, the person's ghost will come back to haunt the patient and take him or her away with him (Delmar-McClure 1985).

Although the concept of brain death is difficult to reconcile with some religious teachings, laws in 39 states upheld brain death standards as of 1988. A precise moment of death cannot be assigned, but a flat line on the brain wave monitor does furnish a visible referent that helps to establish the reality of death.

However, it can be very difficult for family members and even for medical staff to reconcile the contradiction between a brain death pronouncement and obvious signs of respiration in the patient. Family members may feel that their loved one is not "finally" gone until the transplant operation is completed, and there may be a lingering feeling that somehow the patient might still be able to miraculously recover. The family's decision to donate negates the possibility of this miracle occurring, and their recognition of this fact can be very troubling. Fulton, Fulton, and Simmons (1977) clearly illustrated this point in excerpts from interviews with parents who agreed to donate their sons' organs. A father wondered, "O.K., if we, by our decision, are going to terminate his life, where is he in terms of salvation?" A mother experienced guilt that she had somehow willed her child's death, not wanting him to survive and be incapacitated for the rest of his life, and that God responded to her wish.

Before leaving the subject of religious concerns that bear on the issue of organ transplantation, it must be noted that heart transplantation has a special mystical, if not religious, significance that separates it symbolically from other transplant procedures. Interestingly, however, the technology of heart transplantation is less difficult than liver transplantation, and hearts perform a more limited number of functions than do kidneys for the human body. Still, "the heart has always been the site of life . . . and the home of the soul" (Hoffman 1973:xv). Is one still alive and a "real" person when one is "in-between hearts?" The perplexed feelings expressed by this wife of a heart transplant candidate are probably experienced by many: "It's really weird to think of those few moments when his chest will be a big hole, when he has no heart at all" (Schechter 1988:160).

Many ethical concerns about the mechanisms for carrying out organ procurement and distribution are the source of continuing debates.

- Should a donor or donor family be able to specify a preferred recipient?
- Should recipients be told who their donor was?
- Should organs retrieved from American taxpaying citizens be given only to recipients who are also American taxpaying citizens (rather than to foreign nationals who do not pay taxes but who can generously reward their treating hospital)?
- How closely should transplant surgeons be monitored? Can doctors who need to meet annual quotas of transplant procedures be counted on to "play fairly"?
- Should organs be harvested from anencephalic donors (babies who are born with most of the brain missing)?

The last question generated wide debate after Loma Linda University Medical

Center set up an anencephalic procurement/transplant program. Unlike brain-dead accident or trauma victims, anencephalic babies must be maintained until they can be pronounced dead and serve as organ donors, and this may require a number of days. Such practices suggest a slippery slope leading eventually to harvesting organs from other at-risk groups such as patients who are in a permanent vegetative state. Do the possible benefits that grieving parents may derive by donating their baby's organs outweigh the dangers of embarking on this slippery slope? When debate escalated on the issue of harvesting organs from such babies, Loma Linda curtailed its anencephalic procurement/transplant program.

> Sometimes it is said that there are no answers to be found where matters of ethics are concerned. I disagree. There are no easy answers to be found, but an answer of one sort or another is always found, even if it is to do nothing . . . (Caplan 1988:30)

Economic Supports and Constraints

Buying and selling of human organs was explicitly prohibited by PL 98-507, the Organ Procurement and Transplantation Act passed in 1984. However, because of the continuing shortage of donated organs in the United States, rewards such as tax credits for donor families have been suggested (Bassett 1985; Sharpe 1985; Surman 1985). Singapore's 1987 presumed consent law gives priority in transplant access to people who register no objections to donation, that is, those who do not "opt out" (Caplan 1988). To date, all arrangements that border on applying a market model to organ procurement and distribution have generated very little support in the United States.

The extent to which our society can financially afford to make an extensive investment in organ transplantation is a troublesome issue.[2] In 1987, the Oregon legislature was faced with deciding how to commit the state's Medicaid funds for the next two years: Medicaid could either extend its funding for basic health care to include about 1500 persons not covered previously, or continue to fund a program of organ transplantation of bone marrow, heart, liver, and pancreas, for a projected 34 patients. The Division of Adult and Family Services argued for the former choice, and the legislature concurred (Welch and Larson 1988). A 7-year- old boy in Oregon, whose family could not afford to pay for a bone marrow transplant for him, subsequently died of leukemia. It is very difficult to decide whether funds should go to preventive public health programs that potentially benefit many people, or to organ transplant programs that can save lives of people who would otherwise die, but which are limited to serving much smaller numbers of people. In Oregon, this truly proved to be a tragic choice. Some argue that this is an unfair choice because it compares apples and oranges (Newmann 1987); others answer that we must face the fact that we are making allocations from a fixed pie, the health care dollar (Burke 1987). Organ transplantation benefits in this debate from its human interest component; we can be influenced to identify with the individuals portrayed in the media who will die unless they receive transplants, while the unborn babies who might benefit from our spending the same health care dollars on prenatal care for low-income mothers remain an abstract alternative.

Economic support for kidney transplants is well-established; Medicare pays 80 percent of the cost of these procedures, and private insurance or Medicaid typically covers the remaining portion. However, Medicare only will pay for heart transplants that are performed at about 20 designated centers that meet explicit criteria, and the Prudential Insurance Company in mid-1988 became the first private health insurance carrier to limit its coverage to patients who undergo transplantation at a few select hospitals considered to have the best survival rates. These restrictions have implications for the distribution of cadaver organs, increasing the likelihood that organs will be shipped long distances to be used at regional transplant centers that meet third-party payment criteria. Will this make the donor family feel that they are simply turning over a commodity to medical science, rather than participating in making an interpersonal gift? On the other hand, it certainly can be argued that it is more cost-effective to have a limited number of highly successful transplant centers than to have a proliferation of small centers that cannot provide a full range of transplant-related services and will increase the competition for scarce organs.

Providers' and Recipients' Efforts to Influence the Transplant System

Once organs are donated, they must be allocated. The 1984 Transplantation Act stipulated that a transplant network and registry would be established for this purpose, and the United Network for Organ Sharing (UNOS) went into operation in late 1987. This network is charged with maintaining a single national list of all those in the United States who are waiting for a transplant.

> More important, the network, through its broadly representative governance, must develop a system to prioritize the list of potential recipients. The priority system by law must be based on medical criteria, such as the urgency of the individual case and the likelihood of a successful outcome. It must be blind to social criteria. We don't want it weighing the relative value of saving a child with cerebral palsy versus saving an unusually gifted child (Gore 1987:45).

However, surgeons are adamant about maintaining their role in making the final decision about which organ is given to which recipient. The president of UNOS, a surgeon, agrees: "The distribution of organs should be decided by the doctors who take care of these patients, not some technician reading a printout on a computer" (King 1988a:6A). When it appears that norms of specificity rather than generality are being over-emphasized in recipient selection, charges of "medical politics" are quickly raised (King 1988a; Junod 1988).

The basic premise of the total organ transplantation system in the United States is supposed to be that donated organs are "a national resource to be used for the public good" (Gore 1987:45). There is a widespread perception, however, that some are more equal than others in access to transplantation. Cases that receive national media publicity, and wealthy foreign nationals, seem to receive special consideration. If people believe that the system does not operate fairly, they are more likely not to consider donation.

The *Atlanta* magazine in July, 1988, carried a feature story describing the area's "shocking medical war." Other areas of the country are likely to have their own territorial disputes; for example, one report refers to a "turf war" among Texas organ banks (Schechter 1988:162). The Atlanta story chronicles a rift between a leading transplant surgeon and medical school administrators that resulted in the surgeon's decision to establish his own rival transplant program at another local medical institution. The reader glimpses giant egos at work in individuals and organizations that view organ transplantation as an excellent way to "enhance our image." A successful transplant recipient is described as a "walking billboard" for the medical center where he received his transplant (Junod 1988:115). This depersonalized view of patients, and the intense competition for scarce organs between warring programs in the same city, do not contribute in a positive way to public opinion about organ transplantation.

THE INTERPERSONAL FRAMEWORK OF ORGAN TRANSPLANTATION: DONORS AND RECIPIENTS

The "gift of life" via organ transplantation depends on the occurrence of death. The grief attached to that death is likely to be intense, as when a young accident victim dies or a loved one unexpectedly suffers a sudden cerebral hemorrhage. The pain of this grief may, however, be significantly modified by the opportunity to donate the deceased's organs. A mother who donated her three-year-old son's kidneys, eyes, and liver assures us that ". . . even in this dark tragedy, new hope and new life can result . . ." (Bishop 1987:370). In addition, in some cases the donor relatives and the organ recipient develop a unique kind of emotional bonding.

Large numbers of persons who need a transplant die before an organ becomes available. About one-third of the patients waiting for a donor heart, liver, or lungs (or approximately 5,000 patients in 1988) die before an appropriate donor is found.[3] Waiting for an organ that never comes is a painful "Death Row" kind of experience that also strains the coping resources of the patient's family. Receiving a transplant that does not function well, and is eventually rejected is another downside of the so-called miracle of organ transplantation. One writer

(Schechter 1988) likens organ transplantation to a crapshoot; there are inevitable losers as well as winners.

The Donation Experience

What factors are important in making organ donation a positive experience? There appear to be at least three important ingredients in this process:

- The donor relative or family already has thought seriously about this question and has, perhaps unconsciously, decided to donate if ever faced with the situation. Part of this decision is the conviction that this is also what the loved one would want, and this may actually have been discussed with the loved one in the past (Fulton, Fulton, and Simmons 1977).
- At the time when the final decision must be made, the donor family perceives the medical staff involved in the case as compassionate and caring.
- The deceased is to the end treated as a person and maintains his or her identity throughout the donation process.

Although family permission is still necessary even when an individual carries a signed donor card, donor card proponents believe that the cards are useful in generating family discussion about donation, giving family members a sense of each others' wishes. Donor relatives must feel confident that they are making the right decision, and prior consideration of donating helps greatly with this decision at a time of grief and stress.

Mother who donated young son's organs "When I was 12, a friend and I made our own nonlegal wills donating our organs to their respective organ banks . . . Another seed relating to organ donation was planted when I was taking a . . . [class in which there was] a serious class discussion about transplantation . . . (Bishop 1987:370).

Mother who donated baby girl's liver: "I had been involved in organ donation and procurement for about 15 years in the course of my nursing practice . . ." (Bryant 1988).

Wife who donated husband's organs: "I asked my daughter, 'is this really what you want?' and she said 'yes, I think it is what Daddy wants too' " (Buffington 1988).

Compassionate medical staff help ease the pain of the loved one's loss and support the donor relative's feeling that donation is in fact the right thing to do.

Mother who donated young son's organs: "The atmosphere in the intensive care unit was one of extreme caring . . . I was given time to . . . say a very special goodbye to my youngest child . . . The director of the intensive care unit gave the family much consideration . . . He spent time explaining what most likely caused

Jeffrey's death, what kind of medical care was being provided, and the procedure for donating his organs . . . (Bishop 1987:370).

By the same token, non-compassionate staff may jeopardize the donor relative's willingness to go through with the decision:

Wife who donated husband's organs: "Our primary physicians were neurosurgeons—truthful and compassionate. [The one who gave] the second opinion was a blank—if I had a choice I would have preferred to donate *his* organs" (Buffington 1988).

The identity of the donor must be respected through the donation process, a time when the loved one is in a nebulous state between brain-dead life and complete death. Organ retrieval requires more time when several organs are being taken; different retrieval teams may need to fly in from different parts of the country, which extends the trauma of the relatives because they must wait for all of these arrangements to be carried out. Although "the *instant* when life ceases and death begins has already passed," the family learns that "part of the *process* of death is still to occur" (Fulton, Fulton, and Simmons 1977:355).

Mother who donated young son's organs: "I left behind Jeffrey's favorite blue blanket that went everywhere with him and asked the doctor to cover Jeffrey with it following surgery. The doctor assured me he would be cared for as the little boy he was and my wish would be carried out" (Bishop 1987:370).

Mother who donated baby girl's liver: "I needed to be reassured and to know from these professionals who represented authority that she was still my child and she still had an identity. She was still Sarah and up until the end she did not lose that. And that was very compassionately conveyed by both the physician and the nurses and transplant coordinator" (Bryant 1988).

An additional factor helping to make organ donation a positive experience for some donor relatives is the feeling that part of their loved one continues to live, making possible a type of immortality for the loved one. This idea, however, tends to deny the reality of the loved one's death, and this denial could impede family members' healthy resolution of grief.

Donor Relative-Recipient Bonding

Follow-up with donor relatives, informing them about how their gift of life was used, can further contribute to positive feelings about the organ donation experience. The knowledge that another person's life was saved helps make the grief process more bearable:

Mother who donated baby girl's liver: "Through our time of tragedy there has to be something good that can come out of this for someone else . . . It has been two years since our daughter died. Not necessarily does this time of year get any easier for us, but looking back at that decision and knowing that somewhere in [our state] there is a healthy child because of something that we were able to do, helps the grieving process. It makes it a little easier to bear . . . Somewhere in [the state] . . . I have a bond with a mother who has a healthy child as a result of the gift that we were able to make . . ." (Bryant 1988).

For people with deep religious convictions, donating an organ that is life-saving for another person places the loved one's loss in a larger context of "God's plan, which only He knows."

Some transplant recipients and donor families meet and establish a close relationship with each other, as in the case of this young wife who received a liver and a kidney donated by a young girl's parents.

> . . . I do know my donor . . . Debbie's father called my husband and said, "I believe your wife has my daughter's organs. And my husband—what can you tell somebody for giving back life to somebody that you love? I guess it was about three or four weeks before they came to our house and brought pictures of Debbie. They wanted us to know what Debbie was like. It has been a blessing to us and, in turn, maybe it has been a blessing to them and easier for them . . . My husband and I have been in the ministry for 25 years, and they were happy that I had gotten Debbie's organs (Rollins 1988).

The Gift of Life That Never Comes

Patients who receive a new organ and a new lease on life are the success stories of organ transplantation. Patients who wait and never receive the organ they need represent a much less publicized aspect of organ transplantation. It is possible that there would be increased willingness to donate if more people were aware of the experience of those who wait for a gift of life that never comes.

Individuals who have experienced kidney failure may desire a transplant, but if a new kidney is not available they can be maintained for many years by undergoing kidney dialysis therapy. People whose hearts, livers, lungs, or pancreas are failing do not have mechanical assists that can be used for long-term maintenance with satisfactory results. They become increasingly sick physically as they wait for a possible transplant, but they simultaneously must demonstrate psychological and emotional stability in order to be considered a transplant candidate. The patient must be maintained by careful drug therapy and at some points may feel that the agony of needles and IV's simply is not worth the gamble of waiting.

Transplant candidates must come to terms with the fact that their potential gift of life will mean that someone out there has died.

> What bothered Ted was that one day soon—he didn't know when, but it had to be soon—some unsuspecting person would wake up, have breakfast with his or her family, go to work, and die. That unknown someone had Ted's new heart . . . Because a heart can survive no more than four to six hours without blood and oxygen, Ted would probably finish out a day with a heart that had beat in another person that very morning (Schechter 1988:160–161).

While the patient waits for the call that a donor has been found, other patients who have waited shorter periods of time may receive transplants because of closer matches with the donor in body size, blood type, and other factors. The finite time that the patient can wait, about six months in the case of a heart transplant candidate, continues to tick away. The patient's family may begin to scour the newspapers for accident reports containing the key words "critical condition with a head injury"; "what would ordinarily be considered a morbid perversion [becomes] a daily routine" (Schechter 1988:161). Weekends and holidays such as the Fourth of July when automobile accidents are more frequent stir depression when they produce no donors.

. . . The transplant candidate must wait, living out a conundrum worthy of Kafka, living in the hope that someone else—the *right* someone else—will die (Junod 1988:60).

The patient may begin a desperate bargaining with God, begging for a chance to live to see a yet unborn grandchild or to complete some unfinished task.

In his daily rounds with his transplant patients, [the surgeon] breathed an atmosphere of self-examination, repentance, and renewal. He met patients transformed by the imminence of death, worldly men and women singing the virtues of God and family, people with dying hearts who just wanted to *live* (Junod 1988:62).

Patients who are in critical condition are first in line on the computerized network for a transplant, but the surgical survival rate is higher for patients in stable condition; patients who recognize this dilemma may vacillate between worrying that they are too sick and worrying that they are not sick enough. Patients want to maintain unquestioning faith in their physicians' judgment (which is of course what the physician also wants), and even when a donated organ might be judged suitable by other medical professionals, the patient's physician may decide against taking the risk—and the patient continues to wait. Time may eventually run out.

The experts say that patients with hearts as sick as Ted's can feel themselves slipping. They are so in touch with their bodies and especially their heartbeats that when they begin to die, they know it . . . (Schechter 1988:166).

Family members may deny the impending death, continuing to hope against hope that a donor will be found; unfortunately, family members then find it hard to give the understanding support the dying patient needs.

It really bugged Dad that Mom couldn't talk about it. But how could I say, 'Mom, Dad's dying. Why don't you talk about it?' We all hoped he'd get a heart soon. Mom was still totally optimistic (Schechter 1988:166).

Finally, the patient's computerized listing reads "UNOS STAT," a special designation meaning that the patient is on life support with less than twelve hours to live. When there is no response to this emergency call, the patient dies.

Those who are committed to increasing public willingness to donate organs believe that it is inhuman to have a technology that cannot be made available to all who might benefit from it. It is important to stress the word *might*, however. Some people who receive organ transplants do not feel that they have in fact received a gift of life, broadly defined. Quality of life may be severely compromised by the medical and psychological complications they experience. Many undergo transplant rejection and have to repeat the waiting process; as many as half of all recipients of new hearts, livers, kidneys, and other organs eventually will need another transplant, according to recent studies.

> John . . . has mixed emotions about another heart transplant. "I'm going to do it," he says. "The only other option is a black box. Sometimes I wonder about it, though. What am I accomplishing? I might get a few more years out of it, but will I have to go through it again?" (King 1988b:9A).

The strain of transplant complications and rejection is hard on patients; for the medical profession, however, these patients add to the database that is needed to unravel the mysteries of the human immune system—a goal that has implications not only for improving transplant success but also for coping with many other disease processes, including AIDS. In this sense, transplantation remains much more experimental than generally is recognized. For patients, it provides a chance, but not necessarily a cure.

CONCLUSIONS AND IMPLICATIONS FOR PRACTICE

Cadaver organ transplantation in the United States is a complex social system in which macro and micro level forces interact. Individuals and families are asked to make a very personal, emotional decision, agreeing to donate a loved one's organs, at the same time that they are trying to acknowledge and accept a tragic loss in their lives. Hospital personnel experience strain in their effort to facilitate the donation process: the lives of waiting transplant candidates hang in the balance. All who are involved need to be thoroughly convinced that they are participating in a good and worthwhile cause. Unfortunately, many macro level characteristics of the organ transplantation system make some potential donor relatives and hospital personnel question their commitment to this cause.

With the exception of kidney transplant recipients, survival for organ transplant recipients is short in many cases, and about half of all transplant recipients experience chronic rejection of the transplanted organ. Medicine makes constant strides in knowledge and expertise, and soon it may be possible for medical science to successfully manage chronic rejection. Successful management requires not only preventing rejection but also utilizing therapy that does not itself jeopardize patients' longevity and quality of life. If this is accomplished, more patients will want to attempt organ transplantation, further accentuating the persistent discrepancy between demand and supply of transplantable organs. Some already argue that it is un-American to have a medical technology that is not available to all who could benefit from it (Caplan 1988). The imperative of increasing organ donation may compel closer consideration of harvesting organs from sources such as anencephalic babies, which some people in the transplant community already advocate. Ironically, as we more successfully enforce seat-belt legislation and use of motorcycle helmets, raise the legal drinking age, and launch educational campaigns to increase public awareness of the potential for head injury, we simultaneously reduce an important source of cadaver organs for transplantation and must look to alternative sources.

It is not sufficient to call for "greater efforts at public and professional education" and expect that organ donation rates will increase, unless other system characteristics also are addressed. People do not want to contribute a precious resource that will become another weapon in a "turf war among organ banks" or in a "shocking medical war" between competing transplant programs. It is distressing to learn that medical professionals think of successful transplant recipients as walking advertisements for their medical institutions. These dehumanizing aspects of the organ transplantation system are not at all compatible with the donor family's need to preserve the identity of the donor and to feel that they have made possible the most precious gift that one human can give another—life.

Implications for Clinical Sociology

Cadaver organ donation and retrieval strain the emotional resources of the donor family and, often, of medical personnel as well. Doctors, nurses, and allied personnel who are on the scene when organ donation becomes an issue must first be comfortable with their own religious and ethical convictions before they can facilitate a donation decision. They significantly impact both the probability of a donation decision and the family's long-term comfort with a donation decision. The sensitivity of their behavior vis-à-vis family members and the patient shapes the total donation experience for donor relatives.

Several educational and counseling needs should be addressed by clinical sociologists, especially in the following areas:

- An understanding of family systems is important. Family dynamics impact the donation decision: Who are the family members? Is a need for consensus evident?
- It is very important that organ transplant personnel have insight into the grief process and are able to recognize different stages of grieving. Fulton, Fulton, and Simmons (1977) emphasize the significance of identifying (1) a period of "desperate hope," (2) a transitional time period when the situation is gradually redefined as "hopeless," and (3) a period when the redefinition has been accepted and the option of donating can be considered.

- A hospital operates as a bureaucracy and, inevitably, does not respond to all the needs that are important to individuals. The clinical sociologist can identify procedural mechanisms for reducing the strain on donor families, and can provide counseling, as needed, to help individual family members cope with emotional reactions like guilt. The clinical sociologist also can identify cultural differences in religious and ethical outlook that are relevant to individual organ donation decisions, and educate the medical bureaucracy about the function of follow-up with donor families, such as addressing the family's need for information about the outcome of the precious gift they have made possible.
- Because organ harvesting contradicts many tenets of medical training, and because organ transplantation has a dark side of chronic rejection and transplant-related complications, counseling may be needed on an ongoing basis by medical personnel who participate in organ transplantation. Support services also should be available to those transplant candidates and families who endure long waiting periods.

The degree to which patient, family, and medical provider needs are successfully addressed has important ramifications for the overall functioning of the cadaver organ transplantation system that has been outlined in this chapter.

NOTES

1. As of 1988, one-year survival was 95 percent for kidney transplant recipients, 80 percent for heart transplant recipients, 70 percent for liver and pancreas transplant recipients, and 50 percent for heart/lung recipients (King 1988b:8A).

2. In 1988, the cost was highest for liver transplants and heart-lung transplants: $135,000 to $250,000. The most "economical" procedures were kidney transplants, for which the average cost was $25,000 to $35,000 (King 1988b:8A).

3. As of 1988, an estimated 35,000 patients could have their lives extended by heart transplantation or receipt of an artificial heart; 25,000 could benefit from receiving a new kidney; and 12,000 could benefit from receiving a liver transplant. By contrast, in 1987 there were about 1,450 heart transplants, 9,000 kidney transplants, and 1,200 liver transplants performed in the United States (King 1988b:9A).

REFERENCES

Bassett, B. D. 1985. Hearts for sale? *Emory Magazine* 61:31.

Bishop, P. R. 1987. Jeffrey's Story. *American Nephrology Nurses' Association Journal* 14(6):370.

Bryant, M. 1988. Waiting, Giving and Receiving—Families' Experience. Panel discussion presented at Emory University's annual conference on Rehabilitation Issues in Dialysis and Transplantation, Atlanta, GA (April 21).

Buffington, J. 1988. Waiting, Giving and Receiving—Families' Experience. Panel discussion presented at Emory University's annual conference on Rehabilitation Issues in Dialysis and Transplantation, Atlanta, GA (April 21).

Burke, R. M. 1987. We *still* have to deal with allocating organ funds from a fixed pie. *Nephrology News & Issues* 1(9):24–26.

Burley, J. A. and C. R. Stiller. 1985. Emotionally related donors and renal transplantation. *Transplantation Proceedings* 17:123–27.

Callender, C. O. 1987. Organ donation in the black population: where do we go from here? *Transplantation Proceedings* 19(2) Suppl. 2:36–40.

Caplan, A. 1988. With donor organs, where's the give and take? *Nephrology News & Issues* 2(7):30–31.

Delmar-McClure, N. 1985. When organs match and health beliefs don't. *Journal of Adolescent Health Care* 6:233–37.

Fulton, J., R. Fulton, and R. Simmons. 1977. The cadaver donor and the gift of life. In R. G. Simmons, S. D. Klein, and R. L. Simmons, eds. *Gift of Life: The Social and Psychological Impact of Organ Transplantation.* New York: Wiley, 338–76.

Gore, A., Jr. 1987. The national transplantation network: UNOS or NBC? *Nephrology News & Issues* 1(2):44–46.

Hoffman, C. A. 1973. Foreword. In C. A. Frazier, ed. *Is It Moral to Modify Man?* Springfield, IL: Charles C. Thomas, xiii–xv.

Hull, A. R. 1988. What solutions can increase organ procurement? *Nephrology News & Issues* 2(7):15–16.

Izenson, S. B. 1987. Required request laws: A successful state approach to meet the increasing need for cadaver kidneys. *Contemporary Dialysis & Nephrology* 8(5):54–55, 58.

Junod, T. 1988. Tell-tale hearts. *Atlanta* 28(3):58–63, 112–22.

Kaye, M. 1987. The ethics of renal transplantation. *Contemporary Dialysis & Nephrology* 8(5):65–66.

King, M. 1988a. Atlanta transplant surgeon accused of medical politics. *Atlanta Constitution* (February 27):1A, 6A.

———1988b. Transplants: A dark side casts shadow over this century's medical miracle. *Atlanta Journal and Constitution* (July 17):8A–9A.

Kutner, N. G. 1987. Issues in the application of high cost medical technology: the case of organ transplantation. *Journal of Health and Social Behavior* 28 (March):23–36.

Levy, A. S., S. Hou, and H. L. Bush, Jr. 1986. Kidney transplantation from unrelated living donors: Time to reclaim a discarded opportunity. *New England Journal of Medicine* 314(14):914–16.

Manninen, D. L. and R. W. Evans. 1985. Public attitudes and behavior regarding organ donation. *Journal of the American Medical Association* 253:3111–15.

Newmann, J. M. 1987. Organ transplant and neonatal morbidity—are we comparing apples with oranges? *Nephrology News & Issues* 1(9):25.

Nightingale, J. E. 1985. New organ transplant program: The decision tree. *Transplantation Proceedings* 17:137–42.

Plough, A. L. 1986. *Borrowed Time: Artificial Organs and the Politics of Extending Lives.* Philadelphia, PA: Temple University.

Rapaport, F. T. and R. Cortesini. 1985. The past, present, and future of organ transplantation with special reference to current needs in kidney procurement and donation. *Transplantation Proceedings* 17:3–10.

Rollins, M. B. 1988. Waiting, giving and receiving—families' experience. Panel discussion presented at Emory University's annual conference on Rehabilitation Issues in Dialysis and Transplantation, Atlanta, G. (April 21).

Schechter, C. 1988. Dying for a heart. *Texas Monthly Magazine* 16(5):82–87, 157, 159–62, 164, 166, 168.

Sharpe, G. 1985. Commerce in tissue and organs. *Transplantation Proceedings* 17:33–39.

132   ATTITUDES TOWARDS ILLNESS AND DEATH

Sherman, C. E. 1973. Foreword. In C. A. Frazier, ed. *Is It Moral to Modify Man?* Springfield, IL: Charles C. Thomas, xvii.

Simmons, R. G., S. D. Klein, and R. L. Simmons. 1977. *Gift of Life: The Social and Psychological Impact of Organ Transplantation.* New York: Wiley.

Spital, A. 1987. The ethics of using living kidney donors: A reply. *Contemporary Dialysis & Nephrology.* 8(9):44–45.

Surman, O. W. 1985. Toward greater donor organ availability for transplantation. *New England Journal of Medicine* 312(5):318.

U.S. News. 1986. Gallup organ survey results reported. *Contemporary Dialysis & Nephrology* 7:15–16.

Welch, H. G. and E. B. Larson. 1988. Dealing with limited resources: The Oregon decision to curtail funding for organ transplantation. *New England Journal of Medicine* 319(3):171–73.

PART III

Clinical Ethics

Since the 1890s, sociologists in the United States have demonstrated their concern about ethical issues through articles, presentations, interventions, and programs (Fritz and Clark, 1989). These scholars and practitioners have taken on a range of topics. Some have analyzed the development of ethical systems and/or adherence to them. Others have provided passionate and persuasive analyses questioning why sociologists study the less important topics and why they often uncritically accept funds for social science research and practice. Still other contributors analyze case studies to point out ethical dilemmas, make suggestions for resolution, or act to resolve such dilemmas.

This section opens with a case study, "From the Ivory Tower to the Hospital Ward: A Role Analysis of a Clinical Ethicist," by Hammes and Bendiksen. They briefly explain Institutional Review Boards and Institutional Ethics Committees, then discuss the evolving role of a clinical ethicist. One of the authors, Hammes, has been working in this capacity at a tertiary care, community hospital in a small city in the midwest.

Hammes and Bendiksen conclude by presenting an Ethics Consultation Form. This form requires factual information, such as medical and sociological data, and an ethics evaluation which includes identification of relevant ethical principles and advice on courses of action.

Working as an ethicist within an institution is an art that requires a particular environment. To successfully undertake this responsibility, as Caplow (1983:319) has indicated: " . . . requires a certain amount of independence and tolerance from those who engage the [ethicist.] After all, moral efficacy is desirable only when the right questions are being addressed."

The second article in this section is also a case study—Fleming's "Permission to Die." It is based on her work in an urban teaching hospital. Fleming presents the case of a 49-year-old Hispanic man with cirrhosis of the liver and a history of varicose hemorrhage. She documents and analyzes the decision-making processes of those providing the man's medical care, giving particular consideration to social factors.

133

The next article, "Physicians, Patients and Life-Sustaining Medical Procedures" by Dolch, Roberts and Sibley, is about desired physician behavior. The authors begin by briefly describing a Louisiana law that protects the right of patients to refuse life-sustaining medical procedures and allows the withholding and withdrawal of treatment. The authors then analyze views of Louisiana residents who had been asked to imagine that they had a terminal disease. Respondents were asked, given this circumstance, what they would expect of their physician.

The findings of Dolch and his associates support full physician disclosure of information to patients and show that physicians are asked to be helpful by, for instance, identifying organizations that can be of assistance. The authors remind physicians of their enabling role and offer many recommendations to improve medical care for the terminally ill.

The fourth article in this section is Clark's "The Interrelatedness of Loss and Pathological Grief in the Elderly Population." Clark provides a great deal of information about research on grief and abnormal grief reactions like depression, alcoholism, and suicide, and concludes by examining the implications of these findings for clinical intervention. Without explicitly mentioning ethics, Clark raises ethical dilemmas such as age discrimination, a lack of programs, and clinical interventions based on inappropriate research.

The final document in this section is the ethics code of the Sociological Practice Association, the largest national organization of clinical and applied sociologists. The Sociological Practice Association, founded in 1978 as the Clinical Sociology Association, adopted its ethics code in 1982 and revised it in 1985 and 1987. The code states the responsibilities of practitioners: "competence, objectivity in the application of skills and concern for the best interests of clients, colleagues, and society . . . ."

The ethics code, like the codes of other professional associations, presents only basic behavioral guidelines. It may help practitioners avoid legal challenges or professional censure, and it gives interested parties (e.g., clients, students, employers) access to the standards for practice. Clinical sociologists need to do more than simply comply with the guidelines; practitioners have to be self-critical to assure that "they are continuously open to the effects of their interventions on the welfare of [others]" (Corey, Corey, and Callanan, 1988:4- 5).

REFERENCES

Caplan, A. 1983. Can applied ethics be effective in health care and should it strive to be? *Ethics* 93 (January): 311–19.

Corey, G., M. Corey, and P. Callanan. 1988. *Issues and Ethics in the Helping Professions.* 3rd edition. Pacific Grove, CA: Brooks/Cole.

Fritz, J. and E. Clark, eds. 1989. *Sociological Practice: The Development of Clinical and Applied Sociology* VII. East Lansing, MI: Michigan State University Press.

11

From the Ivory Tower
to the Hospital Ward:
A Role Analysis
of a Clinical Ethicist

Bernard J. Hammes and Robert Bendiksen

The practice of medicine and the organization of health care delivery are shaped by social norms and the values held by physicians, nurses, and other health care providers, as well as by patients, their significant others, and public opinion makers. The complexity of providing care is acknowledged by physicians when particular cases present instances of difficult medical-ethical decisions involving conflicting values and moral principles. Identifying unexpressed values in the social context of patients' lives and professional care-giving is a challenge.

In response, a new role of clinical ethicist has developed in hospitals and other health care settings. The function of the clinical ethicist is to educate physicians and nurses about values and ethics and to facilitate ethical discussions in consultations on particular cases. The emergence of this new role and the actual creation of clinical ethicist positions in hospitals provide an opportunity not only to examine role expectations in an organizational setting, but also to consider contributions of clinical sociology to ethical decision-making in the practice of health care.

THE INSTITUTIONAL BACKDROP OF CLINICAL ETHICS

The technical capacity of medicine to care for patients, particularly those with life-threatening illnesses, benefits many patients, but does so in a changed social context of a physician-patient relationship. The people providing medical care to a patient today often do not have long-standing relationships with the people receiving care. While the medical staff may be in an advantageous position to understand the medical implications of a decision, the "right of the patient to decide'' treatment options generally is acknowledged. This setting of great medical/technical capability, provided by people who do not have either a long standing relationship to the patient, or common, unifying, underlying values, has given rise to perplexing ethical decisions in health care institutions.

Consider the following case and the type of issues that it presents:

A 75-year-old male is admitted to the hospital because of dehydration. He has suffered the symptoms of weight loss and diarrhea for almost three weeks. He has had a history of dementia of the Alzheimer's type. He has only short-term memory. His life consists of simple conversations about the present moment. After an extensive workup, he is diagnosed with a cancer for which there is no effective, standard treatment. The only treatment that is considered to have potential benefit is experimental and its effectiveness is not fully known. The relative who has been most involved in this man's care is a grandson. Other members of the family live elsewhere and seem to rely on the grandson to make decisions. The grandson visits his grandfather frequently and is concerned about his welfare; the grandson, however, has not been appointed legal guardian. The grandfather signed a "living will" ten years ago, but the instructions in this "living will" are very general and simply say that no heroics are to be used to prolong life.

While no one case can illustrate all the ethical, legal, social, and human concerns that arise in modern health care, this situation exemplifies common concerns. By examining these general concerns, it is possible to better understand how medical, ethical, and sociological issues have created new expectations for medical professionals and how this type of situation has led to the creation of roles, such as that of clinical ethicist, within health care institutions.

From the family's perspective, and in other cases from both the patient's and family's perspectives, it is important to sort out responsibilities, desires, and fears. In this case, the grandson may raise questions like: Is it my obligation to prolong my grandfather's life? Is my thinking being influenced by my feelings, or by my grandfather's wishes? Which values are most important? For many, if not most families, sorting through questions like these is not only difficult, but also stressful. Often, the asking as well as the deciding can become a source of conflict and tension. Helping patients and families to make these decisions has become an important role and responsibility in health care institutions.

The physicians in such cases also must sort out their ethical responsibilities, which are many. On one hand, physicians have an obligation to prolong life, but they also have an obligation to do no harm. If they treat the patient's disease aggressively, then life may be prolonged by some months, perhaps a year or more, but the side effects of treatment can be many and serious. How should these options be weighed in a patient with this level of mentation? When patients like this are treated in referral hospitals, physicians are often researchers and educators. Entering this patient on an experimental protocol would help medical science to better understand this disease, as well as help educate physician residents who are in training. How should these teaching and research responsibilities influence treatment decisions like this? Physicians today have a growing awareness that they have a role to play in controlling medical cost. Would medical treatment of this patient be financially responsible? And, finally, who should answer these questions? Should the grandson make the decision, even though he is not a legal guardian? Should the physician decide on the basis of the living will? Should the decision be reviewed by someone in the institution or in the courts?

The complexity of these decisions for physicians has made it increasingly stressful and difficult to sort out competing values during the decision-making process. The greater interest and ability of patients and family members to ask clarifying questions, and to make reasonably informed decisions based on personal and family values, comes at a time when medical management of patients is rapidly changing. This presents new challenges for the education of physicians, as well as raising the possibility of ethical consultation for them.

Cases like the one outlined above also present questions for the health care institution. What type of structures and policies should administrators and boards provide to assure good decision- making in cases like this? Which values should the institution follow? Should the institution foster a risk management position or should it foster a posture of promoting patients' rights and responsibilities? To answer these questions would require expertise, time, and money, and involve an individual or a committee to develop new or more sophisticated policies regarding ethical decisions. Committees need to be formed, literature needs to be reviewed, and documents need to be written, in order to form social structures and encourage relationships that will promote sound, ethical decision-making. Health care institutions ought to be concerned about these issues and support staff development in these areas.

The case of the 75-year-old grandfather, and others like it, have generated questions that confront and confuse patients and their families, health professionals, and health care administrators. To respond to these questions, new roles and committees have been created within health care institutions. For example, health care institutions that conduct research on human subjects have federally mandated, local committees, called Institutional Review Boards (IRBs), whose role is to protect human subjects in research (Gray, 1975; Levine, 1986; Veatch, 1986; Rothman, 1987). IRBs have existed for over ten years and are well integrated into institutions involved in research with human subjects. The IRBs review research protocols to determine if they have adequate scientific and ethical merit, and to assure that each patient-subject has given voluntary, informed consent to participate in the research.

It is clear, however, that health care institutions now are faced with ethical issues beyond those involved in the protection of human subjects in research.

A majority of hospitals have formed Institutional Ethics Committees (IECs) (Cranford and Douder, 1984; McCarrick and Adams, 1987), which have several functions: to provide educational programs to institutional staff about ethical decision-making; to develop policies to guide ethical decisions; and to offer advice on cases where the medical and ethical issues are particularly complex (Lo, 1987). In the case cited above, such a committee might be asked by the physician to consider the option of experimental treatment for the patient, and to suggest who should provide the consent or refusal. The decision in the case might be guided by a number of policies previously developed by an IEC. In providing guidance, the IEC could address the needs and concerns of the health professionals, the patients, and the family.

IECs do not, however, fill some roles well (La Puma, 1987). While such committees can and do organize individual conferences and workshops on health care ethics, the members of the IEC are typically busy in their primary practices and seldom have the time to organize a comprehensive educational program. In its primary role as ethics consultant, the IEC has the advantage of bringing together diverse points of view and a wide range of expertise, but it may lose credibility by being distant from the bedside and being under-utilized because of the time required to schedule meetings for deliberation. Moreover, as a committee, the IEC cannot always respond to the broader needs of families and health professionals, as it might involve lengthy discussion for questions to be answered and fears addressed.

To address these additional role-expectations, some health care and educational institutions have created a new position, that of a clinical ethicist (Glover, Ozar, and Thomasma, 1986). Clinical ethicists may be physicians or nurses who have gained additional training in ethics, or they may be chaplains, lawyers, or Ph.D.'s (e.g., philosophers, sociologists) with clinical experience. Whatever their backgrounds, clinical ethicists are being asked to fill the additional educational and consultative roles that arise and cannot be handled by the IECs.

There has not yet emerged a single, well-defined role these persons play in health care institutions, but general expectations abound. Clinical ethicists keep abreast of the current ethical and legal literature, sort out ethical issues that arise in medical decision-making, and provide educational programs in health care ethics. The position of clinical ethicist may be located in the chaplain's department, the administration, a medical education program, or a medical school department. It is likely that the position the role has in the institution will significantly influence how the role is shaped, the credibility it has, and the perspective that is taken in particular cases.

THE POSITION OF CLINICAL ETHICIST: A CASE STUDY

As should be plain, ethical dilemmas in health care have not only raised intellectual and moral issues, they also have created expectations that require new roles in health care institutions. To further explore these roles, the actual development of the role of "clinical ethicist" at a health care facility in a small, midwestern city with a population of 50,000 was analyzed.

Four years ago a new teaching position was created at a nonprofit, 400 bed, tertiary care, community hospital which has 55 physicians in graduate medical training. The position involved teaching medical ethics and related humanities to newly graduated physicians training to be specialists in pediatrics, internal medicine, and general surgery. Because medical faculty, which is part of a 200 physician outpatient clinic, typically participates in the same conferences, this education reaches a much larger group of physicians.

This new role of clinical ethicist was staffed by the senior author, who was educated in the humanities and formally taught in the academic setting, and thus found the clinical setting a major change in role expectations and role enactment. Teaching takes place in two settings at this level of medical education: at the bedside during patient rounds and in monthly conferences. Typically, there are no courses like these in a university undergraduate program or even in the early years of medical school. Rather, teaching in a hospital focuses on cases and topics which are generated by its patient population.

The Medical Education Director and the ethicist quickly decided that the role responsibilities would involve making rounds with nine different teaching services. These included four general medicine services, pulmonary, cardiology, oncology, pediatrics ward and neonatal ICU. In joining these services, contact was established with half of the residents each month, and access was provided to the greatest number of ethical issues in the institution. Since it was difficult to schedule rounds with the surgery residents, one surgery service was followed every other month for a day. This day would involve following the residents while they made rounds early in the day, observing them in the operating room, being with them when they informed families about the outcome of surgery, and reviewing the cases on their service with their attendings (i.e., physicians responsible for one of the teaching services listed above).

Teaching at conferences, while a more familiar setting, was not the same as a university classroom. For one thing, each lecture had to be self-contained. While it was hoped that previous presentations and discussions would be retained, the medical audience was never constant. Moreover, the conferences could not be solely a conceptual analysis of some ethical concept like "informed consent" as the physicians hoped to gain some practical insight into how to improve their practices. This task was no easy matter, since even the newest physician has had considerable experience in patient problems and various approaches to a wide variety of ethical situations.

Initially, the ethicist was limited to making rounds and giving lectures to physicians, which required only a quarter-time position. Over a two year period the role evolved. Nursing staff wanted to have inservices that considered ethical issues. The hospital formed an IEC which required organization of meetings, additional educational responsibilities, policy formation, and eventually participating in a consultation service. In addition, various persons, from inside and outside the hospital, requested outreach educational programs.

The role of ethicist evolved primarily into the roles of educator and facilitator. As educator, the ethicist attempts to help health professionals and those they care for, to understand the ethical issues they face. The ethicist aids others to understand not only ethical principles (narrowly construed), but also issues of communication, history, law, interpersonal relationships, family, religion, and philosophy. This rich understanding of health care ethics, that is the goal of the ethicist as educator, is the reason that from the beginning the role has been formally titled "Director of Medical Humanities." As facilitator, the ethicist acts to improve communication and resolve problems, but the ethicist does not have the authority to make decisions concerning medical care. Rather, the ethicist's role is to help clarify understanding so that the best solution to the ethical questions can be found.

In short, the clinical ethicist role evolved from a part-time position that was focused on educational programs for medical residents to a multifaceted role that involves a wide range of activities both in and out of the hospital. When the role was created, no one anticipated the extent to which it would evolve.

Not unexpectedly, this new, evolving role was a curiosity to the staff. An academically trained person, with a Ph.D. in philosophy, working in a clinical setting was an unfamiliar role to all. Initially, the common question "What do you do as an ethicist?" resulted in difficult and embarrassing interactions. A memorable example of this confusion occurred when the term "ethicist" was heard by a nurse as "anesthetist." The misunderstanding was not even perceived until she expressed surprise that she had not met this new staff member despite long hours in the operating rooms. Over time, the role of clinical ethicist had to be distinguished from the roles of chaplain, therapist, and administrator. Since ethical issues in a clinical setting often involve issues related to these other roles, health professionals would at times turn to the clinical ethicist to resolve these related problems as well.

Resolving the stress of the new role involved much more than clarifying names and function. It took several years to learn what the expectations and limitation of the role were in various settings. Many conflicting expectations became apparent. Working with a range of health professionals, each with a slightly different perspective on patient care, it was often difficult to avoid being pulled into interprofessional rivalry. The most frequent tensions arose when a nurse wanted to discuss a case with the ethicist because she perceived a doctor's decision to be either unethical or not in the patient's best interest. Sometimes such cases turned out to be caused by a misunderstanding of the facts or poor communication. But at times the nurse's judgment was correct, and when this is the case, diplomacy must be used so that the interests of all, especially the patient's, are respected.

Perhaps the most difficult conflict for the ethicist is being asked to comment on a complex case when the physician is clearly looking for support. In this situation, it is important to explore whether the response to the situation is being influenced by a misunderstanding of the ethicist role or guided by a careful consideration of the data and values. Since continuation of the ethicist role is somewhat dependent on the opinion of physicians, and is not explicitly dedicated to act in the patient's best interest, it is important to sort out this potential role conflict. Nowhere in the academic realm does one face a role conflict of this type, that is, where the advice or analysis one gives will literally affect the life or death of a person one has just met. It certainly does test the metal of one's integrity and leads to nights of uneasy sleep.

The clinical ethicist as educator and facilitator, however, is able to minimize role strain and stress for three reasons. First, the ethicist has no institutional authority to make decisions for or about anyone, and in this respect is not a threat to anyone. Second, in most cases, involvement comes at the invitation or consent of the parties involved, and an attempt is made to reach agreement by consensus. Third, the ethicist, not being identified with any of the more traditional health professions, moves comfortably among all of the health professionals in hospital and clinic settings.

An understanding of the role of ethicist has developed and is managed by a constant articulation of the role, as expressed in written reports, oral introductions, and public actions. It is important for the ethicist to adopt a style of self-presentation to the professionals with whom the ethicist is working and to explain behaviors in terms that are mutually understood. For example, since many nurses used the description ''medical'' to refer exclusively to the function of physicians, titles like ''Health Care Ethics'' or ''The Ethics of Foregoing Treatment'' were more appropriate when addressing nurses than a title like ''Ethical Problems of Medical Treatment.''

Moreover, different professions seem to view ethical issues from different vantage points. Physicians as a group consider ethical principles an important factor in patient care, while nurses seem to consider one's relationship with the patient crucial in deciding what is morally appropriate. This difference in viewpoint affects how a case is presented and discussed, as well as how the ethicist needs to listen to the description of a case and existing conflicts.

Ultimately, the success of the role of clinical ethicist hinges on the need for ethical clarification by health professionals and patients, and how the role is managed. Because of the growing complexity and frequency of ethical issues in medicine, health professionals and institutions value the assistance of someone who has time and skill to review the literature, sort out the problems, put together educational programs, and suggest solutions to ongoing problems. This work, however, must be accomplished so that the realities of health care decisions and the complexities of health care values are respected. The work of the ethicist also demands appreciation of the skills of various health professionals and the complex interrelationships that they maintain.

The Expertise of a Clinical Ethicist

Since the role of clinical ethicist involves a collection of activities that can include teaching, ethical consultation, and policy formation, it is impossible to analyze in detail all the forms of expertise that are involved. The role of ethics consultant, however, deserves special attention since it is most often subject to question. Some question the clinical ethicist's claim to expertise. From the halls of academic philosophy comes the argument that there are no moral experts, there is only moral opinion; therefore, no one should claim the role of ethicist (Kock, 1986). There are others, in traditional medical practice, who argue that someone from outside of medical practice cannot adequately understand the medical decision-making process (Wassersug, 1988).

Both of these positions fail to understand the role of the clinical ethicist as educator and facilitator (Thomasma, 1982). Whatever the epistemological status of ethical principles, medical decisions involving complex and conflicting human values must be made. These decisions cannot be put off or ignored, and the best decisions are made by examining both technical factors and the values that are being called into question.

In cases where these issues arise, an appeal to ethical principles like autonomy, beneficence, and truth-telling will not be sufficient to resolve the issues raised. Related questions, like how much certainty is required before a decision can be made, also must be considered. Professional responsibility to patients must be balanced with legal, ethical, and institutional expectations of proper decision-making. Necessary to all of these judgments is knowledge of professional responsibility, legal precedent and statutes, clinical-ethical consensus about similar cases, institutional and professional guidelines and clinical realities, as well as skill in applying this knowledge to specific, concrete cases. It is this combination of skill and knowledge that is at the heart of the role of clinical ethicist. This expertise is a claim neither to ethical truth nor to medical knowledge.

Two points need to be made about the application of the aforementioned skills and knowledge. Many cases are resolved, not through complex reasoning about ethical principles, but by a careful sorting out of data and values. This is not to say that ethical issues are not involved, but rather that decision-makers may not be able to reach an agreement until they have a common understanding of the case. The second point is that even when ethical decisions are considered by parties who subsribe to different ethical theories, most often agreement can be reached about a concrete case. Such a consensus is reached despite theoretical disagreements because the ethical questions involve the application of underlying, commonly held values.

It is important to realize that ethical consultations take different forms. Usually it is the person who asks for the consultation who shapes the task of the consultant. This person has a question and hopes to gain some insight into the answer. Broadly speaking, consultation may be requested for clarification, conflict resolution, or both

Consider the case presented at the beginning of this chapter. A request for an ethical consultation might originate from a number of sources. These might include the physician, the grandson, or a nurse. A consult might involve questions like: Is it acceptable for the grandson to make decisions on behalf of the patient?; To what extent should the living will be considered in this instance?; Should this patient's quality-of-life and treatment costs be considered in assessing the benefits and burdens of treatment? Is the issue, for the person asking the question, legal liability, ethical principle, hospital policy, the decision-making process, or all of these?; and, Is the question being asked to help clarify and assure that good practice is being followed, or is there a serious conflict between the various parties involved?

How these questions are answered will determine the focus of the consultation. Thus, if the grandson is concerned about how his grandfather's quality-of-life should enter into the decision, and for him the issue is clarification, such a consultation would be handled differently from a consult where two physicians disagree with the institution's view of using this patient's living will. Of course, during an ethical consult the clinical ethicist is not blind to ethical issues that are not raised or seen by the parties involved. The consultant has a responsibility to all parties to promote the best ethical decision given the understanding at that time and in that case.

Once the problem is carefully defined, the ethical consultant would more closely examine the relevant data of the case, and the particular values that might have a bearing on the issue. This may require conferring with others, such as an attorney or medical sub-specialist, as well as researching the relevant literature. Based on collected information and further reflection, an answer would be given to the question asked. In some institutions, this work would be guided and recorded on an ethics consultation form which could be reviewed at a later time by an IEC (see Appendix).

It is important to recognize that presently no one is prepared by their training to play this role. Additional training and experience is required. Once acquired, this knowledge and skill can be used for the education of health professionals and patients, the facilitating of complex medical-ethical decisions, and the development of institutional guidelines and policies regarding medical-ethical decisions.

As with any role, some people will acquire the skills and knowledge, and combine them with the appropriate personal qualities, to assume the role well; others will not. This observation raises the question as to whether those people who successfully assume the role should be credentialed in some way. Such recognition seems justified, given the development of the role and the fact that the work of the clinical ethicist can have momentous consequences. But considerations of recognition raise questions about what the credentials would be and who would oversee them. This situation has been discussed in an informal manner by at least one national group, The Society for Health and Human Values, and its importance also is reflected in a newly formed group, The Society for Bioethics Consultation. If the role continues and grows, the issue of credentials will have to be resolved.

CLINICAL ETHICS AS SOCIOLOGICAL PRACTICE

The practice of clinical ethics in medicine is most satisfactory when ethical principles are juxtaposed with data about a patient, the patient's family and community, the medical diagnosis, and the treatment context (Thomasma, 1987). Extreme approaches in ethics would identify absolute moral principles for consistent application, that is do no harm, or, carefully examine the idiosyncratic moral circumstances of specific medical cases to make relative conclusions, as in casuistry analysis (Jonsen, 1986; Jonsen and Toulmin, 1988). Neither of these extremes is adequate, according to Thomasma (1987), because ethical decisions require an examination of moral principles that apply to factors such as the number of people affected and the intensity of medical practice. Thomasma (1987:149) recommends that the social context be examined ". . . to locate a moral problem and the likely values and principles at issue within that locus." By such a sociological analysis, interests and values can be protected as a case is resolved.

Sociological data stand beside medical data in the fact-finding stage of an "ethical work-up." The format for an ethics consultation in the Appendix requires both medical and sociological data in part one. Medical information includes significant past medical history and the course of present hospitalization and treatment. The sociological data include: (1) the patient's marital status, occupation, and religiosity; (2) an assessment of social-behavioral competence; (3) specification of the patient's values, beliefs, wishes, goals, and attitudes about his or her health care, including a statement of advance directives; and (4) the role and involvement of significant others and their values and wishes for the patient's care.

The second part of the ethics consultation form is the ethics evaluation, which includes an assessment of the case, an explanation of ethical principles involved, and advice regarding ethical courses of action. The evaluation may entail clarification of previously unexpressed values and principles or it may involve identifying, explaining, and resolving values that are in conflict within a patient, family, or medical and nursing caregivers. The clarification and assessment of ethical values such as justice, autonomy, and ordinary care, and theories (e.g., deontological and metaphysical), as well as sociological assumptions about, for example, human nature, patient-health provider relationships, and confidentiality, are enhanced by valid and reliable data about the patient and the social context of care.

The role of clinical ethicist in health care is growing as attested to by the creation of new clinical ethicist positions in tertiary care hospitals. Whether the clinical ethicist role will become a well-defined and credentialed role in health care, or will become part of medical problem-solving and decision-making learned in medical education from senior physicians, is yet to be settled. In the meantime, there is a role to be filled and a level of competency and expertise to be learned not only from philosophical ethics, but also from clinical sociology.

REFERENCES

Cranford, R. E. and A. E. Douder, eds. 1984. *Institutional Ethics Committees and Health Care Decision-Making*. Ann Arbor, MI: Health Administration Press.

Glover, J.J. D. T. Ozar and D. C. Thomasma. 1986. Teaching on rounds: The ethicist as teacher, consultant, and decision maker. *Theoretical Medicine* 7(1):13–32.

Gray, B. 1975. *Human Subjects in Medical Experimentation*. New York: Wiley.

Jonsen, A. R. 1986. Casuistry and clinical ethics. *Theoretical Medicine* 7:65–74.

Jonsen, A. R. and S. Toulmin. 1988. *The Abuse of Casuistry*. CA: University of California Press.

Kock, D.F. 1986. Moral philosophers and moral expertise. *Philosophy and Medicine Newsletter*. American Philosophical Association (Fall):2–3.

La Puma, J. 1987. Ethics by committee? (letter) *New England Journal of Medicine* 317(22):1418.

Levine, R. 1986. *Ethics and the Regulation of Clinical Research*, 2nd. ed. Baltimore, MD: Urban and Schwerzenberg.

Lo, B. 1987. Behind closed doors: Promises and pitfalls of ethics committees. *New England Journal of Medicine* 317(1):46–49.

McCarrick, P.M. and J. Adams. 1987. *Ethics Committees in Hospitals*. National Reference Center for Bioethics Literature, Kennedy Institute of Ethics (June).

Rothman, D. J. 1987. Ethics and human experimentation: Henry Beecher revisited. *New England Journal of Medicine* 317(19):1195–99.

Thomasma, D. C. 1987. The Context as a Moral Rule in Medical Ethics. In R. A. Wright, *Human Values in Health Care: The Practice of Ethics*. New York: McGraw-Hill Book Company, 142–56.

———1982. Medical ethics: A clinical base. *Linacre Quarterly* August:266–76.

Veatch, R. 1986. *The Patient as Partner: A Theory of Human- Experimentation Ethics*. Bloomington: Indiana University Press.

Wassersug, J. D. 1988. Invasion of the ethicists. *MD* 28:33–34.

Appendix
Ethics Consultation

Patient's clinic #:
Case referred by:
Patient's age & sex:
Date:
Date of admission:
Statement of ethical conflict(s) or problem(s):

I.   Factual information:
    A.   Medical:
        1.   Significant past medical History:

        2.   Course of present hospitalization:

    B.   Social:
        1.   Patient's marital status, occupation, and religion:

        2.   Assessment of patient's competence (indicate who made assessment):

        3.   Patient's values, beliefs, wishes, goals, and attitudes about his/her health care (indicate source of information, e.g., advance directive, family, nurse, etc.):

        4.   Involvement of significant others and their wishes and values:

Patient's clinic #:
II. Evaluation
    A.   Assessment of the case:

    B.   Explanation of ethical principles involved:

    C.   Advice:

12

Permission to Die: A Case Study in the Social Construction of Reality

Suzanne Fleming

About twenty years ago, I was interviewed in Hebrew, which is not my native language, at Bar Ilan University in Tel Aviv, as part of my application for admission there. I will never forget the question, "When is a person legally dead?" because my interviewers laughed when I answered—as I thought— "when a physician signs the death certificate." They explained that I had, in fact, answered, "When the doctor gives permission to die."

In contemporary America, of course, my answer wouldn't be at all funny. The development of life-sustaining technology has created a situation where physicians often need to decide whether to initiate or continue life-sustaining treatment; that is, whether to permit patients to die. These decisions are the source of difficult ethical, moral, and legal questions—concerning the "right to die," as well as the allocation of scarce medical resources, since there are substantial financial and emotional costs involved in keeping a very sick person alive with expensive technologies, especially when the prognosis is uncertain (Englehardt and Rie, 1986).

Perhaps some of the moral and ethical issues are simply not resolvable to the satisfaction of all. Fox (1986) notes that our culture lacks an appropriate normative paradigm within which to solve the dilemmas that arise out of life-and-death decisions. Nonetheless, having created ways to forestall death, the medical profession was confronted with the need for guidelines to determine when to use them, and the means of implementing their decisions. Developing means was much easier than establishing guidelines for use. The Do-Not-Resuscitate (DNR) and comfort-care-only/no extraordinary measures (NEM) orders are examples of the means developed to carry out the decision to allow the patient to die naturally. DNR means that the patient won't be "coded" or resuscitated in any way if the respiratory and/or cardiac systems fail. NEM orders are given less frequently than DNR orders. An NEM order means that treatment will not be initiated, or that it will be withdrawn. (In the hospital studied, hospital protocols use the acronym NEM to refer to what physicians call "comfort care only." Perhaps the initials stand for "no extraordinary measures," but the substantive meaning of comfort care only is precisely what it says and the order can exclude ordinary treatments such as blood transfusions.)

Concern about life-and-death decisions is not limited to the medical profession. The general public's interest in the "right to die" issue was aroused in 1976 when the Supreme Court of New Jersey approved the removal of a mechanical ventilator from Karen Quinlan as she lay in a coma. (*In re Quinlan*, N.J. 10355, 2d. 647). The Court emphasized that the question did not belong in a law court, but should be decided privately by the involved parties. Since that case, questions concerning life and death decisions have permeated the public domain (Neu and Kjellstrand, 1986). Those of us who have lived long enough to accept our mortality, are thinking about or writing "living wills" in which we express our feelings about life sustaining technology, and possibly organ donation as well. Hospitals have responded to the interest in life and death issues by creating new professional roles, such as ethicists, risk managers, and bio-ethics committees. Much is being written, symposia are being held, and yet, the issues surrounding life and death decisions remain largely unresolved.

A major difficulty in making these decisions is the inability of medical technology to predict the course of disease with complete accuracy. Although most agree that it is appropriate to remove life support in cases of "brain death," that is, when an electroencephalogram indicates no activity at all (AMA, 1985), the majority of cases are not this clear. Problems occur when some amount of brain activity is revealed by examination, despite clinical and behavioral evidence of severe and irreversible brain damage. These cases are problematic because the prognosis cannot be totally supported by objective data, but rests to some extent on the physician's judgement (Anspach, 1987).

The most difficult cases are those where the patient vegetates without meaningful cognitive activity while life continues, possibly aided by mechanical ventilation. Neu and Kjellstraand (1986) state that there is "profound disagreement" in the case of incompetent patients, and the case presented later in this chapter bears out this claim. The American Medical Association (1985:75-76) recognizes that there are times when the social responsibilities of the physician—to prolong life and to relieve suffering—may conflict with each other, but gives no guidelines as to the resolution of the conflict. Physicians who need to decide whether continued aggressive treatment constitutes sustaining life or prolonging the dying process are obliged to some extent to use their own judgement (President's Commission, 1981), therefore, the physician is open to charges of not only mistaken judgement or technique, but also moral misconduct

(Bosk, 1979). This "double jeopardy" may well explain why some of the attending physicians were quite defensive and hostile to my investigation, and why physicians as a group tend to discourage outsiders from participating in the decision-making process.

The need to use non-scientific factors in evaluating medical programs is illustrated by economists' routine use of the "financial worth" or "human capital" approach in cost-effectiveness studies (Landefeld and Seskin, 1985). Nonetheless, a large part of the physician's dilemma is that it is not morally or socially acceptable to use non-scientific factors such as social worth in life-and-death decisions, even though studies show that social and cultural factors are not only used, but must be used, due to the absence of totally reliable, scientifically objective means to decide life-and-death issues (Anspach, 1987; Fox, 1986; Star, 1988).

The use of such factors may not be, *per se,* problematic. It becomes problematic however, because it is covert, and not open to any type of study, supervision, or regulation. Physicians generally act as if the only bases of their decisions are scientific and objective, hiding known social and cultural aspects in medical terminology. Indeed, few of us are even aware of the social construction of our own realities (Berger, 1963). Further, as long as the medical profession continues to claim life-and-death decisions as an integral part of its professional domain, the decision-making process is likely to be the center of some territorial conflict (Star, 1988), and to remain closed to outside investigation.

METHODS

Opportunities to examine the epistemological bases of medical decision-making, are, therefore, rare. I was lucky enough to have such an opportunity, which I present here as a case study, to illustrate how medical uncertainty and sociocultural factors influence and complicate both the do-not-rescusitate (DNR) and comfort care only (NEM) orders. The case of JA is unusual in that one group of physicians made the decision to allow the patient to die, while a different group needed to carry out the decision and implement the NEM and DNR orders. Conflict between the groups revealed some of the non-medical bases of their actions that may otherwise have remained hidden from me.

By working for eighteen months as a researcher and consultant in methods and statistics, for a group of intensive care physicians in an urban teaching hospital, I was in an advantageous position to carry out a case study, an appropriate method for examining the processes of the social construction of reality (Bosk, 1979). During the course of my work, I spent time collecting data in the Intensive Care Unit (ICU), and attended daily rounds, where I observed, and at times felt part of, aspects of the medical staff's behavior and emotions that are usually hidden from lay people.

I became especially interested in the ways that the attending physicians and residents gained consensus on issues related to DNR and NEM orders. My data were gathered by observations and by interviews with nurses, residents, and attending physicians. Most residents spoke to me openly. The ICU residents were easiest to approach, as they were used to seeing me around. I assume that my white coat with my name on it gave me some status, as well as the fact that I addressed their supervising physicians by their first names. ICU attendings assumed my sympathy for their version of reality, and freely expressed their disapproval of medical services, the group that was to implement the DNR and NEM orders.

The medical services residents were quite open, although more guarded than the ICU residents. The medical services attendings were unwilling to discuss JA's case with me because they knew that I was studying death and dying. One attending, KL, who had allowed me to meet with her on another case, as professional courtesy to the ICU department head, told me that she would deny any statements that I attributed to her. My inability to discuss the case openly with these key figures leaves some gaps and unanswered questions in the case analysis.

I was not able to learn why KL was hostile. However, I think that the refusal of the medical services attending to allow a stranger to examine their decision-making process in a life-and-death situation exemplifies their need to keep the process guarded, and within medical circles.

FINDINGS

I first learned of JA one Monday morning in rounds. He had been admitted during the weekend, and was ready for discharge to the floor. This 49-year-old Hispanic man was a local resident who was quite well known to the hospital, due to a history of cirrhosis of the liver caused by alcoholism. His impaired liver had caused the development of varicose veins, or varices, in his esophagus. From time to time, these veins would hemorrhage, causing him to vomit blood, and this was the condition that had caused his current admission to the emergency room.

One way to relieve this type of hemorrhage is to insert a balloon into the esophagus. The balloon is then inflated through a naso-gastral tube, so that it presses against the bleeding vessels. The balloon must be held firmly against the tissues in order to stop the flow of blood. The traditional way to achieve this had been to tie the outside end of the tube to the bed, an uncomfortable and clumsy arrangement. The ICU had recently bought a football helmet to which the balloon could be tied, leaving the bed area clear and relieving some of the discomfort to the patient. Thus, my first view of JA was of a small, emaciated man, lying in bed wearing nothing but a huge black football helmet.

The balloon tamponade is a temporary measure. The varices can be permanently healed through endoscopic sclerosis, a treatment used by gastro-intestinal specialists. The process is fully described by Erkkinen (1986). It can be done even while active bleeding is taking place. Sclerosis of the affected varices treats the active hemorrhage and prevents recurrence of bleeding, provided the patient refrains from alcohol and regains liver function. If the patient continues to drink, the varices and other cirrhosis-related problems will recur. JA had suffered previous episodes of varicose hemorrhage, so it was clear to all that although he had been firmly informed of his own role in his condition, he had not changed his habits.

The balloon tamponade had stopped JA's bleeding by the time his case was discussed in morning rounds, and the resident recommended discharge to the floor for observation before leaving the hospital. The department head nodded his agreement and then asked in an offhanded way, "Why didn't you 'scope him' for varices?" referring to the endoscopic sclerosis discussed above. At the time I knew nothing about the condition or its treatment, but my interest was aroused by the residents' shame-faced responses, which they stuttered and stammered, interrupting each other, addressing the floor and furniture rather than the department head. After waiting some moments the department head said, "Come on," and paused. "You know if he'd been a fine upstanding citizen you would have 'scoped' him." The residents did not defend themselves, and appeared embarrassed. The department head broke the silence and ended the episode by asking for the next case. I wondered why he had not insisted on JA's remaining in the ICU to be "scoped."

When next JA came into the hospital with bleeding varices, he was first admitted to the medical services floor. He was sicker than he had ever been. While he was on the floor, he had been seen by specialists in infectious diseases, gastroenterology, surgery, and neurology. The neurologist's report indicated that there was a possibility that JA may have become so brain damaged as to be considered incompetent.

JA's condition steadily worsened. His bleeding continued, and he lost the ability to breathe on his own. He was placed on a mechanical ventilator and moved into the ICU where a new group of residents had begun their rotation. His situation was very bad—he was unresponsive to stimuli, and he was now bleeding from his stomach, esophagus, and rectum.

The department head suggested a DNR order as soon as the resident had finished her case presentation in rounds. There were no objections, and JA's resident said that she would speak to his closest relative, a niece. She said that the family comprised respectable, hard-working people who spoke English well.

She seemed to be very comfortable with the situation, and refused another resident's offer to speak with the family in Spanish. (She also refrained from using the phrase "let God take him," that an attending physician had suggested.)

She was able to get JA's niece on the phone immediately, and explained simply that the staff needed the family's help in deciding what to do if JA's heart stopped. The niece agreed to come in with her husband right away to discuss the situation, and the resident was warmly praised by the others who had been listening.

The family agreed readily to an order of DNR and also to an order for comfort care only (NEM). Shortly afterward, both orders were entered into the chart, along with an order for morphine, "as needed." The balloon tamponade was removed, and JA was transferred back to the medical services floor.

A couple of days later, one of the residents told me that JA had surprised everybody by surviving the weekend. The family had spoken with the medical service physicians, requesting that JA be removed from his ventilator. In JA's case, the possibility that he would be able to breathe on his own was small, although predicting breathing is very uncertain, as seen in the case of Karen Quinlan who breathed on her own for years after her ventilator was removed (In Re Quinlan, NJ 10355, 2d, 647 (1976)).

I was surprised by the apparent ease with which the family came to their conclusions about the withdrawal of treatment. In all the cases I'd seen, families had shown a great deal of ambivalence and difficulty in making the decision. I asked JA's ICU resident whether JA was a financial and social burden to his family, but she was uncharacteristically reticent. In fact, none of the ICU residents was willing to discuss the social and family issues surrounding JA's case, and I wondered whether the department head's cutting remark to the previous group had been the cause. The ICU attending physicians were voluble and eager to share their opinions on NEM and DNR orders in general, but not in regard to this specific case—like the residents, they avoided any discussion of the social or familial aspects of the case.

JA's medical services resident consulted with the Risk Management Department about the family's request, in accordance with hospital policy. She didn't want to discuss the meeting with me before she talked with her attending. While waiting for JA's resident, I checked JA, and his chart. He lay very still with his eyes closed, connected to his ventilator and to a number of lines. He didn't seem to be producing much urine, although he defecated a steady bloody stream into a rectal tube. His chart contained an order for morphine, which I expected, as well as an order for blood, which I did not expect.

When I double checked the chart, I found that the medical services staff was obeying the transfer orders very literally. The orders stated comfort care only, but did not specify which treatments were to be withheld. At this point I asked the chief resident, who was assigned to medical services, why this was the case. He answered that perhaps JA may want to "venture an opinion on his imminent demise."

Chastened, I reported this interlude to the ICU department head, who refused to accept any intimation of humane motivations on the part of the medical services physicians. It was, he said, simply a matter of specifying treatments in the NEM order. Had the ICU staff written to remove JA's ventilator, he said, medical services would have done so in accordance with the family's request instead of consulting with risk management. Later I found out that hospital policy required that the note list the specific treatments to be withheld.

JA's chart had contained an order for a neurological exam and an electroencephalogram (EEG) that had puzzled me, and I asked the ICU staff about it. They were certain of JA's incompetence, and ventured the opinion that the exam was ordered because of the medical services residents' unrealistic ideas of rehabilitating the patient. An ICU fellow added that had the medical services residents seen JA in the ICU, they would think differently.

However, when JA's resident was finally ready to talk to me, she told me that the examinations had been ordered to satisfy Risk Management, which required the patient be declared incompetent before a decision could be made about the family's request to remove the ventilator. Accordingly, the medical services attending had asked the resident to write orders to discontinue JA's morphine, and also to give him enough blood to keep him alive until the EEG and neurological exam could be completed.

Later the same evening, the consulting neurologist wrote that he was not sure why the evaluation had been ordered, although it "seemed to have something to do with a DNR request." His tentative conclusion was that although the patient could be in the early stages of encephalopathy, he was awake, gravely ill, and "deserving of active medical intervention." He wanted to repeat his examination with an interpreter, and continued that "future medical treatment should be based on the patient's *medical* condition." He suggested a battery of tests, which the resident ordered soon after, as well as more blood. Earlier in the day, the same resident had approved the nurse's progress notes that clearly stated that the patient was not to receive blood.

At eleven that evening, the resident on duty called the attending physician at home to say that JA was alert, moved his hands to shield his eyes, and was no longer bleeding. After the conversation, the resident ordered more blood.

The next day, Saturday, the attending physician asked a student to speak in Spanish to JA, who had now been without morphine for 24 hours. She noted in the chart that she agreed to "continue comfort support, which I interpret to make sure we have provided the best mental status the patient can have." Later,

JA had another EEG, and the neurologist repeated his examination with the aid of a Spanish interpreter. The results were equivocal, JA was responding to some commands but not to others, and the neurologist concluded that the patient was "probably mildly encephalopathic," or brain damaged. He concluded that the need for "active medical intervention" should be evaluated daily. Following the neurology note, the resident wrote that no blood would be given, "for the moment."

On Sunday, two days before the residents were due to rotate to their next assignment, JA's resident summarized the case in an exit note for her replacement. She reviewed his whole history, including the DNR and NEM orders, noting that the question of JA's competence arose after he had been transferred to the floor. "The need to transfuse will be evaluated daily," she wrote.

The neighborhood priest came by on Sunday afternoon. The family had requested that he visit with JA, whom he had never met. Young and sincere, he spoke long and earnestly to JA in American-accented Spanish. JA moaned a few times and moved around in the bed, but otherwise failed to respond. The priest said prayers for JA, but did not give him last rites. Later, he told me that JA's nephew is educated and speaks English well, and that the family is God-fearing and respectable. He asked me to explain JA's condition, and wanted to know whether a liver transplant could help.

On Monday I conferred with the ICU staff, who expressed annoyance with the events on the floor. One physician characterized the neurologist's behavior as the "hedging" of one who was simply unwilling to be held responsible for JA's death, and dubbed him "the neurotic neuro." Neurological consults, according to most of the ICU staff, are a great waste of time, although they are a necessary precaution against possible litigation.

I managed to find JA's resident, who agreed with the ICU staff about the neurologist, although she was angry with them, claiming that JA had been "pushed out" of the ICU because they needed the bed. She characterized the situation as "one big mess." She went on to tell me that the medical services staff had, at one point, reached consensus that JA was incompetent, but the "neurotic neuro" disagreed. He had shouted at her, she said, and demanded to know what the staff was doing for JA. She seemed pleased to be rotating out.

Later in the day JA had another EEG. His nurse informed me that it would be no good, because he had been restless and moving. The nurse was aware of JA's DNR status, but did not know about the NEM order.

JA spent another restless day on Tuesday, and received more blood and more morphine. He was examined by a different neurologist, who wrote a very brief note, stating that JA's prognosis was very poor, and "if he continues to bleed it's 'o,' " meaning zero, or over.

I managed to talk to the chief resident before he also rotated out of medical services. He told me that the medical services plan for JA was to continue to try to get agreement on his mental state, while attempting to wean him from the ventilator. A very short trial had shown that he could draw at least a few breaths on his own. He would receive enough blood to keep him alive indefinitely, assuming no new and violent hemorrhage occured. I asked whether he would be transferred back to the ICU if he did hemorrhage. The chief resident immediately answered that this decision would be up to the next round of physicians, and would say no more.

The next day I found JA's new resident, who told me that he had spoken to the family on the previous day. They had requested that JA be kept free from pain, and that he receive no blood. The new resident was unaware at that time of their earlier request to turn off the ventilator, and the events that followed. Several hours later, I found that the new resident had written an order to discontinue all blood products. The new attending, signing off on the resident's orders, noted that the prognosis was "grim" and that the staff would comply with the family's wishes. JA died the following day.

I felt that the abrupt change in the medical services staff's attitude and behavior could not be attributed to the rotation of personnel alone, and went to find JA's new resident. I learned that he had been brought up to date on the whole story since our last conversation. He explained the events to me as follows: first, the new staff's actions did not represent a change in attitude at all. The first attending physician ordered the neurological evaluations because she felt that JA had never had a fair test of competence. Eventually, the first attending decided that JA was incompetent, and decided to comply with the family's wish, said the resident.

This accounting in no way resembled my own. In my version, Risk Management had required the first neurological evaluation, which was then repeated three times on the neurologist's orders. The first medical services attending and residents had agreed, after some time, that JA was incompetent but were unwilling to act on their decision because of the demands of the "neurotic neuro." The staff ordered blood for JA until their last moments on medical services. It was not until a different neurologist wrote clearly that JA was close to death, and a different set of physicians had rotated onto the service, that the decision was made to act, either on the family's request, or the NEM order—I could not determine which.

I felt comfortable that my version of the event was the correct one—it was, at least, fully documented—and I was able to explain the new resident's version as dissonance reduction. However, the question concerning what finally caused the medical services staff to withdraw treatment remains unanswered.

DISCUSSION

JA's case illustrates the social construction of two conflicting medical realities: one constructed by the ICU staff who made the decision to withhold treatment, and the other made by the medical services staff who were to carry out the decision.

The American Medical Association has stated that all means of life support may be withdrawn "where a terminally ill patient's coma is beyond doubt irreversible and there are adequate safeguards to confirm the accuracy of the diagnosis" (1985:75). The exact meanings of "terminally ill," "beyond doubt irreversible," and "adequate safeguards" are left to the discretion of the parties involved.

Even though physicians' ideal situations are those in which life-and-death decisions are made only on medical, or technological data, the medical facts in most cases are ambiguous. Anspach points out that "when the patient's course is chronic . . . and when, in addition, you do not have concrete, unequivocal evidence of brain damage, you can expect different ideas and prognoses" (1988: 227), and JA's case is an example of a situation about which there were "different ideas." Although it seemed clear to everyone that JA would eventually die, the meaning of "eventually" was unclear. The ICU staff saw it as "sooner," while the medical services staff took the more conservative estimate of "later."

The ICU staff saw a terminally ill, mentally incompetent man, of low social worth. Removal of life support, therefore, was an appropriate course of action. It would not constitute euthanasia, and continuing life support would prolong the dying process and break the Hippocratic mandate to do no harm. The case was quite simple. The prognosis was reliable, the patient was clearly incompetent, and the family members were unanimous in their agreement about withdrawing treatment.

The medical services staff, faced with actually implementing the withdrawal of treatment, drew a much more complex and ambiguous picture. They saw a very sick man, who might or might not be terminal. His mental state was unclear, and was complicated by his pain medication and a language barrier. Withdrawing treatment in this context could well constitute euthanasia.

Both views of reality agreed that JA was a victim, but disagreed about the identity of the offender. The medical services staff blamed the ICU for pushing JA out of its service because his bed was needed. They also blamed the "neurotic neuro" who refused to see JA's situation as terminal. The ICU staff blamed the neurologist for failing to make a decision, or "buck passing," as well as the medical services staff for relying on him. The ICU department head had blamed the group of residents, who had failed to "scope" JA, for being prejudiced, and the "neurotic neuro's" insistence that JA not be denied medical treatment suggests that he, too, suspected that social discrimination played a part in the case.

These separate views of reality support Anspach's (1988) conclusion that medical decision-making is a social process, heavily influenced by the organizational context in which it takes place. In other words, social norms and values are shaped and refined within the organization so that they can be adapted to the specific problems faced by that organization. A brief look at how the two departments faced the problem of medical uncertainty illustrates these propositions.

The ICU is a small unit of 15 beds. It receives extremely ill patients, who need specialized technology and expertise that is available only in the ICU, so there is a heavy demand for admission. Its staff constantly battles with the hospital administration for more space. They like to move their patients in and out very quickly, not only because of the heavy demand for beds, but also because some of the treatments can be harmful if continued for too long. The decision to continue treatment despite the possibility of iatrogenic disease is one of the difficult choices that ICU physicians make daily. Death is commonplace in the ICU, over 40% of ICU patients fail to survive (Bekes, Fleming and Scott, 1988).

ICU physicians work in a stressful environment that is difficult to share with others who have not experienced the same daily routines. ICU attending physicians do not rotate out to other services. They are a much smaller group than the medical services physicians, and work together closely in an emotionally charged atmosphere. Since there are no private rooms in the ICU, all the patients are in full view of the staff at all times. All conversations, no matter how sensitive, are conducted out in the open, and often on the run. Physicians and nurses work among beds that are surrounded with various types of equipment. It is an atmosphere of urgency: everyone seems to be in a hurry. Patients moan, ventilators hiss, and monitors beep.

The atmosphere on the medical services floor is hushed. The patients are hidden from sight in private or semi-private rooms. There are many beds and there is plenty of room. Resources on the floor are not as scarce as in the ICU, and there is much less pressure to move patients out quickly, or to make quick decisions. The patients are not as ill as ICU patients. They need less treatment, and most patients survive the stay. Patients who become seriously ill are transferred to the ICU.

ICU physicians treat gravely ill patients and deal with death very often. They make prognoses about death on a regular basis, and use their own past record to measure their predictive abilities. It is not surprising, therefore, that the ICU staff predicted JA's death, and felt so certain of their diagnosis that they saw no need to back it up with a neurology consultation. Nor is it surprising that the medical services staff treated what was to them a rare event, with great caution. One would expect the ICU staff to make a quick decision, whereas the medical services staff would be expected to take time in deciding JA's mental status.

The intense work environment in the ICU produces a very tightly knit group, whose members feel that other physicians cannot really appreciate what it is like to work with intensive care patients. It is, therefore predictable that they did not feel the need to call a neurologist to pronounce on JA's mental status. The ICU physicians have plenty of opportunity to compare their clinical predictions with the predictions of consulting neurologists, and thus have an empirical basis for their assertion that neurology consults are "a great waste of time." Nevertheless, they often are obliged to call for a neurology consult if a lawsuit seems likely. They therefore, resist calling in a neurologist in a case like JA's where the family members unanimously agree with the physicians' assessment.

JA's social status was low, not only according to social criteria, but also by socio-medical standards. The ICU physicians with whom I worked often told me that they would like to treat acutely ill people who are young enough to enjoy some good years after they recover. JA not only failed to resemble the ideal patient, but also failed to fill the social role of the patient as described by Parsons (1975). He was indifferent, rather than compliant and grateful, and instead of cooperating in his treatment, he continued his unhealthy behavior.

The part played by JA's low social status is difficult to judge. It has been found that blacks and other minorities die disproportionately more often than whites from cirrhosis, which is fifth on a list of six causes of death that account for over 80% of mortality among minorities (Heckler, 1985:5). Could this mean that JA's case is just one example of a wider trend in which "respectable" alcoholics are given full, aggressive treatment at the expense of "non-respectable" alcoholics?

My data cannot answer this question. However, social status seems to have influenced the residents who, when they had the opportunity, did not treat JA with endoscopic sclerosis. Perhaps it influenced the ICU department head to refrain from insisting that JA receive this treatment, but I was unable to find a way to discuss this delicate issue. His status in his family may have influenced his relatives' decision to allow him to die naturally. And I have wondered whether the medical services staff delayed their decision because they felt vulnerable to a charge of prejudice.

Unfortunately, I could find no method to uncover the answers to these questions and so the role of JA's social status in the treatment decisions remains a matter of speculation. It is clear, however, that he did not benefit from aggressive therapy, nor did he have a swift and easy death.

CONCLUSION

The probabilistic nature of medical practice is a major obstacle in making life-and-death decisions. Even though it is seldom possible to have completely reliable, objective data on which to make such decisions, physicians tend to deny the use of non-scientific factors in decision-making. The reconstruction of the events of JA's case by the newly-arrived resident on the medical services floor is an example of this denial, which places a large obstacle in the path of those who would study the use of social and other factors in medical decision-making.

Rather than investigate the use of non-medical factors in decision-making, the medical profession has responded to the problem by attempting to develop reliable prediction instruments that will provide a totally objective basis for decision-making. Anspach's 1988 study mentions some of these instruments, and the ICU where I worked regularly used two others. The Therapeutic Intervention Scoring System, known as TISS, is based on the amount of technology the patient uses (Cullen, Civetta and Briggs, 1974). The other, known as APACHE (Knaus, Draper and Wagner, 1985), is a numeric scale of wellness based on the patient's physiology. The originators of the APACHE, and other investigators who are mentioned by Anspach (1988), are working towards the completion of a reliable prediction instrument that can be used to allocate scarce medical resources in a totally objective manner.

The development of a reliable prediction instrument would appear to do away with the need to use social factors in medical decision-making, thereby preventing discrimination in the allocation of medical resources. In light of the potential of widespread discrimination, the development of objective predictive instruments seems very desirable. But the equitable use of the objective instrument presupposes a full supply of medical resources. This presupposition is simplistic and unrealistic. It has been predicted that medical resources will become more scarce with the "graying of America" (Landefeld and Seskin, 1982), and even a perfect prediction instrument cannot help to decide which of two patients with identical chances of survival will receive the one treatment available.

It can be argued that until our society creates a situation in which there is no scarcity of medical resources, social factors will enter medical decision-making. Perhaps this is good. Rubinstein (1975) uses the holocaust and slavery as examples, of how total rationality in society can cause more human suffering than social policy that allows some irrationality in decision-making. He points out that not only cruelty and hatred are irrational, so are caring, love, and mercy.

It seems, therefore, that discrimination in medical decision-making is inseparable from its roots in social and cultural beliefs and behaviors and will not automatically disappear when objective predictive instruments become available. A first step in its elimination should be to help the medical community to appreciate the social sources of its attitudes and behaviors, through the study of the works of sociologists such as Parsons, 1951, 1975; Fox, 1986; Berger and Luckmann, 1963; and Anspach, 1987.

Current focal points for the introduction of the sociological perspective into the medical setting include voluntary organizations such as Physicians for Social Responsibility; interdisciplinary fields of study such as public health; and new organizational roles such as medical ethicist and risk manager.

It is possible that more focal points for the sociological perspective will be created, as the need to solve the problems of the ethical distribution of medical technology becomes more pressing. Sociologists can contribute not only to the problem-solving process itself, but also can broaden their influence through active participation in those areas of the debate that are currently open to them.

REFERENCES

American Medical Association Division of Communications. 1985. Terminal Illness. In *Refererence Guide to Policy and Official Statements.* American Medical Association, Chicago, IL: 75–76.

Anspach, R.R. 1987. Prognostic conflict in life and death decisions: The organization as an ecology of knowledge. *Journal of Health and Social Behavior* 28 (3): 215–31.

Bekes, C.B., S. Fleming and W.E. Scott. 1988. Reimbursement for intensive care services under diagnosis related groups. *Critical Care Medicine* 16 (5): 478–81.

Berger, P. L. and T. Luckmann. 1963. *The Social Construction of Reality.* New York: Doubleday.

Bosk C.L. 1979. *Forgive and Remember: Managing Medical Failure.* Chicago: University of Chicago Press.

Cullen, D.J., J. Civetta, and B.A. Briggs. 1974. Therapeutic intervention scoring system: A method for quantitative comparison of patient care. *Critical Care Medicine* 2: 57–66.

Englehardt, H.T., and M.A. Rie. 1986. Intensive care units, scarce resources and conflicting principles of justice. *Journal of the American Medical Association* 265: 1159–64.

Erkkinen, J.F. 1986. Injection sclerotherapy: An 'old' technique revisited. *Journal of Intensive Care Medicine* 1 (1): 123–24.

Fox, R.C. 1986. Medicine, science and technology. In Aiken, L.H. and D. Mechanic, eds. *Applications of Social Sciences to Clinical Medicine and Health Policy,* New Brunswick, NJ: Rutgers University Press.

Heckler, M.M. August, 1985. *Report of the Secretary's Task Force on Black and Minority Health.* U.S. Department of Health and Human Services. Washington, DC, U.S. Government Printing Office.

Knaus, W.A., E.A. Draper, and D.P. Wagner. 1985. Apache II: A severity of disease classification system. *Critical Care Medicine* 13:818–26.

Landefeld, J.S. and E.P. Seskin. 1982. The economic value of life: Linking theory to practice. *American Journal of Public Health* 72 (6): 555–66.

Neu, S. and C. M. Kjellstrand. 1986. Stopping long-term dialysis: An empirical study of withdrawal of life-supporting treatment. *New England Journal of Medicine* 314: 14–20.

Parsons, T. 1951. *The Social System.* Glencoe, IL: The Free Press.

———1975. The sick role and the role of the physician reconsidered. *Health and Society.* Summer: 257–78.

President's Commission for the Study of Ethical Problems in Medicine and Biomedical and Behavioral Research. July, 1981. *Defining Death: Medical, Legal and Ethical Issues in the Determination of Death.* Washington, DC: U.S. Government Printing Office.

Quinlan, In re, 70 NJ 10, 355 A.2d 647, *cert. denied,* 429 U.S. 922 (1976).

Rubenstein, R.L. 1975 *The Cunning of History: The Holocaust and the American Future.* New York: Harper and Row.

Star, S.L. 1988. Introduction: The sociology of science and technology. *Social Problems* (Special Issue) 35 (3): 197–205.

13

Physicians, Patients, and Life-Sustaining Medical Procedures: Results and Implications for Death Counseling

Norman A. Dolch, Russell W. Roberts,
and Luella DeFreze Sibley

Louisiana law (1984) protects the rights of patients to refuse life-sustaining medical procedures and includes provisions for the withholding and withdrawal of treatment. The law states that if a patient has a terminal and incurable illness, the patient may refuse medical treatment which would prolong the dying process. To protect the patient who is unable to communicate, such as the patient in a coma, the law provides for a document that the patient may sign, which in the event the patient cannot communicate her or his wishes, will give the patient's physician the authority to withhold life sustaining treatment such as a respirator. The law allows a patient to die from the natural course of a disease rather than be kept alive by unwanted treatment. By signing a living will, the patient is provided by law with a way of irrevocably expressing treatment wishes when comatose or otherwise unable to communicate. If there is no living will, the law provides that certain other people, such as a spouse or siblings, can decide about life-sustaining treatment.

This law encourages Louisiana physicians to discuss such treatment with their patients because it specifically recognizes the right of a competent adult to make an oral or written declaration to a physician. While laws often indicate morally desirable behavior, the behavior may not occur, especially if it is recommended, rather than required. The research that follows is based on a survey of patient reports about their physicians' behavior regarding information about the law. Did they learn about it from a physician? Do they want to know more about it? What do they feel are a physician's obligations in this regard? How would they want a physician to respond to a terminal illness? What difference does physician personality make regarding patients receiving information about the law?

THEORETICAL RELEVANCE

The theoretical relevance of this study is three-fold. First, it includes age stratification theory because the three age categories of 25-44 years, 45-64 years, and 65 years plus are examined. A second point of theoretical relevancy is the literature on the doctor-patient relationship. Third, it examines aspects of closed versus open systems of awareness.

Age Stratification

Age stratification theory (Riley, Johnson, and Forner, 1972) has three distinct characteristics: 1) grouping individuals together on the basis of chronological age; 2) examining how each chronological age stratum differs from others in terms of physical, social, or psychological factors; and 3) looking for the patterning and distribution of social roles. There is increasing interest in social and psychological differences at various stages of adult life, including responses toward death. Schaie and Willis (1986) indicate that some people are concerned about death from an early age, while others may move into old age continuing their one-day-at-a-time approach to life. It is a view largely supported by Schneidman (1978) in a national survey of attitudes toward death. Schneidman found that there seemed to be no age trends regarding thoughts about death. The average respondent was said to think about death only occasionally. Respondents in the 25-29 age group were more fearful than other age groups, and Schneidman suggests that this may be due to persons beginning to recognize their own mortality at about this time in their lives.

Kalish and Reynolds (1976) point out that younger people admit to greater fear of death, but older people think about death more often. In reflecting on this difference, both Kalish (1977), and Schaie and Willis (1984), point out that young persons feel they have their whole lives ahead of them, while older people have more daily reminders of mortality. Cutter (1974) agrees with this reasoning when he says that young people hardly ever think of health, and issues of life and death, because for the most part they are well. Cutter points out that after 40, even the healthy are aware of the temporality of physical well-being.

Recent research by Gesser, Wong, and Recker (1987/1988) showed that the elderly were significantly less afraid of death than middle-aged persons, but not less afraid than the young. The relatively high levels of death and dying anxiety among the young are attributed to the fact that the young have more to lose because they have so much life left to be lived. As indicated by Kastenbaum and Aisenberg (1972), fear and concern about death is probably not a simple correlate of age because there are many factors related to age cohorts such as educational level. Fear and concern about death are one set of considerations; but counseling about a law, awareness of a law's existence, and preferences for physician responses make up another set of considerations that may or may not vary by age cohort.

Doctor-Patient Relationship

As regards the doctor-patient relationship, some writers, like Parsons (1951), view patients as passively acquiescing to professional authority, while others, such as Freidson (1970), view patients as evaluating and making demands on professionals. There is empirical support for Freidson's concepts (Maykovich: 1980) and this study is further support, as it examines the types of responses patients in various age groups desire from their physicians regarding life-sustaining treatment and a terminal illness.

Closed vs. Open Awareness Systems

A third and final point of theoretical relevancy for this study is found in the closed and open awareness systems of Glaser and Strauss (1964). An open awareness system occurs when each interactant is aware of the other's true identity, and his or her own identity in the eyes of the other, and a closed system occurs when one does not know either the other's identity, or the other's view of his or her identity. Closed awareness systems may surround dying patients because physicians often are supported in withholding information by professional rationales such as not destroying a patient's hope. Physicians and other health professionals often talk to dying and terminally ill patients as if they were going to live. Do patients, whether terminally ill or healthy, want information about the right to refuse life-sustaining medical treatment? Do patients want an open awareness context in their interactions with physicians regarding life-sustaining treatment in a response to terminal disease? Keeping in mind these questions, and the questions posed previously regarding age stratification and the physician-patient relationship, the discussion can now turn to methodological considerations.

METHODOLOGY

The sample consisted of 30 patients in each of three separate categories based on age. Young adults, age 25 to 44 years, composed one group, while middle-agers between 45 years and 64 years composed the second group. A third group comprised those persons 65 years or older. These respondents were out-patients of the Comprehensive Care Clinic at Louisiana State University Medical School in Shreveport. An additional group interviewed were nursing home residents

65 years of age or older. Since there were very few males in the sample for any of the age groups, male respondents were dropped from the analysis.

The questionnaire asked patients to report about their physicians' behavior regarding information about the law, such as whether they learned about it from a physician. If they felt that physicians were obligated to tell patients about living wills, then they also were asked how they would want to be informed. Other areas of inquiry included the physician's obligation to tell patients that they may refuse life-sustaining treatment, and whether patients would want to know that they had a terminal disease. A semantic differential of nine adjective phrases was developed to describe the patient's physician so that the role of physician personality, and ability to relate to patients, could be examined for the impact on physician responsiveness and patient desires regarding certain aspects of the law. The adverb pairings were pleasant-unpleasant, active-passive, sharp-dull, rough-smooth, deep-shallow, happy-sad, helpful-unhelpful, interesting-boring, excitable-calm. These formed a physician personality index (see Babbie, 1989:335–361).

ANALYSIS

When respondents were divided into two categories, those who were aware of the law, and those who were not, two questions were significant using a one-way ANOVA. If patients responding to the questionnaire were aware of the law, they were asked if they had learned about the law from their physicians; and all but one said that they had. They also indicated that they wanted to learn more about it. Those who knew about the law and wanted to learn more about it had a mean score of $x = 1.942$ ($N = 52$) compared to a mean response of $x = 1.735$ ($N = 34$) for those who did not ($SS = .881011$, $F = 7.84$, $P = .0064$). Awareness of the law did not influence any of the other responses given, and is not considered an important control variable for the analysis.

Patients were asked whether or not they had a terminal illness at the time the questionnaire was administered. This was considered to be another, possibly important, control variable. There were no significant differences in responses to any of the questions using a one-way ANOVA, including the physician personality index, when accounting for patients who were terminally ill. There was no influence of terminal illness on the responses given.

Table 1 shows a one-way analysis of variance for questions regarding life-sustaining medical procedures and the age groupings of 25–44 years, 45–64 years, and 65 plus years, which correspond to young, middle, and late adulthood. Two significant relationships are reported. There is a significant difference between the age groups regarding whether they would be treated the way that they wanted to be treated if they had a terminal illness and were unable to communicate their wishes ($SS = 1.34$, $F = 3.15$, and $P = .048$). A Duncan analysis of the means for the age groups (df = 82, MSE = .212) indicates that the difference is between young adults (25-44 years) and the other two categories, of middle-aged adults (45-64 years) and older adults (65 years plus). Young adults feel less likely to be treated the way that they wanted. There also was a significant difference between age categories for the physician personality index (SS = 303.108, F = 3.19, P = .04). Older adults are significantly different from the other two age categories, according to a Duncan analysis (df = 83, MSE = 47.543).

Opinions and awareness of life-sustaining medical procedures and the law are reported in Table 2 for persons 65 years plus, differentiated on the basis of whether or not they reside in a nursing home. In addition to the physician personality index, two items are significantly different. Persons 65 years plus in nursing homes (x = 2.0) wanted to know more about the Louisiana law than those 65 years plus (x = 1.72) who were not in nursing homes (SS = .809, F = 9.17, P = .004). The nursing home residents also wanted to discuss medical care to be given in the future should they be unable to speak (SS = .796, F = 4.82, P = .033). Those 65 years plus and in a nursing home (x = 1.88) wanted to do this more than those 65 years plus and not in a nursing home. The physician personality index also was significant between the two groups (SS = 87.98, F = 4.12, P = .048). Persons 65 plus and in nursing homes had a more positive rating for their physician (x = 61.65) than those not in nursing homes (x = 58.78).

DISCUSSION

Patients think it is a physician's obligation to tell them that they may refuse life-sustaining treatment, as indicated by the means in each age category being substantially greater than one with a range of 1.69 to 1.84. Interestingly, patients also thought it was a physician's obligation to tell patients about living wills and to provide living will documents for patients.

If patients had a terminal disease, the survey results also indicated that they would want their physician to do the following: 1) explain how the disease would be expected to kill them; 2) tell them when the disease would be expected to kill them; 3) explain all the treatment possibilities; and 4) discuss the medical care to be given in the future if they were unable to communicate. Also, they believe that if they have a terminal illness, and are unable to communicate their wishes, they will be treated the way that they wanted. This is especially true of middle-aged (45-64 years) and older persons (65 years plus).

Just as age categories had little influence on the results, it mattered little whether someone 65 years plus (in older adulthood) was in a nursing home or not. Whether it came to wanting knowledge about the law, feeling that doctors

Table 1

One-Way Analysis of Variance (ANOVA) for questions regarding life-sustaining medical procedures and age groupings.

	Age Groupings:					
	25–44	45–64	65+	SS	F	P
			Means			
	n=32	n=28	n=26			
1. Did you learn about the law from a doctor?	1.13	1.00	1.00	.152	.65	ns
2. Do you want to know more about it?	1.81	1.79	2.00	.716	3.06	ns
3. Do you think it is a doctor's obligation to tell patients that they may refuse life-sustaining treatment?	1.81	1.75	1.65	.362	.94	ns
4. Do you think it is a doctor's obligation to tell patients about living wills?	1.84	1.86	1.69	.454	1.43	ns
5. Should doctors provide living will documents for patients who want to refuse life-sustaining treatment?	1.81	1.75	1.53	1.146	2.87	ns
6. If you had/have a terminal disease, would you want a doctor to explain how the disease would be expected to kill you?	1.93	1.71	1.80	.756	2.70	ns
7. If you had/have a terminal disease, would you want to know when your disease would be expected to kill you?	1.81	1.65	1.60	.701	1.67	ns
8. If you had/have a terminal disease, would you want a doctor to explain all the treatment possibilities?	2.00	1.92	1.88	.198	1.82	ns
9. Would you want to discuss with a doctor the medical care to be given if, in the future, you should become unable to communicate your wishes?	2.00	1.92	1.88	.198	1.82	ns
10. If you had/have a terminal illness and you became unable to communicate your wishes today, do you think you would be treated the way you wanted?	1.53	1.67	1.84	1.34	3.15	.048
Physician Personality Index	57.53	57.61	61.65	303.108	3.19	.04

Table 2

One-Way Analysis of Variance (ANOVA) for questions regarding life-sustaining medical procedures and the 65-year-plus group who are in nursing homes and not in nursing homes.

| | 65 years plus | | | | |
	nursing home	non-nursing home	SS	F	P
1. Did you learn about the law from a doctor?	1.0	1.20	.177	.79	ns
2. Do you want to know more about it?	2.0	1.72	.807	9.17	.004
3. Do you think it is a doctor's obligation to tell patients that they may refuse life-sustaining treatment?	1.65	1.82	.296	1.45	ns
4. Do you think it is a doctor's obligation to tell patients about living wills?	1.69	1.65	.021	.09	ns
5. Should doctors provide living will documents for patients who want to refuse life-sustaining treatment?	1.54	1.61	.056	.22	ns
6. If you had/have a terminal disease, would you want a doctor to explain how the disease would be expected to kill you?	1.80	1.61	.411	2.08	ns
7. If you had/have a terminal disease, would you want to know when your disease would be expected to kill you?	1.65	1.39	.747	3.09	ns
8. If you had/have a terminal disease, would you want a doctor to explain all the treatment possibilities?	1.88	1.72	.280	1.88	ns
9. Would you want to discuss with a doctor the medical care to be given if, in the future, you should become unable to communicate your wishes?	1.88	1.61	.796	4.82	.033
10. If you had/have a terminal illness and you became unable to communicate your wishes today, do you think you would be treated the way you wanted?	1.84	1.76	.257	.36	ns
Physician Personality Index	61.65	58.78	87.98	4.12	.048

had an obligation to tell patients about refusing life-sustaining treatment, or opinions about terminal illness, place of residency did not matter.

Patients want physicians to give them more information about these matters. In regard to the doctor-patient relationship, the results support Freidson's view (1970) of patients evaluating and making demands on physicians. Regardless of their age group, patients desired their physicians to share information with them about terminating life-sustaining treatment and having a terminal illness. Patients desire open awareness systems rather than closed awareness systems.

Physicians scored high on the personality index with mean scores ranging from 57.53 to 61.65 out of a possible 63 points. That there were third and fourth year student physicians in the Comprehensive Care Clinic speaks well for their training. With this positive outlook, as indicated by the physician personality index, patients will respond to physicians.

RECOMMENDATIONS

Several recommendations emerge from the data and other considerations also come to mind which could be incorporated into a medical practice to deal with issues of life-sustaining medical treatment. The survey itself suggests: a) telling people about living wills; b) telling people about terminal diseases and treatment possibilities; and c) discussing medical care to be given when patients are unable to communicate their wishes.

Physician Death Anxieties

To talk to their patients about issues of death and dying, physicians must first face their own mortality and death so that emotions of fear, shock, and horror are not transmitted to their patients (Barrow, 1986). It is a point also made by Kubler-Ross (1969:12), who advocates that physicians make an all-out effort to contemplate their own deaths, and to deal with their anxieties about death. A physician who is still dealing with grief issues surrounding someone in his or her personal life is not going to be very responsive to patients regarding death. To talk about living wills, organ donation, and life-sustaining medical procedures, physicians should first formulate their own views on these subjects (Kinzel, 1988). Since psychotherapeutic techniques can assist in clarifying personal thinking about such matters, physicians would be well advised to seek professional consultation to be sure that they are fully prepared to respond to their patients and assist them in viewing death as a life event.

Physician-Patient Decision Making

We suggest that physicians always be cognizant of their role, and the role of the patient, in the decision-making process regarding current or future terminal illness. Wanzer, et al. (1984) and Rouse (1988) provide some guiding thoughts in this regard, as well as concerning improved communication with patients. They point out that perfect mechanisms are lacking, but that a written statement prepared in advance (e.g., the living will) can be helpful to a physician with respect to patient preference. Patients also might indicate a proxy, and this person could be given power of attorney. In terms of the physicians' role, physicians must not let their personal values and unconscious motivations influence their responses. If the physician is not an expert on a particular disease, then he or she should consult with experts. Physicians cannot ignore legal constraints, liability concerns, and the fact that there are monetary considerations regarding life-sustaining treatment.

Using Pamphlets

Regardless of whether physicians feel personally comfortable discussing issues of death and dying, a practical method to deal with issues of life-sustaining medical treatment is the use of pamphlets on the state law placed in the waiting area; or better yet, handed to patients in the examining room as something that the physician wants patients to know. Pamphlets explaining living wills also could be made available, and the survey clearly indicated that sample forms of living wills should be available, too. Having more in-depth material, or a reading list of resources available at the local library, is another possibility. Pamphlets and more detailed booklets are available from the Society for the Right to Die, 250 West 57 Street, New York, NY 10107.

Legal Advice

From the local bar association, a practitioner could obtain a list of attorneys who will take referrals about legal questions. Also, physicians can make available information pamphlets on various types of terminal illnesses, which can be obtained from groups like the American Cancer Society.

Support Groups

For those who might benefit from or request it, a physician should be able to put patients in contact with support groups for terminal illnesses and other types of medical conditions. For those who need more help dealing with issues than the physician can give, a list of board-certified social workers, certified clinical sociologists, licensed psychologists, psychiatrists, and ministers should be developed for referral, with special attention paid to particular expertise like grief counseling.

Other Professionals

Referral of patients to other professionals for counseling, such as clinical sociologists or social workers, is indicated when any one of several conditions exist

(Kinzel, 1988). If a patient has great difficulty with, or a total lack of willingness to talk about, issues of death and the use of life-sustaining medical procedures, then referral might help. Patients with unresolved grief issues certainly will benefit from referral. A patient might benefit from referral if she or he has extreme difficulty talking with other family members because of feelings like anger or fear or some family life situation. Sometimes a patient will have rational ideas which conflict with religious beliefs. Obviously, this list of reasons for referral is not exhaustive. Physicians who refer patients who might benefit from counseling are less likely to do harm than those who don't.

A few comments seem appropriate at this point regarding patients who have terminal illnesses. Regardless of their age, terminally ill patients in our sample expected their physicians to answer their questions and talk with them about treatment modalities and their wishes. Quality death refers to those patients who accept the fact of their own death and find a sense of peace and strength to see them through this final life experience. Physicians need to remember that they are enablers in this process and that referral resources are available.

CONCLUSION

Issues such as life-sustaining medical practices are apt to remain controversial, according to Atchley (1988), because our society, as yet, has no clear-cut, moral ethic that dying persons, their families, or physicians can fall back on. The research reported is from a survey of female clinic and nursing home patients from different age groups, their desires regarding information on Louisiana's law, and their physicians' responses to life-sustaining medical procedures. Regardless of the patients' ages, they wanted information about the law and felt that their physicians should give them information on it as well as on any terminal disease they had. In examining persons 65 years of age and older who were in nursing homes compared to those not in nursing homes, there was not much difference in the results. Nor was there much difference between the young (24–44 years), middle-aged (44–65 years), and older, non-nursing home adults (65 years plus). The fact that physicians are perceived very positively by all age groups means that they are in a good position to assist patients to determine and express their wishes regarding life-sustaining procedures. Practical measures were suggested for doing this, such as providing patients with pamphlets to read. The roles of physician and patient in decision-making were examined. Finally, physicians were seen as enablers, who could help their patients make decisions regarding their lives and the use of life-sustaining medical procedures, a point that any person who deals with issues of death and dying should know about, and that seems to be consistent with Louisiana's law.

REFERENCES

Atchley, R. C. 1988. *Social Forces and Aging: An Introduction to Social Gerontology*, 5th ed. Belmont, CA: Wadsworth Publishing Company, 221–38.

Babbie, E. B. 1989. *The Practice of Social Research*. Belmont, CA: Wadsworth Publishing Company, 389–403.

Barrow, G. M. 1986. *Aging, the Individual and Society*, 3rd ed. New York: West Publishing Company, 363–87.

Cutter, F. 1974. *Coming to Terms with Death: How to Face the Inevitable with Wisdom and Dignity*. Chicago: Nelson-Hall Company, 103–22.

Freidson, E. 1970. *Professional Dominance: The Social Structure of Medical Care*. New York: Atherton Press.

Gesser, G., P. T. P. Wong, and G. T. Recker. 1987/1988. Death attitudes across the life-span: The development and validation of the death attitude profile (DAP). *Omega* 18:113–28.

Glaser, B. G. and A. L. Strauss. 1964. Awareness contexts and social interaction. *American Sociological Review* 29:669–79.

Kalish, R. A. 1977. *The Psychology of Human Behavior*, 4th ed. Monterey, CA: Brooks/Cole Publishing Company, 280–82.

Kastenbaum, R. and R. Aisenberg. 1972. *The Psychology of Death*. New York: Springer Publishing Company, 40–112.

Kinzel, T. 1988. Relief of emotional symptoms in elderly patients with terminal cancer. *Geriatrics* 43:61–68.

Kubler-Ross, E. 1969. *On Death and Dying*. New York: Macmillan, 1–121.

Louisiana. Act No. 382, Senate Bill No. 271, 1984, Regular Session.

Maykovich, M. K. 1980. *Medical Sociology*. New York: Alfred Publishing 135–77.

Parsons, T. 1951. *The Social System*. Glencoe, IL: Free Press.

Riley, M. W., M. Johnson, and A. Forner. 1971. A sociology of age stratification. In Vol. 3 of *Aging and Society*. New York: Basic Books.

Rouse, F. 1988. Legal and ethical guidelines for physicians in geriatric terminal care. *Geriatrics* 43:69–75.

Schaie, K. W. and S. L. Willis. 1986. *Adult Development and Aging*, 2nd ed. Boston: Little, Brown, 470–81.

Schneidman, E. S. 1978. National survey of attitudes toward death. In R. Fulton, E. Markusen, G. Owen, and J. L. Scheiber, eds. *Death and Dying: Challenge and Change*. Reading, MA: Addison- Wesley, pp. 23–33.

Wanzer, S. H., et al. 1984. The physicians responsibility toward hopelessly ill patients. *The New England Journal of Medicine* 310: 955–59.

14

The Interrelatedness of Loss and Pathological Grief in The Elderly Population

Elizabeth J. Clark

The percentage of aged persons in the population has increased dramatically since 1900. At the turn of the century, there were three million persons over age 65; today there over 29 million, one-third of whom are over age 75 (Fowles, 1987). In 1900, life expectancy was 47 years. Today it is extended beyond 70.

The increasing longevity of Americans has helped to foster a growing interest among social and medical scientists in the biological and behavioral aspects of the aging process, and the social role of the elderly person (Butler and Lewis, 1982; Cox, 1984; Peterson and Quadagno, 1985). However, despite the impetus that geriatrics and gerontology have received, they still lag behind the study and care of other age groups. Research specific to aging is needed to understand the concerns and problems of this age group, to serve as a predictive model of the behavior that accompanies old age, and as a basis for implications for current and future social policy.

One example of empirical work that needs to be broadened to include the aged is the field of thanatology. Although much attention currently is being devoted to death-related subjects, the interest has been predominantly with the younger segments of the population, with those persons over age 65 excluded from the research. This exclusion usually is justified on the basis of attenuation of response—a belief that the elderly cannot respond accurately. An implied reason, however, appears to be that loss and grief in later life are viewed as normal and expected, and, therefore, not as problems of major concern. As a result, little actually is known about how the elderly view death, how they adapt to various losses, the coping mechanisms they use, and the special death-related problems they encounter and must overcome.

THE AGE FACTOR AND LOSS AND GRIEF

Loss is a constant factor in the lives of the aging. The longer a person lives, the more personal losses he or she experiences. For the elderly, many losses may accumulate suddenly, be in rapid succession, or occur with frequent repetitions. (Goodstein, 1984).

There are four general categories of loss (Peretz, 1970:5): 1) loss of a significant loved one; 2) loss of some aspect of self; 3) loss of external objects; and 4) developmental loss. An elderly person may have to face several types of loss at the same time. For example, an older woman who becomes widowed (loss of a loved one), loses her social role as wife (loss of an aspect of self), and may no longer be able to maintain her home financially (loss of an external object).

THE "NORMAL" GRIEF RESPONSE OF THE ELDERLY

Bereavement is the total response to loss. *Grief* includes the subjective feelings—the intense emotions and physical symptoms—caused by the loss. *Mourning* is the process of grieving, of expressing grief.

Beginning with Lindemann's classic study in 1944, the characteristics of normal grief have been well documented (for example, see Bowlby, 1961 and 1980; Parkes, 1972; Schoenberg, et al., 1970). It now is agreed that grief is a process, not a solitary event, and that the intense mourning process usually lasts from 6 to 48 months (Goodstein, 1984). In addition, there is a symptomatology of grief which is common to the normal grieving process. It includes the following clinical symptoms (Carr, 1985: 1286):

1. Denial
2. Sighing and crying
3. Feelings of weakness
4. Decreased appetite
5. Weight loss
6. Difficulty concentrating
7. Difficulty breathing and talking
8. Sleep disturbances
9. Preoccupation with thoughts of the deceased
10. Sense of the presence of the deceased
11. Identification with the deceased
12. Withdrawal of interest in the outside world
13. Expressions of anger
14. Self-reproach

This "normal" pattern of grief appears to be altered for the elderly. Goodstein (1984:1) notes that the manifestations of mourning in elderly persons often follow "devious patterns of grief," and "may appear to be physical ailments, anxiety syndromes, and even senile dementia." Kozma and Stones summarize the differences between elderly grief and "normal" grief in the following ways (1980: 230):

1. Old people may express grief more through somatic problems than through psychological difficulties.
2. There is no evidence that intensity of grief varies significantly with age.
3. Available evidence, although meager, suggests that grief may be more prolonged in older people than in their younger cohorts.
4. Older bereaved are lonelier than either younger bereaved or older married persons far into the postbereavement period.

The uncharacteristic patterns of grief in the elderly may mask the significance of the loss, the existence of the grief, and the implications for appropriate intervention.

Despite a disproportionate number of losses experienced by those in older age categories, research efforts regarding the grief response of the elderly have been few and inconclusive. Old age is generally a time of diminishment, which may include diminished health, diminished income, diminished social support, diminished resources, and diminished self-esteem. Taken together, these factors may precipitate an abnormal or pathological mourning experience for the elderly person.

PATHOLOGICAL GRIEF REACTIONS IN THE ELDERLY

There are four basic tasks which a grieving individual must accomplish if mourning is to be completed. These are (Worden, 1982: 11–16):

1. To accept the reality of the loss;
2. To experience the pain of the grief;
3. To adjust to an environment in which the deceased is missing; and
4. To withdraw emotional energy and reinvest it in another relationship.

Incomplete grief tasks can impair growth and further development. Carr (1985) notes that if not resolved, grief can develop into depression or pathological mourning. In any age group, abnormal grief may appear in various forms, and it is given numerous labels, such as pathological grief, unresolved grief, complicated grief, delayed grief, exaggerated grief, or complicated bereavement

(Worden, 1982: 5-8). In addition, there are many problems which may be manifestations of unresolved grief. Depressive disorders, alcohol abuse, and suicide are some of the most serious consequences of loss in the elderly, and are frequently interrelated.

DEPRESSIVE DISORDERS AND THE ELDERLY BEREAVED

Depression is the primary mental disorder of the aged. A study by Kay and Bergmann (1980) found that 4 percent of the men and 11 percent of women over age 60 manifest depression of at least moderate severity. The symptoms of depression may be apparent or hidden. Common indicators of the presence of depression include (Butler and Lewis, 1980: 70): feelings of helplessness, sadness, lack of vitality, frequent feelings of guilt, loneliness, boredom, constipation, sexual disinterest, impotence, insomnia, early morning fatigue, marked loss of appetite, hypochondriasis, somatic symptoms, and sleep disturbances.

Both research and clinical experience stress the role of loss as a psychosocial correlate to depression. Reactive depressive symptoms are expected to be present in the normal grief process, but some persons seem to become "stuck" in the depressive, withdrawal stage of the grieving sequence (Martin, 1981). Since persons who have experienced previous depressive episodes are more likely to experience major depression, rather than normal grief, at the time of loss, evaluating the individual's past clinical history may be helpful in judging the current reaction (Carr, 1985).

Adult grief and its expression are complicated by cultural influences and societal expectations, and the elderly appear to be particularly vulnerable to these constraints. Butler and Lewis (1982) note that older persons in the United States today do not receive the necessary cultural support for grief and mourning, and that lack of this support can prolong depression and leave grief unresolved. This may, in turn, contribute to maladaptive behaviors, such as alcoholism and suicide in the elderly bereaved.

ALCOHOLISM AND THE ELDERLY

Alcoholism and suicide in later life have not been adequately studied by gerontologists and social scientists (Cox, 1984). Snyder and Way (1979) have pointed out that older Americans are less likely to drink than younger Americans, and are more likely to be moderate rather than heavy drinkers. But they also list the major causes of alcoholism in the elderly as follows: loneliness, retirement (with a loss of self worth), and recreational activities which encourage drinking.

Zimberg (1974) has identified two types of older alcoholics: those for whom alcoholism has been a lifelong pattern, and those for whom alcoholism appears to be a reaction to the stresses of aging. For many of the elderly, one of the stresses which accompanies the aging process is conjugal bereavement, and several researchers (Bailey, Haberman, and Alkne, 1965; Butler and Lewis, 1982) have found that elderly widowers have the highest rate of alcoholism of all age groups.

Alcohol abuse and suicide often go hand in hand. Clinicians have noted a high prevalence of alcohol abuse by persons attempting suicide in every age group. Boekelheide (1978) notes that approximately 25 percent of all persons who commit suicide have alcoholism. It also has been noted that there is an increase in alcohol abuse among the suicidal elderly (Kahne, et al., 1973). Alcohol is a depressant and, therefore, can increase depressive symptoms. With regard to suicide, the risk factor of alcoholism may interact with other risk factors. Murphey, et al., (1979) found that in a study of 50 random cases of suicide where alcoholism was a risk factor, 26 percent of the sample had experienced the loss of a close personal relationship within six weeks of their death. There were 24 subjects in the study who were over 55 years of age.

GERIATRIC SUICIDE

Miller (1979) estimates that at least 10,000 people 60 and older commit suicide in our country each year. There is a disparity between male and female suicide rates at all ages, but the differences become more pronounced in later life. Aged women do not have a disproportionately high rate of suicide. Suicides for women peak during middle age (50–54), not old age (Barrow, 1986). Females 65 and over have a suicide rate of 6.1/100,000, significantly lower than the national average of 12/100,000. In contrast, the high suicide rate for older men in our country is a critical problem. Males aged 65–74 have a suicide rate of 28.4 those aged 75–84 have a rate of 41.4 and the rate for men 85 and over increases dramatically to 50.2/100,000 (Statistical Abstracts, 1985).

There is currently no satisfactory explanation for why suicide is much more prevalent among older men than women. It is recognized that many of the factors that influence suicide in general are experiences typical of aging, such as loss of a loved one and physical illness.

Stenback (1980) summarized a number of studies which attempt to explain why the elderly commit suicide and found that depression was a major factor. Yet, depression, the mental state most frequently associated with suicide in old age, is at least as common among women as among men (Miller, 1979). McConnell (1982) links suicide in elderly men to widowhood and its resultant social isolation and loneliness. She argues that the absence of a cohesive support network during the postbereavement period is likely a contributing factor to the high suicide rate for elderly men. Most researchers concur that the widowed population is at considerable risk for suicide, but there is debate as to whether the death of the spouse is sufficient cause. Miller (1979) claims that no one factor is in itself suicidogenic, but sees a clustering of vital losses, often occurring in close temporal proximity and decreasing the individual's ability to cope, as increasing the likelihood of geriatric suicide. Vital losses related to suicide in the elderly fall into five broad categories (Miller, 1979: 7):

1. Economic (loss of a job or income);
2. Physical (loss of a limb or good health);
3. Social (loss of a best friend or a cherished neighborhood);
4. Psychological (loss of self-esteem or confidence); and
5. Emotional (loss of a spouse or child).

Still, only a small minority of older people who experience multiple losses commit suicide. Others may turn to less obvious forms of life-threatening behavior. According to Butler and Lewis (1982), suicide may be "subintentional" or passive. It may be a long-term process of "suicidal erosion" or chronic suicide which may include not eating, not taking medicines, delaying treatment, taking physical risks, or drinking too much. Passive suicide is frequently related to depression and giving up the will to live.

Suicide may not be the only consequence of psychologically giving up on life. Studies suggest that if a person responds to life with hopelessness, depression, and submission, a biological change that encourages the development of an existing disease potential may be triggered and result in the onset of physical illness (Butler and Lewis, 1982; Carr, 1985). This loss of health may constitute a vital loss and may perpetuate the loss-depression-illness cycle.

Butler and Lewis (1982) maintain that the depression-based suicidal tendency is perhaps the most treatable cause of suicide, yet there has been little attention to appropriate clinical intervention for elderly persons who may have suicidal tendencies. Despite tragic consequences, geriatric suicide has gone relatively unnoted in our society, intervention programs, and research.

Suicide is a complex behavior which is difficult to predict and prevent, but that has not stopped health care professionals from marshalling resources to deal with the increasing adolescent suicide problem. This is another example of our country's valuing youth and devaluing the aged, a form of age discrimination based on stereotypical thinking that only youth have great potential, and that the elderly already have lived their productive years. Health care in an aging society involves an array of issues, such as cost-effectiveness, allocation of scarce resources, and priorities for the delivery of services and basic research (Callahan, 1986). A major challenge for future policymakers will be how to strike an appropriate balance between care for the aging and health care for the rest of the population (Fuchs, 1984).

IMPLICATIONS FOR CLINICAL INTERVENTION

What strategies for intervention can be developed by gerontologists and related clinicians to address these serious concerns about the treatment of, and provision of services for, our elderly population? First, we must overcome our own stereotypical thinking. We must reexamine our thoughts about when an individual becomes old, what that really means, and what the elderly can and do contribute to society. Next, we must be more conscientious about including elderly subjects in our research. It is no longer acceptable to exclude subjects over the age of 60 from our research designs, and yet assume that our findings are relevant to these older age groups. We need a better understanding of the elderly with respect to death-related subjects, and we need more research specifically directed toward this goal. What are the elderly's thoughts about loss, grief, death, and euthanasia? What can we, as a society, learn from their death-related experiences and concerns?

Next, we need to reexamine both the content and the format of our clinical interventions for the elderly who are terminally ill and bereaved. Many people in the helping professions seem to be basing their strategies on incomplete or outdated theories about loss and grief in the elderly population. We must understand the differences between, and the different needs of, young and old widows, older widows and widowers, and those persons who are chronically and terminally ill. We must recognize, and sanction, the grief process of the elderly, and must develop programs which will facilitate their adaptation to loss and prevent pathological mourning. The interrelatedness of loss, depression, alcoholism, and geriatric suicide has to be further explored and addressed.

We also must evaluate the social context of the thanatologic experience for the elderly. What resources are available to help meet these challenges, and what resources need to be developed? Litwak (1985) emphasizes the complementary roles of informal networks and formal systems when designing interventions for the elderly. The informal network includes family, neighbors, friends, and community organizations like churches, and augments the formal systems of health care and service delivery. Interrelated services and services that encompass death-related problems frequently are lacking because these areas consistently receive low priority.

Last, but certainly not least, is the need for advocacy, based on research and clinical intervention specific to the elderly population. This may include such actions as obtaining community support and funding for an elderly widowers' support group, or lobbying for research dollars for geriatric issues. Such advocacy also means being aware of, and contributing to, pending legislation at state and local levels that affects on the psychosocial well-being of our elderly.

Age discrimination has long been of interest to gerontologists, yet seldom have we linked ageism with lack of concern about death-related issues and the elderly. Geriatric thanatology, just by virtue of the growing number of elderly in our country, will demand more attention in the future. As health care and service providers, we must move quickly to eliminate existing deficits, and to develop positive approaches for intervention on various levels. Only when these goals are met will geriatric thanatology be elevated to the same level as thanatology for other age groups.

REFERENCES

Bailey, M., P. Haberman and H. Alksne. 1965. The epidemiology of alcoholism in an urban residential area. *Quarterly Journal Studies of Alcohol* 26:13.

Barrow, G. 1986. *Aging, the Individual and Society*. 3rd ed. St. Paul, MI: West Publishing Company.

Boekelheide, P.D. 1978. Evaluation of suicide risk. *American Family Practitioner* 18(6): 109–13.

Bowlby, J. 1980. *Attachment and Loss III: Sadness and Depression*. New York: Basic Books.

—— 1961. Process of mourning. *International Journal of Psychoanalysis* 42:317–40.

Butler, R. and M. Lewis 1982. *Aging and Mental Health*. St. Louis, MO: C.V. Mosby Company.

Callahan, D. 1986. Health care in the aging society: A moral dilemma. In A. Pifer and L. Bronte, eds. *Our Aging Society: Paradox and Promise*. New York: Norton and Company, Inc.

Carr, A. 1985. Grief, mourning and bereavement. In H. Kaplan and B. Sadock, eds. *Comprehensive Textbook of Psychiatry IV*. Baltimore, MD: Williams and Wilkins.

Cox, H. 1984. *Later Life: The Realities of Aging*. Englewood Cliffs, NJ: Prentice-Hall

Fowles, D. 1987. *A Profile of Older Americans*. Long Island, CA: American Association of Retired Persons.

Fuchs, V. 1984. 'Though much is taken': Reflection on aging, health and medical care. *Milbank Memorial Quarterly/Health and Society* Spring: 164–65.

Goodstein, R. 1984. Grief reactions and the elderly. *Carrier Foundation Letter* #99 (June): 1–5.

Kahne, M., et al. 1973. Discussion: suicide in the aging. *Journal of Geriatric Psychiatry* 6:52.

Kay, D. and K. Bergmann 1980. Epidemiology of mental disorders among the aged in the community. In J. Birren and B. Sloan, eds. *Handbook of Mental Health and Aging*. Englewood Cliffs, NJ: Prentice-Hall.

Kozma, A. and M. Stones. 1980. Bereavement in the elderly. In B. Schoenberg, ed. *Bereavement Counseling: A Multidisciplinary Handbook*. Westport, CN: Greenwood Press.

Lindemann, E. 1944. Symptomatology and management of acute grief. *American Journal of Psychiatry* 101: 141–48.

Litwak, E. 1985. *Helping the Elderly*. New York: Guilford Press.

McConnell, K. 1982. The aged widower. *Social Work* 27(2): 188–89.

Martin, B. 1981. *Abnormal Psychology*. 2nd ed. New York: Holt, Rinehart and Winston.

Miller, Marv. 1979. *Suicide After Sixty: The Final Alternative*. New York: Springer.

Murphey, G., et al. 1979. Suicide and alcoholism: interpersonal loss confirmed as predictor. *Archives of General Psychiatry* 36:65.

Parkes, C. 1972. *Bereavement*. New York: International Universities Press.

Peretz, D. 1970. Reaction to loss. In B. Schoenberg, et al., eds. *Loss and Grief: Psychological Management in Medical Practice*. New York: Columbia Uiversity Press.

Peterson, W. and J. Quadagno 1985. *Social Bonds in Later Life: Aging and Interdependence*. Beverly Hills, CA: Sage.

Snyder, P. and A. Way 1979. Alcoholism and the elderly. *Aging* (January–February): 8–11.

Schoenberg, B., A. Carr, D. Peretz, and A. Kutscher, eds. 1970. *Loss and Grief: Psychological Management in Medical Practice*. New York: Columbia University Press.

Statistical Abstracts. 1985. 105th edition. Washington, DC: Department of Commerce, Bureau of the Census, 74.

Stenback, A. 1980. Depression and suicidal behavior in old age. In J. Birren and B. Sloan, eds. *Handbook of Mental Health and Aging*. Englewood Cliffs, NJ: Prentice-Hall.

Worden, J. 1982. *Grief Counseling and Grief Therapy*. New York: Springer.

Zimberg, S. 1974. The elderly alcoholic. *The Gerontologist* 14: 221–24.

15

Ethical Standards of Sociological Practitioners

Sociological Practice Association

PREAMBLE

Clinical and applied sociologists respect the dignity and worth of the individual and honor the preservation and protection of fundamental human rights. They are committed to increasing knowledge of human behavior and of peoples' understanding of themselves and others and to the utilization of such knowledge for the promotion of human welfare. While pursuing these endeavors, they make every effort to protect the welfare of those who seek their services or of any human group, or animal(s) that may be the object of study. They use their skills only for purposes consistent with these values and do not knowingly permit their misuse by others. While demanding for themselves freedom of inquiry and communication, clinical and applied sociologists accept the responsibility this freedom requires: competence, objectivity in the application of skills and concern for the best interests of clients, colleagues, and society in general. In the pursuit of these ideals, clinical and applied sociologists subscribe to the following principles: 1) Responsibility, 2) Competence, 3) Moral and Legal Standards, 4) Public Statements, 5) Confidentiality, 6) Welfare of the Student, Client and Research Subject, and 7) Regard for Professionals and Institutions.

PRINCIPLE 1.

Responsibility

In their commitment to the understanding of human behavior, clinical and applied sociologist value objectivity and integrity, and in providing services they maintain the highest standards of their profession. They accept responsibility for the consequences of their work and make every effort to insure that their

Adopted, September, 1982; Revised, August, 1985; Revised, June, 1987; Revised, January, 1989.
1. The model for this draft is the 1977 APA approved Ethical Standards of Psychologists.

services are used appropriately. The clinical or applied sociologist is committed to avoid any act or suggestion that would support or advance racism, sexism or ageism.

a. *As scientists,* clinical and applied sociologists accept the ultimate responsibility for selecting appropriate areas and methods most relevant to these areas. They plan their research in ways to minimize the possibility that their findings will be misleading. They provide thorough discussion of the limitations of their data and alternative explanations, especially where their work touches on social policy or might be construed to the detriment of persons in specific age, sex, ethnic, socioeconomic or other social groups. In publishing reports of their work, they never suppress disconforming data. Clinical and applied sociologists take credit only for the work they have actually done.

Clinical and applied sociologists clarify in advance with all appropriate persons or agencies the expectations for sharing and utilizing research data. They avoid dual relationships which may limit objectivity, whether political or monetary, so that interference with data, human participants, and milieu is kept to a minimum.

b. *As employees* of an institution or agency, clinical and applied sociologists have the responsibility of remaining alert to and attempting to moderate institutional pressures that may distort reports of clinical or applied sociological findings or impede their proper use.

c. *As teachers,* clinical and applied sociologists recognize their primary obligation to help others acquire knowledge and skill. They maintain high standards of scholarship and objectivity by presenting information fully and accurately.

d. *As practitioners,* clinical and applied sociologists know that they bear a heavy social responsibility because their recommendations and professional actions may alter the lives of others. They are alert to personal, social, organizational, financial, or political situations or pressures that might lead to misuse of their influence.

e. *As employers or supervisors,* clinical and applied sociologists provide adequate and timely evaluations to employees, trainees, students, and others whose work they supervise.

PRINCIPLE 2.

Competence

The maintenance of high standards of professional competence is a responsibility shared by all clinical and applied sociologists in the interest of the public and the profession as a whole. Clinical and applied sociologists recognize the boundaries of their competence and the limitations of their techniques and only provide services, use techniques, or offer opinions as professionals that meet recognized standards. Clinical and applied sociologists maintain knowledge of current scientific and professional information related to the services they render.

a. *Teaching.* Clinical and applied sociologists perform their duties on the basis of careful preparation so that their instruction is accurate, current and scholarly.

b. *Professional Development.* Clinical and applied sociologists recognize the need for continuing education and are open to new procedures and changes in expectations and values over time. They recognize differences among people, such as those that may be associated with age, sex, socioeconomic, and ethnic backgrounds. Where relevant, they obtain training, experience, or counsel to assure competent services or research relating to such persons.

c. *Professional Effectiveness.* Clinical and applied sociologists recognize that their effectiveness depends in part upon their ability to maintain effective interpersonal relations, and that aberrations on their part may interfere with their abilities. They refrain from undertaking any activity in which their personal problems are likely to lead to inadequate professional services or harm to a client; or, if engaged in such activity when they become aware of their personal problems, they seek competent professional assistance to determine whether they should suspend, terminate or limit the scope of their professional and/or scientific activities.

PRINCIPLE 3.

Moral and Legal Standards

Clinical and applied sociologists' moral, ethical and legal standards of behavior are a personal matter to the same degree as they are for any other citizen, except as these may compromise the fulfillment of their professional responsibilities, or reduce the trust in clinical or applied sociology or clinical or applied sociologists held by the general public. Regarding their own behavior, clinical and applied sociologists should be aware of the prevailing community standards and of the possible impact upon the quality of professional services provided by their conformity to or deviation from these standards.

a. *As teachers,* clinical and applied sociologists are aware of the diverse backgrounds of students and, when dealing with topics that may give offense, treat the material objectively and present it in a manner for which the student is prepared.

b. *As employees,* clinical and applied sociologists refuse to participate in practices inconsistent with legal, moral and ethical standards regarding the treatment of employees or of the public. For example, clinical and applied sociologists will not condone practices that are inhumane or that result in illegal or otherwise unjustifiable discrimination on the basis of race, age, sex, religion, national origin, sexual orientation or disability in hiring, promotion or training.

c. *As practitioners,* clinical and applied sociologists avoid any action that will violate or diminish the legal and civil rights of clients or of others who may be affected by their actions.

d. *Both as practitioners and researchers,* clinical and applied sociologists remain abreast of relevant federal, state, local and agency regulations and Association standards of practice concerning the conduct of their practice or of their research. They are concerned with developing such legal and quasi-legal regulations as best serve the public interest and in changing such existing regulations as are not beneficial to the interest of the public.

PRINCIPLE 4.

Public Statements

Public statements, announcements of services, and promotional activities of clinical and applied sociologists serve the purpose of providing sufficient information to aid the consumer public in making informed judgments and choices. Clinical and applied sociologists represent accurately and completely their professional qualifications, affiliations and functions, as well as those of the institutions or organizations with which they or the statements may be associated. In public statements, providing sociological information or professional opinions or providing information about the availability of sociological products and services, clinical and applied sociologists take full account of the limits and uncertainties of present sociological knowledge and techniques.

a. *Announcement of Professional Services.* Normally, such announcements are limited to name, academic degrees, credentials, address and telephone number and, at the individual practitioner's discretion, an appropriate brief listing of the types of services offered, and fee information. Such statements are descriptive of services provided but not evaluative. They do not claim uniqueness of skills or methods unless determined by acceptable and public scientific evidence.

b. In announcing the availability of clinical or applied sociological services or products, clinical or applied sociologists do not display any affiliations with an organization in a manner that falsely implies the sponsorship or certification of that organization. In particular, and for example, clinical and applied sociologists do not offer SPA membership as evidence of qualification. They do not name their employer or professional associations unless the services are in fact to be provided by or under the responsible, direct supervision and continuing control of such organizations or agencies.

c. Announcements of training activities give a clear statement of purpose and the nature of the experiences to be provided. The education, training and experience of the clinical or applied sociologists sponsoring such activities are appropriately specified.

d. Clinical and applied sociologists associated with the development or promotion of devices, books or other products offered for commercial sale make every effort to insure that announcements and advertisements are presented in a professional, scientifically acceptable, and factually informative manner.

e. Clinical and applied sociologists do not participate as clinical or applied sociologists for personal gain in commercial announcements recommending to the general public the purchase or use of any proprietary or single-source product or service.

f. Clinical and applied sociologists who interpret the science of sociology or the services of clinical or applied sociologists to the general public accept the obligation to present the material fairly and accurately avoiding misrepresentation through sensationalism, exaggeration or superficiality. Clinical and applied sociologists are guided by the primary obligation to aid the public in forming their own informed judgments, opinions and choices.

g. As teachers, clinical and applied sociologists insure that statements in catalogs and course outlines are accurate and sufficient, particularly in terms of subject matter to be covered, bases for evaluating progress, and nature of course experiences. Announcements or brochures describing workshops, seminars, or other educational programs accurately represent intended audience and eligibility requirements, educational objectives, and nature of the material to be covered, as well as the education, training and experience of the clinical or applied sociologists presenting the programs, and when clinical services or other professional services are offered as an inducement make clear the nature of the services, as well as the costs and other obligations to be accepted by the human participants in the research.

h. Clinical and applied sociologists accept the obligation to correct others who represent the clinical and applied sociologist's professional qualifications or associations with products or services in a manner incompatible with these guidelines.

PRINCIPLE 5.

Confidentiality

Safeguarding information about an individual or group that has been obtained by the clinical or applied sociologist in the course of teaching, practice, or research, is a primary obligation of the sociologist. Such information is not communicated to others unless certain important conditions are met.

a. Information received in confidence is revealed only after most careful deliberation and when there is clear and imminent danger to an individual or to society, and then only to appropriate professional workers or public authorities.

b. Information obtained in clinical or consulting relationships, or evaluative data concerning children, students, employees, and others are discussed only for professional purposes and only with persons clearly concerned with the case. Written and oral reports present only data germane to the purposes of the evaluation and every effort is made to avoid undue invasion of privacy.

c. Confidential materials may be used in classroom teaching and writing only when the identity of the persons involved is adequately disguised.

d. The confidentiality of professional communications about individuals is maintained. Only when the originator and other persons involved give their express permission is a confidential professional communication shown to the individual concerned. The clinical or applied sociologist is responsible for informing the client of the limits of the confidentiality.

e. Where research data are being made public, the clinical or applied sociologist assumes responsibility for protecting the privacy of the subjects involved if confidentiality has been promised or called for by the nature of the research.

PRINCIPLE 6.

Welfare of the Student, Client and Research Participant

Clinical and applied sociologists respect the integrity and protect the welfare of the people and groups with whom they work. When there is a conflict of interest between the client and the clinical or applied sociologist's employing institution, clinical and applied sociologists clarify the nature and direction of their loyalties and responsibilities and keep all parties informed of their commitments. Clinical and applied sociologists inform consumers as to the purpose and nature of evaluation, treatment, educational or training procedures and they freely acknowledge that clients, students or participants in research have freedom of choice with regard to participation.

a. Clinical and applied sociologists are continually cognizant of their own needs and of their inherently powerful position vis-a-vis clients, students and research participants, in order to avoid exploiting their trust and dependency. Clinical and applied sociologists make every effort to avoid dual relationships with clients and/ or relationships which might impair their professional judgment. Examples of such dual relationships include treating employees, supervisors, close friends or relatives. Special care is taken to ensure that clients, students and research participants are not exploited in any manner, e.g., sexually, politically, economically, emotionally or socially.

b. Where demands of an organization on clinical or applied sociologists go beyond reasonable conditions of employment, clinical and applied sociologists recognize possible conflicts of interest that may arise. When such conflicts occur, clinical and applied sociologists clarify the nature of the conflict and inform all parties of the nature and direction of the loyalties and responsibilities involved.

c. When acting as a supervisor, trainer, researcher, or employer, clinical and applied sociologists accord informed choice, confidentiality, due process, and protection from physical and mental harm to their subordinates in such relationships.

d. Financial arrangements in professional practice are in accord with professional standards that safeguard the best interests of the client and that are clearly understood by the client in advance of billing. Clinical and applied sociologists are responsible for assisting clients in finding needed services in those instances where payment of the usual fee would be a hardship. No commission, rebate, or other form of remuneration may be given or received for referral of clients for professional services, whether by an individual or by an agency. Clinical and applied sociologists willingly contribute a portion of their services to work for which they receive little or no financial return.

e. The clinical or applied sociologist attempts to terminate a clinical or consulting relationship when it is reasonably clear that the consumer is not benefiting from it. Clinical and applied sociologists who find that their services are being used by employers in a way that is not beneficial to the participants or to employees who may be affected, or to significant others, have the responsibility to make their observations known to the parties involved and to propose modifications or termination of the engagement.

PRINCIPLE 7.

Relationships with Professionals and Institutions

Clinical and applied sociologists act with due regard for the needs, special competencies and obligations of their colleagues in sociology, other professions, and the institutions or organizations with which they are associated. Special care is taken to insure that colleagues are not exploited in any manner, e.g., sexually, politically, economically, emotionally or socially.

a. Clinical and applied sociologists understand the areas of competence of related professions, and make full use of all the professional, technical, and administrative resources that best serve the interest of consumers. The absence of formal relationships with other professional workers does not relieve clinical or applied sociologists from the responsibility of securing for their clients the best possible professional service, nor does it relieve them from the exercise of foresight, diligence, and tact in obtaining the complimentary or alternative assistance needed by clients.

b. Clinical and applied sociologists respect other professional groups and cooperate with members of such groups.

c. Clinical and applied sociologists who employ or supervise other professionals or professionals in training accept the obligation to facilitate their further professional development by providing suitable working conditions, consultation, and experience opportunities.

d. As employees of organizations providing clinical or applied sociological services, or as independent clinical or applied sociologists serving clients in an organizational context, clinical and applied sociologists seek to support the integrity, reputation and proprietary rights of the host organization. When it is judged necessary in a client's interest to question the organization's programs or policies, clinical and applied sociologists attempt to affect change by constructive action within the organization before disclosing confidential information acquired in their professional roles.

e. In the pursuit of research, clinical and applied sociologists give sponsoring agencies, host institutions, and publication channels the same respect and opportunity for giving informed consent that they accord to individual research participants. They are aware of their obligation to future research workers and insure that host institutions are given adequate information about the research and proper acknowledgment of their contributions.

f. Publication credit is assigned to all those who have contributed to a publication in proportion to their contributions. Major contributions of a professional character made by several persons to a common project are recognized by joint authorship, with the researcher or author who made the principle contribution identified and listed first. Minor contributions of a professional character, extensive clerical or similar nonprofessional assistance, and other minor contributions are acknowledged in footnotes or in an introductory statement. Acknowledgment through specific citations is made for unpublished, as well as published material that has directly influenced the research or writing. A clinical or applied sociologist who compiles and edits material of others for publication publishes the material in the name of the originating group, if any, and with his/her own name appearing as chairperson or editor. All contributions are to be acknowledged and named.

VIOLATIONS:

Procedures Governing Alleged Violations of Ethical Standards

When a clinical or applied sociologist, who is a member of the Sociological Practice Association, violates ethical standards, clinical and applied sociologists who know firsthand of such activities should, if possible, attempt to rectify the situation. Failing an informal solution, clinical and applied sociologists bring such unethical activities to the attention of the Chair of the Ethics Committee. The Ethics Committee will consider the matter and the Chair of the Ethics Committee will forward the recommendation of the Committee to the Executive Board of the Sociological Practice Association for disposition.

PART IV
Special Populations and Special Problems

As Straus (1984:61) has noted, "many or most problems encountered in social life, from the personal to the societal levels, can best be understood and dealt with as 'social problems.'" He further advocates the use of sociological intervention, defined as "reconstructing the operational definitions of the situation with references to the multiple, interacting layers of social context framing any particular case." The six chapters contained in this section explore a variety of special populations and social problems specific to each.

Kabele, in "The Shared Microworld of the Mother and Oncological Child Patient of Pre-School Age," reports on his work as a clinical sociologist in a Child Oncology Clinic in Prague, Czechoslovakia. Using a case example of a four year old girl at a critical life-and-death juncture as a starting point, he describes the community of the clinic and the joint microworld of the mother and child created within this setting. In normal circumstances, the mother-child relationship as expressed by the shared microworld is asymmetric, with the mother being in a position of dominance. As the illness progresses, there is a shift from mother dominance to child dominance as the child becomes passively resistant and, eventually, escapes into "another world."

Kabele presents a stochastic model of stress in the illness process, and using this conceptual model and his clinical experience, he describes his intervention strategies for mobilizing the clinic's auto-therapeutic and self-help potential.

In "Facing Death with Children," Bendiksen discusses the special problems that dying children and their family members face. He examines the socio-emotional phenomenon of bonding between parent and child and looks at their special needs within the social and cultural context in which coping must take place. He further extends his analysis to bereavement—defined as the sociological adjustment to loss—from both the adult and childhood perspectives, and presents guidelines for sociologically-based intervention.

The population addressed by the third chapter in this section focuses on cancer survivors, specifically on family members whose loved ones are in remission from cancer. In "Coping with Uncertainty: Family Members' Adaptation During Cancer Remission," Nathan notes that once cancer patients and their families survive the initial diagnosis and treatment phases, they become part of a different category—families who are living at exceptional risk. Despite the increasing number of families touched by cancer, little research has been conducted to identify those factors which enhance resistance to the distress that comes from living with uncertainty. Nathan provides a theoretical model to show the proposed relationships between background variables, coping strategies adopted by family members, and successful adaptation to living with cancer remission.

In "Testicular Cancer: Passage to New Priorities," Gordon's research also focuses on cancer survivors. He emphasizes a particular type of cancer—testicular cancer—in which illness is seen as the social and psychological phenomena that accompanies an undesirable physiological process. Using qualitative methodology, primarily intensive interviewing, Gordon studied the problems and problem-solving strategies of 17 men diagnosed with testicular cancer. Common problems they faced included health anxiety, social isolation, and short-term sexual dysfunction. Yet, the experience of having had cancer and recovered had some positive outcomes as well, such as viewing the experience of cancer as a turning point, almost a rite of passage, and consequently, feeling more in control of their lives, more assertive in their decision-making, and developing greater feelings of empathy for others. Gordon concludes that there is supportive evidence that men with more positive long-term outcomes have accepted the identity of cancer survivor and have integrated it with their other identities.

"Role Performance After Loss" by Ferguson, Ferguson, and Luby, focuses on the multitude of problems that women face when widowed at a young age. The authors have developed a Theory of Alternatives, based on biopsychosocial role theory, to provide a structure to help widows adjust to their new situation and to examine alternatives. Using a complement of seven interdependent life vectors, and adding a time dimension to role theory, the client is encouraged to assess her past and present situation and to make realistic decisions.

The purpose of Ishii-Kuntz's chapter, "AIDS: Toward an Effective Education on Safer Sex Practices," is to highlight the contributions that sociological research can make in the prevention of AIDS. Previous research has indicated that college students generally have not been concerned about AIDS nor have they changed their level of sexual activity because of it. Using a sample of heterosexual college students, Ishii-Kuntz conducted a survey to determine if knowledge and concern about AIDS would lead to changes in sexual behavior. Her results show that knowledge about AIDS did not contribute to changes in sexual practices, but concern about getting AIDS did.

Based on these findings, the author presents implications for education about

AIDS: 1) concern about AIDS should be increased not only among students, but among those to whom students turn for information; 2) young people need a reasonable conception of risk; and 3) there is a need to improve the kinds of messages about AIDS provided to young people.

Sociologists tend to have early knowledge of emerging social problems (Freedman, 1982). Research about emerging problems is important, as is the development of intervention strategies to address these problems (Straus, 1984). As evidenced by the work presented in this section, clinical sociology has a great deal to contribute.

REFERENCES

Freedman, J. 1982. Clinical sociology: What it is and what it isn't—a perspective. *Clinical Sociology Review* 1:34–49.

Straus, R. 1984. Changing the definition of the situation: Toward a theory of sociological intervention. *Clinical Sociology Review* 2: 51–63.

16

The Shared Microworld of the Mother and Oncological Child Patient of Pre-School Age

George Kabele

The long-term effects arising from the operation of a stochastic source of intense stress—in the present case, malignant tumor disease—perceptibly co-determine the dynamics of the mother–child relationship. This area of research has been underexplored, and the obstacles encountered in this type of research are formidable:

1. The mother and child experience the clashes and conflicts with adverse fortune as a life-drama of a preeminently intimate character describable only with great difficulty;
2. The swiftly changing spectrum of events, bound up with various social settings, make empirical investigation an extremely difficult task which moreover cannot always be justified on ethical grounds; and
3. We still lack simple and unobtrusive techniques for the study of the dyadic relationship operative in a natural environment.

My professional experience was gained at the Child Oncology Clinic in Prague, Czechoslovakia. After establishing rapport with mothers and children, I facilitated the provision of mutual help and social support within the dyadic mother–child relationship and within the broader community of the ward. Through my natural participation in the lives of the children and their mothers, I was able to share in, and at the same time, help to co-create their microworld. I used the ensuing experience in laying the groundwork for my conceptual activity designed to shape the life of the ward community so as to mobilize its auto-therapeutic and self-help potential.

Following established practice, the Child Oncology Clinic encouraged the hospital residency of mothers wishing to look after their older children, especially children in the terminal phase of disease. My goal was to utilize the mothers' potential support not only for their own children, but for other children on the ward as well. A mother in the helper's role thus acted in a capacity beyond that of her own child-oriented personal involvement.

METHODOLOGY

I had the chance to experience the drama of the battle against oncologic disease with numerous mother–child couples. The course of such drama was recorded after a certain lapses of time, and the notes were subjected to qualitative content analysis. The results of the analysis revealed the presence of a specific covert model inherent in the dynamics underlying the relationship between mother and the oncological child-patient, and it is the experience relating to this model that is reported here.

Case Example One—Otitis

For more than a year, four-year-old Jane, suffering from Neuroblastoma, received treatment at our clinic. The therapy was complicated by adverse reactions to therapy, and several relapses aggravated in one case by the onset of variola. This was the time when Jane first reached a critical life-and-death juncture. A complicating factor was that for the past six years, Jane's mother, who had left school at the secondary level and was not employed, had looked after her son who suffered from a mild form of cerebral palsy.

In late August, Jane was given a dose of cytostatics. Based on a previous experience, her mother expected the occurrence of leucocyte and thrombocyte losses for Jane. On the 10th day, Jane was given a blood transfusion. She complained of earache and was sent to the ENT clinic. The ENT findings were negative, so Jane and her mother went home.

On the 13th day post-treatment, Jane developed severe otitis. She arrived at the clinic with a high temperature and in acute pain. The doctors prescribed more efficient antibiotics. Jane was in great distress, and her irritability and sensitiveness increased steadily. The doctors were confronted with the dilemma of whether to perform surgery to alleviate the pressure. The operation would be fraught with risk because Jane could bleed to death due to thrombocyte deficiency. The other option—no operation—entailed the threat of acute sepsis.

Complicating the medical dilemma was Jane's mother's emotional state. After some hesitation, she agreed to meet with me for a private talk. During the course of the conversation, she criticized the ENT doctor, who she was convinced had injured Jane during the examination. She was overwhelmed with the "crucial yes-no dilemma of the operation." Apart from this, she regretted not having met with the "distance healer" prior to Jane's admission to the clinic. She described in detail how she had met this man, and how he had won her confidence. This discussion appeared to help her calm down.

In the afternoon the doctors decided to wait for the effect of the antibiotics and not risk undertaking the operation unless absolutely necessary. Jane's complaints grew less intense as she became more exhausted. The doctor in charge was convinced that Jane's pain could not be as bad as she described, and attributed her state to her mother's presence which added to the mutual distress. The doctor decided to give Jane a sedative which he felt would help ease the crisis. After that, Jane's mother gradually calmed down, too.

By the 14th day, Jane's condition had not changed; she was still in a state of quiescence. Her mother was relatively calm in the morning and preoccupied with her duties of child care. However, her anxiety began to increase rapidly, and she became worried about Jane's apathy. She asked to meet with me and expressed hope that the end would come quickly so that, as she put it, "we would no longer have to torture Jane." This touched off a long discussion about euthanasia, for which the mother heartbrokenly pleaded.

By the 15th day Jane's condition had not improved, but there was no onset of sepsis. In talking with me, the mother expressed utter despair, but I could sense that her hopes had been secretly revived.

On the 16th day, a slight improvement was recorded in Jane's condition. While no longer sedated, Jane nevertheless dodged any attempt at communication, especially with her mother. On the 18th day, further aggravation resulted as Jane developed alkalosis, and her feet became swollen.

On the 20th day, to everyone's amazement, including the doctors', Jane's condition improved dramatically. The operation was then scheduled to take place in four days. The mother ascribed the improvement to the effect of the "healing" as she had managed to contact the "healer."

The operation was successfully performed on the 26th day, but Jane refused to walk postoperatively. The doctors diagnosed no somatic cause. The mother looked for her own solution to the problem. She bought Jane a pair of roller skates, and, surprisingly, this lured Jane out of bed.

By the 27th day, Jane attempted to walk, began to communicate, and tried to join other children for games. Her mother was depressed and in the blackest of moods, and asked how long this spell of improvement would last. As Jane got stronger, the mother became more depressed. By the 32nd day, Jane refused any help at all from her mother, and her mother had to ask others to feed her child. Her interpretation of the child's attitude was that Jane was angry with her because she did not protect her against painful medical interventions.

In the days that followed, Jane's condition continued to improve, and as recovery proceeded, the mother-child crisis lessened. For a long time the ear still was not properly healed, a fact which seemed to account for the recurrence of minor crises in the couple's relationship. On discharge from the clinic, both mother and child were looking forward to their return home. Both of them knew, of course, and the mother reminded me of the fact, that within a fortnight they would have to come back to the clinic for another treatment of cytostatics.

Much later I learned that during the crucial period reported here, Jane's mother was experiencing a severe identity crisis. She felt she was losing her main identity (the role of mother), and the prospect of her own future worried her. Jane, she reasoned, was going to die, and she needed to think about her own future. As she lacked special or professional skills, she could not envision a future for herself, and these and other questions weighed heavily on her mind.

STRESS AND MALIGNANT DISEASE

Viewed from the medical standpoint, the dynamics of the progress of malignant tumor disease is expressible in terms of Figure 1 (Kabele, 1987). The process is comparable to a closed circuit in which the patient moves from one condition to another.

Several points in the figure require some added explanation. As it happens, in a number of cases, the patient's acute complications are attributed to causes other than malignant tumor growth, and it is only after a certain period of time that the suspicion of tumor formation finally crystallizes. Up until then, the patient is treated as if suffering from another, less serious disease. This situation corresponds to what we term the state of "False Diagnosis." Active therapy (State IIa) following a thorough examination of the child usually is accompanied by grave complications such as impairment of hemopoiesis and the ensuing immunological insufficiency, serious disturbances in the intake and digestion of food, local necroses due to the escape of cytostatics at the injection site, and impairment of the function of other affected organs which themselves require treatment (State IIb). Palliative treatment is the term referring to a situation in which cure of the original disease is no longer the aim of therapy, but instead attention is concentrated on the complications of the disease. If the malignant disease progresses despite the numerous changes in therapy plans, the possibilities of active therapy become exhausted. In some cases, the next step is mere dissimulation. The purpose of palliative treatment is to make dying compatible with human dignity.

The model illustrates the course of disease as a stochastic source of repeated stress-loads. The stress-load is generated by each new progression from one state to another. The model further reveals the features of recurrence which, together with the cyclical character of cystostatic treatment (repeated series of injections), decisively determine the time-scale of the disease and the course of

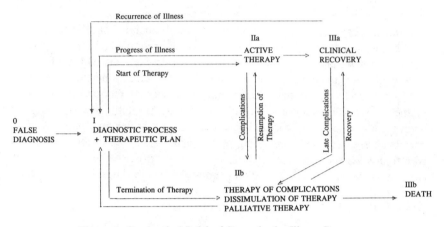

Figure 1. Stochastic Model of Stress in the Illness Process

treatment. For a child constantly moving in the vicious circle of transitions—between active therapy, changes in therapy plan and the treatment of complications—time-perception gradually begins to be dominated by cyclical time, replacing the linear, ascending time characteristic of childhood. This brings us closer to the dynamics of the actual course of the disease as an affliction which at the given moment functions as the leitmotif of the child's biography and the family history.

In practice, this means that the course of illness is conceived as a sequence of topical stress-loads, suffering and ominous problems which in equal measure interfere with the patient's physical and psychological existence and disrupt the psychological integrity and normal course of life of many other persons involved. Finally, the unity of the family's social world is threatened. The range of the stress-loads is extremely varied and encompasses manifestations of the illness, the stress of the therapy and attendant complications (Katz, 1984).

Of crucial importance for the process shaping the destiny of an oncological child-patient, the mother and the entire family are the accumulation and synergy of the effects of different stress-loads primarily determined by the malignant disease as well as by factors generated by other sources (McCubbin and Figley, 1983). Phobias, anticipatory pathological reactions, exhaustion, disintegration of the future horizon, the sense of physical and psychological failure, communication barriers, erosion of the framework of the defense of self-integrity, the twists and warps of extreme moods, envy and preconceived judgment of other people all are features connected with long-term exposure to the strain and stress of malignant tumor disease.

THE FAMILY OF THE ONCOLOGICAL CHILD-PATIENT

The mother and oncologic child patient of pre-school age constitute a closely interconnected couple in the course of joint hospitalization. The mother usually assumes the role of the family specialist in problem-solving connected with the illness and in shaping the couple's distinctive relationship with the clinic. To a considerable extent, the mother generally monopolizes the provision of social support to the child during the major crises. The couple creates a micro-world of their own, existing as an entity in its own right both in the community of the clinic and in the family. This changes the family system in that the husband–wife relationship ceases to function as the center of gravity in the family. Along with the changing pattern of family life, the status of other members of the family changes, too. The change primarily affects the neglected, and therefore frequently jealous, siblings.

THE COMMUNITY OF THE CLINIC

At the time when the clinic's official accommodation capacity was 50 beds (but in actual fact 60 children and eight mothers were hospitalized there), the basis of the clinic community was formed by 25 personnel, 200 children undergoing intensive medical treatment, and 30 accompanying mothers. Relationships formed speedily among everyone involved in the dramatic duels with illness.

For the hospitalized mothers and children, the clinic acquired the spirit and character of Goffman's (1961) total institution, in which the hospitalized soon perceive that their entire life is shaped by the "here and now." Mothers and children find themselves in a subordinate position and are "compelled to play the expected game" so as to ensure the smooth functioning of the clinic and avoid negative treatment. The threat they face is the possible withdrawal of certain advantages or privileges.

Newcomers to the clinic are the object of increased curiosity, but within a relatively short time the newness wears off, the interest wanes, and once the newcomer's problem is "settled," the initial tide of curiosity ebbs away.

RISE OF THE SHARED MOTHER-AND-CHILD MICROWORLD

The joint microworld shared by the couple is the creation of the mother and child (Berger and Luckermann, 1967), and is the result of sharing daily reality during face-to-face encounters, coping with the ordinary problems of life, and coping with challenging new problems.

The basis is the process of sharing everyday reality through immediate mother–child contacts. In the process of subtle communication and the exchange of stimuli of which most participants are not fully aware, the mother's and the child's "now, here, and there" become identical and reciprocal. At the same time, there exists a correspondent relationship between the contents of their perceptions, a relationship repeatedly renewed and reaffirmed. Everyday reality is, hence, experienced as a matter of course, as something not requiring additional verification.

Most of the sectors of everyday reality are in normal circumstances perceived as problem-free by the mother-and-child couple. The problematic sectors motivate the couple's effort to transform them. This mode of behavior is communicative and meaningful, but if the application of available routines proves ineffective in problem-solving, the couple is still confronted with the persisting problems. As a rule, the couple undergoes change and the shifts bound to occur in the basic relational structures involve a change of routines, convictions and values. The normal course of socialization is governed by a specific temporal order controlling the discovery of new and, hence, at least temporarily intractable problem sectors. The socialization process is determined by the child's biological and mental development, as well as by the distinctive childhood and adolescent model shared by the specific culture.

The joint mother-and-child microworld is, moreover, characterized by the presence of permanently and mutually delimited spheres: the sphere of incontestable realities as distinct from the sphere of incontestable notional constructs; and, again, the sphere of doubtful, indeterminate phenomena. The actual sense of the mother's negotiation of reality with the child resides in the search for lines of demarcation. The imperative need here is the identification of elements of truth versus elements of fiction—in other words, the definition of the distinction between what is the legitimate experiential finalization of reality and what, on the contrary, is subjective fallacy, deception or pretense.

To a considerable extent, pre-school children still lack the capacity of spontaneous differentiation between reality and fiction. Apart from this, we ought to take into account the key role that imagination and fantasy play in children, just as in adults, in coping with the stress-loads of illness. Without them, no situation-definition is possible, given the lack of reliable information. But while imagination may help a good deal, it also may prove detrimental.

Mother and child complete their joint microworld by "shadow realities" (Rosenblatt and Wright, 1984). Certain notions, facts and circumstances cannot actually be shared by the couple. They are blocked by the values, longings and principles shared and professed by the couple, giving greater credibility to everything that is in consonance with them. In contrast, everything that is at variance with such values, longings, and principles, must be ousted "into the shadow sphere." Thus, mothers believing in a spartan education of the child are prone to disguise any mode of conduct contradicting such principles in the web of rationalizing arguments, or they may totally dodge such principles in their consciousness.

The effects of malignant tumor disease on the creation of the joint microworld shared by the mother-and-child couple can be examined. If the course of the illness is complicated and adverse, rather than favorable, the following features emerge:

- demands placed on coping with new problems accumulate at a fast rate;
- the sphere of doubtful, indeterminate phenomena broadens, the intersphere boundary becomes controversial, and often mother and child are no longer certain of what they can or cannot believe; and
- the sphere of shadow realities gains in prominence, while the sphere of shared realities becomes more restricted.

Thus, for the mother-and-child couple, the shared universe is reduced to the present, their destinies get "estranged,"and they frequently regard themselves as passive victims of a totally treacherous world.

THE SHIFT OF SYMMETRY IN THE MOTHER-AND-CHILD RELATIONSHIP

In normal circumstances, the mother–child relationship as expressed by the shared microworld is asymmetric. Mother controls the child and retains her position of dominance in the nexus of mutual relations. Aggravated by the physical condition of the child, the relations usually develop in the following sequence:

Mother's dominance → Child's dominance →
Child's passive resistance → escape into "another world"

The dominant position is based on the prevalence of the child's demands for stimuli, on the mother's care and support and offer of stimuli, and on the mother's capacity to enforce the child's obedience. The illness, however, changes the normal demand-based pattern into an offer-based pattern, motivates the mother, and reduces the variety and number of the child's realizable wishes. The range of procedures available to the mother for the enforcement of obedience becomes more constrained. As a result, she finds herself in a position of strategic disadvantage and enforces her will with considerable difficulty. Even at a young age, the child manages to assert his or her own influence with remarkable skill and sophistication.

The shift from mother dominance to child dominance generally entails the phase of obvious power competition. The child is armed with a broad range of active and passive strategies. Active strategies include the clamor for positive experience and for all manner of compensations, the setting of limits to the mother's care and behavior, expressions of pain, distress and negative emotions, and actual aggression. The boundary between active and non-active strategies is fairly vague, for different strategies often are combined to enhance final impact. Thus, not infrequently, the child demands something with great verve and insistence, the mother finally gives in, but then the child rejects the hard-won result of the battle.

Mothers, too, can and do apply the same range of strategies, but they are clearly in a position of strategic disadvantage for two reasons. Their major constraint is adherence to the generally accepted moral code, and they are constantly faced with the dilemma of whether the child's actions and wishes are merely a power-seeking maneuver or an authentic expression of the child's needs and difficulties. What then are the mother's defense strategies? Apart from the threat of sanctions put into effect in extreme cases, mothers may seek recourse to ruse (diverting the child's attention, disguising their true intent), manipulate information ("ration" truth, seek recourse to lies, suppress information on true reality), or, in a harmless situation, they may adopt "burnt-child-dreads-the-fire" tactics. The most effective strategies of defense include compromise solutions and compensation agreements.

"Bad" children—and this is how children with a markedly aggravated health condition were described (in a subdued voice) in the ward—may feel the compulsive need to assert their influence by hurting people. Symptomatically, this need finds an outlet particularly if the mother is present. The mother's action is not motivated by the desire to triumph in the clash with the child, or to defend her position at all costs. The mother can offer the child genuine aid and support only if she accepts her own defeat, fighting a rearguard battle to prepare the ground for later remedial action when she regains her position once the child's condition improves. The child's opposition vis-à-vis the mother (and here passive resistance is the most frequent mode of strategy) is to a certain extent justified. From the child's point of view, the mother really is something of a "fence-sitter." She serves the child's interest, but, at the same time, complies with the interests of the personnel of the ward as she lets her child be controlled by their power and presses the child to cooperate in the painful therapy procedures. Both the child and the personnel, therefore, have reason to be dissatisfied with the mother's conduct.

Children in the terminal phase frequently "escape into the other world." This escape is an experience *sui generis*, a phenomenon not solely attendant on the period of quiescence. As a rule, children restrict their contacts with the world spontaneously, and their communication, if retained, begins to reflect the predominance of nonverbal components. The impression thus created is one of spiritual life continued in a form defying our grasp. In any case, children loathe being disturbed while sunk in their own world, inaccessible to the outsider.

THE BLOCKING OF COMMUNICATION AND EXCHANGE OF STIMULI BETWEEN MOTHER AND CHILD

With regard to communication in the mother–child microworld, the working term "cycle-formation" was coined. This refers to a specific process occurring in different areas of communication within the mother-and-child couple. The mother–child communication is set in the context of other areas such as child–social surroundings, mother–social surroundings, mother-and-child social surroundings, mother per se and child per se. In all of these areas, a disturbance of the exchange of stimuli may occur in the form of an autotelic and repeated circulation process. Thus, a specific communication area may acquire a cyclical character if the stimuli and responses of the mother and child are such that both are compelled to repeat the same partner-influencing strategies even if such strategies prove inefficient. Moreover, in mother and child, the "cycle-formation" process also may occur at the level of inner dialogue (communication with one's self). Thus, in the state of eustress or distress, they may tend to revert, time and again, to a single event, or reflect on one problem without any major change. Not every cycle-forming act, however, disturbs communication within the couple; indeed, cycle-forming may be part of the normal process by which losses are experienced by both partners. In this way, the acts themselves communicate meanings that are often incommunicable in other forms. Hence, they may form an integral part of numerous rituals. Nevertheless, if cycle-forming manifestations occur over a long period of time, and if their emergence in the life of the couple becomes unpredictable and "defies control," they may begin to function as a formidable disturbance factor detrimental to the shared microworld. As a result, the couple's microworld ceases to be a sphere of shared trust, safety and naturalness, and its order begins to disintegrate.

The cycle-forming processes have a paroxysmal character, and with occurrences of longer duration, they tend to expand to the remaining communication spheres. In other words, they are subject to generalization. This tendency, of course, is not the sole aspect that gives plausibility to the obvious analogy with the model of the genesis of epileptic paroxysm. The following factors—individually or in combination—seem to share in the rise of the cycle-forming process:

1. Inclination toward cycle-formation (analogous to paroxysmal "readiness"). This varies with individual couples and individual spheres, and is not always easily deducible from the mother's and the child's personality structures.
2. Stimuli which trigger the autotelic circulation of stimuli and responses. The connection with source problems (see below) is frequently fairly loose.
3. Source problems (analogous to the epileptic focus). These are activated in the course of the cycle-forming process and include actual or anticipated suffering, past and present wrongs and grievances, uncontrolled or discarded problems, and previous failures.

GROWTH OF THE BOUNDARIES OF THE MICROWORLD SHARED BY
MOTHER AND CHILD

In the community of the clinic, both mother and child protect their microworld,
and not everyone is admitted to share their world. To preclude undesirable
interventions, the mother usually shoulders the burden of the care for the child,
a role which, in actual fact, she is expected to perform in the ward. Both mother
and child have a number of good reasons for seclusion. In their own closed
world, they need not compare their plight with the destinies and attitudes of
other people, and, hence, they retain their privacy. By the same token, this
seclusion reduces the possibility of missteps or transgressions on the mother's
side, such as "acting out of role," and this prevents the mother from crying or
complaining about standards of care.

As the health condition of the child deteriorates, the following changes in the
couple's relations with their surroundings generally are observable:

Normal give-and-take relations with the sourroudings	→	Withdrawal into the couple's secluded world	→	Attempts to escape, and pulsation of the couple

To recall a point made earlier, the couple has good grounds to shut themselves
off in a secluded world of their own. However, from the account given above,
it also follows that with the child's deteriorating condition, neither mother nor
child can feel really happy in this isolated, self-contained world. It usually is
the mother, but sometimes also the child, who is prone to attempt a flight from
this isolation. Yet, outside the microworld they feel uncomfortable, and both
share the compulsive need to renew immediate contact. As such attempts are
repeated, we witness a specific spatial pulsation of the couple.

DISTURBANCE OF THE CONTROL OF INTERPERSONAL DISTANCE

Each mother-and-child couple continually keeps check on the mutual interpersonal distance (Lewis, 1986). Depending on the concrete situation, the distance
between mother and child is sometimes very close. At other times they drift
apart while enforcing their differing views and wishes, and they are unable or
unwilling to project themselves in order to get the feel of each other's situation.
The imaginary scale of interpersonal distance can be presented in terms of three
models of mutual contacts scaled to the respective degree of cohesion. The most
cohesive model is the "WE" model. It controls the couple's relationship if both
mother and child are exposed to the same stimuli and live through the same
experience, or if the close relationship is strengthened by shared experience on
the basis of empathy and mutual reflection.

A less cohesive relationship is the "I–YOU" model in which the mother and child act as partners in negotiations in games and/or minor conflicts. Finally, the greatest distance between mother and child occurs in the "I–SHE" model which entails an unequal status of the two partners. In this model, one partner is envisaged as an instrument mediating the fulfillment of the other partner's wishes, the consent being obtained by means of power.

In normal circumstances, the mother should be able to progress with the child from one model to another. The central role should be played by the "I–YOU" relationship which functions as the motor force of socialization. However, the stress factors connected with the adverse course of the illness motivate the reduction or enlargement of interpersonal distance. The couple insulates itself in closed, inward-looking world of its own, and, hence, mother and child are maneuvered into the "WE" type of attitude.

Usually, the mother assumes the active role, which causes a shift in the balance of power within the couple. Then the child's growing domination or resistance gradually establishes the "I–SHE" relationship. Mother enforces the child's compliance with therapy requirements. This state of affairs, in turn, motivates the renewal of the shared feeling of togetherness, the "WE" feeling from which the couple frequently lapses into the other extreme of the "I–SHE" relationship. With the child's aggravating condition, the "I–YOU" relationship, which plays a key role in the formation of the shared microworld, is excluded from the process of interaction.

In the terminal phase, with the child returning from the forays into the "other world," the "WE" relationship naturally gains the upper hand. The mother and other relatives and close friends should not prevent the child's attempts to escape. If this condition is met, a sense of mutually shared tenderness and conciliation pervades the final act during which the mother parts with her child.

CONCLUSION

The account presented here of the dynamics governing the relationship between the mother and the oncological child patient remains, like all other descriptions of this relationship, no more than a tentative model. Even if verified by research, the model only can represent half of the actual truth. Each individual case involves a unique drama whose character is shaped by the insidious nature of the illness, by the personality structures of the mother and the child, and by the idiosyncratic traits of the entire family. It is a drama in which elements of tragedy prevail, and it is the tragic aspects that our model seeks to emphasize. In light of the model, the world of childhood oncology may strike the outsider as a totally inhuman world. The truth, of course, is that the tragic aspect of the illness gives this world a superhuman dimension. It is a world which often defies the horizons of our comprehension. Yet the battle waged by mother and child alike is a pre-eminently human battle, for the price of human life is best gauged by the courage, endeavor and skill mobilized by love for the sake of its preservation.

REFERENCES

Berger, P. and T. Luckermann. 1967. *The Social Construction of Reality.* Harmondsworth, England: Penguin Books.

Goffman, E. 1961. On the characteristics of total institutions. In *Asylums: Essays on the Social Situation of Mental Patients and Other Inmates.* Garden City, NJ: Doubleday, 1–124.

Kabele, J. 1987. Mother and the oncological child patient. *Family Research I.* Praha: VUSRP, 38–47.

Katz, E. and S. Jay. 1984. Psychological aspects of cancer in children, adolescents and their families. *Clinical Psychological Review* 12(21): 525–42.

Lewis, J. 1986. Family structure and stress. *Family Process* 25: 235–47.

McCubbin, H. and C. Figley. 1983. Coping with Catastrophe. In *Stress and the Family*, Vol. 2. New York: Brunner/Mazel.

Rosenblatt, P. and S. Wright. 1984. Shadow realities in close relationships. *The American Journal of Family Therapy* 12(2): 45–54.

17

Facing Death With Children[1]

Robert A. Bendiksen

Facing death with children challenges everyone. Each of us is acutely aware that some children die, and that children are forced at times to deal with the deaths of adult relatives, siblings, close friends, and pets. As adults, we are faced with the reality of dying children and children who are bereaved. We want to know how we might help, or at least not increase the hurt when death enters the lives of children. Death, however, challenges our sense of fairness. According to Charlie Brown, "The way I see it, we die in the same order we were born. It's the only fair way of working it!" (Schulz and Hall, 1965:1).

The conditions associated with children and death have changed from very common exposure to infrequent occurrences in the United States and other economically developed countries. Death was a frequent event in the middle ages, especialy when the "black death" ravaged Europe (Kastenbaum, 1972). Aries (1962) claims that the value of children was low in prior centuries because infant and childhood mortality was so high (de Mause, 1974). Goldscheider (1971) notes that there is a correlation between the concept of children as valued individuals and decreasing death rates. Young people in the nuclear age, however, experience death and death imagery in a unique way (Fulton and Owen, 1988; Lifton, 1987).

The facts of death are different from our wishes and hopes, even in today's world of advanced medical technology;. Each year, 17 million children in the world die; that is approximately 40,000 children per day. In the last three decades there has been a gradual improvement in health conditions. However, serious setbacks in some economically developing countries have led UNICEF to claim that there is a "silent emergency" in infant mortality (Grant, 1982). In the United States and other wealthy countries the mortality rate of children is low, but children continue to die at a high rate in countries where critical care medicine and public health practices are limited (Grant, 1985).

Childhood death is an experience that most American families have been spared in recent decades. In 1988, about 10 out of every 1,000 live newborn infants in the U.S. died before one year of life elapsed. The first month of life remains the most hazardous, as the death rate in that month is twice the rate of the remaining months of the first year. Congenital anomalies lead the list of causes of death for these infants, but many other problems are present for other babies that die. SIDS (Sudden Infant Death Syndrome or Crib Death), a yet to be explained phenomenon, is the leading cause of death in infants from one month to one year. Accidents, when combined, rank first in causes of death of all children up to 15 years old (Haub and Kent, 1988; Markusen, et. al., 1977–78; National Center for Health Statistics, 1988; Swoiskin, 1986).

The United States spends over eleven percent of its gross national product on health care, a figure unmatched by other nations. Yet, the United States in 1985 ranked 17th in infant mortality, a condition related to poor perinatal health care that is especially prevalent among the poor (Grant, 1985:133). Poverty affects both white and non-white families, but poverty among non-whites is exceptionally high in the United States. Differences in poverty levels are reflected in large differences in infant mortality rates. While both non-white and white infant mortality rates are much reduced, non-white children continue to die at a rate that is twice the white infant death rate. Non-white infant mortality lags behind white infant mortality by fifteen years. There have been improvements in infant mortality among all groups, but the disparity between the death rates of various ethnic and socioeconomic groups in the United States remains.

Deaths of infants are difficult for parents, siblings and others because of the great expectations and positive cultural meanings associated with the birth of a child. Peppers and Knapp (1980) estimate that as many as one-third of all pregnancies result in miscarriages, abortions, stillbirths, and neonatal deaths. Pediatricians and maternal health care providers are becoming interested in the bonding process between parents and their new infant, and greater parental involvement with newborns is being encouraged even when an infant is dying. Early reports of appreciative parents who were allowed to hold their dead child is encouraging pediatricians and pediatric nurses to drastically change the norms of patient care in their hospitals.

Children who are dying appear to make sense of their dying just as adults do. They manage the information available to them in different ways, however, depending on their cognitive maturity. When we take time to listen to children who are dying, we discover that they often have a degree of awareness of their condition that is not easily appreciated by their parents, medical and nursing caregivers, and others. The child's awareness of dying ought to be recognized and taken into account as childhood diseases such as leukemia or AIDS progress. The increasing involvement of parents, family members, and medical care-givers in shared decision-making does not reduce legal responsibility, but rather widens the base of concern and understanding.

Recent research (Bowlby, 1980) confirms that adult and childhood mourning are similar, although earlier researchers (Freud, 1943; Klein, 1944) have debated this issue. Children who lose a close relative or friend through death are bereaved. They experience grief and express it through mourning behavior that may take the form of personal or shared ritual. Their individual experiences with bereavement are affected by a variety of factors such as: (1) their developmental level; (2) their experiences with past bereavements; (3) the presence of role models; and (4) adult definitions of appropriate behavior. The resolution of grief in children is important, but the long-term effects of grief are not clearly understood, in spite of extensive research (Bendiksen and Fulton, 1976). Helping a child who is mourning is difficult. To be a friend to a child confronted with death may mean simply being there. We may want to listen to and affirm the child's expression of feelings and thoughts, especially when parents and other close relatives are unable to help because of their own grief.

FACING THE DEATH OF A CHILD

The death of a fetus or child takes place in a social context of medical meanings and institutionalized responses. Associated role expectations define "appropriate" attitudes and behavior whether one faces the death of a fetus, new-born, or older child (Behnke, Setzer and Mehta, 1984; Limbo and Wheeler, 1986; Bluebond-Langner, 1978). The social construction of the meanings of illness comes into sharp focus with the "new" causes of childhood death such as AIDS (Grossman, 1988; Fulton and Owen, 1988; Shilts, 1987) or SIDS (Markusen et al., 1977–78).

The socio-emotional phenomenon of bonding between parent and child is difficult to describe with accuracy, but it appears to involve a number of elements that give meaning to the new relationships. Klaus and Kennell (1976) claim that bonding includes: (1) planning the pregnancy; (2) confirmation of the pregnancy; (3) acceptance of pregnancy; (4) fetal movement when the mother perceives the fetus as separate from herself; (5) delivery; and (6) the seeing and touching of the infant that confirms the reality.

The bonding process between parent and child is similar for both parents, but important differences remain. The father, for instance, is more likely than the mother to anticipate the birth of the child in an intellectual way. The mother-to-be, on the other hand, has the advantage of being the first to be in physical contact with the growing fetus. This is particularly evident during the spontaneous movements of quickening. The attachment of both mother and father tend to equalize later when each holds the child and makes eye contact with the responding infant—"My child!" The two "miracles" of childbirth are the total environmental change from living in water to breathing air and the socio-emotional attachment of bonding, which in common-sense terms is a profound "hello!" The importance of the second miracle is evident when death occurs at the beginning of life. In human terms, "You can't say 'good-bye' until you say 'hello' " (Hartigan, 1981).

Research on attachment behavior between parent and child has been accumulating for decades (Bowlby, 1969), but the work of Klaus and Kennell (1976) has focused the thinking of the pediatric and maternal care community by presenting a strong case for the importance of bonding to medical practice. The research and theoretical framework of bonding provide a perspective for pediatric care of infants who are critically ill and dying. The sensitivity of medical and nursing personnel to the growing relationship between parent and child allows the caregivers to encourage attachment even as separation through death threatens.

Grief is an intense emotional experience precipitated by the loss of another, particularly through death. We express our grief and mourning with, or in spite of, others. The bereaved parents are often at a loss when trying to understand what has happened and to explain it to others. The death of a child may be the first experience of intense grief for many young parents. They may prefer to grieve alone, even when they are surrounded by people who care and want to help, because so few people know what such a loss entails.

The stages of grief have been outlined in detail by many (e.g., Lindemann, 1944; Kubler-Ross, 1969), but essentially they involve the shock and disorganization of realizing something is wrong—one's plans and expectations are not coming true with the new baby. All parts of one's self are torn apart in the mental and emotional confusion asociated with the loss of another who is part of one's self. Grief also includes the attempts to come to terms with the loss by learning to live without the one who has died. Parents may never completely let go emotionally, and may prolong their grief by maintaining what Peppers and Knapp (1980) call "shadow grief." As time passes, the loss is less evident, but grief is re-experienced for many at an anniversary or an unanticipated event such as meeting a mother with a newborn baby.

Deaths associated with the beginning of life are not alike in their impact on surviving parents. Grieving differs in important ways depending on whether the loss is due to a miscarriage, a stillbirth, the death of a newborn infant, sudden infant death syndrome, or diseases such as AIDS. The mother's response to the death of her child is very intense, regardless of the cause of that death. She has a close relationship with the fetus throughout pregnancy and invests herself physically and emotionally in the development and delivery of the child. The father also experiences a very intense initial response if the baby dies at full term or later, as fathers become attached in ways similar to mothers when the child is born. An important difference between the parents has been noticed in fathers' reactions to miscarriage, as initially they seem to respond with limited intensity. Perhaps significant bonding has not yet occurred for the father (Peppers and Knapp, 1980).

Individual differences in grief responses are common, and patterns are limited in their predictive value. The struggle to adjust to the death of a fetus or child is both painful and comforting, in that the separation tears, while identification with the child unites (Furman, 1978). Mother and father may experience different degrees of emotional attachment in "incongruent bonding," and they may also express their grief incongruently due to differences in male and female role expectations (Peppers and Knapp, 1980). Davidson (1977:265) studied 15 mothers whose fetuses were born dead or whose infants died in the first 24 hours of life. These mothers were thwarted at three points as they sought to deal with their recent loss: "(1) when trying to confirm, perceptually, whom they had lost; (2) when reaching out to others for emotional support; and (3) when trying to test their feelings against the perceptions of others." It is no wonder that communication problems and other difficulties arise in the weeks and months that follow the death of a child.

Bowie (1977) reported in a diary-like format how she and her husband were isolated from their newborn son who died after many days in intensive care. She and her husband found it very difficult to obtain information or opinions about their son's condition even when direct quesitons were asked. Bowie (1977:11) notes, "When faced with hard lay questions regarding medical decisions, the medical profession closed in its ranks." This is not a uniquely American experience as Giles (1970) and Cullberg (1972) report similar types of behavior from physicians in Australia and Sweden.

Klaus and Kennell (1976:215) claim that the task for the physician and nurse is "(1) to help the parents digest the loss and make it real, (2) to ensure that normal grief reactions will begin and that both parents will go through the entire process, and (3) to meet the individual needs of specific parents." Helping to make death real for the parents may involve allowing parents to visit their critically ill infant, and to hold the baby even after the infant has died. They also may be helped by having a funeral service for the baby in the hospital if the mother is unable to leave. The supporting professionals should visit with the parents right after the death, again in two or three days, and again three to six months later. The advantage of the third visit is that any evidence of pathological grieving might be discovered and the parents helped by referral to grief counselors. "Helping parents through these experiences is an extremely difficult assignment, but we have been rewarded by the thanks and expressions of appreciation parents have relayed to us later," report Klaus and Kennell (1976:217).

Norms of hospital life are undergoing changes as human values are brought into balance with the management of diseases. Rules that have prevented children under 16 from visiting patients, because of historical problems of communicable diseases, have been eliminated or significantly revised. Furman (1978) is of the opinion that the age of siblings is the major factor in determining their involvement in near and after death settings:

> Adolescents should decide for themselves. Elementary grade children are helped by attending a service but not helped by seeing a malformed dead body. Children under school age are particularly not helped by seeing their dead brother or sister, but they are sometimes helped by being in the company of the parents at the time of the funeral.

Nurses are providing an essential support system to parents and siblings at the death of fetuses and infants, as illustrated by the highly successful "Resolve through Sharing" program developed at Lutheran Hospital-LaCrosse in Wisconsin (Smiley and Goettl, 1981; Limbo and Wheeler, 1986).

FACING DEATH AS A DYING CHILD

Much has been written about the dying child in recent years by psychiatrists (e.g., Easson, 1970), psychologists (e.g., Zelligs, 1974), nurses (e.g., Gyulay, 1978), and other helping professionals. These clinicians have described their own professional and personal experiences with cases, taking as their theoretical context developmental psychology (e.g., Anthony, 1971; Nagy, 1948; Loneto, 1980). Infants who are dying appear to have a degree of understanding that is without words, but full of behavioral meaning as they respond to disease symptoms, treatment procedures, pain, social isolation, and the responses of adults.

Easson (1970) claims that an infant of five or six months may react to the way people treat him or her in response to the disease condition. Children around age four respond to changes in their sense of self as they are dying. Not long afterwards, between the ages of four and five, they are able to respond to the significance of the diagnosis of their condition. Between the ages of five and seven the significance of the prognosis is responded to by children. By the time children are six and seven, they are quite capable of responding to changes in their social role relationships.

Bluebond-Langner (1978) concurs in her participant observation study of leukemic children ages three to nine in a pediatric unit of a hospital. The understanding that dying children have of their prognosis, as well as what other, critically ill children understand, cannot be easily determined by talking openly with children about their condition. Critically ill children are involved in a socialization process of becoming aware of factual information about their treatment and of associated meanings of self identity. At the time of the diagnosis, children view themselves as well. The first stage of awareness of their condition is in learning that "'it' is a serious illness," and that they are "seriously ill."

The second stage occurs when they learn the names of drugs and their side effects; children at this stage believe that they are "seriously ill and will get better." The third stage involves understanding the purposes of treatment and procedures, and children believe that they are "always ill and will get better." The fourth and fifth stages both involve a series of relapses and remissions, with death itself marking the final stage. In the fourth stage the children believe that they are "always ill and will never get better," while in the fifth stage they understand that they are dying.

The concept of "mutual pretense", as a type of "awareness context," developed by Glaser and Strauss (1965), is a very helpful way of describing how children who are dying interact with adults. The adults in the Glaser and Strauss study tended to move from "closed awareness," "suspicion awareness," and "mutual pretense" to "open awareness," where patients discussed their condition with others when it was appropriate or necessary. The children in their study, and in Bluebond-Langner's study, tended to maintain "mutual pretense" rather than move toward openness. Children may be able to know the truth about their condition, but they cannot change the rules by which the adults play. Children may be close to being open and need an "open awareness context," but adults often are traumatized by a child's openness and honesty. It is not easy to make sense of dying when one is a child. It is also difficult to make sense of dying when one is the parent, or medical or nursing caregiver, of a dying child. Children and adults have their own needs that should be respected (Bluebond-Langner, 1977).

The difficulties in facing death as a dying child are associated with the elaborate medical and nursing care that allows them to live considerably longer than they would have only a few decades ago. Kidney disease treatment, for example, now includes dialysis and transplantation (Simmons, Klein and Simmons, 1977). Medical experimentation is conducted on children who are ill so that the efficacy of drugs and treatment procedures are identified (Van Eyes, 1978; Gray, 1975). Specialization in treatment means that a child who is dying from a chronic disease, such as leukemia or AIDS, can expect to confront numerous people who perform countless tasks "on" him or her, often without a basic respect to deal with the situation sensitively, openly, and honestly.

The social construction of meaning that children are bound to participate in with their parents and others adds to the complexity of care for all concerned. The challenge for physicians and other health care professionals is to provide sensitive death counseling and social and psychological support both in the hospital setting (Behnke, Stezer, and Mehta, 1984) and in home care (Martinson, Nesbit, and Kersey, 1985). The challenge for adults involved with dying children is to learn how to listen well and to be available for open conversations, even when they would rather avoid or postpone discussing a topic like death.

Children's books and stories are recommended as therapeutic metaphors when intervening with seriously ill children (Husbans and Brouddhus, 1984). Pollach (1986) reminds us that childhood sibling loss makes the death of a child a family tragedy. Share (1972) is particularly helpful in distinguishing between "protective" and "open" approaches of communication in families with dying children.

FACING DEATH AS A SURVIVING CHILD

Research on grief and mourning has included dying and bereaved adults as well as bereaved children. Kubler-Ross (1969) describes the characteristics of adult dying patients who respond to a fatal diagnosis with shock and denial. As the reality of life's limitations sink in, the patient feels rage and anger, often expressing it in diverse ways. The struggle to maintain life manifests itself in bargaining for survival. With the awareness of the full reality of impending death, the patient may become depressed and withdrawn. But a patient can come to accept impending death, given time and the close companionship of a caring relative, friend, or professional caregiver.

Grief is a psychological reaction to loss, particularly through death. The personal adjustment to loss involves disruptive emotions and moods as one copes with a radically changed present and future reality. For the dying person, the inner response to a fatal diagnosis is fraught with anxiety and fear. It is also a time of redefinition of self in light of changes in ability, mobility, and social relationships. The greatest stress, however, may well be the loss of a life plan— a sense of the future that is drastically changed. Perhaps the greatest difficulty of impending death is the grief associated with coming to terms with the loss of one's hopes and plans. The struggle to come to terms with impending death in children may take various forms, but we now know that it, too, is grief.

Mourning is the expression of loss that includes inner and outer realities. Each of us has developed personally meaningful, patterned ways of expressing who we are and how we relate to and interact with others. The inner reality of mourning the death of a significant other person is the personal way we have developed to come to terms with death and other losses. The outer realities of mourning are the socially relevant, ritualized patterns of coping that guide our public behavior. Mourning a death often means that public customs of mourning are followed. It is hoped that each person who is grieving will be helped in his or her mourning process through the public expression of concern and the affirmation of support. Rosen (1984–85) points to social prohibitions against mourning childhood sibling deaths that limit healthy recovery.

Bereavement is the sociological adjustment to loss, where social norms and values define behavioral expectations. The typical pattern of bereavement in American society prescribes mourning customs that principally include people who are directly related to the person who has died. In some traditions, it is limited to only the immediate relatives, while in others a wide group of relatives and friends are full participants in bereavement. The bereaved are expected to grieve and mourn in ways appropriate to the family, ethnic or religious group, or community. Children and teenagers are often full participants in mourning and bereavement rituals in traditional cutures, but are less evident in modern funeral and memorial services. The effectiveness or ineffectiveness of funerals in helping adults and children cope with bereavement depends on shared definitions and the expressions of thoughts, feelings, and behaviors that are socially and personally meaningful.

The grief and mourning of children is becoming increasingly evident (Bendiksen and Fulton, 1976; Bowlby, 1980; Zambelli et al., 1988). Bowlby (1980), in his comprehensive third volume of *Attachment and Loss*, brings together much of the research on children in a theoretical framework that challenges traditional Freudian assumptions while complementing symbolic interaction theory in sociology. Bowlby's new paradigm for explaining the mourning of children takes the perspective of cognitive psychology and human information processing. This type of cognitive psychology complements the social constructionist approach that attends to the awareness of meanings in a person's social situation and the interaction that results. For Bowlby, mourning in both adults and children involves a "defensive exclusion" of information that is similar to what Kubler-Ross (1969) calls "denial" and Lifton (1988) describes as "psychic numbing." The healthy or unhealthy nature of this "defensive exclusion" depends on its intensity and longevity in the struggle with coming to terms with the death.

Evidence is mounting that it is possible for young children to mourn in a manner similar to healthy adults. This occurs when the relationship between the child and his or her parents has been reasonably secure before the death. The child has been a participant in the awareness of what has been taking place in the time during and after the death, with information appropriately shared in response to the questions asked. The child has participated in funeral rites or the memorial service, and the on-going relationship with the surviving family members has involved a "comforting presence" with an assurance of continued relationship. If this has not been possible, then a trusted surrogate has been available to provide this type of support.

Guidelines for providing support to children are suggested by many authors; Lonetto (1980:189) summarizes:

1. Children are ready and capable of talking about anything within their experience;
2. Use the language of the child, not the sentimental symbols we find so easy to utter;

3. Don't expect an immediate and obvious response from the child;
4. Be a good listener and observer;
5. Don't try to do it all in one discussion; that is, be available;
6. Make certain that your child knows that he or she is part of the family, especially when a death has occurred; and
7. One of the most valuable methods of teaching children about death is to allow them to talk freely and ask their own questions.

The long-term effects of childhood bereavement are difficult to document, which explains why most studies involve comparison groups drawn from available populations such as hospital patients. Bendiksen and Fulton (1976), however, compared the impact on children of the death of a parent to the divorce of parents among the general population in Minnesota in a longitudinal study begun by other researchers in 1954. Their results indicate that the experience of divorced parents has a greater impact on children than the death of a parent. Both types of childhood family disruption are traumatic, but the long-term impact of the death of a parent on a child appears to be mediated by their families in ways that parental divorce precludes.

Support groups are becoming available to children who experience bereavement and other types of family disruption. One example is an interdisciplinary counseling program of clinical intervention for childhood bereavement in Montclair, New Jersey (Zambelli et al., 1988). This four-year-old program has two groups, one a creative arts group for children led by an art therapist, and the other a group for their parents facilitated by a social worker. A positive mourning experience for the children is most often found when the child has a parent in the companion group, which ". . . implies that the child in grief must be considered within the context of the family system and that the value of therapy is redoubled when offered as part of an interdisciplinary intervention" (Zambelli, et. al., 1988:41).

Fox (1984–85) reminds us that counseling support of children ought not be limited to the period immediately following a family death, but also should be available when anniversary reactions rekindle what Peppers and Knapp (1980) call "shadow grief." Death education in elementary, middle, and secondary schools is more common today than in the past (Ulin, 1977), but teachers and school administrators, as well as other professionals, are seeking opportunities to develop support skills for dying and bereaved children.

CLINICAL SOCIOLOGY IMPLICATIONS

For many today, the death of an elderly relative is an occasion for the barest acknowledgment of a death and most expeditious disposal of the body. Miscarriages, abortions, stillbirths, and neonatal deaths share in the minimal public

recognition accorded devalued elderly adults. Children today experience few deaths in their families, and those deaths that do occur tend to be minimized in their impact, leaving children alone in their grief. Such "low grief" deaths (Fulton, 1970) result from perceptions of minimal loss, and desires for muted grief and minimal mourning and bereavement. In the case of a fetus or newborn, the death may be considered "low grief" because life has not yet "really" begun, while for elderly persons death comes after a full life, and possibly a prolonged illness, and is perceived as inevitable.

The death of a developing child, or a young husband or wife, on the other hand, is perceived as premature and unjust. The social and emotional needs of the survivors, adults and children alike, are acknowledged as "high grief," having an infinitely great impact. Whether these "high grief" deaths are actually more traumatic than "low grief" deaths for the the people involved is questionable. Consider, for instance, how "improper grief" might be expressed by individuals in their roles as health care professionals or even friends and lovers, who are not expected to mourn because they are not considered the "bereaved," that is, the proper recipients of concern and social support.

A clinical sociology approach to grief and bereavement broadens our understanding by linking the individual's socio-emotional needs at the time of loss with the social and cultural context in which coping takes place. The professional cooperation beginning to emerge in the medical and nursing care given to dying adults and children, and their families, can be expected to continue. Health care professionals are responding to new directions in holistic health by acknowledging their own humanity in the practice of their professions. Resistance by certain professionals, and others in authority, should not deter dying patients and family members from asserting their concerns and expressing their needs. Consulting clinical sociologists can assist in designing organizational responses, and providing case-by-case assessments which aid medical and nursing care providers, and families, in coping with death, grief, and bereavement.

The clinical sociologist brings an appreciation of the roles of socio-economic status, family organization and interaction, professional issues in health care delivery, and social and psychological responses in death, grief and, bereavement. Symbolic interaction theory in sociology sensitizes one to the constraints of social expectations, and the ways in which people construct and reconstruct the reality that is their world. For social constructionists, facing death with children means understanding and coping with dying, death, grief, and bereavement in different ways. For the child who is dying, learing to cope means learning how to die and how to live in the time remaining. For the medical and nursing caregivers, effective helping means honoring the person while managing the disease and its effects. For the bereaved child, coping with death means learning to live in a world that is very hard to understand. As clinical sociologists, our task is to increase public awareness of the private loss of death, and to enhance the support of dying and grieving children and the adults who care for them.

NOTES

1. This chapter is a revised and updated version of "Children and Dying" written by the author and published as Chapter 7 of Leming and Dickinson's *Understanding Dying, Death, and Bereavement*, New York: Holt, Rinehart and Winston, 1985: 175-206. Permission granted for revision and republication by Holt, Rinehart and Winston, Inc.

REFERENCES

Anthony, S. 1971. *The Discovery of Death in Childhood and After*. New York: Basic Books.

Aries, P. 1962. *Centuries of Childhood: A Social History of Family Life*. New York: Alfred A. Knopf.

Behnke, M., E. Setzer and P. Mehta. 1984. Death counseling and psychosocial support by physicians concerning dying children. *Journal of Medical Education* 59: 906-08.

Bendiksen, R. and R. Fulton. 1976. Death and the child: An anterospective test of the childhood bereavement and later behavior hypothesis. Chapter 19 in R. Fulton in collaboration with R. Bendiksen, *Death and Identity*, rev. ed. Bowie, MD: The Charles Press.

Bluebond-Langner, M. 1978. *The Private Worlds of Dying Children*. Princeton, NJ: Princeton University.

Bowie, W. K. 1977. Story of a first born. *Omega* 8:1-17.

Bowlby, J. 1969. Attachment. Vol. 1 of *Attachment and Loss*. New York: Basic Books.

——— 1980. Loss, sadness and depression. Vol. 3 of *Attachment*. New York: Basic Books.

Cullberg, J. and S. Karger. 1972. Psychosomatic Medicine in Obstetrics and Gynecology, 3rd International Congress, Basel, Switzerland.

Davidson, G. W. 1977. Death of the wished-for child: A case study. *Death Education* 1:265-75.

deMause, L. 1974. The Evolution of Childhood, in *The History of Childhood*. New York: Harper and Row.

Easson, W. M. 1970. *The Dying Child: The Management of the Child or Adolescent Who is Dying*. Springfield, IL: Charles C. Thomas.

Fox, S. 1984-85. Children's Anniversary reactions to the death of a family member. *Omega* 15:291-305.

Freud, A. and D. T. Burlingham. 1943. The Shock of Separation. In *War and Children*. New York: Medical War Books.

Fulton, R. 1970. Death, grief and social recuperation. *Omega* 1:23-28.

Fulton, R. and G. Owen. 1988. AIDS: Seventh Rank Absolute. Chapter 19 in I. B. Corless and M. Pittman-Lindeman, *AIDS: Principles, Practices, and Politics*. New York: Hemisphere.

Fulton, R. and G. Owen. 1987-88. Death and society in twentieth century america. *Omega* 18:379-94.

Furman, E. P. 1978. The death of a newborn: Care of the parents. *Birth and the Family Journal* 5:214-18.

Giles, P. F. H. 1970. Reactions of women to perinatal death. *Australian and New Zealand Journal of Obstetrics and Gynecology* 10:207-10.

Glaser, B. G. and A. L. Strauss. 1965. *Awareness of Dying*. Chicago: Aldine.

Goldscheider, C. 1971. *Population, Modernization and Social Structure*. Boston: Little, Brown.

Grant, J. P. 1982. Interview on "All Things Considered," National Public Radio, February 1.

Grant, J. P. 1985. *The State of the World's Children*. New York: Oxford University Press.

Gray, B. H. 1975. *Human Subjects in Medical Experimentation*. New York: Wiley.

Grossman, M. 1988. Children with AIDS. Chapter 13 in I. B. Corless and M. Pittman-Lindeman, *AIDS: Principles, Practices and Politics*. New York: Hemisphere.

Gyulay, J. 1978. *The Dying Child*. New York: McGraw- Hill.

Hartigan, J. M. 1981. Maternal-Infant Bonding: Differences in Bonding/Grieving Response to Neonatal Death, Stillborn and Miscarriage. Session III of Resolve Through Sharing Core Team Training Program at La Crosse Lutheran Hospital, La Crosse, Wisconsin.

Haub, C. and M. M. Kent. 1988. *1988 World Population Data Sheet*. Washington, DC: Population Reference Bureau.

Husbans, E. and D. A. Brouddhus. 1984. Children's books and stories as therapeutic metaphors: An intervention with seriously ill children. *Paedovita* 1:17–21.

Kastenbaum, R. 1972. The kingdom where nobody dies. *Saturday Review of Science* 5:33–38.

Klein, M. 1944. A contribution to the theory of anxiety and guilt. *International Journal of Psychiatry* 23:114–23.

Kubler-Ross, E. 1969. *On Death and Dying*. New York: Macmillan.

Lifton, R. J. 1987. *The Future of Immortality and Other Essays for a Nuclear Age*. New York: Basic Books.

Limbo, R. K. and S. R. Wheeler. 1986. *When a Baby Dies: A Handbook for Healing and Helping*. La Crosse, WI: Lutheran Hospital La Crosse/Gunderson Clinic, Ltd.

Lindemann, E. 1944. Symptomatology and management of acute grief. *American Journal of Psychiatry* 101:141–48.

Lonetto, R. 1980. *Children's Conceptions of Death*. New York: Springer.

Markusen, E., G. Owen, R. Fulton, and R. Bendiksen. 1977–78. SIDS: The survivor as victim. *Omega* 8:277–84.

Martinson, I. M., M. E. Nesbit, and J. H. Kersey. 1985. Physician's role in home care for children with cancer. *Death Studies* 9:283–93.

Nagy, M. 1948. The child's theories concerning death. *Journal of Genetic Psychology* 73:3–27.

National Center for Health Statistics: Births, Marriages, Divorces, and Deaths for 1987. *Monthly Vital Statistics Report*, 36 (12), DHHS Pub. No (PHS) 88–ll20. Public Health Service, Hyattsville, MD.

Peppers, L. G. and R. J. Knapp. 1980. *Motherhood and Mourning: Perinatal Death*. New York: Praeger.

Pollach, G. H. 1986. Childhood sibling loss: A family tragedy. *Annuals of Psychoanalysis* 14:5–34.

Rosen, H. 1984–85. Prohibitions against mourning in childhood sibling loss. *Omega* 15:307–16.

Schulz, C. and K. F. Hall. 1965. *Two-by-fours: A Sort of Serious Book about Children*. Anderson, IN: Warner.

Shilts, R. 1987. *And the Band Played On: Politics, People, and the AIDS Epidemic*. New York: St. Martin's.

Simmons, R. G., S. D. Klein, and R. L. Simmons. 1977. *Gift of Life: The Social and Psychological Impact of Organ Transplantation*. New York: Wiley.

Share, L. 1972. Family communication in the crisis of a child's fatal illness: A literature review and analysis. *Omega* 3:187–201.

Smiley, C. and K. Goettl. 1981. Resolve Through Sharing Core Team Traning Program. Paper presented at La Crosse Lutheran Hospital, Wisconsin.

Swoiskin, S. 1986. Sudden infant death: Nursing care for the survivors. *Journal of Pediatric Nursing* 1:33–39.

Ulin, R. O. 1977. *Death and Dying Education*. Washington, DC: National Education Association.

van Eys, J. 1978. *Research on Children: Medical Imperatives, Ethical Quandries and Legal Constraints*. Baltimore, MD: University Park.

Zambelli, G. C., E. Clark, L. Barile, and A. F. de Jong. 1988. An interdisciplinary approach to clinical intervention for childhood bereavement. *Death Studies* 12:41–50.

Zelligs, R. 1974. *Children's Experience with Death*. Springfield, IL: Charles C. Thomas.

18

Coping With Uncertainty: Family Members' Adaptations During Cancer Remission

Laura E. Nathan

In the story of Damocles and Dionysius, Damocles admired the wealth, power, and happiness that Dionysius had as ruler. In an effort to show Damocles what his life was like, Dionysius invited Damocles to be his guest at a banquet, and to experience a monarch's situation. When Damocles arrived, he was placed on a couch of velvet, surrounded with gold and silver objects and with servants to attend to his desires. At first Damocles reveled in this situation, but later he glanced up and saw a sword above his head, dangling from the ceiling, held by a single horsehair. Confronted with danger and risk, Damocles immediately asked that he be allowed to leave. Threatened with impending doom, he could no longer enjoy the state that he had envied.

When cancer patients are in remission, they and their families are in positions similar to that of Damocles. When they are undergoing treatment for cancer, patients and their families typically focus on recovery. However, once the disease is under control, for a significant time at least, the patient is not considered cured. Rather, remission is a time of limbo, a period when patients and their families wait to see if additional treatment is needed. Like Damocles, cancer patients and their families see a situation that looks enviable (i.e., where freedom from disease is the norm), but with remission, the everpresent fear of recurrence is like a sword suspended overhead.

REMISSION

Remission is defined as the "complete or partial disappearance of the signs and symptoms of disease in response to treatment" (American Cancer Society, Inc., 1985:15). As indicated above, remission does not necessarily imply a cure, it is merely a time when the disease is under control. Remission is in many respects a hopeful time, for it signals to all that the acute crisis of cancer is over. It is a time when both patients and family members can begin to refocus their energies on aspects of their lives not related to cancer.

Although remission is generally greeted with hope and happiness, it also can be a time of unusual stress. People who have had cancer are at high risk for recurrence of the same type of cancer. Moreover, former cancer patients are at higher than normal risk for developing a second primary cancer (Laszlo, 1987). The threats of recurrence and growth of a new primary cancer bring the potential for illness and more treatment for patients, and the prospect of major life adjustments and anticipatory grief for family members. On a personal level, remission means that patients and family members continue day-to-day life with a cloud looming overhead. Consequently, these individuals must, either consciously or unconsciously, develop strategies for dealing with the threat of cancer.

Aside from strictly personal or psychological challenges, remission also can be a time of interpersonal and social stress. Throughout the cultural history of the United States, patients in general, but especially cancer patients, have been held accountable for their illnesses (Patterson, 1987). Accordingly, cancer patients, even those in remission, have had to bear the stigma of the disease. Some people are afraid to be around cancer patients, even when they are in remission (Nathan, 1988). Similarly, people often find it uncomfortable to be around cancer patients' family members, typically because they are unsure of what to say. Further, employers are sometimes unwilling to hire people who have had cancer (Frankfurt, 1987), and former cancer patients often experience discrimination in securing affordable and comprehensive health insurance (Crothers, 1987). In sum, cancer patients and their families face a host of potential stressors, even when the cancer is in remission.

Until recently, researchers "have mainly been concerned with the crisis of diagnosis of cancer and the crisis of death from cancer. The adaptive process that takes place between these two events has been neglected" (Clark, 1984:168). Recently, however, survivorship has become a topic of major importance. In fact, the 1987 American Cancer Society Conference on Human Values and Cancer was devoted to survival, recognizing the "obvious advantages and the special problems which go hand in hand with survival" (Holleb, 1987:1). While the use of the term survivorship casts the remission period in a most positive light, remission is a chronic condition requiring special kinds of adjustments. Both premorbid factors and characteristics of a patient's illness influence the choices of strategies employed by family members for handling remission. In addition to identifying the indicators associated with family members' selections of coping strategies, we need to more clearly articulate the impact of specific strategies on the other aspects of their lives.

FAMILIES OF CANCER PATIENTS

Researchers are beginning to recognize that life threatening illness in general, and cancer in particular, is a family matter (Barbarin, 1987; Cohen, 1987; Fobair, 1987). With the understanding that the development of a disease such as cancer can have serious consequences for patients and their significant others, investigators are focusing attention on the psychosocial morbidity of family members resulting from their experiences with a relative's cancer. Cancer places the continuity of family life in jeopardy, and the threat is shared by all. What can make the cancer experience particularly difficult for family members is that they typically are called upon to assist and comfort the patient at times when they themselves are most needy. For relatives of long-term survivors, providing yet not receiving emotional support can have a lasting and debilitating effect.

Stress is a part of life, and "a predictable aspect of family development and change over the life span" (Figley and McCubbin, 1983:v). Some stresses within families are considered normal due to the large number of families who live with them as everyday difficulties (e.g., stresses over family finances and those relating to achieving a balance between work and home). Others are considered normative since they are life transitions experienced by many (e.g., the stress accompanying the birth of a child or that associated with remarriage and the blending of families). In contrast to the normative stresses with which families are confronted, some situations present extraordinary stresses. A catastrophic stress is "a sudden and extreme threat to survival which is associated with a sense of helplessness, disruption, destruction, and loss" (McCubbin and Figley, 1983:220). Living with chronic illness, or, in particular, living with cancer or the threat of cancer, qualifies as a stress of this sort. Extraordinary stresses typically have an impact on all members of the family unit. In fact, sometimes a "catastrophe" within the family has a greater impact on other family members than it does on the victim (Figley, 1983).

The emotional impact of cancer reverberates throughout the family, and family members' reactions to cancer, both upon initial diagnosis and over an extended period of time, may be similar to those of the cancer patient. Responses may, at various points, include denial, shock, fear, anger, depression, anxiety, and guilt (McKhann, 1981). This is understandable, for all times, even during the remission period, a family member's cancer can stimulate intense emotions related to the uncertainty of survival and the possibility of loss (Lauria, Whitt, and Wells, 1987; McKhann, 1981). Further, because people are linked by virtue of belonging to a family, individuals' reactions to stress will likely have a bearing on how others in the family are affected.

However, not all family members will necessarily respond the same way to a relative's cancer. The impact that cancer has on family members will vary with personality and other factors, yet the greatest variation in response to cancer is related to the role that a person has vis-a-vis the patient. "For example, the treatment of a child introduces significant challenges to the parents and other family members, and the treatment of a parent may cause adjustment problems in a child" (Dobkin and Morrow, 1985/86:24). Further, "siblings of cancer patients experience emotional and developmental conflicts" (Quinn and Herndon, 1986:46). Yet, it is spouses who often are particularly affected, since they are the ones most likely to be overloaded by the additional burdens created by the cancer. Further, "spouses struggle with their fears and shattered dreams" (Quinn and Herndon, 1986:46).

Family distress associated with cancer treatment and the unpredictability of the disease can affect all aspects of well-being, including interpersonal relationships, intellectual functioning, and the ability to accomplish tasks, and may result in a variety of negative consequences such as psychosomatic problems, sleep and mood disturbances, eating disorders, and sexual dysfunction (Barbarin, 1987). Cancer is a stressful event for everyone, yet both in the acute phase and over time, this burden is not equally shared. It is the relative closest to the cancer patient who, along with the patient, typically bears the brunt of the strain (Holland, 1973).

From early on in the cancer experience, both patients and family members are concerned with the effects of the disease and its treatment on the quality of life. Certainly, normal living is compromised during the treatment phase, but the impact of cancer may have long-term effects, as well. Over the course of time, the financial strain of treatment and other expenses associated with the cancer may result in the lowering of the family's life-style (Dobkin and Morrow, 1985/86:24; Kaplan, 1982). This and other changes in family circumstances may threaten essential values and aspirations for members. Adjustments in living, and the patterns of coping initially adopted by families are important, as they often persist during remission and beyond.

Under normal circumstances families ideally are thought of as a refuge from the troubles of everyday life. When a crisis strikes, it is the family that is counted on to rally around the victim. As a result, the expectations placed on family members during the cancer experience can be enormous. With illnesses like cancer, family members are frequently enlisted to help insure that the patient's treatment protocol is carried out (Lauria, Whitt, and Wells, 1987). Similarly, relatives often are called upon to be caretakers, for at least a short period of time, and it is presumed that family members will offer solace. While it is true that families can serve to alleviate some of the emotional trauma associated with cancer, excessive and prolonged stress may undermine the protective effect of even the strongest family.

As is clear from the above discussion, patients have many needs throughout the natural history of the cancer experience, and the family frequently is asked to be a mainstay of care. But family members also have needs during the course of the illness and its aftermath. The desire for information is typically great when a family member has cancer. Like the patients themselves, family members seek information about the disease, and what to expect with respect to both treatment and prognosis (Northouse and Northouse, 1987). Family members who have been working prior to the cancer diagnosis will likely continue to work, and that work will be more crucial than ever, given the financial threat posed by cancer and its treatment. Moreover, work is important for some family members because it allows them to spend part of their time focusing on something other than the relative's illness. In a similar fashion, attending school offers a respite to family members who are students. Perhaps the greatest need of family members, however, is to be able to continue life as normally as possible, with time for entertainment, relaxation, and even vacations. In recognition of the lot of family members when faced with a relative's cancer, the Tulsa, Oklahoma chapter of the national cancer support group, Make Today Count, drafted a Bill of Rights for relatives. A key principle of this document is the conviction that relatives of cancer patients must take care of their own needs. This premise is sound, since there is evidence that family members who put their own lives on hold while taking care of patients are at high risk for burnout, with detrimental effects for both patients and caretakers (Nathan, 1986). Yet it is not always easy for healthy family members to find time to address their own concerns.

As suggested earlier, when a person is ill, his or her responsibilities are usually transferred to others. Thus, serious illness often produces changes in the family system. The ways in which family tasks are redistributed can have a marked impact on individuals and the family unit. According to Vess, Moreland, and Schwebel (1985), problems associated with the reallocation of family roles are related to many factors, including the normal responsibilities of the patient, the abilities of other family members to take on those jobs, and the availability of outside resources. Further, a family's method of assigning roles to individuals will influence how both the individuals and the family will weather the cancer experience. Families who redistribute roles based on individuals' efforts and abilities, i.e., those who employ an achieved method of assigning roles, undergo limited family disruption. Further, people in these families experience less role conflict and role strain over time than individuals whose families employ a reallocation pattern based on ascribed characteristics (Vess, Moreland, and Schwebel, 1985).

Vess, Moreland, and Schwebel (1985) also explored three family redistribution patterns and their effects. The patterns they identified were the nuclear redistribution pattern, where the responsibilities of the patient were taken on and shared by all members of the nuclear family; the external redistribution pattern, where people outside the nuclear family were enlisted to take on some of the patient's former tasks; and the overload distribution pattern, where the bulk of the work fell to one person (in their study, the spouse) and others were, at most, marginally involved in assuming the patient's roles. They found that the nuclear reallocation pattern was the best for families, resulting in the lowest levels of family conflict and the greatest levels of cohesion.

Communication between family members throughout the cancer experience is an important consideration. With so much to be concerned about, and people responding in different ways at different times, there are many possibilities for misunderstanding. For some people, verbalizing fears and talking about problems gives those fears and problems lives of their own. Thus, some family members may have a general resistance to talking or may be unwilling to listen to others who have a desire to talk. As in other stressful situations, family members may decrease communication in an attempt to guard against painful thoughts (Northouse and Northouse, 1987). Those who are able to communicate with other family members are generally at an advantage, since open communication typically eases stress and aids in overall family adaptation while closed communication can interfere with family bonds (Vess, Moreland, and Schwebel, 1985; Northouse and Northouse, 1987). Although the bulk of the literature on communication in the family emphasizes the benefits of open communication, there is evidence that, for some, avoiding discussion of the cancer and its accompanying threat may be a positive coping mechanism.

It is important to keep in mind that "adaptational demands are placed on family members throughout the course of the disease" (Dobkin and Morrow, 1985/86:38). Although it is the acute phase of any phase of any illness that is typically the major focus, the end of treatment for cancer also may mean a significant adjustment for family members. Nagging worries often accompany the relief associated with the end of cancer treatment. There can be fear among family members about factors that may complicate recovery. Worse still is the looming threat of recurrence. Gotay (1987) makes mention of symptom consciousness, where evidence of symptoms like those associated with the cancer results in intense anxiety. This condition, one prevalent in cancer survivors, also can exist for family members. Another concern related to the transition following the acute illness stage is that sometimes, in an effort to cope with the active phase of a disease, family members and others close to the patient will prepare for the worst. In doing so, they may experience anticipatory grief, and even rehearse in their minds what they think life will be like after their loved one dies. If this method of coping is used, then remission comes as a surprise and these family members face further adaptational demands.

Difficulties in coping with a family member's cancer may be so severe that personal problems arise. Children who have close relatives with cancer are at risk for problems in school, while adult family members may have problems in their work environments (Kaplan et al., 1973 cited in Kaplan, 1982; Barbarin, 1987). Further, illness and substance abuse have been documented in studies of surviving relatives (Kaplan, et. al., 1973 cited in Kaplan, 1982).

Not all of the consequences of cancer experienced by the family are negative. In fact, sometimes family members gain an increased appreciation for one another, and the crisis situation can result in greater family cohesion (Holland, 1973). Parents with intact marriages who have had children survive cancer have noted a positive impact on their marriages in the long run (Foster, O'Malley, and Koocher, 1981, cited in Dobkin and Morrow, 1985/86). As expected, the strength of the family unit prior to the cancer diagnosis is predictive of what will happen to that family as a result of the cancer experience (Wellisch, 1987). In general, those families with strong and functional relationships fare better than those whose relationships are initially less healthy.

THEORETICAL MODEL: COPING STATEGIES AND THEIR CONSEQUENCES

For both patients and family members, the process of adjusting to cancer remission is not the same as that of adapting to cancer. When a diagnosis of cancer is given, there is the fact of the disease to be reckoned with. Treatment procedures are recommended, and families are confronted with the focus and activity inherent in the acute phase of care. With remission, there is no precise time at which the patient is well. The remission phase begins following treatment, and will continue indefinitely, or until the cancer recurs. For most types of cancer, patients who remain disease-free for five years after treatment are considered "cured" (American Cancer Society, Inc., 1985:9), yet there is no guarantee that that person will remain cancer free. The remission phase, then, is a process of adapting, not to terminal disease, but to uncertainty.

As cancer remission becomes an increasingly common experience, the need increases for research that will clarify the nature and scope of problems with which family members are faced following the conclusion of cancer treatment. One of the greatest challenges in discussing families of cancer patients and cancer survivors, is attempting to generalize about their experiences and how they can attempt to cope with the circumstances presented by the illness. People's cancers are very different from one another. Owing to the variety of diseases that are called cancer, it is impossible to say that all cancer survivors and their families will develop a particular coping strategy or need a specific kind of resource or support service to help them in their adaptation to living

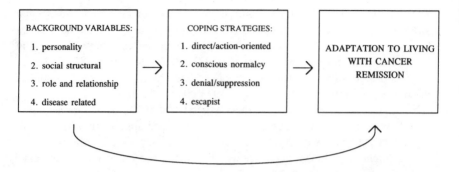

Figure 1. Theoretical model showing the proposed relationship between background variables, the coping strategies adopted by family members during cancer remission, and successful adaptation to living with remission.

with remission. Further, by virtue of our unique personalities and the social statuses and roles that we have, we as individuals experience threats such as cancer in ourselves or in a loved one in very personal ways. Despite recognition of these individual differences, it is nonetheless important to identify the factors related to the adoption of specific kinds of coping strategies, as well as the impact of particular strategies on people's day-to-day lives. Once we identify at least some of these general relationships, we can begin to develop interventions that will be helpful to broad categories of people.

Many factors will influence a family member's overall adjustment to living with cancer remission. Based upon what is currently known about cancer patients and their families, the following model of adaptation is proposed (see Figure One). This model takes into account three categories of variables: background variables, types of coping strategies as intervening variables, and the outcome variable of adaptation to cancer remission. It is proposed that the background variables will influence adaptation to remission both directly and indirectly, through specific coping strategies. It is further predicted that coping strategies will be more strongly associated with overall adaptation than will the background variables.

Four major background variable classifications are considered in this model: psychological and personality variables, social structural and demographic features, role and relationship indicators, and disease related factors. In the individual or psychological realm, it is expected that the selection of specific coping strategies and overall adaptation to living with cancer remission will be influenced by a person's general level of adjustment and coping skills prior to the family member's diagnosis. Drawing upon the work of Quinn and Herndon

(1986), it also is proposed that a person's level of self-esteem and sense of mastery prior to the crisis of a relative's cancer will affect coping styles and adaptation to uncertainty.

Psychological and personality factors are, to some extent, shaped by demographic characteristics that themselves help define a person's position in the social system. Factors such as a person's sex, educational status, and occupation, as well as the family's socioeconomic status, race, and ethnicity, are suggested as predictors of the coping strategies that will be adopted and of overall adaptation. Age and stage of life also are viewed as potentially potent indicators, as are religious identity and religiosity. Marital status is seen as an important independent variable both in and of itself, and because of role and relationship factors that come into play when the cancer patient is one's spouse.

According to the proposed model, roles and relationships prior to the cancer diagnosis and during the treatment phase will influence coping and adaptation during cancer remission. As suggested earlier, a family member's response to a relative's cancer will, to some extent, be a function of the role relationship of that person to the patient. This will likely also hold true for responses relating to the uncertainty of remission. Further, the roles in the family of the cancer patient and other family members prior to the cancer diagnosis are seen as potential predictors of coping strategies that are adopted for living with remission. Likewise, family composition and the roles and functioning of various family members may influence individual coping and adaptation.

The quality of relationships before the cancer diagnosis also is viewed as a possible predictor in the proposed model. In general, bonds among family members and, more specifically, the kinds of relationships that a given person has with others in the family, are suggested as factors leading to choice of coping strategies and adjustment to remission. While connections between family members are seen as key indicators, the proposed model does not negate the potential importance of relationships with friends. Friendships may play a role in preference for particular coping strategies and can thus affect adaptation to remission. Additionally, relationships with health care providers both prior to the patient's cancer diagnosis and throughout the treatment stage may lead to the adoption of specific coping behaviors and an accompanying level of adaptation.

Finally, the model put forward here suggests that several disease-related factors will help determine both the coping mechanisms that are employed by family members, and individuals' adaptations to living with cancer remission. The specific diagnosis, including type and stage of cancer, and the prognosis, can profoundly affect coping strategies. The types and length of treatment, treatment side effects, and the patient's degree of disability and pain will all have an impact on family members' understanding of the situation. A recurrence following a period of remission also can influence coping and adaptation, for once a cancer has recurred, there can be an increased sense of helplessness. In addition to the disease-related variables mentioned above, the time elapsed since completion of treatment is seen as a predictor of coping and adaptation in this model. According to Bard (1987:4) "the period immediately following the conclusion of active treatment is a particularly difficult time." This is the time that Mullan (1985), in discussing seasons of survival, refers to as the time of extended survival, a time which he states is dominated by fear of recurrence. The coping strategies employed at this stage may be different from those used at other times.

The process of coping involves coming to terms with adverse circumstances. Strategies for coping with the uncertainty brought about by a family member's cancer remission may take the form of attitudes toward the cancer remission or specific behaviors that are used in response to the situation. Strategies for coping may be conscious or unconscious, and they may be individual or interpersonal in nature. Not all coping patterns are necessarily healthy, so some coping strategies will result in lower overall adaptation to living with remission. The proposed model includes four general coping patterns or strategies: the direct/action-oriented pattern of coping; the strategy of conscious normalcy; the denial/suppression strategy; and the pattern of escapism. While these patterns are not necessarily mutually exclusive, certain modes of coping are more or less compatible with other proposed patterns.

Using the direct/action-oriented strategy for coping with a family member's cancer remission means fully recognizing the situation and doing one's best to address that reality. In employing an action-oriented strategy, the family member acknowledges his or her own needs as well as those of the patient in remission. This direct pattern of coping is a problem-solving mode, where individuals address the difficulties inherent in the situation. One action that clearly lies within the realm of this coping strategy is the seeking and obtaining of information related to the disease. This may take the form of enrolling in a course, surveying the literature on the topic, or talking to people with expertise on the subject. In any case, it is an effort to gain control of the situation by better understanding what is likely to lie ahead. Straightforward attempts to gain emotional support also qualify as action-oriented behaviors. Becoming a member of a support network, such as an "I Can Cope" self-help group sponsored by the American Cancer Society, is an example of such action-oriented conduct, as is seeking support from friends, neighbors, and other family members. Enlisting the aid of professional helpers, including psychotherapists, and drawing upon the social services and organizations that are available in the community, also signals a direct pattern of coping. Additionally, a willingness to engage in open and empathic communication within the family, including discussion of how roles will be reallocated in the family should the patient be unable to fulfill his or her normal responsibilities, indicates an action-oriented mode of coping.

The conscious normalcy pattern of coping is similar to the direct/action-oriented mode in that the reality of the situation is acknowledged. The difference, however, is that rather than actively confronting that reality, those who employ the conscious normalcy strategy choose to more or less put that reality to the side and continue life, to the greatest extent possible, as it was before the cancer diagnosis. Resuming employment or schooling is seen as a part of this coping style, as is participating in social occasions. Living in the present is central to this form of coping. Diversions from the responsibilities of everyday living, such as exercise or recreation, going to the movies, or even short holidays, are in keeping with the conscious normalcy form of coping.

A third pattern of coping with remission, the denial/suppression mode, is quite different from the strategies described above. This pattern involves attempts to handle the situation by not facing the true circumstances. It may involve out-and-out denial of the cancer and subsequent remission, or acceptance of the facts with a simultaneous need on the part of the family member to suppress his or her own feelings. An unwillingness to communicate with other family members about the disease and remission is suggestive of the denial strategy, as are efforts to retreat into oneself and remain isolated. Likewise, a fatalistic attitude signals that one has given up on gaining some control over the situation as it exists. Further, placing blame on others for the circumstances that have resulted from cancer and remission also can be understood as an attempt to keep oneself distracted from the real issues. Also included in the denial/suppression coping style is the submerging of one's own needs, supposedly for the benefit of the person in remission.

Finally, the escapist strategy is an attempt to distance oneself from all reality—especially the realities of cancer, cancer remission, and the changes that have taken place or lie ahead as a result of the family member's cancer. The primary escapist route is through the use of substances, especially drugs or alcohol. Adopting a pattern of escapism may make any given day seem easier. In terms of long term adaptation, however, this strategy is probably the least productive.

The theoretical model presented in this chapter sees both background variables and coping strategies as leading to the outcome variable of adaptation to cancer remission. To date, there is no one agreed-upon indicator of adjustment to cancer, let alone consensus on what constitutes adaptation to remission for family members. When researchers begin to further explore family members' experiences with cancer remission, the conceptualization and measurement of adaptation will undoubtedly be major foci. For the model proposed here, adaptation is viewed as having a number of potential components. Maladjustment to cancer remission may be revealed in diminished health for the family member, or it may be evidenced in work related factors, such as increased absenteeism or impaired job performance. On an emotional or psychological level, poor adaptation may surface as depression or reduced self-esteem. On the other hand, improved relationships within the family, increased family cohesion, and a heightened sense of general satisfaction with life point to successful adaptation.

Although little research has been done with families of cancer patients, information available on the patients themselves makes it possible to begin speculation about which background variables and coping strategies will lead to successful adaptation for family members. For example, there is evidence that cancer patients in prestigious occupations garner greater social support and adapt better to cancer than do patients in less highly ranked occupations (Clark, 1984). Other research (Worden and Sobel, 1978, cited in Fobair, 1987) supports the notion that an active coping style assists patients in maintaining positive outlooks. It is anticipated that having a highly prestigious job and adopting an active coping style will likewise lead to better adaptation for family members. More systematic research is needed to test the variables and proposed relationships suggested in the theoretical model herein presented. Future research will also undoubtedly uncover additional determinants of family members' adaptations to cancer remission.

SOCIETAL RESPONSE TO THE IMPACT OF LIVING WITH RISK

Once former cancer patients and their families survive the initial diagnosis and treatment phases, they become part of a different category: families who are living with exceptional risk. Given the persistent threat of additional cancer, these families may need support services and organizations to help them perform effectively in their daily lives. Just as Cicely Saunders and others (1981) developed the modern hospice concept to address the special needs of dying patients and their families, innovative organizational responses need to be developed and made available to families living with the threat of cancer recurrence.

Some resources currently are available to cancer patients and their families. For instance, there are organized support groups in a number of places, information can be obtained by those who are determined to get it, and therapeutic intervention is a possibility for many. Unfortunately, what exists generally is available in piecemeal form rather than being part of a coordinated system of resources and services. Support groups should be convenient to all and easy to locate, and tangible support services, such as legal and financial counseling for cancer patients and their families, should be readily available. Counseling and therapy should be available to everyone, not just those who can afford them, and psychosocial interventions might be more effective as preventive measures than as responses to crises. Patients and their families should have easy access to information about cancer and its sequelae, and a central mechanism should be established to refer patients and their families to the desired resources. While it is clear that not all patients or family members will need the same types and levels of intervention, resources need to be made available, and families deserve to be offered assistance in adapting to cancer remission. Moreover, once resources are established, it is necessary to let people know about them, for unless available resources are adequately publicized, the fact of their existence will have little impact on the adjustment that people make to living with uncertainty.

The needs of cancer patients are beginning to be addressed in innovative ways. A national magazine is being published for people living with cancer, and a National Coalition for Cancer Survivorship has been established. Each of these efforts is a means of linking cancer patients, of focusing on the shared aspects of the experience, and of acknowledging that in many ways cancer is a continuous, lifelong condition. While the experiences and concerns of family members are recognized through these vehicles, both the magazine and the coalition have patients as their primary focus. It is possible that a parallel publication or organization designed specifically for family members would be useful to many.

In an effort to meet patients' needs, the American Cancer Society has developed a variety of visitor programs that link up new cancer patients with people who have experienced and adapted to cancer and its consequences. These visitor programs seem to be helpful to both the new patient and the long-term survivor. The new patient gets valuable advice about living with cancer and the visitors benefit from the process of supporting others. Although no visitor programs currently exist for family members, it is possible that such programs would be very helpful to family members adapting to the remission period.

At issue for patients and family members is the quality of life while living with the aftermath of disease and the specter of recurrence. While each patient and family member will experience the cancer and remission in an individual way, these are not just personal problems. The consequences of cancer are felt by the entire society, and are thus public matters in addition to private concerns. Research needs to be undertaken to clearly identify those factors that come from living with uncertainty. While research can provide the information about the resources that are needed, only the commitment of a caring society can provide the impetus to move from knowledge and scattered resources to coordinated and coherent public policy.

CONCLUSION

Current projections of cancer incidence highlight the need for increased insight into the impact of cancer on patients and their families. Statistics show that nearly one in three Americans alive today will develop some form of cancer, more than one in every five Americans will die of cancer, and cancer will occur in nearly three out of four families (American Cancer Society, 1988; Renneker, 1988). Given the large number of people who will be affected by cancer, and particularly the increased number of survivors (American Cancer Society, 1988), research on the psychosocial consequences of cancer survival is essential. Once we understand both the factors that influence which coping strategies are adopted by individuals with a family member at high risk for cancer recurrence, and the consequences of the various coping strategies that are employed, we as a society can begin to formulate policy and develop services designed specifically to address the difficulties resulting from this increasingly common circumstance of modern life.

REFERENCES

American Cancer Society. 1988. *Cancer Facts and Figures-1988.* New York: American Cancer Society.

American Cancer Society. 1985. *Cancer Word Book.* New York: American Cancer Society.

Barbarin, O. A. 1987. Psychosocial risks and invulnerability: A review of the theoretical and empirical bases of preventive family-focused services for survivors of childhood cancer. *Journal of Psychosocial Oncology* 5(4):25–41.

Bard, M. 1987. Psychosocial Perspective on Surviving: A Definition. In American Cancer Society, ed. *Proceedings of the Fifth National Conference on Human Values and Cancer—1987.* San Francisco, CA: American Cancer Society, 2–5.

Clark, E. J. 1984. Social Assessment of Cancer Patients. In American Cancer Society, ed. *Proceeding of the National Conference on Practice, Education and Research In Oncology Social Work.* Philadelphia, PA: American Cancer Society, 164–69.

Cohen, J. 1987. Cancer Survival and Psychosocial Impact. In American Cancer Society, ed. *Proceedings of the Fifth National Conference on Human Values and Cancer—1987.* San Francisco, CA: American Cancer Society, 14–17.

Crothers, H. 1987. Health Insurance: Problems and Solutions for People With Cancer Histories. In American Cancer Society, ed. *Proceedings of the Fifth National Conference on Human Values and Cancer—1987.* San Francisco, CA: American Cancer Society, 100–109.

Dobkin, P.L. and G.R. Morrow, 1985/86. Long-term side effects in patients who have been treated successfully for cancer. *Journal of Psychosocial Oncology* 3(4):23–51.

Figley, C. R. 1983. Catastrophes: An overview of family reactions. In C. R. Figley and H. McCubbin, eds. *Stress and the Family Volume 2: Coping With Catastrophe.* New York: Brunner/Mazel, 3–20.

Figley, C. R. and H. McCubbin. 1983. *Stress and the Family Volume II: Coping With Catastrophe.* New York: Brunner/Mazel (preface).

Fobair, P. A. 1987. The Adaptation Process in Surviving Cancer. In American Cancer Society, ed. *Proceedings of the Fifth National Conference on Human Values and Cancer—1987.* San Francisco, CA: American Cancer Society, 6–10.

Foster, D.J., J.E. O'Malley, and G.P. Koocher. 1981. The parent interviews. In Gerald P. Koocher and J.E. O'Malley, eds. *The Damocles Syndrome: Psychosocial Consequences of Surviving Childhood Cancer.* New York: McGraw-Hill, 86–100.

Frankfurt, J. 1987. Work and School—The Crucibles of Survival; Employment Problems of the Cancer Survivor. In American Cancer Society, ed. *Proceedings of the Fifth National Confer-*

ence on Human Values and Cancer—1987. San Francisco, CA: American Cancer Society, 88–92.

Holland, J. 1973. Psychologic Aspects of Cancer. In J.F. Holland and E. Frei III, eds. *Cancer Medicine.* Philadelphia, PA: Lea and Febiger, 991–1021.

Holleb, A. I. 1987. Forward: Fifth National Conference on Human Values and Cancer. In American Cancer Society, ed. *Proceedings of the Fifth National Conference on Human Values and Cancer-1987.* San Francisco, CA: American Cancer Society, 1.

Kaplan, D. M., A. Smith, R. Grobstein, and S. Fischman. 1973. Family mediation of stress of posed by severe illness. *Social Work* 18:60–69.

Kaplan, D. M. 1982. Intervention strategies for families. In J. Cohen, J. W. Cullen, and L. R. Martin, eds. *Psychosocial Aspects of Cancer.* New York: Raven Press, 221–33.

Laszlo, J. 1987. *Understanding Cancer.* New York: Harper and Row.

Lauria, M. M., J. K. Whitt, and R. J. Wells. 1987. Protocol for Survival in Childhood Cancer: Family System Interventions. In American Cancer Society, ed. *Proceedings of the Fifth National Conference on Human Values and Cancer—1987.* San Francisco, CA: American Cancer Society, 114–20.

McCubbin, H. and C. R. Figley. 1983. Bridging normative and catastrophic family stress. In H. McCubbin and C. R. Figley, eds. *Stress and the Family Volume 1: Coping With Normative Transitions.* New York: Brunner/Mazel, 218–28.

McKhann, C.F. 1981. *The Facts About Cancer.* Englewood Cliffs, NJ: Prentice Hall, 41–55.

Mullan, F. 1985. Seasons of survival: Reflections of a physician with cancer. *The New England Journal of Medicine* 313(4):270–73.

Nathan, L.E. 1986. Families of cancer patients. Paper presented at the annual meeting of the Society for the Study of Social Problems, New York (August).

———1988. Understanding cancer: Personal, interpersonal, and social considerations. In M. Renneker, ed. *Understanding Cancer.* Palo Alto, CA: Bull Publishing Company, 257–62.

Northouse, P. G and L.L. Northouse. 1987. Communication and cancer: Issues confronting patients, health professionals, and family members. *Journal of Psychosocial Oncology* 5(3):17–46.

Patterson, J. T. 1987. *The Dread Disease.* Cambridge, MA: Harvard University Press, 12–35.

Quinn, W.H. and A. Herndon. 1986. The family ecology of cancer. *Journal of Psychosocial Oncology* 4(1/2):45–59.

Renneker, M. 1988. Introduction to cancer. In M. Renneker, ed. *Understanding Cancer.* Palo Alto, CA: Bull Publishing Company, 2–4.

Saunders, C., D. Summers and N. Teller, eds. 1981. *Hospice, The Living Idea.* London, England: Edward Arnold Publishers, Ltd.

Vess, J. D. Jr., J. R. Moreland, and A. I Schwebel. 1985. A follow-up study of role functioning and the psychological environment of families of cancer patients. *Journal of Psychosocial Oncology* 3(2):1–14.

Wellisch, D. K. 1987. Surviving and its effects on the family. In American Cancer Society, ed. *Proceedings of the Fifth National Conference on Human Values and Cancer—1987.* San Francisco, CA: American Cancer Society, 59–62.

Worden, J. W., and H. J. Sobel. 1978. Ego strength and psychosocial adaptation to cancer. *Psychosomatic Medicine* 40(8):585–92.

19

Testicular Cancer:
Passage to New Priorities

David F. Gordon

Although studies of cancer survivors have been increasing in recent years, very little research has been done on survivors of testicular cancer. This is a serious omission for several reasons. First, although testicular cancer is relatively rare in the general population,[1] it is the most common cancer affecting white men between the ages of 20 and 34 and the second most common cancer affecting them between the ages of 35 and 39 (National Cancer Institute, 1987). These are the ages at which most men are making commitments to their careers, spouses, and families, and a life-threatening disease could have serious effects on these commitments. Second, because of its location, it is possible that testicular cancer will have serious effects on feelings about masculinity, sexuality, and having children. Finally, testicular cancer is highly curable.[2] This, combined with onset at an early age, means that men who have had testicular cancer can be expected to live for many years. Thus it is possible to examine the long-term psychosocial effects of testicular cancer, and what we learn may apply to other forms of cancer as they become more curable.

The few existing studies of these psychosocial consequences have found that, despite some problems associated with sexual functioning, most men who have had testicular cancer make positive long-term adjustments (Gorzynski and Holland, 1979; Tross, et al., 1984; Rieker, et al., 1985). This is consistent with studies of the long-term quality of life of other cancer survivors (de Haes and Knippenberg, 1987). A major question is *how* testicular cancer survivors make positive long-term adjustments. This is especially important for developing clinical approaches for those men (and other cancer survivors) who do not arrive at positive adjustments.

This study was undertaken to identify the post-treatment effects of testicular cancer on the lives of men and those close to them, the processes by which

234

positive adjustments are made, and to develop recommendations for clinical intervention based on this information. It was found that, in most cases, testicular cancer created a transitional phase which allowed men to reassess their lives. The outcome of this reassessment almost unanimously was regarded as an improvement. Although the disease did have negative effects, these were neither as severe nor as related to sexual function as might be expected. The following sections will provide a description of the methods used in the study, a presentation of the findings, a theoretical interpretation of these findings, and a discussion of their clinical implications.

METHODS

The general focus of this study is the experience of a particular illness, in which the illness is seen as a social and psychological phenomenon that accompanies some undesirable physiological process or state (Conrad, 1987). Conrad (1987:18) points out, "The qualitative approach is still probably the most appropriate for examining topics as subjective and fluid as illness experience." Qualitative methods were thus chosen for the present study, in which the focus is on processes of adjustment, and because other studies of testicular cancer survivors primarily have been quantitative. Because this is a relatively unexplored area of inquiry, an attempt will be made to let the men speak for themselves as much as possible, and to use the inductive method to interpret their experiences.

Face-to-face, intensive interviews were conducted with 17 men who have had testicular cancer at some point in their lives.[3] These men were selected by several methods. Some were identified through a tumor registry at a local cancer center. Others had participated in a support group for testicular cancer and were identified by the group's organizer. Still others were found by word of mouth and referrals by acquaintances.

All but one of the interviews were done in the homes of the men. Five of the interviews included husband and wife jointly. Each interview lasted between one and one-and-a-half hours. In most cases the conversation continued after the formal interview was finished. These conversations were recorded in field notes. An interview guide was used, but the men were encouraged to talk about whatever they considered important. The goal of the interviews was to discover how testicular cancer patients interpret various aspects of the experience rather than to discover how widely these interpretations are distributed among such patients (McCraken, 1988).[4]

TESTICULAR CANCER

When a testicular tumor is discovered the affected testicle is removed in what is called an orchiectomy. If there is suspicion that the tumor has metastasized to the abdominal lymph nodes, an additional operation, called a lymph node dissection, is performed to remove these lymph nodes. It is common for the nerves that control ejaculation to be damaged during this operation. When this occurs the patient experiences a dry ejaculation, which is a normal ejaculation except that there is nothing ejaculated. This condition can reverse itself after several years, or it can be permanent. Depending on the type of cancer cell found in the testicular tumor, surgery can be followed by radiation or chemotherapy to kill any cancer cells left in the body. A newer approach, used in some cases in which the tumor is in an early stage, is to forgo therapy following surgery. Instead, the patient is monitored closely to watch for any further evidence of cancer (Sogani, et al., 1984; Pizzocaro, et al., 1986).

Testicular tumors frequently have very mild symptoms, or no symptoms at all. Very few men perform or even know about testicular self-examination (Cummings, et al., 1983). Of the 17 men interviewed, only one, a physician, discovered his tumor by self-examination. Consequently, many testicular tumors are discovered when the testicle is accidently bumped or when the tumor is advanced enough to cause noticeable pain or swelling. Even then, they are frequently misdiagnosed by family doctors (Murphy, 1983). This leads to a continuation of the discomfort, further growth of the tumor, and frequently, to more drastic treatment than would have been necessary earlier. Most of the serious medical aspects of testicular cancer are caused by such delays. One man said:

> And actually the doctor treated me for two-and-a-half months of something he thought it was, which I'm still a little upset about . . . So two-and-a-half months earlier, perhaps, if he'd sent me to a urologist instead of trying to correct the problem as a medical, just a regular medical doctor, I might have avoided, nowadays, that extra surgery. That, after finding out all the facts later, that I might have been able to avoid it, that kind of upsets me. You know because I have a scar from here to here and it's gonna be there, forever.

In other cases the man himself caused the delay by not seeking medical attention. The obvious clinical implication here is that men and physicians need to be better informed about testicular cancer, and attentive to the possibility of contracting it. Regular testicular examinations performed by men themselves, and by doctors during routine checkups, would detect many testicular tumors much earlier. This would eliminate the most serious physical consequences of testicular cancer, and perhaps prevent the most serious psychosocial consequences as well.

THE RITE OF PASSAGE

The most remarkable aspect of the experience of testicular cancer is the turning point that it provides in men's lives. Several men spoke about the experience as dividing their lives into before and after stages. "Sort of a transitional thing.

And, other than that, it's like before cancer, after cancer.'' Or, as another said, ''And that's the pivot point. I'm not sure how much causality is involved, but it is a pivot point that I can see.'' This pivot point is also seen by the men's families:

> But that, even in our family, at some points, a lot of times we'll talk to each other. We'll say, gee, was that before Dad had cancer or after, you know.

Even those men who did not explicitly interpret their lives as being divided by this experience did, in fact, point out major changes in their approaches to life following the cancer. The more positive changes include: 1) being more actively in control of one's life; 2) being more relaxed about life in general; and 3) being more empathic toward others. The more negative changes include: 1) being more anxious about one's health; and 2) feeling somewhat stigmatized and isolated from others.

CONTROL

Not surprisingly, the discovery of cancer was shocking and terrifying:

> When he mentioned the word "cancer," I fainted. They had to revive me. I fell right off the table. That's how frightened I was.

The fact that it is *testicular* cancer, and is highly curable, in most cases initially means very little, since few men know anything about testicular cancer. "When I heard cancer, having cancer, of course you think terminal . . ." Wives reacted in a similar manner. "Yeah, you say cancer and it's like I was panicky. All I could see is being left here with these two boys to bring up alone."

The specific location of the cancer does make a difference in adding to the fears of its consequences:

> I think I broke out in an absolute cold sweat and went blank and was more frightened than I can remember being. Um, not just the thought of cancer . . . but the thought of losing a testicle, I think, is devastating to a man, especially a young man, just every aspect of it.

Despite the initial shock and fear created by the diagnosis, in the long run men were able to overcome these feelings to a great extent. Furthermore, the experience of overcoming these feelings provided them with leverage for improving their lives in other ways. This process is very much like a rite of passage (Van Gennep, 1960). Having faced and conquered their fears they emerge with a greater sense of control over, and a more relaxed attitude toward, their lives. The process was expressed most insightfully by one of the men:

> I was scared. And saying well, it is me, and unless I deal with that I'm always going to be running. . . .That almost mystical experience of saying, hey, this is me. And if it hadn't been for the cancer I don't think I would have had that. And I think it's helped me in a lot of other things in dealing with my life, of having a greater sense of personal responsibility, not wanting to run quite so much.

When asked to characterize the experience in general he replied:

> I would rather have spent the weekend in Philadelphia. Yeah, I mean, scary. Just this frightening experience. At the same time, though, a sense of amazement at my own capacity for having gotten through it. And sort of the recognition that I was capable of dealing with more things than I thought I was. . . . Yeah, being forced to stay in there, being forced into a situation where you had to then assert yourself against it.

The increased sense of confidence and control manifests itself in a number of specific ways. Some become more willing to take risks:

> As far as dealing with the world, yes, I do find differences now with how I'll deal with things. I found that even in business I'm willing to take more risks now. I don't feel the need to cling to a (quote) secure position. I'm more willing to say go for it, who cares. In my home life, too, I've done things that are maybe more adventuresome than most people would do.

A young academic decided to stay in his home town instead of going to wherever the job openings in his field were. He said:

> Rather than going where the members of my field would have me go, I decided to stay in _____. That makes it my choice instead of someone else's.

It also helped men make changes in their personal lives:

> Before I'd even got cancer I would say I was not being faithful to my wife. And I think I was doing things that I shouldn't have. . . . But that stopped me from doing anything like that, which I'm glad it did. . . . Uh, so that changed my outlook and changed my attitude about life and some practices of things that I was doing.

Men were not always sure that the cancer itself was responsible for their changed approach:

> I suspect that I do things now because I know how important today is and not so much worrying about what traditionally other people do or what I should do. Like starting my own business, five, six years ago. I decided not to wait until I was sixty or sixty-five and be sorry that I didn't do what I really wanted to do. Whether having cancer had something to do with that or not, I can't specifically say, but I think my frame of reference has changed a little bit.

Some of this change resulted from their awareness that they were approaching maturational turning points in their lives, apart from the cancer, especially concerning their own mortality. These greater senses of control over life seemed to be a more prominent issue among the men who had testicular cancer in their 30's and 40's than those who had it in their 20's. Even granting that there is a maturational effect at work, it is clear that having survived testicular cancer focused and accelerated the effect:

> So there's that sense of having to go through that, facing death right there, and consciously having to do it, whereas prior to that time I had never done that. . . . I guess what I'm trying to say is a lot of things which you come up against over a period of time have been compacted into one extremely intense period of time.

RELAXED APPROACH

Another outcome of this rite of passage is a reassessment of priorities and a more relaxed attitude toward life in general. This is closely related to the greater sense of control which puts one more at the center of one's life. It also is related to the greater awareness of mortality:

> I don't think I'm as eager to go to the warehouse and kill myself anymore as far as really hustling something. I feel like, you know, got to take a little time easy because I've been hustling it so long, so far in my life, that it kind of woke me up and said, hey, if you don't settle down you could die tomorrow and have no time of relaxation.

A statement by another man combines several related points:

> And now, when I really don't care about something I really try not to get involved in it. And if I do care I'll really show that care. I'm not as afraid to lose financially or business-wise. I always feel it's not the end of the world. I can always regroup and do something again. And the same thing goes for cars or houses or things like that. While I love material things and I strive for them to make my life and my children and wife's more comfortable and have all the stuff, it's not as critical to me as it used to be.

EMPATHY

This brings us to the third major outcome of the rite of passage, a greater feeling of empathy for others. This was the most widely-shared outcome among these men. They all expressed feeling this way, and most of them had acted on these feelings:

> But I have a better feeling and emotional feeling for people. I feel sorry for them, and I want to help them. Which I'm sure my experience has brought me to, because I never really had that in me, where I felt that. I didn't care if anyone was sick. You know, I didn't care about helping them. But I don't feel that way anymore. I'm glad.

There is a special concern for other cancer sufferers. Several of the men have become volunteers for the American Cancer Society or for other cancer organizations. Those who have not, however, often help others on an informal basis as the opportunity arises. For example:

> I am very aware of the word "cancer." And very aware of when I hear someone has cancer. My partner's wife just had a cancer operation a week ago or two weeks ago, and I felt like I could give him counseling about some of the problems. What bothers me the most, and my wife, is when we go through the cancer center and we see the other people. The people less fortunate than you.

HEALTH ANXIETY

Another universal response reported by the men is lingering anxiety about their health. There is fear of recurrence of testicular cancer as well as fear of other forms of cancer. Everyday aches, pains, and coughs take on new, sinister meanings. A physician talking about his own case said:

> Little aches and pains aren't just aches and pains anymore. While they're there you worry. Even though people say, oh, it's just a pain that will go away, until it does, there is always an element of worry there.

Another man said:

> If I happen to get a cold and I have a cough, most people say, "Oh, I've got a cough and no big deal." My immediate thought is, oh, God, here we go again. That's something starting up.

Even though the feelings of anxiety decrease as time passes, they are never entirely gone:

> I don't think it ever leaves your mind. It's always there. Not all the time, but of course, more times than others, like we said, whenever there's a pain here and there. Um, it's been an ordeal, I tell ya.

This anxiety peaks when men see their oncologists for regular checkups. Even those who claim not to worry at other times become very anxious prior to checkups:

> I have a very high level of anxiety, and I'll still sweat and get all upset when I go back for my tests.

SOCIAL ISOLATION

Anxiety over being alone seems to be part of the reason that men who have had testicular cancer feel set apart from others. This is a burden that ultimately they must bear alone. As one man put it, having had cancer, "almost puts you in a different group of people. . . . I realized that you are alone." Some of the men have attempted to overcome this feeling by interacting with other cancer patients in their volunteer work, or participating in a testicular cancer support group that lasted for several weeks. This participation not only provided some relief from the feeling of social isolation, it also allowed the men to compare physical symptoms, which led to reduced anxiety about these symptoms.

OTHER PROBLEMS

A variety of other, more specific problems remain for men who have had testicular cancer. Somewhat surprisingly, only a few men encountered problems of infertility resulting from the lymph node dissection. Some of the men did not have lymph node dissection, and many of those who did had already had their children prior to the surgery. Several of these men said that they regarded the surgery as a "fancy vasectomy." Even those who desired to have children and could not had made adjustments to this situation. One man married a woman who did not want to have children. One couple decided not to try to have a second child.

A serious problem for those men who had had their children prior to the testicular cancer was in helping their children cope with the fact that their father had cancer. In one case a son blamed himself for his father's cancer. In the same family, both sons and their mother became overly concerned about the possibility of the sons getting testicular cancer. The mother said, "We were running to the doctor for every mosquito bite, practically." In another family the man's daughter had problems adjusting. His wife said:

> The middle child was having nightmares. People with knives, him dying. All kinds of . . . , and she wasn't concentrating at school. She was a mess, really, for a while.

In another case the father worried about the effect of his appearance while undergoing chemotherapy. He said:

> I didn't want my son to see me. I really didn't, because I looked so bad. And he didn't see me, and at five years old he was kind of shuffled around from one grandmother to another. It was very bad on him emotionally. And him not seeing me but knowing I might die, and he also was becoming very disruptive because of that.

Aside from problems of infertility, there were also problems in sexual functioning and feelings of loss after the orchiectomies. The problems of sexual functioning, however, were either short-term problems following surgery and treatment, or were episodic and were not seen as serious by the men.

Although many of the men expressed a sense of loss regarding their removed testicle, this did not generally make them feel less masculine. In the cases where it did have some effect on feelings of masculinity, the men were able to deal with this with the support of their wives. A man who had gotten married after having testicular cancer said:

> Sexually I'm able to function as well as I could before. It still feels good. I don't feel self-conscious about expressing my sexuality . . . I don't even worry about it so much, because I don't have any questions about my masculinity.

INTERPRETATION

The experience of having and recovering from testicular cancer has the paradoxical result of making men feel more in control of their own lives and more assertive in their decision-making. At the same time it does not seriously or permanently affect their feelings of masculinity or expression of sexuality. It could be said that men come out of the experience exhibiting more masculine characteristics than before it occurred. At the same time, these men exhibit more empathy toward others, a characteristc that in our society generally is associated with femininity. This indicates that the increased assertiveness and self-confidence experienced by the men are not merely attempts to cover up doubts about masculinity by exaggerating masculine characteristics. Although the disease has long-term negative consequences, when men attempt to give meaning to their experiences they concentrate on the positive consequences it has had for their self-concepts. Furthermore, the positive outcomes enabled the men to cope effectively with the negative outcomes. It is therefore important to understand the sources of these positive outcomes so that they may be fostered.

It is useful to think of the experience of testicular cancer as movement to a new status (Van Gennep, 1960; Glaser and Strauss, 1971). The men recognized this even when they were disturbed by this new status. One man who was trying to forget his status as a cancer survivor, and who was reluctant to be interviewed, agreed to do so because of an obligation he felt as a cancer survivor. The crucial question is, what can be done to ensure that a positive self-concept accompanies this new status? This question can be addressed by examining the kinds of experiences common to the men whose self-concepts improved. This will be done in terms of the four processes of self-concept formation discussed by Rosenberg (1979).

The first process of self-concept formation is reflected appraisals (Rosenberg, 1979), the idea that we tend to think of ourselves in ways that reflect the thoughts that our significant others have of us. This process was prominent in the men's explanations of how they were able to maintain their feelings of masculinity and wholeness despite physical disfigurement. As described by one of the men, his wife was very important at this point:

> I went from a 215 pound healthy, running athletic guy down to 150 pounds, smooth as an egg, no hair, bald, skin lesions, vomiting, just a really decrepit person. And yet she could kiss me, hug me, make love to me, with no feelings any different than she did when I was normal and healthy. . . . I say what did I do to deserve such a wonderful person that she could really not see the facade and really still love me. And she just showed me that so much, that really was the point that, well the whole ability to get through it I think was her support and her feeling of her, of that non-changing love regardless of physical condition.

Men without wives turned to women friends, relatives, or old friends for support. These sources of support are not always available in a crisis, however. Even some of the married men did not rely on their wives for support. When asked if he discussed his fears with his wife one man said:

> No, I didn't want her to have to worry about it. She had enough on her mind and it just didn't seem necessary to burden her with it.

This approach can make the wife's efforts to provide support difficult. The wife of another man who took this approach said:

> So here I am trying to figure out, what's he thinking and how am I supposed to make him feel better?

In another case the relationships between a man and his woman friend, and between the man and his parents, became strained because of the disease. He felt that none of them gave as much support as he needed:

> I think the relationship got totally strained, with the girl, and that's, even with my

family I feel, inside I feel real alone because I don't feel like anyone really understands what I went through.

It cannot be assumed, therefore, that adequate social support will exist for men in this position. It is important, then, that opportunities for counseling and psychosocial support be provided. Some of the men did request and receive professional counseling. Others said they would have liked to have had some counseling. Those who did receive counseling had mixed opinions about its effectiveness. The type of social support that was desired most, however, was the opportunity to talk with other testicular cancer patients. The men who had done this found it very helpful, and those who had not done it wished that they had. Fellow patients provided practical advice, inspiration, and a unique kind of support:

And that really helped. I felt like I wasn't alone. Because you cannot tell your wife, your mother, your brothers, or anyone else, what it's like to go through cancer. Or what it's like to go through chemotherapy, unless you talk to someone who knows.

Counseling or peer support for wives, womenfriends, children, and others close to the patient also need to be made available. As we have seen, significant others of the patient also have fears and problems of adjustment in the face of this disease. Furthermore, they may need advice or emotional support to help them provide support for the cancer patient. As one man pointed out:

It would have been nice if somebody could have met with my wife while I'm going through surgery or afterwards, or while I was sleeping in the hospital. . . . Now I come up with a question and my wife's already heard it and perhaps she can convey it so, there could be a lot of support just through your spouse or through family members, you know, where they could have known the answer. Just putting them at ease is important too.

The second process of self-concept formation is self-attribution, drawing conclusions about ourselves by observing our own behavior and reactions (Rosenberg, 1979:70). This is the primary process by which the men became more confident and assertive, as well as more relaxed about life. It is crucially important here that patients are active participants in their own treatment, especially in making decisions. Different individuals were active in different ways. Some were active by asking for information or seeking out information about the disease on their own. One challenged his doctor's choice of therapies. Another said he did everything his doctors told him:

. . . so someone couldn't come back and say, well you had a chance and you didn't take it. We could have saved you, but you said the hell with it. And *I decided* to go through it. Every bit of the chemotherapy.

Decisions of this magnitude cannot be made in an informational vacuum, though:

The doctor said, you make the decision. Preventive or to go, and we sat around talking, we couldn't make a decision. He gave us two weeks to make a decision.

> We thought about it. We went back. Finally we sat down and he left the room and we talked to the head nurse of the chemo department. . . . So, given those circumstances or those statistics, that I may never have to have it . . . I said, well I'll wait and see, hoping that I'll never have to have it.

The testicular cancer patient should be given every opportunity to participate in his own treatment. This means that a patient should have access to reliable information about the disease and treatment alternatives, so that he is able to make well-informed decisions about his illness and about his life (Conrad, 1987:14). A patient should have routine access to a medical library, which several patients sought out on their own, and access to health professionals with whom to consult. There also should be an assessment made of the patient's belief system because not every man with testicular cancer has the same needs (see also Bindemann, 1987). It would be inappropriate to force unwanted information on a man who prefers to "control" the situation by following his doctor's orders.

There is some suggestive evidence that the men with more positive long-term outcomes have accepted the identity of cancer survivor and have integrated it with their other identities. To the extent that this identity has positive implications, we can expect it to lead to an overall increase in self-esteem through Rosenberg's principle of psychological centrality (Rosenberg, 1979). Such acceptance also would allow men to make social comparisons with other cancer patients and survivors that would lead to less negative implications for themselves than comparisons with the non-cancer population might (Rosenberg, 1979):

> I saw other people in the hospital with cancer with no one, I mean no one. I mean their wives or girlfriends had abandoned them, and I felt bad for them.

The acceptance of this identity also leads to a willingness to face the fears of the cancer survivor. Without this acceptance, the men might never be able to gain a sense of control from having defeated the disease. Finally, acceptance of the cancer survivor identity will increase a man's likelihood of seeking out other survivors and breaking down feelings of isolation. As Mullan (1985:271), himself a cancer survivor, has pointed out:

> Patients with cancer, whether recently diagnosed and being treated or previously diagnosed and relatively stable, have more in common with one another than they do with people who have not experienced cancer.

He goes on:

> For better and worse, physically and emotionally, the experience leaves an impression. No matter how long we live, cancer patients are survivors—at once wary and relieved, bashful and proud (1985:272).

Acceptance of the cancer survivor identity generally occurs without any specific intervention, but it might be useful for counselors of testicular cancer patients to include this as a consideration.

CONCLUSION

We have seen that having testicular cancer is still a terrifying experience for men and those close to them, despite its high rate of cure. It can lead to long-term anxiety about health and feelings of social isolation, as well as short-term sexual dysfunction. When the proper conditions are present, however, these problems can be minimized, and several positive outcomes can be realized. In particular, when social support provides consistent and positive reflected appraisals of the men, they suffer little or no damage to their self-concepts or feelings of masculinity. When the conditions of a man's treatment allow him to interpret his role in his cure as active, and he faces up to and conquers his fears, the result is enhanced self-confidence and greater feelings of control over his life. Finally, when a man adopts the identity of cancer survivor and uses other cancer survivors as a comparison group, he feels more positively about his own life. Eventually, the cancer survivor is able to normalize his life in a way which includes, but does not dwell on, this identity. As this was stated by a physician writing about his own testicular cancer (Fiore, 1979:288):

> Much of the intensity of that period decreased as my chances improved and I returned to some of my worrying about the future. The experience of clear priorities and sense of personal power that comes from facing a life-and-death struggle, however, will continue to be a positive influence in my life, enhancing the quality, if not the quantity, of that life.

Several clinical implications follow from this analysis. 1) Both men and physicians need to be better informed about testicular cancer and testicular exams. 2) Patients should be allowed and encouraged to actively participate in their own cures. This can be facilitated by giving them access to valid information about the disease. 3) A variety of coping resources should be available for the patient to choose from, such as psychosocial counseling for all family members, financial advice, and sex and fertility counseling. 4) Patients should be given the opportunity to speak with other testicular cancer patients, especially men who have completed their own treatments. Men also should be given the opportunity to help other patients once they, themselves, have recovered. This gives them an opportunity to feel active in relation to the disease (Cox, 1979), allows an opportunity to provide "repayment" for the help they received, and also encourages acceptance of the cancer survivor identity.[5]

As further progress is made in curing cancer, we can expect more and more people to find themselves in positions similar to those of present testicular cancer survivors. The results of this study provide a basis for cautious optimism regarding the long-term psychosocial outcomes for those cancer survivors.

NOTES

1. The overall rate of testicular cancer is 2 per 100,000 (American Cancer Society, Guide for Speakers/Presenters on Testicular Self-Examination).

2. The present rate of cure is approximately 90 percent (American Cancer Society, 1988:17).

3. The ages of the men at the time of interview ranged from 27 to 58 years (average = 38). The ages at the time of diagnosis ranged from 24 to 40 years (average = 32). The time since treatment at the time of interview ranged from 1 to 24 years (average = 6.4). At the time of the interview 16 of the men were married and 13 of the men had one or more children. In terms of surgery and treatment, all had orchiectomies, 14 had lymph node dissections, 7 had chemotherapy, 2 had radiation therapy, 3 had received both chemotherapy and radiation therapy, and 5 had neither chemotherapy nor radiation therapy.

4. All of the interviews were conducted by the author, who has had testicular cancer himself. This status was advantageous to the research. It was possible to use an insider's knowledge to frame questions and probe for more details. Often, the discussion of common experiences or feelings reminded men of the details of their own experiences. Knowing that they would be talking to a fellow survivor also motivated the men to participate in the interview. Most of the men appreciated that someone was taking the time to do such a study. Others had never spoken to another man who had had testicular cancer and were eager to do so. The two men who had the most negative reactions to the testicular cancer were also the most pessimistic about any good coming from this study. They both agreed to participate nonetheless. As one of them said,

> You know, when you called up, if you hadn't said you had had it yourself I never would have agreed to talk about it. But since you said you had it yourself I felt a sort of obligation.

5. These recommendations are consistent with those made by Fiore (1979) and by Mullan (1985) in their discussions of their own cases. They are also consistent with a recent review of the literature by Northouse and Northouse (1987) in which they found that the major communication issues from the patient's point of view are maintaining a sense of control, seeking information, disclosing feelings, and searching for meaning.

REFERENCES

American Cancer Society. 1988. Cancer Facts & Figures—1988.

_____. n.d. *Guide for Speakers/Presenters on Testicular Self-Examination*.

Bindemann, S. 1987. Psychological impact of cancer: Its assessment, treatment, and ensuing effects on quality of life. In N. K. Aaronson and J. Beckmann, eds. *The Quality of Life of Cancer Patients*. New York: Raven Press, 227–38.

Conrad, P. 1987. The experience of illness: recent and new directions. In J. Roth and P. Conrad, eds. *Research in the Sociology of Health Care, Volume 6*. Greenwich, CN: JAI, 1–31.

Cox, B. 1979. The cancer patient as educator and counselor. In J. Tache, H. Selye, and S. Day, eds. *Cancer, Stress, and Death*. New York: Plenum, 75–85.

Cummings, K., D. Lampone, C. Mettlin, and J. Pontes. 1983. What young men know about testicular cancer. *Preventive Medicine* 12:326–30.

De Haes, J. and F. Van Knippenberg. 1987. Quality of life of cancer patients: Review of the literature. In N. Aaronson and J. Beckmann, eds. *The Quality of Life of Cancer Patients*. New York: Raven, 167–82.

Fiore, N. 1979. Fighting cancer—one patient's perspective. *The New England Journal of Medicine* 300(6):284–89.

Glaser, B. and A. Strauss. 1971. *Status Passage*. Chicago: Aldine.

Gorzynski, J. and J. Holland. 1979. Psychological aspects of testicular cancer. *Seminars in Oncology* 6(1):125–29.

McCracken, G. 1988. *The Long Interview*. Newbury Park, CA: Sage.

Mullan, F. 1985. Seasons of survival: Reflections of a physician with cancer. *The New England Journal of Medicine* 313(4): 270–73.

Murphy, G. 1983. Testicular cancer. *CA-A Cancer Journal for Clinicians* 33(2):100–104.

National Cancer Institute. 1987. Testicular Cancer—Research Report.

Northouse, P. and L. Northouse. 1987. Communication and cancer: Issues confronting patients, health professionals, and family members. *Journal of Psychosocial Oncology* 5(3):17–46.

Pizzocaro, G., et al. 1986. Orchiectomy alone in clinical stage I nonseminomatous testis cancer: A critical appraisal. *Journal of Clinical Oncology* 4(1):35–40.

Rieker, P., S. Edbril, and M. Granick. 1985. Curative testis cancer therapy: Psychosocial sequelae. *Journal of Clinical Oncology* 3(8):1117–26.

Rosenberg, M. 1979. *Conceiving the Self.* New York: Basic Books.

Sogani, P., et al. 1984. Orchiectomy alone in the treatment of clinical stage I nonseminomatous germ cell tumor of the testis. *Journal of Clinical Oncology* 2(4):267–70.

Tross, S., et al. 1984. A controlled study of psychosocial sequelae in cured survivors of testicular neoplasms. *Proceedings of the American Society of Clinical Oncology* 3(March):74 (Abstract C–287).

Van Gennep, A. 1960. *The Rites of Passage.* Chicago: University of Chicago Press.

20

Role Performance After Loss

Tamara Ferguson, Jack Ferguson, and Elliot D. Luby

How do you feel, and what do you do, when you are in your forties and your companion, your husband of twenty years, dies suddenly? What do you do when your husband, who was central to all of your roles, leaves you alone to shoulder the responsibilities of a life-style that was designed for two adults and their children?

The emotional and physiological responses to loss have been well documented (Freud, 1957; Marris, 1958; Gorer, 1959; Parkes, 1964; Maddison and Viola, 1968; Furman, 1974; Glick, 1974; Greenblatt, 1978). Somatic distress, restlessness, insomnia, a flare up of previous illnesses, a sense of unreality, intense preoccupation with images of the deceased, feelings of guilt, and hostile reactions in relation to other people are all universal responses to loss (Lindemann, 1944).

What is unique to the problems of the young widow is that she has to adjust her behavior to her new situation, modify her expectations and performance in most of her roles, because her loss is not only emotional, but financial, social, sexual, and in her parental role, and may require her to move and go back to work (Lopata, 1973, 1979; Ferguson, Kutscher, and Kutscher, 1981a).

Role theory can help the widow to evaluate her situation. Roles have been defined in many ways, but the basic elements of role theory are the expectations about self and others of a person occupying a certain position (Biddle, 1986). Other theorists have added the concept of enactment (Linton, 1936; Davis, 1948; Sarbin and Allen, 1968). In this chapter we shall define roles as the enactment of the self and other expectations of a person holding a certain position—that person's rights and obligations. The problems with role theory are: (1) that it is not clear which roles should be considered when analyzing the

An earlier version of this chapter was presented at the International Conference on Grief and Bereavement in Contemporary Society, sponsored by Cruse, London, England, July 12–15, 1988.

role-set of a person (Merton, 1968: 422-438); (2) it does not lend itself to evaluate change over time; (3) roles are not clearly related to emotions and physiological states; and (4) it does not provide us with a definition of a healthy personality.

We propose a biopsychosocial role theory, the Theory of Alternatives, to attempt to deal with the current limitations of role theory. We shall summarize this theory, and explain how it provides a structure for the widow to come to terms with her emotional responses and seek new opportunities.

The theory emerged after trying to operationalize Erikson's theory of the psychosocial development of children (Ferguson, 1962; Baker & Ferguson, 1972; Ferguson, Kutscher and Kutscher, 1981a; Ferguson et al., 1981). One of the three surveys which led to the development of our Theory of Alternatives was a survey of 100 young widows, and we shall refer to that study in this chapter (Ferguson, Kutscher, and Kutscher, 1981a). The basic assumptions of the theory have been tested in three surveys (Ferguson, Ferguson, and Luby, forthcoming). We propose that to function in a society a person has to achieve a sense of attainment.

A SENSE OF ATTAINMENT

> The knowledge that you are achieving your self expectations and other expectations for all your basic biopsychosocial needs, or life vectors, and that you are able to negotiate expectations and performance with yourself and others when expectations are not met.

By self-expectations we mean what you want for yourself and will do for others, in other words, your rights and obligations (Banton, 1965). Other expectations are what you believe other people want for themselves and will do for you— their rights and obligations.

Seldom are all our expectations achieved. Daily, we have to negotiate rights and obligations with ourselves and others. The knowledge that one has a schema to think through problems, deal with emotional responses, and negotiate differences of opinion with others, appears to be an important feature of the healthy personality.

INTERACTIONS BETWEEN TWO PERSONS

Figure 1 represents the interaction between two persons, ego and alter, in this case a woman and her husband. The problem when ego interacts with alter is that only performance is observable and that ego has to infer alter's expectations and motivation from his performance.

The long arrow from alter to ego shows that alter's performance indicates to ego what alter will do for her and wants in return. The small arrow at the base of the upper triangle shows that ego has to decide whether alter's performance tallies with her expectations. The long arrow from ego to alter indicates that in turn ego's performance reflects the result of her deliberation.

The two short arrows which are directed to the base of each triangle indicate how cultural expectations learned from others may further influence ego's and alter's expectations. Alter may offer drugs to ego, but this conflicts with ego's cultural expectations and she refuses. On this particular matter, there is majority agreement, but there is less agreement within the culture when it comes to some of the other decisions that a person faces.

When there is role complementarity, when both ego and alter are satisfied with their own performance and the performance of the other person, there are no problems. But when this is not the case, as is frequent, conflict occurs.

Interaction between husband and wife is not limited to one area of behavior, but covers their physiological, social, and spiritual needs. These basic needs are interdependent and run through the course of their lives. We have entitled them life vectors.

COMPLEMENT OF LIFE VECTORS

By life vectors we mean the basic biopsychosocial needs that are institutionally defined and sanctioned by the individual. These needs are latent in a person and run through the course of his or her life. Although certain life vectors appear more crucial at one period of our lives than at others, the period at which they are being activated depends on maturation and the culture in which a person lives. The following needs are interdependent and have been derived through research from Malinowski (1956) and Erikson (1958), among others.

COMPLEMENT OF LIFE VECTORS

Health	Occupation
Nutrition	Finance
Shelter	Parenthood
Motor Development	Art
Speech	Law and Order
Education	Politics
Social Life	Religion
Love and Sex	Ethics

Survival is a prime concern of the infant and the older person, thus Health, Nutrition, Shelter, and Motor Development (Exercise) are crucial to their wel-

EXPECTATIONS

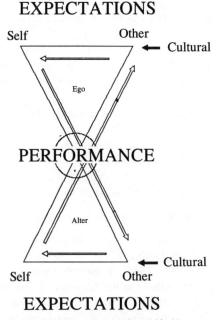

EXPECTATIONS

Figure 1. Interaction in One Life Vector

fare. Learning to communicate with others through Speech and acquiring an Education starts at an early age. In adolescence Social Life, Love and Sex, the choice of an Occupation, and Finance become increasingly important issues, and a desire for Parenthood is a concern of the young adult. A commitment to Art as a medium of expression, respect for Law and Order, and interest in Politics, Religion, and Ethics, may start at an early age or become more significant later in life.

DISBELIEF, ANGER, AND GUILT

Cooley (1956) has pointed out that the performance of others is for us a looking-glass that reflects our behavior and helps us to evaluate it. Our survey of widows has shown that even in marriages where a high level of conflict prevailed, the husband was at least a reflector. But what happens when through death this looking-glass is shattered? Figure 1 may help us to understand the feelings of disbelief and unreality that a widow experiences when suddenly there is no feedback from her husband when she performs.

Figure 1 also may help us to understand the feelings of anger and guilt experienced by the widow. The sudden removal of her husband can be interpreted by the widow as a betrayal, as evidence that her own behavior was objectionable, or both. It is difficult for the widow to decide if her husband has let her down, or if his death was triggered by her own carelessness, or both, and she may alternate between feelings of anger and guilt.

In an effort to make sense of her feelings, the widow reminisces and retraces her behavior in all of her life vectors, but she no longer has her mate's ongoing performance to create a dialogue. Instead there is an interior monologue which may lead to brooding.

Figure 2 shows that expectations that are not achieved create physiological and emotional stress and that the widow (ego) can either rationally and objectively assess her new situation, and by negotiating expectations and performance regain her equilibrium or, because of habitual and unproductive cognitive methods of dealing with stress, perform in a manner that does not solve her problems and may even compound them, for she worries that she is not more effective.

DEFENSE MECHANISMS AND PATTERNS OF REACTION

Freud identified a number of unconscious defense mechanisms that a person uses to avoid confronting a painful reality, but his definition of these concepts changed many times (Vaillant, 1986). Even now there is little consensus on the "empirical understanding of defense mechanisms" (Vaillant, 1986: xiii). Beck makes a distinction between internal and external events and suggests that a person's problems are derived largely from "erroneous premises and assumptions" (1976:3). It is the meaning that a person attaches to events that is distorted and has to be corrected, and emotional reactions occur because of this thought distortion.

We make a clear distinction between expectations, which exist in the mind and may be unconscious, preconscious, or conscious, and behavior, which is observable. This makes it possible to differentiate clearly between the situation in which ego finds herself, her assessment of this situation, her emotional and physiological responses, and her performance.

We call defense mechanisms habitual and unproductive cognitive methods for dealing with unmet expectations, because even if they momentarily relieve stress, they are not culturally acceptable: they deny an objective reality and distort performance.

DEFENSE MECHANISMS
Habitual and Unproductive Cognitive Methods
for Dealing With Unmet Expectations

Regression: *Ego focuses on a set of expectations held at an earlier stage of development.*

The widow behaves as if she were still a child and powerless.

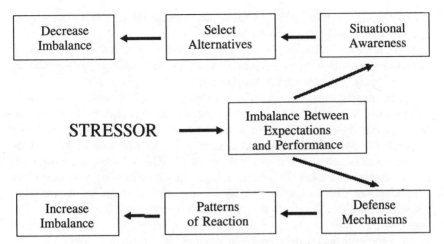

Figure 2. Response To Imbalance in One Life Vector

Fixation:	*Ego is obsessed by certain past expectations.* The widow cannot give up thinking about her previous losses.
Denial:	*Ego refuses to recognize certain performances.* The widow refuses to recognize that she has to change her life-style.
Rationalization:	*Ego maintains that her expectations are reasonable.* The widow buys an expensive car that she cannot afford.
Projection:	*Ego attributes to another a derogatory expectation she holds of herself.* The widow believes that other women despise her because she is a widow.
Identification:	*Ego adopts the expectations of another.* The widow believes she has cancer because her husband died of cancer.
Displacement:	*Ego transfers an expectation about a person to another person or to an object.* The widow who was jealous with respect to her husband is jealous if her son dates.

Our list of defense mechanisms and definitions is derived from Freud. This list of defense mechanisms is tentative, but we have selected those that appear to apply to the widow's problems.

The methods of thinking presented above are unproductive because in all of these cases the widow's emotional response is not tempered by objective reality, and thus leads to performances that are not culturally acceptable.

Horney explains that a person who has been submitted to contradictory expectations when he was a child may move towards, against, or away from people. She says that a person will move towards people and become dependent if he "accepts his own helplessness, and in spite of his estrangement and fears tries to win the affection of others and lean on them". He will move against people if "he accepts and takes for granted the hostility around him, and determines consciously or unconsciously to fight. He implicitly distrusts the feelings and intentions of others towards himself". He will move away from people if "he wants neither to belong nor to fight, but keeps apart. He feels he had not much in common with them, they do not understand him anyhow," and instead he builds a world of his own (1945: 42–45).

Horney's description of different types of unproductive behavior has been translated into the following patterns of reaction. Patterns of reaction are habitual and observable performances that are unproductive because even if they make ego feel better momentarily, they do not improve her excessive reliance on, contempt for, or avoidance of, others.

PATTERNS OF REACTION
Habitual and Observable Performances
That Are Unproductive

Brutalization:	*Ego physically or verbally forces a performance on another.*
	The widow quarrels with her favorite son.
Victimization:	*Ego submits to the performance of another, although it is contrary to her expectations.*
	The widow goes to live with relatives she dislikes.
Self-Brutalization:	*Ego forces a pseudo-performance upon herself: she eats or drinks too much, stops eating, or takes drugs.*
	The widow gains forty pounds.
Insulation:	*Ego physically or verbally withdraws from the situation.*
	The widow shies away from her former friends.

Horney does not include self-brutalization in her classification of types of behavior. We call it a pseudo-performance for it seems to occur when ego does not know who to blame or how to behave. Figure 2 shows that when the widow responds in such a manner, she increases the imbalance between her expectations and her performance.

In her role of single woman, the widow's rights and obligations are different from when she was a married woman. There is no longer a division of labor in the family and she can no longer consult her husband for advice. Instead she finds that everyone is giving her advice: her relatives, friends, and professionals. The problem is that this advice can be contradictory, and she should question the integrity and expertise of her advisers before making up her mind. Moreover, while her advisers will focus on one or more of the widow's life vectors, only she can be aware of all of her basic needs and decide on a new life-style and priorities.

When the widow responds with patterns of reaction to the performance of others, her behavior prevents further meaningful interaction with them because they do not know how to interpret and respond to her behavior. They may react emotionally to her demands and the problem gets lost in the shuffle.

SITUATIONAL AWARENESS AND SEEKING ALTERNATIVES

Instead of responding to her loss with unproductive expectations and performance, the widow can try to assess her situation more objectively.

First, she can come to terms with the feelings of anger and guilt triggered by her loss by retracing her past interaction with her husband in each of her life vectors. This helps her to differentiate between the sorrows and the joys in her life, and realize that her husband's death, even if it was accidental, was not due to a single event since his physical health, his temperament, and his satisfaction with life did not stem per se from their interaction.

Allowing herself to grieve, and then move on, allows the widow to evaluate her present situation more realistically. Thomas emphasizes the importance of looking at the subjective and objective elements of a situation and he states that our definition of the situation intervenes between the situation and the response. He believes that "if men define situations as real, they are real in their consequences" (1931: 189).

Our concept of life vectors helps the widow to assess her past and present situations because they run through the course of her life. The various life vectors have been grouped under the following seven themes to emphasize their interdependence and that the widow's sense of attainment is based on meeting her basic biopsychosocial needs. Education, Occupation, and Speech have been grouped together under "Doing the Work You Like" to emphasize that she may have to be retrained to get the job she wants, and should discuss her options with others. Housing and Finance have been listed under "Options in Savings and Spending" because the widow's house is often her biggest financial asset and whether or not to move is a primary consideration. Social Life and Love and Sex are grouped together under "To Love and Be Loved" because the widow's attachment to others does not have to be limited to her family roles. Parenthood has been listed under "Your Children and Their Future" for she may be reluctant to face that she has to help her children, in particular her favorite son, to become independent.

Health, Nutrition, and Exercise have been grouped together under "Taking Care of Your Body" because in middle age the plans that the widow makes depend on the state of her health. Interest in Art, Law and Order, and Politics can broaden her outlook on life and make her feel that she is part of the world. And finally, although perhaps this should come first, to be at peace with herself, the widow has to come to terms with the existential crisis that her loss has created and face up to her religious and ethical principles. In our book we outlined, under each of these themes, the main problems that widows with very different backgrounds experienced (Ferguson, Kutscher and Kutscher, 1981b).

INTERDEPENDENCE OF LIFE VECTORS

Doing the Work You Like	Taking Care of Your Body
Education	Nutrition
Occupation	Exercise
Speech	Health
Options In Saving and Spending	Be Part Of This World
Finance	Art
Housing	Politics
	Law
To Love and Be Loved	At Peace With Yourself
Social Life	Ethics
Love and Sex	Religion
Your Children and Their Future	
Parenthood	

CONCLUSION

The Theory of Alternatives provides a structure for the widow to assess her situation more objectively, as a first step, retracing past behavior in each of her life vectors. This allows her to see that her situation has changed over the years and not to confuse the past with the present. Only when the widow recognizes the differences between her expectations and those of others, and is able to negotiate expectations and performance, can she make decisions that are realistic.

Our survey of 100 young widows supports our theoretical position. The main proposition was that women who were egalitarian in their occupational, educational, social life, love and sex, and parental roles, who made about the same number of crucial decisions as their husbands and experienced low marital conflict in these roles, would adjust better than dominant and dependent women to their new positions as single women. This proved to be the case, for egalitarian women tended to listen to advice and still make up their own minds, while dominant women did not realize that their situation had changed, and dependent women looked for another mentor.

What role theory has lacked in the past is a means of evaluating the entire domain of roles that an individual is capable of enacting. It has traditionally either dealt with one role at a time—such as occupation—or used the concept of role at such an abstract level that further specification and measurement became impossible. Not all roles are necessarily enacted simultaneously, but we must be able to know which ones are active, and which are affecting other roles.

We have added a time dimension to role theory because a person can retrace expectations and performance in the past for each life vector, assess the present situation, and foresee some of the consequences of future goals before trying to achieve them.

Although there is a wide range of emotions, in stressful circumstances guilt and blame appear to eclipse other emotions, and by emphasizing that only performance is visible, we have clarified how emotions relate to role theory.

Role theory can be useful for therapy because it divides culture into institutional structures. Instead of generalities, it provides specific roles within behavior areas. It allows us to look simultaneously at all life vectors and to understand how people's health, as well as their social and spiritual problems, have influenced their expectations and performance.

Finally, this role theory has provided us with a definition of the healthy personality that can be operationalized. We have devised interview schedules that allow us to trace the social development of a person and his or her mode of interaction with significant others in each life vector (Ferguson, Ferguson, and Luby, forthcoming).

REFERENCES

Baker, J. and T. Ferguson. 1972. *Identity and Separtism*. A Research Report Prepared for the University of Detroit.

Banton, M. 1965. *Roles: An Introductory to the Study of Social Relations*. New York: Basic.

Beck, A. 1976. *Cognitive Therapy and The Emotional Disorders*. New York: International Universities Press.

Biddle, B. J. 1986. Recent developments in role theory. *Annual Review of Sociology* 12:67–92.

Cooley, C. H. 1956. Human nature and the social order, rev. ed. In *The Two Major Works of Charles C. Cooley*. Glencoe, IL: The Free Press.

Davis, K. 1948. *Human Society*. New York: Macmillan.

Erikson, E. H. 1958. The psychosocial development of children. In J. M. Tanner and B. Inhelder, eds., *Discussions on Child Development: The Proceedings of the Third Meeting of the World Health Organization Study Group on the Psychobiological Development of Children, Vol 3*. New York: International Universities Press.

Ferguson, T. 1962. An Exploratory Study of the Repetitive Pattern of Maternal Deprivation. Unpublished Master's Essay. New York: Columbia University.

Ferguson, T., A. H. Kutscher, and L. G. Kutscher. 1981a. *The Young Widow: Conflict and Guidelines*. New York: Arno Press.

——1981b. A practical guide for young widows. In Ferguson T., A. H. Kutscher and L. G. Kutscher. *The Young Widow: Conflict and Guidelines*. New York: Arno Press, 105–37.

Ferguson, T., C.E. Schorer, G. Tourney, and J. Ferguson. 1981. Bereavement, stress, and rescaling therapy. In O. S. Margolis et al., eds. *Acute Stress*. New York: Columbia University Press.

Ferguson T., J. Ferguson, and E.D. Luby (forthcoming). *Life Histories for Therapy and Research*.

Freud, S. 1957. Mourning and melancholia. In J. Strachey, trans., *The Standard Edition of the Complete Psychosocial Works of Sigmund Freud*. Vol 14. London: Hogarth Press, 243–60.

Furman, E. 1974. *A Child's Parent Dies (Studies in Child Bereavement)*. New Haven: Yale University Press.

Glick, I. O., R. S. Weiss, and G. M. Parkes, 1974. *The First Year of Bereavement*. New York: Wiley and Son.

Gorer, G. 1959. *Death, Grief and Mourning in Contemporary Britain*. London: Cresset.

Greenblatt, M. 1978. The grieving spouse. *American Journal of Psychiatry* 135: 43–47.

Horney, K. 1945. Our inner conflicts. In *The Collected Works of Karen Horney*. Vol. 1. New York: Norton.

Lindemann, E. 1944. The symptomatology and management of acute grief. *American Journal of Psychiatry* 101:141–48.

Linton, R. 1936. *The Study of Man*. New York: Appleton-Century.

Lopata, H. Z. 1973. *Widowhood in an American City*. Cambridge: Shenkman.

—— 1979. *Women as Widows*. New York: Elsevier.

Maddison, D, and A. Viola. 1968. The health of widows in the year following bereavement. *Journal of Psychosomatic Research* 12: 297–306.

Malinowski, B. 1960. Basic needs and cultural responses. In *A Scientific Theory of Culture and Other Essays*. New York: Galaxy, 91–119.

Marris, P. 1958. *Widows and Their Families*. London: Routledge.

Merton, R. K. 1968. *Social Theory and Social Structure*, enlarged ed. New York: Free Press.

Parkes, C. M. 1964. Recent bereavement as a cause for mental illness. *British Journal of Psychiatry* 110: 198–204.

Sarbin, T. R. and V. L. Allen. 1968. Role theory. In G. Lindzey and E. Aronson, *The Handbook of Social Psychology*, 2nd ed., Vol 1. Reading: MA: Addison-Wesley, 488–567.

Thomas, W. I. 1931. The relation of research to the social process. In *Essays on Research in the Social Sciences*. Washington, DC: The Brookings Institution.

Vaillant, G. E. 1986. *Empirical Studies of Ego Mechanisms of Defense*. Washington, DC: American Psychiatric Press.

21

AIDS: Toward an Effective Education on Safer Sex Practices

Masako Ishii-Kuntz

Over the past eight years, Acquired Immune Deficiency Syndrome (AIDS) has reached epidemic proportions and attained widespread social significance. The total number of AIDS cases on record in the United States is well over 50,000 and 56 percent of these AIDS patients have died (Centers for Disease Control, 1988). And the curve is rising dramatically. By 1991, according to estimates from the Centers for Disease Control (1988), the number of AIDS cases may exceed 270,000, and 179,000 will have died because of the disease (Institute of Medicine, 1986). Past research has resulted in an increased understanding of the etiology and pathogenesis of AIDS, and the modes of transmission of the causal agent. Biomedical research, however, has yet to discover an effective therapy or vaccine. In the absence of a vaccine or satisfactory drug for AIDS, it is clear that control of the spread of AIDS is only possible through social measures. The Institute of Medicine (1986:27) states that "Social science research can help develop effective education programs . . . (that) contribute to the design of policies that reduce the public's fear of AIDS and that help eliminate discriminatory practice toward AIDS patients." Additionally, social science can identify the important factors which contribute to the development of educational programs on safe sexual practices.

The purpose of this study is to present how sociological research can contribute to education on safe sex practices, which may be one of a few effective avenues in the prevention of AIDS. Specifically, we will examine how knowledge of AIDS transmission, and concern about the disease, influence the extent of safe premarital sexual practice among heterosexual college students. In the

Support for this research was provided by the Intramural Research Grant of the Academic Senate at the University of California, Riverside.

259

United States, persons with AIDS have, by and large, been homosexuals or bisexual men. There are, however, reports which indicate that AIDS is spreading into the mainstream heterosexual population. For example, the Centers for Disease Control (1988) estimates that the pool of infected heterosexuals probably exceeds 250,000 people. Although many of the infected heterosexuals are intravenous drug users and the female partners of either bisexual men or intravenous drug users, approximately 30,000 heterosexuals without identified risks also carry AIDS (Boffey, 1988). It also was reported that by 1991 the overall number of AIDS cases will probably increase ninefold, but the number of cases involving heterosexuals will increase about 20-fold (Koop, 1987).

It is clear that AIDS is no longer a disease that is confined to certain populations, such as homosexuals and IV drug abusers. Indeed, AIDS can be transmitted by both males and females and has spread rapidly in the heterosexual population in Central Africa (Dickson, 1987; Quinn, et al., 1986). Although the conditions in Africa may be vastly different from the United States, the increasing rate of AIDS cases among American heterosexuals warrants an investigation. This study focuses on the younger population, i.e., college students who are heterosexuals. Given that about one-quarter of all AIDS cases are among persons between the ages of 20 and 29 (Macklin, 1988) and the incubation period of AIDS can be up to 5 years or more (Institute of Medicine, 1986), a large proportion of current AIDS patients originally may have been infected during their late teen years. The findings of this study, therefore, may provide important implications for effective educational programs to alleviate the sexual transmission of the AIDS virus among younger generations.

KNOWLEDGE AND CONCERN ABOUT AIDS

The AIDS virus—also known as "human immunodeficiency virus," HIV—is transmitted from one person to another in blood or semen. Certain sexual practices, engaged in mainly by homosexual and bisexual men, often produce semen and blood that is passed between partners. These practices can be changed. Previous studies have documented that homosexuals who are concerned about AIDS and receive intensive AIDS education are likely to alter sexual practices considered at high risk (Brown, 1986; Feldman, 1985; Winkelstein, et al., 1987). Winkelstein, et al. (1987), for example, document a 60 percent reduction in high-risk sexual practices in their sample of San Francisco homosexuals. Feldman (1985) also reports a significant change in both the number of partners, and the participation in high-risk sexual behavior, in a sample of New York City homosexuals. Similarly, Romanowski and Brown (1986) found a sharp reduction in cases of rectal gonorrhea and other sexually transmitted diseases among homosexuals in Alberta, Canada, which may be associated with changes in sexual practices among these men. Because of a shorter incubation period than AIDS, it is easier to track these sexually transmitted diseases for short-term data. Based on these findings, it is possible to assume that the transmission of AIDS within homosexual groups has probably decreased (Koop, 1987).

The findings with respect to changes in sexual practice among homosexuals present evidence that increased concern and intensive education encourage practices of safe sex. This implies that effective education on safe sex for young people may involve raising their concern and knowledge about the disease. But do concern and knowledge about AIDS actually influence the sexual behavior of younger heterosexuals? This is the major question addressed in this study.

Past research reports relatively little change in premarital sexual behavior among young heterosexuals due to AIDS. Simkins and Eberhage (1984) and Simkins and Kushner (1986) found no changes in self-reported rates of sexual activity among college students. Based on a sample of 232 college students at a midwestern university, Simkins and Eberhage (1984) found that the majority of their respondents were not concerned about AIDS and their levels of sexual activity had not been affected by fears of infection. This is consistent with the portrayal of college students in the campus media (The Chronicle of Higher Education, 1987; The Guardian, 1988). According to Hirshchorn (1987a, b), AIDS has not resulted in behavioral changes among college students.

More recent studies, however, show that the degree of concern about AIDS among young heterosexuals is on the rise (Carroll, 1988; Asquith, 1988). Carroll (1988), for example, found that among sexually active students, over half reported that they have altered their sexual practices as a result of concern about AIDS. This is confirmed by the finding that close to half of the college students in Iowa, due to AIDS, are more likely to use condoms when having intercourse (Whitbeck and Simons, 1988).

Increased knowledge and concern about AIDS among college students can be predicted to encourage students to engage in safer sex practices. Our study includes permissive attitudes toward premarital sex and extensive sexual experience as antecedents to knowledge and concern about AIDS. The extent of sexual experience can be viewed in terms of frequency of premarital sexual intercourse, number of partners, and various forms of sexual practice. It seems logical that people who have extensive sexual experience and active sexual relationships will perceive themselves at risk of getting AIDS. It can be predicted that the more permissive the student's attitude about sex, the more likely he or she will be to be concerned about AIDS and to have accurate knowledge about the disease, which, in turn, will produce a change in sexual behavior. This is presented in a path analytic model, predicting changes related to length of time before intercourse (Figure 1), inquiry about partners' past sexual history (Figure 2), and the use of condoms (Figure 3).

A factor which may be helpful in developing an effective educational program on safe sex is knowledge of the sources of information on AIDS. The National Health Interview Survey (1988) reports that the main source of AIDS information for the general public is television, followed by newspapers. With respect to college students, Whitbeck and Simons (1988) also reported that students in Iowa receive most of their information about AIDS from television. Other sources of information, such as parents, schools, and churches, contribute minimally to students' knowledge about AIDS. Television also was found to be a principle source of information on AIDS in a California sample of college students (Asquith, 1988). Behavioral change, however, does not occur unless the information provided by various sources increases concern about AIDS. We will, therefore, examine the extent to which various sources of AIDS information influence students' concern about getting the AIDS virus.

METHODS

Sample

The data for the study were obtained from a survey conducted with a sample of undergraduate students enrolled in sociology courses at the University of California, Riverside (N = 450). After approval of the university's Human Subjects Committee, a 12-page questionnaire was administered to various classes. The face sheet of the questionnaire gave an overview of the project and explained the delicate nature of the questions. Students were told that they could stop at any point and skip questions they were not comfortable answering. Since some of the questions dealt with explicit sexual behavior, it was important to guarantee confidentiality, and, to do this, the questionnaire was proctored like an exam. The subsample used for this study includes those students who have had sexual experience and those who are single and not involved in steady relationships. This resulted in 120 males and 167 females. In the sample, over half of the students (65.8 percent) were concerned with the possibility of getting the AIDS virus. Over 80 percent of the students had accurate knowledge about AIDS transmission through sex.

The sample obtained is not random; however, random; numbers were used to choose class numbers listed in the departmental class schedule. With the consent of the instructor, questionnaires were administered until we reached a reasonable sample size for analysis.

Measurement

The independent variables in this study include attitudes about premarital sex and sexual experience. The intervening variables are knowledge and concern about AIDS. Perceived change in various sexual behaviors is the dependent variable.

Sexual experience—Determining the sexual behavior of students involved a summation of four items designed to measure frequency and level of sexual experience. These items reflect the number of lifetime sexual partners, with a 7-point response range from one to more than ten, and the frequency of intercourse during the past six months, with a 7-point response range from not at all to daily or more often. The frequency with which students engaged in oral sex, and in anal sex, also was measured. The five response categories for these items ranged from "never, and I wouldn't permit it," to "frequently." Overall, the higher the score on this scale, the more sexually experienced the respondent. The scale of sexual experience is found to be internally consistent with a Cronbach's alpha coefficient of .77.

The permissiveness of attitudes toward premarital sex—Attitudes toward premarital sex were measured by a five-item Guttman scale developed by Reiss (1980):

1. I believe that petting is acceptable before marriage if the couple is in love.
2. I believe that petting is acceptable before marriage if the couple feels strong affection for one another.
3. I believe that sexual intercourse is acceptable before marriage if the couple is in love.
4. I believe that sexual intercourse is acceptable before marriage if the couple feels strong affection for one another.
5. I believe that sexual intercourse is acceptable before marriage even if the couple does not feel particularly affectionate toward one another.

The Reiss Sexual Permissiveness Scale has been used extensively in research in the United States as well as in other countries (Reiss, 1980). The scores for each response (1. disagree or 2. agree) were added to create a scale which yielded a Cronbach's alpha coefficient of .74. High scores on the scale indicate more permissive attitudes toward premarital sex.

Knowledge about AIDS—Knowledge about AIDS was defined as a student's degree of certainty with respect to his or her knowledge of AIDS transmission. Four items included in this study asked students if AIDS can be transmitted by: deep or "french" kissing, by saliva, by semen, and by vaginal fluid. Response categories were "I know this is true," "I believe this is true but I am not sure," "I believe this is false, but I am not sure," and "I know this is false." A knowledge scale was created by the summation of these items, which yielded a Cronbach's alpha coefficient of .63. High scores on this scale indicate more certainty that AIDS cannot be transmitted by the above methods.

Concern about AIDS—Students' concern about AIDS was assessed by asking

"How worried or concerned are you about the possibility of getting AIDS?" Students answered this question by choosing one of the response categories which ranged from (1) not concerned at all to (4) very concerned. Students also indicated the degree to which they agree or disagree with the statement, "AIDS is a problem in California so I need to worry about it." These two items were combined, and the higher score indicated more concern about AIDS.

Change in sexual behavior—The extent to which AIDS has resulted in changes in sexual practices among college students was measured by three items:

> Because of AIDS, I have increased the length of time I date someone before engaging in sexual intercourse.
> Because of AIDS, I am more likely to ask a potential sex partner about his/her sexual history.
> Because of AIDS, I am more likely to use condoms when having intercourse.

Response categories were: "This is not at all true for me," "This is not very true for me," "This is somewhat true for me," and "This is true for me." From these responses, the prevalence of safe sex practices can be identified.

Sources of AIDS information—Various sources of AIDS-related information, such as television news or other programming, print media, discussions, with parents, classes in school or church, and discussions with friends, were measured by the extent to which they contributed to students' knowledge about AIDS. Response categories for these items were: "Contributed nothing," "Slightly contributed," "Contributed somewhat," and "Strongly contributed."

RESULTS

The data were analyzed in two steps. First, path analysis was used to test the hypothesized relationships. Second, sources of AIDS information were examined with respect to their impact on concern about the disease. All the analyses were performed separately for males and females.

Figure 1 presents the path diagram predicting change in length of time before intercourse. As can be seen, for both males and females, the level of sexual experience and the permissiveness of attitudes toward sex are not significantly related to knowledge and concern about AIDS. It is also clear that accuracy of knowledge about sexual transmission of AIDS fails to predict change with respect to time before intercourse. But male and female students who are concerned about AIDS are found to be delaying intercourse with their partners.

A similar pattern was found with respect to the likelihood of asking about a partner's sexual history and using condoms when having intercourse. Figure 2

Figure1. Path Model Predicting Change Related to Length
of Time Before Intercourse Among College Students

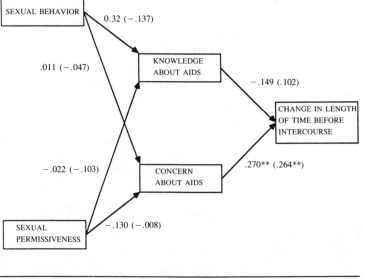

Note: Path coefficients for females are in the parentheses.
*p < .05; **p < .01.

shows that having accurate knowledge about the sexual transmission of AIDS
has a slightly negative effect on the likelihood of asking about a partner's sexual
history. On the other hand, the male and female students who are concerned
about AIDS are most likely to inquire about a partner's sexual history.

As can be seen in Figure 3, students who are concerned with the disease are
most likely to use condoms when having intercourse. Again, the level of knowledge about the sexual transmission of the AIDS virus was found to be a non-
significant predictor of condom use.

The results of examining how various sources of AIDS-related information
influence the degree of concern about AIDS among college students are shown
in Table 1. Both male and female students were more likely to be concerned
about getting the AIDS virus if television and their parents contributed to what
they knew about the disease. Other sources, such as print media, class discussions, church, and friends, were found to have no significant effect on concern
about AIDS.

In summary, it is clear that concern about AIDS encourages both male and
female students to practice safer sex. Knowledge about AIDS, on the contrary,
does not contribute to changes in sexual practice. With respect to the sources

Figure 2. Path Model Predicting Likelihood of Asking About
Partner's Sexual History Among College Students

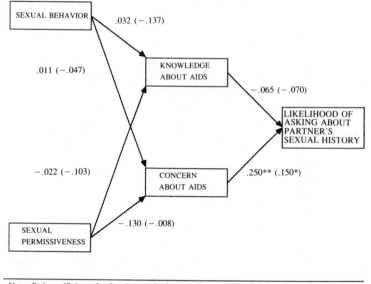

Note: Path coefficients for females are in the parentheses.
*p<.05; **p<.01.

of AIDS-related information, students who obtained information from television
and discussions with parents are most likely to be concerned about AIDS.

DISCUSSION

The students in the sample were apt to express concern about the possibility of
getting AIDS. Their concern also was found to delay sexual intercourse, increase the likelihood of asking about a potential partner's sexual history, and
increase the use of condoms. Knowledge about AIDS did not encourage such
changes.

   The findings on the relationship of knowledge to action deserve special comment. First, it may be that the more accurate the knowledge students have about
AIDS, the more likely they will be to think that because they are heterosexual
they are at low risk. This may result in less concern about AIDS. But the more
accurate the knowledge students have on the transmission of the AIDS virus,
the more likely they will be to practice safer sex. Second, the limited effect of
knowledge on changes in sexual practice, as shown in this study, may be explained, in part, by the very basic questions used in our knowledge measure.
That is, the knowledge questions included here reflect issues frequently discussed in the media. The responses to the questions included in our question-

Figure 3. Path Model Predicting Likelihood
of Condom Use Among College Students

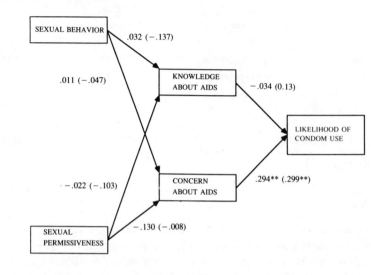

Note: Path coefficients for females are in the parentheses.
*p < .05; **p < .01.

naire, therefore, may be considered common knowledge. Consequently, the level of knowledge based on these questions may neither alter sexual behavior nor produce concern about AIDS.

Our analysis of the effect of sources of AIDS information on the degree of concern also is noteworthy. Television was acknowledged as the strongest influence on male students' concern. Parents are viewed by female students as an important information source affecting their concern about AIDS. Since concern about AIDS was found to be linked with changes in sexual practice, we can predict that information from television news and parents encourages safer sex practices among college students.

This study has limitations, one of which is the use of a nonrepresentative sample. The questions investigated in this study are so important, however, that one cannot await for a national study on this issue. Implications derived from this study may be considered suggestions for further investigations using a more representative sample.

WHAT CAN WE DO? CONCLUSIONS AND IMPLICATIONS FOR EDUCATION

Clearly, it may be many years before the discovery of an effective vaccine or

Table 1

Contributions of Various Sources of Information to Concern about AIDS
(Standardized Regression Coefficients)

Source	Males	Females
Television news or other programming	.207**	.131*
Print media (magazines, newspapers)	−.064	−.032
Discussion with parents	.168*	.197**
Classes in school	−.100	−.046
Church	.060	−.027
Discussion with friends	−.023	.074

*p ≤ .10; **p ≤ .05;

treatment for AIDS. In the interim, education to encourage safer sex practices is one of the most important ways to prevent and contain the spread of the disease. Most professionals agree that there is a need for AIDS education in schools and colleges (Yarber, 1987). Our findings have several implications for developing an effective educational program for the younger population.

First, concern does appear to promote safer sex practices among students. Educational efforts should be directed not only at the discussion of safe sexual practices, but also at increasing students' concern about AIDS. According to our findings, increased concern may result from accurate knowledge about AIDS and the ways in which the disease is transmitted. However, presenting the experiences of AIDS patients and the serious nature of the epidemic may be more effective in spurring concern about the disease. Our findings with respect to condom use, show that females are slightly more likely to encourage condom use during intercourse. This indicates a need for expanding the conception of condom use from a primarily male contraceptive form to a more universal safe sex practice.

It also is important to note that such behavioral change as condom use may be fostered by delaying intercourse until later in a relationship or discussing sexual histories prior to intercourse. Therefore, increasing young people's comfort in talking about sex with a potential partner will increase the probability of safer sexual practices. This may be best accomplished in interactive educational settings such as schools, which up to this point have rarely been viable sources for information about AIDS.

Our findings with respect to the various sources of information on AIDS are also thought-provoking, and may benefit education on safer sex practices.

Television is clearly one of the major sources affecting the degree of concern about AIDS. Discussions with parents also were found to raise concern about the disease. These findings imply that television and the family play key roles in AIDS education and prevention, and safer sexual practices among younger people.

In summary, our findings imply that educational efforts with these relatively low-risk students should focus on three areas. First, concern about AIDS should be increased not only among students, but among those to whom students may turn for information: parents, teachers, and clergy. Second, it is important that young people have a reasonable conception of risk. As concern increases, behavioral change clearly follows. Finally, as sources of AIDS-related television information, producers and parents should consider their potential impact on concern about AIDS and on the changes in behavior that are necessary to prevent the spread of the disease. The lack of correspondence between other sources of information, such as print media, classes in school, church, and friends, and the degree of concern about the disease suggests that efforts should be directed at improving the kinds of messages about AIDS provided by formal and informal sources.

With a few exceptions, notably the Assistant Secretary of Health and the Surgeon General of the U.S. Public Health Service (see U.S. Department of Health and Human Services, 1986 and Windom and Koop, 1987), national policymakers have not provided leadership in instituting education on safe sex practices (Macklin, 1988). Most of the debate at the policy level has focused on the advisability of mentioning condom use in public school sex education or advertising condoms on public television. Former Education Secretary William Bennett, echoing the position of the Reagan administration, has consistently argued that teachers and parents should emphasize abstinence as the best safeguard against AIDS, and that to promote the use of condoms suggests to younger Americans that adults expect them to engage in sexual intercourse (Bennett, 1987). This attitude does not take into account that about 28 percent of younger Americans between the ages of 12 and 17 are currently sexually active, and about 70 percent of teenage girls and 80 percent of teenage boys have had at least one coital experience (Yarber, 1987). The *essential* question to be discussed by the policymakers is not whether or not condom use should be encouraged, but how to promote educational programs to increase concern about AIDS and safer sexual practices among our young people.

The next step in this research is the investigation, using a similar model, of a younger population like high school students. Public education on safer sex at an earlier age may prevent a significant proportion of younger people from becoming infected with AIDS.

REFERENCES

Asquith, D. 1988. Student responses to the AIDS epidemic. Paper presented at the Pacific Sociological Association annual meetings, Las Vegas, Nevada.

Bennett, W.J 1987. AIDS and the Education of Our Children: A Guide for Parents and Teachers. Washington, DC: Department of Education.

Boffey, D.M. 1988. "Spread of AIDS abating, but deaths will still soar." *New York Times,* February 14, pp.1,36.

Carroll, L. 1988. Concern with AIDS and the sexual behavior of college students. *Journal of Marriage and the Family* 50:405–11.

Centers for Disease Control. 1988. January 18. AIDS Weekly Surveillance Report. Atlanta, GA: Centers for Disease Control.

Dickson, D. 1987. Africa begins to face up to AIDS. *Science* 238:605–607.

Institute of Medicine, National Academy of Sciences. 1986. *Confronting AIDS: Directions for Public Health, Health Care, and Research.* Washington, DC: National Academy Press.

Feldman, D.A. 1985. AIDS and social change. *Human Organization* 44:343–48.

Hirschorn, M.W. 1987a. Persuading students to use safer sex practices proves difficult even with the danger of AIDS. *The Chronicle of Higher Education* June 10:30.

———1987b. AIDS is not seen as a major threat by many heterosexuals on campuses. *The Chronicle of Higher Education* April 29: 1,32,33.

Institute of Medicine, National Academy of Sciences. 1986. *Mobilizing against AIDS: The Unfinished Story of a Virus.* Cambridge, MA: Harvard University Press.

Koop, C.E. 1987. Teaching children about AIDS. *Issues in Science and Technology* 4:67–70.

Macklin, E.D. 1988. AIDS: Implications for families. *Family Relations* 37:141–49.

National Center for Health Statistics. 1988. AIDS knowledge and attitudes for December 1987. *Advance Data* 153, May 16.

Quinn, T.C., et al. 1986. AIDS in Africa: An epidemiologic paradigm. *Science* 234:955–63.

Reiss, I. L. 1980. *Family Systems in America,* 3rd ed. New York: Holt, Rinehart and Winston.

Romanowski, B. and J. Brown 1986. AIDS and changing sexual behavior. *Canadian Medical Association Journal* 134:872.

Simkins, L. and M.G. Eberhage. 1984. Attitudes toward AIDS, Herpes II, and Toxic Shock Syndrome. *Psychological Reports* 55:779–86.

Simkins, L. and A. Kushner. 1986. Attitudes towards AIDS, Herpes II, and Toxic Shock Syndrome: Two years later. *Psychological Reports* 59:883–91.

United States Department of Health and Human Services. 1986. Surgeon General's Report on Acquired Immune Deficiency Syndrome. Washington, DC: United States Public Health Service.

Whitbeck, L. B. and R. L. Simons. 1988. AIDS in the heartland: Knowledge, concern, and perceived behavioral change among college students. Paper presented at the Midwest Sociological Society annual meeting, Minneapolis, MN.

Windom, R.E., and C. E. Koop. 1987. *No-Nonsense AIDS Answers.* Chicago: Blue Cross/Blue Shield Association.

Winkelstein, W., et al. 1987. The San Francisco Men's Health Study: III. Reduction in Human Immunodeficiency virus transmission among homosexual/bisexual men, 1982–1986. *American Journal of Public Health* 76:685–89.

Yarber, W.L. 1987. School AIDS education: Politics, issues, and responses. *SIECUS Report* 15:1–5.

PART V

Organization and Structure as Sociological Variables

With the resources available to them, health care administrators and professionals seek to provide the best possible care for their patients and clients. Yet, problems in financing, ethics, advanced technology, and coordination of health care delivery notwithstanding, these same health care professionals have tended to view social organization and structure as residual variables or as parameters that are taken for granted.

In contrast, clinical sociology emphasizes organizational and structural variables in conceptualizing, researching, recommending, and implementing changes in health care delivery. This is exemplified in the following four chapters which provide a sociological perspective on illness and loss and prescribe organizational solutions to role problems. They represent various theoretical constructs, research methods, and intervention strategies. Socio-medical problems include cancer, Alzheimer's Disease, and grief, while organizational contexts range from face-to-face interaction and role behavior to organizational and social structure.

Gear and Haney in "The Cancer Patient after Diagnosis: Hospitalization and Treatment" focus on transitions to the role and status of "cancer patient" after the initial diagnosis. Becoming a medical patient for any reason may involve uncertainty and loss of control, as well as altered self image and personal identity. Cancer treatment, particularly in tertiary care facilities, includes proliferation of complex technologies, fragmentation of care, acute rather than chronic care orientation, and independent caregivers who frequently do not treat the whole person. Gear and Haney ask how a cancer diagnosis can be prevented from becoming a "master status" that overwhelms the patient, how patients can be more involved in decision-making, and how staff can increase management of patient care rather than management of only the patient's disease. The authors recommend creation of a new role, Case Management Coordinator, to facilitate organizational changes in hospitals.

Clark, in "Intervention for Cancer Patients: A Clinical Sociology Approach

271

to Program Planning,'' describes a problem solving implementation for cancer patients in a mid-sized community hospital. Clark was hired to determine the feasibility of developing and implementing a comprehensive intervention program for cancer patients. Program planning included an organizational assessment of the hospital, assessment of community resources, development of hospital and community advisory committees, and a survey of cancer patients. The success of this sociologically designed program appears to be due to the care with which Clark utilized a broad-based organizational approach that included all the significant role players in the program, existing resources and networks, and meaningful sociological data. Articulation of role concepts and labeling theory provided a "language" that facilitated changes in perception and expectations by the staff.

Johnson in "The Sociology of Alzheimer's Wings in Nursing Homes" also reports on a problem solving implementation. Based on a symbolic interactionist assessment of Alzheimer's Disease (AD), Johnson designed and implemented a low stimulus environment for chronic Alzheimer's patients in a nursing home. The nursing staff was selected and trained in AD patient care, and was encouraged to reframe the situation from "dying from " to "living with AD," and from caring for "patients" to caring for "residents with AD." In effect, the staff members became specialists in caring for people with AD and they became part of the AD network in the community. Preliminary results from this program suggest positive changes for AD residents in the final two stages of AD when compared to a traditional nursing home environment and even the AD residents' own homes.

Kalekin-Fishman and Klingman in "Rituals and Ideology: The Case of the Funeral in Non-religious Kibbutzim" examine the role of mourners and the significance and efficacy of established funeral rituals. Like Blauner (1966), they find that funerals are not mere rituals, but significant adaptive structures. Non-religious kibbutzim are communal organizations that value equality, common responsibility, organic belongingness, direct democracy, and non-exploitation of others. Kalekin-Fishman and Klingman have a functionalist perspective which leads them to expect the funeral to reinforce communal identity as mourners' needs are assuaged. The authors find that both mourners and kibbutzim are only partially served by these funeral rituals, where value inconsistencies and potential conflicts are to be found. The kibbutzim are encouraged to re-examine the ritual of the funeral in order to resolve moral paradoxes in the social structure. Mourners, the authors conclude, are best served in the short run by the intervention of "trained ritual specialists."

Social expectations, in the form of role definitions, frame the way that patients and their health care providers interact with one another. Roles of patient, physician, and nurse, as well as medical technologist, chaplain, clinical sociologist, counselor, and others, are socially constructed by people who enact these roles, who respond to these roles, and who shape the normative structure and organization of health care delivery. Any analysis of organizations which serve the ill, the aged, the dying, or the bereaved, must include sociocultural factors (Bendiksen, 1976) and what Straus (1984:53) identifies as "total social context" including both "macro" and "micro" viewpoints.

REFERENCES

Blauner, R. 1966. Death and social structure. *Psychiatry* 29: 378–94.

Bendiksen, R. 1976. The sociology of death. In R. Fulton, ed., *Death and Identity*. Bowie, MD: Charles Press, 59–81.

Straus, R. 1984. Changing the definition of the situation: Toward a theory of sociological intervention. *Clinical Sociology Review* 2: 51–63.

22

The Cancer Patient After Diagnosis: Hospitalization and Treatment

Elizabeth Gear and C. Allen Haney

Despite optimism over improvements in survival rates, a significant proportion of those diagnosed with cancer will not survive the disease following intensive treatment efforts (Bailar and Smith, 1986).[1] This is particularly true for patients with types of cancer in which the symptoms mimic those of other disorders, or are difficult to detect in the early stages (e.g., ovarian epithelial carcinomas and pancreatic cancer). Others, for whom prognosis is somewhat more favorable, may undergo hospitalizations, surgery, and months of out-patient treatments which temporarily may halt the progression of disease, or may be followed by a period of remission, prior to recurrence and death. Those whose diagnosis is optimal may be hospitalized and undergo surgery, may undergo a course of radiotherapy or chemotherapy, or may only be required to submit to periodic follow-up examinations and testing following surgery. A proportion of those diagnosed with cancer will be considered survivors, currently determined by a disease-free period of at least five years, but they must continue to live with the fear of recurrence.

Numerous researchers and laypersons have observed that the diagnosis of cancer significantly changes every aspect of the individual's life. Frequently, discussions center on the social, psychological, and physical effects of the disease and the uncertainty of treatment outcome. These notwithstanding, a significant aspect of having cancer, and one often taken for granted, is that the person diagnosed with cancer becomes a "cancer patient"—a status which frequently takes primacy over most of the other statuses in the individual's life.

Although therapies vary, it is not uncommon for patients to undergo one or more hospitalizations for surgery, treatment, complications of treatment, and disease symptoms. Treatment following the initial surgery generally consists of chemotherapy, radiotherapy, a combination of these, or immunotherapies administered in an out-patient chemotherapy unit or radiotherapy section. On the average, treatment lasts from three to twelve months and is given in weekly or monthly cycles. During treatment, patients also may undergo numerous radiologic tests (x-rays of chest and gastrointestinal tract, ultrasound, computerized tomography scan, magnetic resonance imaging, etc.), be required to have blood and other fluid samples drawn two to four times monthly, and be scheduled for monthly appointments in an out-patient clinic or oncologist's office for examinations during this process.

At the same time, then, that the individual is faced with the crises posed by a life threatening disease, the individual must also, for an unspecified and potentially lengthy period of time, negotiate his or her status and roles within and relative to the health care organization. Particularly for those with cancer, organizational practices, as they relate to the status and roles of the patient may function to compound the threats produced by the disease. These threats include uncertainty, loss of control, altered self image, and, perhaps more important, loss of personal identity.

It is a basic premise of sociology that to understand human behavior and patterns of social relations one must take into account the structural context in which these occur. Further, it is argued that these social arrangements must be viewed in relation to material factors such as physical environment (including the biological), technology, and resources. Finally, it is argued that these structures, material factors, and patterns of social relations are not static, but emergent and interactive (Straus, 1985). Clearly, to neglect the experience of hospitalization and treatment, and particularly the impact of the internal organizational structure and the social relations within that structure, is to fail to examine a major portion and context of the experience of many of those diagnosed with cancer.

This chapter will focus primarily on factors common to the treatment experience initially following diagnosis in a cancer center or a general hospital with a cancer program. While the issues of recurrence, experimental or homeopathic treatments, survivors' rights, and terminal care also are important areas of focus, detailed treatment of these subjects is largely outside the scope of this chapter.

THE SOCIAL CONTEXT OF CANCER DIAGNOSIS AND TREATMENT

So there is something worse, after all, than your man turning away from you.
Your own body turning away, running away with a crazy new life of its own
(Lynch and Richards, 1986:10).

Perhaps the most devastating impact of illness and aging, and particularly of cancer, is the betrayal of one's own body. Cancer is defined as "invasive," the treatment as an attack on the disease, and the patient is defined variously as victim or valiant fighter, and frequently, as the battleground over which this war with cancer is fought (Sontag, 1978).

The effects of the physical betrayal are widespread and synergistic. Individuals may be subject to repeated disruption and reorganization of life activities, plans, and goals, and may be faced with significant financial strain resulting from both the costs associated with treatment and with the negative impact on their ability to predict or maintain a consistent work life (Sourkes, 1982). In turn, the identity derived from life activities may be threatened, and may result in an altering or loss of social relationships (Donnelly, 1987; Haney and Raffoul, 1986). Additionally, both diagnosis and treatment carry the potential for discrediting and stigmatizing the individual. Patients may blame themselves or be blamed for having incurred the disease and in some instances, for the failure of treatment (Abrams and Finesinger, 1953; Bard, 1970; Patterson, 1987). Finally, both the societal and organizational roles of the ill, regardless of the illness, may require that individuals submit to further social and physical capacity reduction, in addition to that already caused by the disease which they seek medical help to alleviate (Freidson, 1970; Parsons, 1972). In the case of cancer, it is unclear whether those who survive ever cease to be patients (American Cancer Society, 1988).

THE ORGANIZATIONAL CONTEXT OF CANCER TREATMENT

Many of the threats to the self which result from the treatment process, such as physical and social contamination, identity stripping, and loss of control, derive from the manner in which health care delivery is structured (Goffman, 1961; King, 1962; Mechanic, 1976; Strauss, 1970). Hospitals and treatment centers are perhaps best defined as quasi-bureaucratic, complex organizational structures characterized by multiple lines of authority. More to the point of this analysis, health care organizations are characterized by two interacting types of structures: bureaucratic and professional. This divergence in organizational structure may be particularly characteristic of, and most pronounced in, large cancer centers, the majority of which are state or university institutions which employ highly specialized, professional staff. Oncologists, for example, are trained and generally board certified in one or more traditional areas of medicine as well as an area of cancer diagnosis and treatment, e.g., obstetrics and gynecology (OB-Gyn), gynecologic oncology. A number of oncologists are, in addition, board certified surgeons. This additional training and certification is also common among nurses and social workers employed in cancer centers and programs.

While the bureaucratic structure tends to constrain the professionally ordered division of labor, professional occupations, defined by licensed autonomy, are specifically antibureaucratic (Freidson, 1986). Hospitals and treatment centers also may be rather rigidly departmentalized according to professional orientation, even when interdisciplinary work is attempted. Yarbro (1985) attributes much of the failure to achieve optimal interdisciplinary efforts in cancer research and treatment, the objective of the federally supported, National Cancer Institute's (NCI) Cancer Centers Program, to resistant bureaucratic and professional structures. The cancer patient becomes the focus of these structures and the multiple departmental, professional, and personal orientations within the organization. Rather than being the determinant, cancer patients are primarily the recipients or objects of activity.

Technology and the Generalized Delivery of Services

Hospitals and treatment centers tend to operate and be guided by the requirements of the organization, establishing rules and procedures which facilitate the delivery of services, and not infrequently, adversely affecting individuals being treated there (Perrow, 1965; Titmuss, 1965). While technological innovations have in some cases functioned to improve the quality of care (e.g., Bollis infusion pump), the proliferation of complex technologies now required in health care also has served to increase the fragmentation of care. As Strauss, et al., (1985:5) illustrate:

> During patients' hospitalizations, they are frequently moved to and from specialized machine areas where machines are used to do tests, monitor the course of diseases, or provide treatments. . . . In addition, a constant stream of workers comes and goes, performing tasks on patients. The scheduling of work for diagnostic tests and monitoring of illness status, treatments, and general nursing care is complex; there is a high likelihood that schedules will go awry since each machine area and patient care unit has its own schedules and contingencies.

Similar fragmentation of care also tends to characterize out-patient facilities (Garrett, Ashford, and Savage, 1986; Gross, 1986). The routine of out-patient clinics, laboratories, treatment and diagnostic radiology units, patient service departments, patient care and surgical areas is likely to be unfamiliar to patients, as are the physical layout of the organization, the significance of uniforms and titles, the language used by both medical and non-medical personnel, the meaning and purpose of various tests and procedures, and even the particular smells, sights, and sounds which characterize treatment facilities (Blumberg, Flaherty and Lewis, 1980; Gross, 1986; King, 1962; Samora, Saunders, and Larson, 1961; Strauss, 1970). As a consequence, patients are unlikely to be familiar with the rules and authority structures governing either patients or organization staff. Patients also may be ill-equipped to evaluate the treatment options and medication orders to which they must give consent (Tagliacozzo and Mauksch, 1972).

Hospitals and clinics are organized for "getting work done" from the staff point of view; only infrequently are they set up to minimize the patient's confusion. He fends for himself and sometimes may even get lost when sent "just down the corridor." Patients are often sent for diagnostic tests from one service to another with no explanation, with inadequate directions, with brusque tones. This may make them exceedingly anxious and affect their symptoms and diagnosis. After sitting for hours in waiting rooms, they become angry to find themselves passed over for latecomers—but nobody explains about emergencies or priorities (Strauss, 1970:14).

Gross' (1986) observation of the development of what he terms a "veteran community," or a group of patients who have, through common experience, become knowledgeable regarding both organizational and treatment practices, also suggests that much of the information patients obtain regarding the treatment setting is experiential in nature.

The manner in which health care services are provided tends to be consistent with the industrialized, technological society of which it is a part, characterized by bureaucratic organization and mass production (Taylor, 1970). In this way, the organization, or more accurately, each department, service, and patient care area, is geared toward the provision of goods and services in a generalized manner rather than the meeting of the specific needs of individual patients.

Consider, also, patients' daily schedules. As the official standardization of meal-times, medication times, visiting hours, and—occasionally—bedtime suggests, the temporal location of daily events such as eating, taking medications, having visitors, and going to sleep applies to all patients *together*. . . . That each patient gets his medicine when medications are given suggests that standard medication times are 'social facts' which apply to each part of the system only because they apply, first of all, to the system as a whole. The act of giving a patient his medication is only a part, and a particular manifestation, of the act of administering medications at that time of day in general . . . (Zerubavel, 1979: 107–108).

Not discounting the rationale guiding some hospital and clinic policies, such as the requirement that "valuables" be secured upon admission, the need to meet governmental reporting requirements, or the necessity of providing treatment, tests, and examinations to a large number of patients, it has been suggested that the organizationally regimented, and sometimes arbitrary procedures, used to implement these policies also may negatively impact on the individual's sense of social cohesion, separate the individual from sources of support, and result in numerous assaults on the self (Goffman, 1961; Roth, 1957; Taylor, 1970). This particularly may be true for those cancer patients whose treatment requires multiple admissions and clinic visits (Fotes, 1985; Garrett, Ashford, and Savage, 1986).

Goffman (1961) observed more than a quarter century ago that in organizations charged with caring or providing for large numbers of people there is a tendency to find justifications for actions and procedures relative to the generalized distribution of services, regardless of their effects on the individuals being cared for.

> In total institutions . . . the various rationales for mortifying the self are very often merely rationalizations, generated by efforts to manage the daily activity of a large number of persons in a restricted space with a small expenditure of resources (Goffman, 1961: 47).

To illustrate, the practices most often justified, on the basis of the requirement of close monitoring of bodily functions over patient comfort, are those of intensive care units. It is therefore justified, given the need for proximity to specialized equipment and personnel, to place patients in a ward-like environment. In addition, however, patients, including those who are incapacitated but conscious, are often left lying in bed only semi-clad so that the patient's body (breasts, buttocks, etc.) is exposed to all other hospital personnel, including hospital management, housekeeping, transport, and supply personnel, who walk through the unit.

It also could be argued that hospitals and treatment centers are neither designed nor physically constructed with the needs of ill persons in mind. Hospital size, for example, is calculated on the basis of the number of beds and not the number of rooms. While a view exists that sharing a room with another cancer patient provides the individual with support, this observation may reflect responses to imposed situations, rather than the understanding of the types of supportive relationships generally found to facilitate coping with the disease and treatment (Clark, 1983; Dunkel-Schetter, 1984; Gross, 1986; Rofe, Lewin, and Hoffman, 1987).

Treatment areas, among the areas most frequented by cancer patients, also seem to be constructed with little regard for the physical and social needs of those receiving treatment, and may be the last areas to undergo renovation as the following vignette illustrates:

> A 35-year-old hospital manager, on touring the new out-patient chemotherapy unit shortly after it opened in 1987, continually remarked that she "must have died and gone to heaven." There were actually three separate units, each large with a central nursing station completely surrounded by individual, private rooms. All of the staff expressed agreement with her sentiments. By comparison, the old unit which she said "had been there for most of her five years at the hospital and probably long before that," consisted of two rooms full of "ortho type chairs" and a third room with a row of metal beds against each wall and an isle about two and one-half feet wide between the rows. These rooms were connected by a hallway that doubled as a waiting area. "The first time I saw it," she recalled, "I was angry." "I remember thinking to myself, chemo is our stock 'n trade! You'd think we could do better than this, especially with all the money we spend on other things like that new auditorium and the hospital lobby." And she explained, "Chemo can make people sick you know. But here they were in beds only four inches apart and no room for family and friends to sit by you. And I'll tell you, even if I *weren't* on chemo, I'd probably throw up if I were lying that close to someone who did."

Similar observations have been made regarding the physical environment af-
forded indigent patients, and those with diseases of unclear etiologies which are
frequently subject to experimentation and segregation (Albrecht, 1984; Fox,
1959; Patterson, 1987; Strauss, 1970). There are, of course, notable exceptions
(Clark, 1984; Davis, 1980; Dawe, 1985; Garrett, Ashford, and Lewin, 1987;
Klagsbrun, 1970; Weld and Greer, 1986). It is interesting to observe, however,
that many of these modifications in organizational practices and patient environments established to meet the social and emotional needs of patients have been
viewed as "experimental" (as opposed to existing "proven" methods), and
frequently required that outside funding be obtained. Further, these programs,
particularly those attempting to recognize the patient's involvement, have tended
to be conducted under the direction of the staff and the center, on issues defined
as salient by staff (Brownlea, 1987). In only rare cases has patient input been
solicited or considered.

Acute Care Orientation

Hoffman's (1974) analysis of the responses of patient care staff to stroke victims
suggests that many hospital practices, and by implication many of those involving cancer patients, may be partially explained by an acute care or disease
orientation rather than an orientation to the needs of the person who is ill. Her
observations suggest that tasks not directly related to the treatment and cure of
disease or injury to the body may be defined as outside the realm of medical
activity.

This is consistent with Glaser and Strauss' (1965) observations of the difficulties encountered by staff in meeting the needs of dying patients. Further, contrary
to assumptions which might be made about cancer treatment facilities, these
institutions are not established to provide hospice and terminal care services.
In large cancer centers particularly, when a medical decision is reached that
nothing further can be done, the patient frequently is discharged to the referring
physician and hospital, to a hospice, or sent home. Only recently, as survival
rates have begun to increase, has significant attention been directed toward the
inclusion of physical and social rehabilitation, and measures to reduce the disa-
bling effects of treatment, as part of cancer treatment programs (Hickey, 1986;
MacVicar and Winningham, 1986).

In cancer treatment, the negative effects of treatment on patients, or "side-
effects," such as complaints of pain, nausea and vomiting, fatigue, and hair
loss (alopecia), while of considerable significance to patients' self image and
ability to conduct normal life activities, may be viewed by staff as predictable
and common accompaniments to treatment and medically insignificant. Care
practices generally are prioritized on the basis of severity of illness, defined in
terms of acute physiological condition and degree of threat to bodily function-

ing. While there appears to be a general agreement, on the part of both patients and staff, on the need to prioritize patient care activities on the basis of severity of illness, Tagliacozzo and Mauksch (1972) observed that a lack of consensus may occur between patients and staff over the priority assigned to a particular patient's condition. Similarly, Strauss, et. al. (1985) have suggested that the priority assigned to "care work", such as attending to patients' complaints of pain or elimination needs, relative to other instrumental or technological nursing functions, may run counter to the patient's expectations and serve to increase the patient's sense of dependency and lack of control.

Perhaps most consistently defined as outside the scope of medical care, or deemed of secondary importance, have been the social and emotional needs of patients (Schulman, 1972). It may not, in fact, be unreasonable to suggest that social and psychological needs, such as emotional support, positive self esteem, and a sense of personal control are more effectively met by traditional sources of support, and barring these, professionals whose primary training and occupational responsibilities are geared toward meeting those needs. However, accessibility to traditional sources of support may be limited by care and treatment practices (Twaddle and Hessler, 1987). Further, the defined separation in functions also may serve to promote a focus on illness, to the exclusion of the social and psychological impact of both life-threatening illness and treatment on the individual (Bloom, 1981), and lend itself to erroneous and negative assessments of patients (Lorber, 1981; Leidermann and Grisso, 1985).

> Mr. H. was a 58-year-old blue-collar worker and a bachelor, diagnosed with advanced prostate cancer. Mr. H. expressed the belief that he was to blame for the advanced state of his disease because he didn't detect the problem and go to the doctor sooner. Mr. H. was almost incapacitated and had to be transported daily to treatment and diagnostic testing areas on a stretcher. Despite the fact that lying on a stretcher was particularly painful, there were frequently delays of 30–45 minutes before Mr. H. was returned to his room. During most of his hospital stay, Mr. H. wore only a short, cotton hospital gown and, because of edema in both legs, elastic stockings up to his thighs which the nurses changed for him each morning. Each day during his treatment a "tech" would come to draw blood and frequently this process also inflicted pain. Mr. H. generally exhibited depression and on days when the chemotherapy had made him particularly ill, when he had been unable to urinate by himself, had had the stockings placed on him by a female nurse, had been transported and left on a stretcher for 45 minutes, and had blood drawn in a particularly painful series of attempts, Mr. H. became tearful as well. The nurses generally expressed the feeling that Mr. H. was overly emotional and demanding and the physician ordered a "psych consult" because Mr. H. was exhibiting depression.

In contrast to the view which may be produced by an acute care orientation, it appears more accurate to suggest that the problems experienced by cancer patients may result from both the demands placed on them by their on-going social activities and roles, their predictable responses to disease symptoms, treatment, and care activities (Clark, 1983; Haney and Raffoul, 1986; Leshan, 1964; Strauss and Glaser, 1975).[2]

Professional Autonomy and the Role and Status of Patient

Strauss, et al. (1985) emphasize that work involving human beings differs from work on inanimate objects in that human beings react and become part of the process. One of the most frequently noted phrases in the health care literature is, in fact, "the management of the patient" (not "the management of patient care"), implying a social relationship characterized by dominance of one over the other. As Emerson notes, ". . . power is a property of the social relationship, it is not an attribute of the actor." (1962:32) The person, then, has not become the disease, but rather, a patient to be managed (Davies, 1976; Freidson, 1986).

One of the consequences of professional activity in health care, and arguably, of any occupation claiming or accorded professional status and autonomy whose activity involves caring for, acting on behalf of, regulating or instructing sentient human beings, is the tendency of professionals to assume a superordinate role over those for whom activity is being performed. This tendency may be present precisely because the authority and status accorded professionals do not derive from the characteristics of the individual, but are vested in the position, and legitimized by a societally recognized authority to act, based upon a differential, and collective, level of expertise (Freidson, 1986; Goode, 1957; Simmel, 1965).

The potential for the development of a paternalistic attitude toward those who are ill is not, however, confined to the medical profession. It also may be exhibited by those seeking the recognition of professional status, those acting in association or accordance with the directives of professionals, and by nonprofessional care givers such as relatives. Lynch, for example, records the following encounter during her search for information prior to deciding to undergo a mastectomy.

> I try to find out what a mastectomy looks like so I call the American Cancer Society. The woman on the other end tells me that books with pictures of cancer treatments aren't considered suitable for non-medical people (Lynch and Richards, 1986:16).

For each patient, however, the experience is unique and first-hand. Failure of the professional or organization staff to provide adequate information may function to increase uncertainty and decrease the individual's sense of predictability and control. Unwillingness to explain professional decisions, or the attitude that patients are incapable of understanding or do not require information, functions to ". . . in essence refuse (the patient) the status of a responsible adult or person in the full sense of the word (Freidson, 1986:149)."

Paternalism, defined as those behaviors which transgress patient self-determination, or can be characterized as interference in a manner inconsistent with patient goals, may have the greatest potential for being directive and intrusive when exhibited by those assuming professional status (Lomas, 1981; Marzuk, 1985; Perry and Applegate, 1985). However, those areas where the opportunity for the expression of inappropriate parental behaviors appears to be greatest, are those which lie largely outside the dominance of the medical profession, and exist in groups striving for professional status which must establish this status by demonstrating an autonomy and control ascribed to greater knowledge or expertise.

Strauss, et al. (1985) noted this tendency in the expansion of nursing activities into patient education. They suggest that the directive and limited format frequently utilized in patient education mitigates against patient involvement and reduces the likelihood that patients' informational needs will be met. Similarly, professional recognition by non-physicians may be sought through inclusion in decision-making and a broadening of the definition of care activities. These efforts also may function to promote a view of patients as persons to be managed and for whom decisions should be made (Mayer, 1986; Russell, 1984).

Likewise, while crisis intervention generally is considered valuable in helping the patient focus on the source of problems, the value of this approach is in facilitating patient action and coping (Capone, et. al., 1979; Clark, 1984). Failure on the part of staff to explain or to question the necessity of specific hospital and care practices, a source of frustration frequently cited by patients, may in turn limit the patient's ability to cope with problems, and function to increase feelings of helplessness or loss of control underlying frustration over care practices, and may serve to underscore the dominance of staff over patients (Weld and Greer, 1986).

Tagliacozzo and Mauksch (1972) concluded that patients generally perceive the definition of their role in the organization as unclear and limited to responsibilities such as cooperation. Yet it was observed that patients differentiated hospital personnel in a manner suggesting that patients hold expectations of the nature of the relationship between themselves and health care personnel which differ from the child–parent relationship and the generalized service mode. In addition, the frequency of association, particularly in out-patient settings, which tend to operate on a regular business week schedule allowing recurring patient contact with the same nurses and support staff, also serves to promote the development of familiar, interpersonal relationships. It appears then, that in addition to the more limited organizational roles, a role of helped person exists for those without selected resources (e.g., medical expertise) that is not a child role, nor a traditional client role, where dependence is situation and ability specific. However, this role relationship may be in conflict, for both patients and staff, with that of the organizational and legal roles of patient and staff.

IMPLICATIONS FOR INTERVENTIONS

An obvious, but perhaps impossible, solution to some of the problems described herein might begin with preventing one's cancer diagnosis from becoming a master status. That would mean preventing the diagnosis from becoming the over-arching attribute, identity, or designation used to define the individual. Following Scheff's (1963) argument regarding the so called mentally ill, during those experiences and circumstances which occur in times of ambiguity and heightened anxiety, the role of cancer patient or cancer survivor might seem to be the only one open to the individual. Furthermore, it may be seen by others as a less confusing or more expedient way in which to guide interaction with the ill person. For the ill person this designation could, at least initially, help structure behavior and provide meanings disrupted by the disease. In the long run, however, this process will likely ill serve all concerned. Certainly the current organizational role of patient mitigates against the provision of information and against the involvement of patients in the decision-making process by defining the individual as incapable of either, on the basis of physical illness. This reduces the possibility that the individual's goals or needs in coping with the disease and treatment process will be met.

There is little question that in a treatment facility there are countless goals to be pursued, and all manner and level of personnel charged with their attainment. Too often, however, the goals of the patient may be overlooked. Even a cursory examination of the various job descriptions in a cancer facility reveals that the overall well-being of the patient is difficult to find specified anywhere. Further, it is unfortunate that, to a great extent, those employees who do seem to have the most patient contact and to care more for the entire person are those with the least authority to intervene on the patient's behalf. While it is understood that nothing can take the place of a genuine concern for protecting the dignity and autonomy of the patient, it is unrealistic to believe that this will evolve under the present system of medical care and medical education in which this is rarely taught, seldom learned, and of marginal priority.

Medicine is oriented to the most rapid and efficient intervention possible in the disease process. It can be observed that few cancer care facilities have hospice counseling or care as a major emphasis. Similarly, until recently, relatively little provision was made for meeting the rehabilitation needs of those surviving cancer. It would appear that the main goal is cure, even when cure is not a realistic outcome. This perspective may be contrary, however, to both the nature of the disease and, from a sociological perspective, to the patient's best interest. While significant delays in seeking help may affect the treatment outcome, there appears to be little clinical indication for requiring patients to make life-altering and potentially life-threatening decisions within hours or even days following diagnosis (Blumberg, Flaherty, and Lewis, 1980). Patients may need time; time to be reassured by others, time to assess alternatives open to them, time to adjust to the manifold changes required by the disease, and time to decide what part they will play in the drama unfolding around them.

Further, health care delivery is generally structured to meet organizational needs. As such, greater emphasis is placed upon the management of the patient than on the coordination of care activities. An approach to service delivery which defines functional areas of responsibility, and the interrelationship of these functions relative to a common goal, would seem to be a more effective approach than defining relationships on the basis of hierarchial structure. If one accepts the premise that one of the requirements for making rational decisions, and for rational behavior, is adequate information, then it would not seem inconsistent with organization goals to aid in the development of a better informed patient population.

While significant organizational change is desireable, the most realistic approach to the problems identified herein appears to be a greater reliance upon patient advocates or case management coordinators, who are vested with the authority to intervene on the patient's behalf and charged with a responsibility to provide information about organizational structure and services, to make resources available which meet patient goals and needs, and to provide for greater continuity in patient care (Clark, 1984). While the concept of advocacy has been much used, what is suggested here is the development of an autonomous and authoritative role, rather than the attachment of the role to an existing organizational position. Additionally, in devising any type of intervention it is suggested that the most important, and most frequently neglected task, is to accurately identify the needs of patients (Bos, 1987; Clark, 1984).

What is required for the resolution of problems resulting from the current system of health care delivery is a recognition that health care delivery is a service, and that the treatment of cancer is likely to be a long term process with an outcome which is uncertain and often, at best, life-prolonging. Further, during most of the process the patient may be expected to be sentient and functional. As such, the requirements of the structure and orientation of the cancer care organization are vastly different from both the current structure of health care delivery and from those charged with the delivery of short-term, and generally effectual, acute care.

NOTES

1. The term cancer is used throughout to refer to a group of over 200 "oncological diseases" (see Raven, R.W., 1985). It also should be noted that patients may be diagnosed as having two or more different oncological diseases simultaneously and may concurrently be suffering from a non-oncological condition, e.g., heart disease, diabetes.

2. Green, et al. (1987) suggest that crying, for example, may be indicative of behavioral abnormality only insofar as no causal linkage can be established between the bahavior and the nature of events or circumstances preceding the emotional response, and physiological determinants can be ruled out. Similarly, Leshan (1964) has described the emotional devastation produced by the significant duration of severe pain.

REFERENCES

Abrams, R.D. and J.E. Finesinger. 1953. Guilt reactions in patients with cancer. *Cancer* 6:474–82.

Albrecht, G.L. 1984. Large urban public hospitals: An analysis of competing explanatory paradigms. *Research in the Sociology of Health Care* 3:221–25.

American Cancer Society. 1988. The cancer survivors' bill of rights. *NCCS Networker* Spring 1988:3.

Bailar, J. and E. Smith. 1986. Progress against cancer? *New England Journal of Medicine* 314:1226–32.

Bard, M. 1970. The price of survival for cancer patients. In A. Strauss, ed. *Where Medicine Fails.* New Brunswick, NJ: Transaction Books, 99–110.

Bloom, J.R. 1981. Cancer care providers and the medical care system. In P. Ahmed, ed. *Living and Dying With Cancer.* New York: Elsevier North Holland, Inc., 253–72.

Blumberg, B., M. Flaherty, and J. Lewis, eds.. 1980. *Coping With Cancer. A Resource for the Health Professional.* Bethesda, MD: U.S. Department of Health and Human Services. NIH Publication No. 80-2080.

Bos, G. 1987. Sexuality of gynecologic cancer patients: Influence of traditional role patterns. In N.K. Aaronson and J. Beckmann, eds. *The Quality of Life of Cancer Patients.* New York: Raven Press, 207–13.

Brownlea, A. 1987. Participation: Myths, realities and prognosis. *Social Science and Medicine* 25 (6): 605–14.

Capone, M.A., et al. 1979. Crisis intervention: A functional model for hospitalized cancer patients. *American Journal of Orthopsychiatry* 49:598–606.

Clark, E.J. 1983. The role of the social environment in adaptation to cancer. *Social Work Research and Abstracts* 19:32–33.

———1984. Intervention for cancer patients: A clinical sociology approach to program planning. *Journal of Applied Sociology* 1 (1):83–96.

Davies, J. 1976. Impact of the system on the patient–practitioner relationship. In J.W. Cohen, B.H. Fox, and R.N. Isom, eds. *Cancer: The Behavioral Dimensions.* New York: Raven Press, 137–44.

Davis, M.Z. 1980. The organizational, interactional, and care-oriented conditions for patient participation in the continuity of care. *Social Science and Medicine* 14:39–47.

Dawe, N.A. 1985. An oasis for cancer patients. *RN* 48 (10): 32–33.

Donnelly, S. 1988. Human selves, chronic illness, and the ethics of medicine. *Hastings Center Report* 18 (2):5–8.

Dunkel-Schetter, C. 1984. Social support and cancer: Findings based on patient interviews and their implications. *Journal of Social Issues* 40 (4): 77–98.

Emerson, R.M. 1962. Power-dependence relations. *American Sociological Review* 27 (Feb):31–40.

Fotes, Y. 1985. A plea for humanism. In S.C. Gross and S. Garb, eds. *Cancer Treatment and Research in Humanistic Perspective.* New York: Spring Publishing Company, 207–15.

Fox, R.C. 1959. *Experiment Perilous: Physicians and Patients Facing the Unknown.* Glencoe, IL: Free Press.

Freidson, E. 1970. *The Profession of Medicine.* New York: Dodd, Mead.
———1986. Professional dominance and the ordering of health services: Some consequences. In P. Conrad and R. Kern, eds. *The Sociology of Health and Illness. Critical Perspectives.* 2nd ed. New York: St. Martin's Press, 146–55.
Garrett, T.J., A. Ashford, and D. C. Savage. 1986. Oncology clinic attendance at an inner city hospital. *Cancer* 58 (3):793–95.
Glaser, B.G. and A.L. Strauss. 1965. *Awareness of Dying.* New York: Aldine.
Goffman, E. 1961. On the characteristics of total institutions. In *Asylums: Essays on the Social Situation of Mental Patients and Other Inmates.* Garden City, NJ: Doubleday, 1–124.
Goode, W.J. 1957. Community within a community: The professions. *American Sociological Review* 22 (April):194–200.
Green, R.L., T.W. McAllister, and J.L. Bernat. 1987. A study of crying in medically and surgically hospitalized patients. *American Journal of Psychiatry* 144 (4):442–47.
Gross, E. 1986. Waiting at mayo. *Urban Life* 15 (2):139–64.
Haney, C.A. and P.R. Raffoul. 1986. Four psychosocial stressors among cancer patients. *The Cancer Bulletin* 38 (5):244–47.
Hickey, R.C. 1986. Historical basis for cancer rehabilitation at the University of Texas M.D. Anderson Hospital and Tumor Institute. *The Cancer Bulletin* 38 (5):239–40.
·Hoffman, J.E. 1974. Nothing can be done: Social dimensions of the treatment of stroke patients in a general hospital. *Urban Life and Culture* 3:50–70.
King, S.H. 1962. *Perceptions of Illness and Medical Practice.* New York: Russell Sage Foundation.
Klagsbrun, S.C. 1970. Cancer, emotions, and nurses. *American Journal of Psychiatry* 126:1237–44.
Leidermann, D.B. and J. Grisso. 1985. The gomer phenomenon. *The Journal of Health and Social Behavior* 26 (3): 222–32.
Leshan, L. 1964. The world of the patient in severe pain of long duration. *Journal of Chronic Diseases* 17:119–26.
Lomas, H.D. 1981. Paternalism: Medical or otherwise. *Social Science and Medicine* 15F (2–3):103–106.
Lorber, J. 1981. Good patients and problem patients: Conformity and deviance in a general hospital. In P. Conrad and R. Kern, eds. *The Sociology of Health and Illness.* New York: St. Martin's Press, 395–404.
Lynch, D. and E. Richards. 1986. *Exploding Into Life.* New York: Aperture Foundation.
MacVicar, M.G. and M.L. Winningham. 1986. Promoting the functional capacity of cancer patients. *The Cancer Bulletin* 38 (5): 235–239.
Marzuk, P.M. 1985. The right kind of paternalism. *New England Journal of Medicine* 313 (23):1474–76.
Mayer, D.K. 1986. Cancer patients' and families' perceptions of nurse caring behaviors. *Topics in Clinical Nursing* 8 (2):63–69.
Mechanic, D. 1976. *The Growth of Bureaucratic Medicine. An Inquiry Into the Dynamics of Patient Behavior and the Organization of Medical Care.* New York: John Wiley and Sons.
Parsons, T. 1972. Definitions of health and illness in the light of american values and social structure. In E.G. Jaco, ed. *Patients, Physicians, and Illness: A Sourcebook in Behavioral Science and Health,* 2nd ed. New York: Free Press, 107–127.
Patterson, J.T. 1987. *The Dread Disease. Cancer and Modern American Culture.* Cambridge, MA: Harvard University Press.
Perrow, C. 1965. Hospitals, technology, structure, and goals. In J. March, ed. *Handbook of Organizations.* Chicago, IL: Rand McNally, 910–71.

Perry, C.B. and W.B. Applegate. 1985. Medical paternalism and patient self-determination. *American Geriatric Society Journal* 33 (5):353–59.

Raven, R.W. 1985. The development and practice of oncology. In S.C. Gross and S. Garb, eds. *Cancer Treatment and Research in Humanistic Perspective.* New York: Springer Publishing Company, 65–79.

Rofe, Y., Hoffman, M. and Lewin, I. 1987. Affiliation patterns among cancer patients. *Psychological Medicine* 17:419–24.

Roth, J.A. 1957. Ritual and magic in the control of contagion. *American Sociological Review* 22:310–14.

Russell, C.A. 1984. The team approach: Should we or shouldn't we? In *Proceedings of the National Conference on Practice, Education, and Research In Oncology Social Work—1984.* New York: Professional Education Publication. American Cancer Society, 71–73.

Samora, J., L. Saunders, and R.F. Larson. 1961. Medical vocabulary knowledge among hospital patients. *Journal of Health and Human Behavior* 2 (Summer):83–92.

Scheff, T.J. 1963. The role of the mentally ill and the dynamics of mental disorders: A research framework. *Sociometry* 26 (Dec.): 436–53.

Schulman, S. 1972. Mother surrogate—After a decade. In E.G. Jaco, ed. *Patients, Physicians and Illness: A Sourcebook for Behavioral Science and Health,* 2nd ed. New York: Free Press, 233–39.

Simmel, G. 1965. On superordination and subordination. In T. Parsons, et al., eds. *Theories of Society. Foundations of Modern Sociological Theory,* one-volume edition. New York: Free Press, 540–51.

Sontag, S. 1978. *Illness As Metaphor.* New York: Farrar, Straus, and Giroux.

Sourkes, B.M. 1982. *The Deepening Shade: Psychological Aspects of Life-Threatening Illness.* Pittsburgh, PA: University of Pittsburgh Press.

Straus, R.A. 1985. Using social theory to make sense out of life. In R.A. Straus, ed. *Using Sociology.* Bayside, NY: General Hall, Inc., 4–22.

Strauss, A.L. 1970. Medical ghettos. In A.L. Strauss (ed.). *Where Medicine Fails.* New Brunswick, NJ: Transaction Books/Aldine Publishing Company, 9–26.

Strauss, A.L., S. Fagerhaugh, B. Suczek, and C. Wiener. 1985. *Social Organization of Medical Work.* Chicago, IL: The University of Chicago Press.

Strauss, A.L., and B. Glaser. 1975. *Chronic Illness and the Quality of Life.* St. Louis, MO: C.V. Mosby.

Tagliacozzo, D. and H.O. Mauksch. 1972. The patient's view of the patient's role. In E.G. Jaco, ed. *Patients, Physicians, and Illness: A Sourcebook for Behavioral Science and Health,* 2nd ed. New York: Free Press, 172–85.

Taylor, C.D. 1970. *In Horizontal Orbit: Hospitals and the Cult of Efficiency.* New York: Holt, Rinehart and Winston.

Titmuss, R.M. 1965. The hospital and its patients. In A.H. Katz and J.S. Felton, eds. *Health and the Community.* New York: Free Press, pp. 341–42.

Twaddle, A.C. and R.M. Hessler. 1987. *A Sociology of Health,* 2nd ed. New York: MacMillian.

Weld, M. and G.E. Greer. 1986. Support groups in a cancer hospital. *The Cancer Bulletin* 38 (5):251–255.

Yarbro, J.W. 1985. Cancer research and the development of cancer centers. In S.C. Gross and S. Garb, eds. *Cancer Treatment in Humanistic Perspective.* New York: Springer Publishing Company, 3–15.

Zerubavel, E. 1979. *Patterns of Time In Hospital Life.* Chicago, IL: University of Chicago Press.

23

Intervention for Cancer Patients:
A Clinical Sociology Approach
to Program Planning

Elizabeth J. Clark

The incidence of cancer continues to rise every year with recent data suggesting that one in four Americans alive today will develop cancer, and that two out or three American families will be affected by the disease (American Cancer Society, 1983). While only certain types of cancer can now be cured, medical advances have extended survival time considerably. Approximately two million Americans have had cancer and are alive five years after detection, and long-term survival is now possible for one in three cancer patients (Davis and Milone, 1983). Therefore, it has become increasingly important to understand how people live with, and adapt to, the illness of cancer. This includes viewing cancer from a sociological perspective: recognizing the social problems which accompany a diagnosis of cancer; understanding the impact of various social factors on cancer adaptation; and determining how the social environment of cancer patients should be structured to effect positive adaptation.

In view of these issues, this chapter will focus on the application of sociological concepts to a hospital intervention program for cancer patients.

PROGRAM PROPOSAL

The hospital involved is a non-profit, 450-bed acute care community hospital which was the recipient of a small grant from the American Cancer Society to determine the feasibility of developing and implementing an intervention program for cancer patients that could serve as a model for other community hospitals. Specifically, a program was to be developed which would demonstrate that comprehensive cancer care could be provided at the community hospital level and did not necessitate referral to a university-affiliated medical center. The initial funding was for six months, with a possible one year renewal period, and was to be used for the salary of a health care professional to direct the effort. Although the hospital had been searching for a nurse to fill this role, because of previous experience in program planning and health care, the author, a clinical sociologist, was hired.

From its inception, the program had strong support from a small group of physicians who had written the original grant proposal. Despite this proposal, which was very basic, these physicians had few preconceived ideas about how the program should be structured or implemented. They were mainly interested in providing support for cancer patients, and were cooperative and readily amenable to most suggestions. This lack of specifics allowed for a great deal of flexibility and creativity regarding program design.

PROGRAM PLANNING

As an initial phase in program planning, it was essential to understand the social system of the hospital and the community it served. This involved organizational assessment and community analysis.

Organizational assessment.   Several characteristics of the hospital were important factors for program planning:

1. The hospital was a mid-sized, acute care, general hospital which had good rapport with, and acceptance by, the community. Community members had strong representation on the hospital board.
2. As found in most hospitals, there was a system of dual authority (Ver Steeg and Croog, 1979); however, the hospital administrators were more dominant than the medical staff. This frequently led to conflict regarding authority, patients' needs, services, and program support. The nursing department was also a strong force in the hospital hierarchy.
3. It was the largest community hospital in the geographic area and acted as a referral center for outlying, smaller hospitals in the district. Approximately 800 newly diagnosed cancer patients were seen at the hospital each year.
4. The hospital was service-oriented, with little emphasis on research. The two exceptions to this were quality assurance surveys and certificate of need studies.
5. It was a teaching hospital with medical residents and student interns of various disciplines. Also, the hospital had its own nursing school, and

the hospital nursing staff was composed predominantly of graduates of this program.

6. The hospital served people of various ethnic and class backgrounds, with the largest minority group composed of Puerto Ricans. Class stratification determined access to particular hospital services and facilities. Room accommodations ranged from several elaborate suites to four-bed wards. There was a large clinic population and clinic patients were seen primarily by the medical residents.

7. The hospital served as a self-contained cancer treatment center and was staffed by surgical and medical oncologists, radiation therapists, and allied health professionals.

8. While there were several specialty units, such as dialysis and coronary care, there was no oncology unit. Patients with cancer were found on all patient units, except the obstetrical and psychiatric units. The development of a specialty unit for cancer patients was not favored by the administration nor by the majority of the medical staff or nursing personnel. Administration felt that it was not economically feasible; physicians and nurses opposed it on the basis of being too depressing for both patients and staff.

Community analysis. Since the assessment of community resources was another important step in the program planning phase, the health care delivery system of the community was analyzed. All community health agencies which provided services for cancer patients were contacted, and information was collected on their organizational structure, requirements for service delivery, and referral patterns. A goal of the program design was to avoid a duplication of services both within the hospital and within the community. Four agencies, the local unit of the American Cancer Society, the Homemaker Agency, the Visiting Nurse Association, and the American Red Cross, were particularly active in providing services for cancer patients.

Development of support. To facilitate planning, an advisory board of key hospital personnel was established. This included not only the physicians who had initially supported the idea, but also representatives from other hospital services such as nursing, administration, and rehabilitation. By including these people on the advisory board, an exchange of ideas was effected, but their inclusion also served the purpose of keeping them from feeling threatened by the possibility of a new program encroaching on their territory.

Also, a similar group, called the Community Liaison Committee, was formed. This group was composed of members of various community agencies and churches, as well as cancer patients and family members of cancer patients.

Once again, incorporating these persons into the formative process facilitated program planning, not only by providing ideas and information, but also by developing awareness and support within the community.

Research basis. As noted, the hospital was not research oriented. Being a community hospital, the emphasis was on providing patient care, and any research undertaken was generally done so in a secondary sense. In view of this, research regarding cancer patients was not seen as a primary focus by the hospital or the medical staff. However, due to the requirement of progress reports by the funding source, concomitant research was seen, if not as an instrumental component, at least as an acceptable part of the program design.

To examine the needs and problems of cancer patients and to determine the levels of social support and adaptation to their illness, demographic, medical, social, and psychological data were gathered by using a needs assessment form and conducting ongoing psychosocial assessments (Clark, 1980).

The problem identification phase of the program had been designed to assess the most frequently reported problems of cancer patients. The results showed that cancer patients have to contend with a wide variety of problems, many of which have a social basis. The areas of occupational and financial problems were particularly salient. Also ranked high were interpersonal problems, and problems with illnesses of other family members (Clark, 1983).

In the area of needs assessment, counseling and education regarding the diagnosis and treatment of cancer were the needs most frequently identified. These findings served as the guidelines for clinical intervention. Additionally, based on past research findings (Abrams, 1966; Mages and Mendelsohn, 1979; Weisman, 1979; Wortman and Dunkel-Schetter, 1979), it was decided that the patient and the family should be seen as the unit of care, and that continuity of care, beginning at diagnosis (when possible) and extending as long as necessary, would be important.

PROGRAM IMPLEMENTATION

The issues of staffing patterns, staff education, and the determination of referral mechanisms had to be addressed before the implementation phase of the program could begin.

Multidisciplinary staffing. For a cancer treatment program to be comprehensive, a combined treatment modality approach is essential. Therefore, it was determined that the program had to be multidisciplinary in scope. Care was taken to draw upon existing resources, including available personnel. However, additional program staff eventually was hired. Due to the diverse needs of cancer patients, two social workers, two oncology nurses, and a health educator were added over a two year period.

From the start, it was decided that an identity of the program separate from the Social Service Department should be maintained. This was justified because the Cancer Care Program was more specialized and narrower in focus (i.e., worked only with cancer patients) than a traditional hospital social service program, while at the same time it was broader and more comprehensive than traditional hospital social work (with continuity of care, extensive follow-up including home visits and a medical emphasis). Hospital policy and reimbursement procedures frequently dictate the training and educational background of social service staff. The separateness of the program provided a mechanism for multidisciplinary staffing.

Referral patterns.   Since the hospital functioned according to the traditional medical-intervention pattern (Freidson, 1973), with the staff's work organized by the physician's orders, it was apparent that the program would have to operate, at least initially, by physician referral.

Staff education.   Education of both the hospital staff and the community was an important first step in implementation of the program. It was necessary to alert staff, agencies, and the community to the availability of the program, while at the same time enlisting their support. An extensive educational program was developed. Presentations were made for the various services in the hospital, including most nursing units, the nursing school, and the medical staff. Additionally, numerous presentations were made at the community level during the first year of operation. At each presentation, the philosophy, the available services, and the referral mechanism for the program were stressed. Also stressed was the need for a comprehensive team approach composed of both hospital and community personnel.

Educating persons about the needs and problems of cancer patients was another issue. It was emphasized that the goal of the Cancer Care Program was to help persons successfully adapt to the illness of cancer. Therefore, a strong differentiation was made between the Cancer Care Program and a terminal or hospice program.

Impact of labeling.   In light of the goals, cancer was viewed as a chronic illness - as a disease which often can be successfully treated and controlled. The staff was concerned about the negative effects that can occur when someone is labeled a "cancer victim," and therefore, an attempt was made to remove some of the stigma of cancer as a disease. Cancer is the most feared disease in this country. While it kills fewer people than cardiovascular disease, it is equated with death and is clearly our most dreaded disease (Davis and Milone, 1983). In Sontag's analysis of this social attitude toward cancer, she notes (1978: 7–8), "As long as a particular disease is treated as an evil, invincible predator, not just a disease, most people with cancer will indeed be demoralized by learning what disease they have. The solution is hardly to stop telling cancer patients the truth, but to rectify the conception of the disease, to de-mythicize it." It was felt that one way of doing this was to use the word "cancer" in the name of the program, calling it simply the "Cancer Care Program." This elicited negativism from some of the hospital staff, particularly nurses, who felt that patients would prefer a less readily identifiable term such as "oncology." However, after talking with many cancer patients and asking their opinions, it was decided that the difficulty seemed to be with the professionals. The patients generally felt that it was not only acceptable, but useful for them in learning to deal more directly with their illness. As a result, the word "cancer" was retained in the program name. Also, "Cancer Care Program" was included as part of staff members' name tags. If staff members could show ready acceptance of the word "cancer," it was felt that it might help to remove some of the negativism that usually accompanies the word.

A second reason for including the word "Cancer Care Program" on staff name tags was to emphasize a part of the program's philosophy. In order for cancer patients to be referred for services, they had to be aware of their cancer diagnosis. Despite recent compelling evidence that patients wish to be told the truth regarding their illness (McIntosh, 1974 and Novak, et al., 1979), some physicians still maintained the opposite. By identifying themselves as part of the Cancer Care Program, staff did not fall into the trap of trying to deceive the patient. Physicians realized that patients would need to be told their diagnosis of cancer before intervention could begin.

PROGRAM CONTENT

Based on the goal of successful adaptation to cancer, the program content had several main components. These were education and information, coordination of services, counseling, general assistance and tangible support services, referral and follow-up, and patient advocacy. Additionally, several unique features of the program should be mentioned.

Continuity of care.   To assure continuity of care, one worker was assigned to each patient/family unit at the time of diagnosis and continued working with them throughout the intensive treatment phase. The same worker was responsible for follow-up when the patient left the hospital, and saw patients at outpatient appointments and made home visits as necessary.

Home visits or seeing patients outside of the hospital setting are somewhat unusual for hospital employees. However, many of the physicians' private offices were located adjacent to the hospital, and physicians were amenable to outpatient follow-up taking place in their offices. Initially, hospital administration was reluctant to agree to this arrangement because there was no insurance reimbursement procedure established for outpatient follow-up off hospital premises. However, due to the separate outside funding there was no charge for the services of the Cancer Care staff, and this problem eventually was overcome with staff permitted to see patients in the physicians' offices and at the patients' homes.

Coordination of care. Coordination of patient care was an area of major importance. Hospital personnel and physicians were an integral part of the Cancer Care team, invited to weekly team meetings, patient conferences and asked to record on a multidisciplinary Cancer Care Progress Note Sheet on the patient's hospital chart. Also, since patients often see several medical specialists during the same time period, coordination of their outpatient care can be difficult. In an attempt to facilitate this process when patients left the hospital, the Cancer Care staff sent discharge summaries to each physician concerned with the care of the patient. This summary included an overview of the patient's and family's current psychosocial functioning, potential problem areas, services needed and arranged for from community agencies, and the dates of all follow-up appointments. This idea was well received by physicians who frequently kept these summaries in their office files for ready reference. The discharge summaries also served the purpose of legitimating the Cancer Care Program and demonstrating that psychosocial rehabilitation was an integral and needed component of comprehensive care.

Another effort at coordination of care involved a system established in the oncologists' private offices. Once a patient was referred to the Cancer Care Program, the patient's office chart would be marked with a special sticker placed on the outside cover. This included the name of the Cancer Care staff member following the patient. As mentioned above, the Cancer Care worker periodically would meet the patient in the physician's office for follow-up purposes. If the staff member was not present for the visit, but a problem had arisen, the physician's office would notify the Cancer Care Program. The staff member would then get in touch with the patient as soon as possible.

Coordination of care also involved community agencies, which maintained close contact with the agencies providing services for referred patients. Written referral notices were sent to the agencies, and periodic exchanges of information took place. Additionally, some members of community agencies, such as the Visiting Nurse Association representative, were invited to participate in team meetings, and Cancer Care staff met with other personnel at the agencies' location as needed.

Accessibility of care.   Another important consideration was that patients have access to the Cancer Care Program on a 24-hour basis. A long-range paging system was implemented for the hospital to reach the Cancer Care staff at home. Also, patients were given the workers' home phone numbers. Hospital personnel initially were skeptical of this practice, fearing that staff would be inundated with calls and lose all privacy. That fear, it turned out, was unwarranted. The service seldom was abused, but patients frequently did mention how secure they felt knowing that they "could" call someone at any time if a need arose.

Patient advocacy.   Patient advocacy took many forms. Most often it entailed helping the patient manage bureaucratic problems (frequently those precipitated by our own hospital's billing procedures), dealing with occupational concerns, and finding needed resources.

One feature of the program came about unexpectedly and resulted not only in augmenting resources for patients, but in providing good publicity for the program and the hospital. During the process of the community education presentation, several groups expressed an interest in making contributions to the Cancer Care Program. However, they wanted this money to be used to enhance the lives of cancer patients. They indicated that they did not want their donations used for research, hospital equipment, or hospital expenses. Later on, it was determined that in order to avoid awkwardness, physicians' bills also should be excluded. Monies contributed went into a Cancer Care Discretionary Fund. On many occasions, after careful exploration of available family and community resources, it was found that there simply was no established mechanism to provide the needed financial assistance. The discretionary fund was invaluable in these instances. For example, it was used to pay rent and utility bills, to buy food and clothing, and to provide prostheses for patients who did not have adequate insurance coverage.

The services made possible by the fund garnered very positive word-of-mouth publicity for the hospital. Since the Cancer Care Program was a hospital service, the provision of money for the services needed was often seen as the hospital returning something tangible to the community. This created a reciprocal effect and donations to this fund increased from various sources including churches, organizations, and individuals. One church group held a benefit program with the proceeds going to the Cancer Care fund. Needless to say, having these monies available was a tremendous asset in assisting cancer patients with financial problems.

Patient education. Patient education was a continual part of the intervention and support provided by the Cancer Care Program. Basic education about cancer was essential because many patients and their families have misconceptions about cancer in general, about treatment modalities, and about prognoses and future possibilities.

One of the first steps of intervention involved helping patients and their families understand as much as they could about the patient's specific type of cancer and the necessary treatment regimen. This had the effect of reducing fear, and helping the patient and the family to actively participate in the treatment process. Patients also were encouraged to ask questions of their physicians, and other health care personnel, to obtain needed information.

A second area of patient education involved the availability of community resources. If patients had no previous experience with cancer, they usually were not aware of the varied services available to facilitate adaptation. Based on information obtained during the program planning phase, a Cancer Resource Information Booklet was compiled which contained a description of all applicable community resources, and relevant information about each resource such as the referral procedure, hours of operation, and required needs tests (Clark, 1980).

Since the community had a large Puerto Rican population, this booklet also was translated into Spanish. Later on, some physicians mentioned that many of their older patients of Slavic descent did not read English. A retired nun volunteered to translate the booklet into Slovak so that this small group of patients also would have accessibility to community resource information.

Additionally, an educational program on home nursing was established in conjunction with the American Red Cross. This program was offered weekly at the hospital, and family members of patients who were about to be discharged were invited to attend. There was no fee for this service.

Counseling component. Counseling and support were a major part of the intervention program, and there are a variety of counseling techniques available to help the cancer patient adjust to and cope with the problems produced by the illness, its treatment, and possible recurrence. The two techniques used most frequently by the Cancer Care staff were crisis intervention and reality-based counseling.

A crisis can be defined as "acute, and often prolonged, disturbance to an individual or to a social network as the result of an emotionally hazardous situation" (Klein and Lindemann, 1961: 284). Most persons have no habitual problem-solving mechanism for cancer related crises, and, particularly at the time of diagnosis, they literally do not know how to think about their problem or how to evaluate reality or the outcome of the crisis and possibilities for problem-solving (LoGuidice and Clark, 1980). Crisis intervention counseling helps the patient develop the necessary adaptation mechanisms to cope with crisis situations which accompany cancer.

Reality-based counseling is especially effective for dealing with low self-esteem, lack of self-confidence, feelings of inadequacy, and the sense of isolation, withdrawal, and depression that linger after the initial crisis has passed. One major goal of reality-based counseling is to get the patient responsibly and meaningfully involved in activities that hold some promise for success. Another goal is to help the patient maintain, strengthen, or re-establish close relationships with other people (Glasser, 1965; Glasser and Zunin, 1973).

Both techniques, crisis intervention and reality-based counseling, emphasize the evaluation of resources available within the individual and within the social network at that particular time, facilitate the seeking of needed information, and are oriented toward restoration of pre-illness levels of psychosocial functioning.

PROGRAM ACCEPTANCE

The Cancer Care Program was well accepted by both the hospital staff and the community. More importantly, it met its goal of providing comprehensive care for cancer patients.

Indicators of success.   After six months of operation, the Cancer Care Program was evaluated by the funding source. They were pleased with the progress and decided to extend funding for an additional 12 month period. At the end of that year, it was determined that not only had the program met the goal of demonstrating that comprehensive cancer care could be provided at the community hospital level, but it had exceeded their expectations. By that time, the program had been so well received both in the hospital and in the community that the hospital decided to continue fully funding the program as it existed. The program later was used as a basis for a grant application for federal funding which eventually was awarded.

In a short period, it became obvious that the Cancer Care Program was helpful to physicians as well as to patients. The number of referrals continued to increase. In the three year period during which the author directed the Cancer Care Program, 600 patients and families were referred for services. Also, as the program became more established, and patients learned more about its function, they asked their physicians to make referrals or called the Cancer Care office themselves. In this case, the primary physician would be asked to approve the referral. Seldom was any difficulty encountered in getting approval. Eventually, many of the oncologists requested that their patients be referred automatically to the Cancer Care Program.

Factors contributing to success. In evaluating the process of the development and implementation of the Cancer Care Program, several factors were found to be instrumental in its success.

First of all, the outside funding was invaluable. While initially it was not a large sum, it did serve the purpose of offsetting some of the traditional barriers frequently encountered within a hospital setting. It definitely allowed for more flexible staffing patterns and greater provision of services.

Establishing a broad base of support for the Cancer Care program was also important. In this particular situation, both hospital and community support were essential. In fact, the community support for the program was so great that the hospital would have had difficulty in discontinuing the program when the outside funding ended without straining the relationship between the hospital and the community agencies, who saw themselves as integral parts of the program, as indeed they were.

Instead of bringing about unnecessary change, the program tried to work within pre-existing systems. It was important to spend enough time analyzing the structure and function of the existing social system to be able to enlist, rather than alienate, the support of key personnel and services. The problem of the referral system illustrates this process. As mentioned above, it was realized initially that the Cancer Care Program, like most other hospital services, would need to operate by physician referral for services. This was a concern for some physicians who were uncertain about the necessity for, and usefulness of, the program. By structuring the program so that physicians could decide which of their patients were referred to, and followed by, Cancer Care, their concern that they would lose control of their patients' care was alleviated. They were not accustomed to any ancillary service being involved in patient care without their request. For this reason, every effort was made to keep the physician aware of the developments, problems, and concerns of the patient and his or her family.

Going through the proper channels also was important in the implementation of the program. This became particularly evident when one idea had to be completely revised, not because it lacked merit, but because the staff had neglected to get approval from a minor hospital committee. The committee was offended by having been overlooked and refused to give approval for the original idea.

Problems encountered. Since the Cancer Care Program did not always follow traditional pathways, numerous problems were encountered during the development of the program. Occasionally the program would be caught in the middle— between the physicians who saw the need for the rapid development of services for their patients, and the hospital administrators who were cautious due to concerns about cost containment and the limited outside funding period for the program.

Other problems were related to staffing and staff functions. The structure of the program required staff schedules to be flexible. Staff members, often unexpectedly, had to be available on evenings or weekends. This necessitated the use of compensation time for the staff. The personnel department had been accustomed to hospital staff working during specified shifts with strict guidelines for any overtime work. A separate system had to be developed for the Cancer Care staff, so that they were able to begin work at noon if they had worked the previous evening or to take Monday off if they had worked the previous Sunday.

The multidisciplinary staffing pattern in the program created some conflict with the nursing department. All of the other nurses in the hospital reported to the nursing administrator, and she felt that the oncology nurses in the Cancer Care Program should also report to her. Since the oncology nurses would not be performing bedside nursing functions, but primarily would be doing patient assessments, education, and outpatient follow-up, this problem finally was resolved with the oncology nurses reporting to the Director of the Cancer Care Program.

Another problem occurred because in the program staff roles tended to overlap. While role obligations and performances usually are strictly specified in hospital settings, in the Cancer Care Program roles became blurred, and sometimes social workers educated patients about chemotherapy and made physical assessments, and nurses did counseling. This required intensive training in all areas of oncology so that the Cancer Care staff could function in the various capacities whether these involved the psychosocial or medical aspects of care.

One area in which the Cancer Care Program was never completely successful was in the education of nurses with regard to the nurses' impact on the attitudes, and subsequent adaptation, of cancer patients. Of all hospital personnel, nurses spend the most time with the patients. Many nurses were not able to move beyond the idea of equating cancer with death, and they often were negative about the benefits of chemotherapy. These attitudes inadvertently were communicated to the patients. Nurses generally only see patients when they are very ill and hospitalized, and their attitudes are based on these experiences. While Cancer Care made an effort to relate to nurses the successful adaptation that patients made once discharged from the hospital, or between admissions, some of the nursing staff could not overcome their negativism. They frequently complained if there were several cancer patients on their particular unit, and occasionally were outspoken when a chemotherapeutic treatment with difficult side effects was ordered for a patient. This made it more difficult for the cancer patient and family members to maintain a positive outlook. This problem probably could have been overcome with the establishment of a separate oncology unit where nurses were specially trained in oncology, and where staffing was done with those who had chosen this area of specialty.

CONCLUSION

This chapter has described a problem-solving intervention program for cancer patients that was developed and implemented at a mid-sized community hospital. The program used a community interactional approach and focused on changes that could be made in the health care delivery system, and within the social environment of cancer patients, to bring about a higher level of adaptation to cancer.

This chapter also has attempted to show some of the possible roles of clinical sociology in a traditional medical setting. Clinical sociology includes direct intervention to effect positive change within a social system, thereby contributing to the resolution of a social problem. Clinical sociologists use a variety of techniques to facilitate change. With regard to the Cancer Care Program, one of the major contributions the sociologist made was insisting that research be an integral and continuous part of the overall program design. As a result, the program was grounded in research, and data collection in various forms was conducted throughout.

The basic research looked at cancer in a sociological context. Needs assessment and problem identification were important first steps in program design. Sociological practice skills, such as organizational assessment and community analysis, were essential for program planning. Also, knowledge of the roles and contributions of various health professionals and health organizations was imperative in the program planning phase. Social concepts, such as the role of social support in illness adaptation, and labeling theory (with its far-reaching effects), were used to plan the structure and the content of the program. Diagnostic skills drawn from qualitative research were used to determine intervention strategies. Counseling techniques were based on a social network perspective that included viewing both patient and family as the unit of care, and recognized the negative impact that a diagnosis of cancer can have on the interpersonal relationships of patients.

It is important to note that the role of the clinical sociologist did not end with the research or with the program planning, but continued through the implementation phase. This included the administrative management of the program, and the hiring and training of multidisciplinary staff.

In summary, the clinical sociologist acted as a change agent, using a sociological perspective as the basis for intervention. This included intervention at a macro level, the community; at an organizational level, the hospital; and at a micro level, the individual cancer patient and family system.

REFERENCES

Abrams, R. 1966. The patient with cancer - his changing pattern of communication. *New England Journal of Medicine* 274 (6):317–22.

American Cancer Society. 1983. *Cancer Facts and Figures*. New York.

Clark, E. 1980. *Comprehensive Cancer Care: A Model for Community Hospitals*. Hershey, PA: Pennsylvania Division of the American Cancer Society.

———1983. The role of the social environment in adaptation to cancer. *Social Work Research and Abstracts* 19:32–33.

Davis, A. and L. Milone. 1983. The fight against cancer - the 1982 legislative front. *Cancer Investigation* 1(1):101–107.

Freidson, E. 1973. *Profession of Medicine*. New York: Dodd Mead.

Glasser, W. 1965. *Reality Therapy*. New York: Harper and Row.

Glasser, W. and L. N. Zunin. 1973. Reality therapy. In R. Corsini, ed. *Current Psychotherapies*. Itaska, IL: Peacock.

Klein, D. C. and E. Lindemann. 1961. Preventive intervention in individual and family crisis situations. In G. Caplan, ed. *Prevention of Mental Disorders in Children: Initial Explorations*. New York: Basic Books.

LoGuidice, J. and E. Clark. 1980. Counseling techniques for life-threatening illness. In P. Tretter, et al., eds. *Psychological Aspects of Radiation Therapy*. New York: Arno Press.

Mages, N. and G. Mendelsohn. 1979. Effect of cancer on patients' lives: a personological approach. In G. Stone, et al., eds. *Health Psychology*. San Francisco, CA: Jossey-Bass, 255–84.

McIntosh, J. 1974. Processes of communication, information seeking and control associated with cancer: a selected review of the literature. *Social Science and Medicine* 8:167–68.

Novak, D., R. Plummer, R. Smith, H. Ochtill, G. Morrow and J. Bennett. 1979. Changes in physicians' attitudes toward telling the cancer patient. *Journal of the American Medical Association* 241 (9):897–900

Sontag, S. 1978. *Illness as Metaphor*. New York: Farrar Straus Giroux.

Ver Steeg, D. and S. Cobb. 1979. Hospitals and related health care delivery systems. In H. Freeman, et al., eds. *Handbook of Medical Sociology*. Englewood Cliffs, NJ: Prentice-Hall, 308–46.

Weisman, A. 1979. *Coping with Cancer*. New York: McGraw-Hill.

Wortman, C. and C. Dunkel-Schetter. 1979. Interpersonal relationships and cancer: a theoretical analysis. *Journal of Social Issues* 35(1):120–55.

24

The Sociology of Alzheimer's Wings in Nursing Homes

Christopher Jay Johnson

The author designed and implemented the "Low Stimulus Alzheimer's Disease Nursing Home Wing," using a symbolic interactionist theoretical model. The units have been in operation since 1985. The two nursing home sites where units are built are part of the writer's research and demonstration project for Affiliated Nursing Homes, Incorporated, of Alexandria, Louisiana. These nursing home wings are constructed to maximize daily functional capacities, compensate for disabilities, and enhance the self-respect of Alzheimer's Disease (AD) residents. This chapter describes the philosophy and clinical approach for the development and training of staff, selection of residents, pre-admission procedures, and admission procedures. The sociological importance of the interaction of staff and family with AD residents, and the significance of role changes in the ongoing care of the AD residents also are explored. Finally, this chapter discusses clinical sociological interventions with staff and residents.

BACKGROUND TO ALZHEIMER'S DISEASE

It has been estimated that about 15 percent of the U.S. population over age 65, or 4.4 million persons, suffer from what is called "senile dementia" (Heston and White, 1983). Dementia is a deterioration in intellectual performance that involves the progressive loss of memory and is severe enough to interfere with work and social activities. It is the slow, progressive loss of a person's problem-solving skills and abilities for abstract thought. Alzheimer's Disease (AD) is the most common form of dementia, accounting for about 50 percent of all dementia cases. AD is a concern for gerontologists because it is said to be the fourth leading cause of death among elderly. AD affects 22 percent of persons over 80 years of age. Half of all current nursing home residents are affected by AD. Two to four million Americans are reported to be affected by AD, which could mean that one in three of us will face this in an older relative (Gwyther, 1985). However, this author has not found any studies which have quantified the false-negative and false-positive rates with regard to the diagnosis protocol for AD patients. Another problem is that the literature has not adequately identified the duration period of the disease, primarily due to inaccurate knowledge of the onset of the disease (Stage 1). Hence, there are inaccuracies in studies of the incidence and prevalence of the disease.

AD is a brain disease causing loss of recent memory, confusion, and poor judgment. There are no known causes or cures for AD at the present time. We do know that AD is *not* a normal part of aging, hardening of the arteries, a vitamin deficiency, a direct result of stress, a lack of oxygen to the brain, or a host of other reversible cognitive symptoms. "Today, AD and senile dementia is regarded as one disease. Over the last few years, both terms have been discarded in favor of dementia of the AD type, abbreviated DAT or, alternatively, senile dementia of the AD type, abbreviated SDAT" (Heston and White, 1983:15). Unfortunately, many medical practitioners label patients with such diagnostic headings as OBS (Organic Brain Syndrome), without being more specific. The disorder diagnosed as OBS could be any of a number of problems, such as Pick's Disease, Normal Pressure Hydrocephalus, Creutzfeldt-Jakob Disease, and other irreversible dementias which present somewhat different disease processes and disabilities in the victims (Zarit et al, 1985; U.S. Dept. of Health, 1984).

Stages of Alzheimer's Disease.   There appear to be four distinct stages in AD (see Figure A). They progress from a minor short-term memory loss to a complete loss of bowel and bladder function, memory, and speech. Throughout all four stages, there is a steady mental and physical deterioration.

A person in the first stage of Alzheimer's Disease is typically still living at home and functioning fairly well. He or she is beginning to have trouble driving, however, and will have difficulty internalizing complex new tasks or information, which limits the amount of learning that can be accomplished. Instructions will need to be repeated several times and even written down on paper. At this point relocation to an acute care setting can make the person with AD more confused and disoriented.

In the second stage, persons with AD can be especially difficult to understand. They will claim that no one has taken care of them that day, when in fact they have forgotten all of the assistance already given them. They often will lose their money and personal belongings because they put them in a "safe place" and then forget where they are. They often accuse family members of stealing these "lost" items. These persons cannot function alone for many safety reasons and need a great deal of nursing assistance. During this stage, there is frequent wandering. They may wander off and not be able to find the way back. They often will refuse to carry out personal hygiene tasks because they think they have already completed them or the prospect is frightening to them. Catastrophic reactions, in which the patients do not understand, or feel frustrated, are common. These actions are a sign that these persons are overwhelmed. Nursing home care is usually the obvious choice for special care toward the middle part of this stage of AD.

In stage three, even the routine activities of dressing, eating, and going to the bathroom become difficult, and these persons need more and more help in all of their everyday activities. This deterioration continues until they are totally dependent upon another person or nursing home staff for their care.

In the fourth stage, persons with AD require total assistance with the activities of daily living. They become bedridden and incontinent during this stage. Often these persons lose the ability to eat and need to be fed through a nasogastric tube. Death usually results from complications due to immobility or respiratory infections.

SOCIOLOGICAL CONSEQUENCES OF ALZHEIMER'S DISEASE

Most clinicians understand that, for the care-giver, living with and caring for a person with AD can create an emotional turmoil which turns an ordinary day into a "thirty-six hour day" (Mace and Rabins, 1981). As the dementia progresses, the general day-to-day care-giving becomes so stressful and dangerous, for both the family caregiver and person with AD, that a doctor's or family's decision on nursing home placement usually becomes necessary. Nevertheless, clinicians need to be reminded that persons with AD are members of families, and that these families have different styles of communicating and interacting. Within each family there are various levels of intimacy between family members and the person with AD. Hence, we have a social dimension to the disease that does not decrease in importance as the disease progresses.

Prolonged terminal illnesses change the social and emotional makeup of a family. Family members go through a bereavement process after hearing the prognosis, and experience what often is referred to as an "ongoing funeral" during the years of caring and grieving for the person with AD. As the person with AD begins to lose the ability to perform daily tasks, the care-giver has to pick up the slack and perform roles that are uncommon to him or her. For example, as the person with AD becomes less capable of eating or dressing unaided, the care-giver, who may be a spouse or child, must change roles and become a parent to the person with AD, who is now in the child ego state. This change in roles can be a stressful adjustment for the family. Family members go through a host of feelings, including anger at the victim, God, or the situation. Guilt is also commonly expressed in the idea that the caregiver is being punished for something or surrounding the quality of care-giving. The guilt may be compounded when nursing home placement is imminent because people may tell the caregiver, "You should be able to take care of your loved ones." Depression may be experienced by the person with AD and his or her family after hearing the prognosis, and by the care-givers in trying to face the economic and social realities of dealing with AD. Because AD lasts from approximately seven to fifteen years, care-givers face the expense of long-term care without sufficient financial remuneration.

SYMBOLIC INTERACTIONISM AND ALZHEIMER'S DISEASE

"We live in a meaningful world because our environment is not merely physical; it is also symbolic. A symbol is something that can meaningfully represent something else" (Robertson, 1987:144). Many things can be symbols—a smile, a gesture, a style of clothing, or a picture hanging on a wall. A symbol has meaning because a person attributes meaning to it, or because many people agree on its meaning. A local nursing home, for example, represents a nursing home simply because some people share the same interpretation of an otherwise meaningless design. However, people with dementia, and others may not share these interpretations because they have their own meaning systems. Words are also symbols, attached to agreed-upon meanings, and language is the richest and most flexible system of symbols. People define and interpret their unique social worlds through their use of language and symbols. Hence, while life may seem to be meaningless, it is transformed into meaningful patterns through a process of social interaction by which a person, during his or her lifespan, acquires selfhood and learns the culture. In this chapter these processes are encompassed in a theoretical approach called symbolic interactionism, which explains the interaction between persons with AD and their society or environment.

Symbolic interactionism is used here to describe the distinctive features of the typical AD resident role in traditional nursing homes versus the role of an AD resident in a "Low-Stimulus AD Nursing Home Wing." As the reader begins to understand the effects of the changes in staff or family attitudes, staff-AD resident interactions, and social environment that are suggested here, these processes and how they operate within the framework of symbolic interactionism will become clear. It then will be apparent that the person with AD does not respond to care-givers directly, but rather to the meaning that is placed on their actions (Mead, 1934).

George Herbert Mead (1863–1931) pointed out that socialization is never complete. He distinguished between what he called the "I" (the impulsive, self-interested self) and the "me" (the socialized self that is conscious of social norms, values, and expectations). The "I," he stated, is never completely under control of the "me." For the person without brain disease, the "me" is usually dominant over the "I." In contrast, for the person with AD, the "I" may dominate the "me." This is because the person with AD often reacts to the acts of others or to the environment without rationally controlling his or her impulsive, emotionally-charged behavior, thus the acts of significant others and the environment need to altered to accommodate this behavior. However, it seems that all humans have the ability to violate the rules and expectations of others. Moreover, the behaviors that are rule-breaking or considered behavioral problems in one setting may be acceptable in another environment. People interpret the behaviors of others in different ways. Clinicians view the dysfunctional behavior of persons with organic brain syndrome of the AD type as caused exclusively by irreversible factors. However, the *symbolic* effect of changed care-giver *interactions* and modified environments on the acts of persons with AD are only beginning to be understood. The author's research has found that what is traditionally thought to be organically-induced behavior in persons with AD may be influenced by numerous sociological forces.

TRADITIONAL NURSING HOME CARE OF AD PATIENTS

Traditional nursing home staff is trained, if it is trained at all, to deal with AD residents as "problem patients." The AD patients are conceptualized as the most difficult residents to manage. The emphasis of staff training is on AD patients' "frailties" and deficits in cognitive abilities. These homes usually employ a medical model, which assumes that AD patients' deficits are caused exclusively by brain disease and are therefore inevitable and untreatable. This assumption has been criticized by some researchers in America (Brody, Cole, and Mose, 1973; Hellebrandt, 1978; and Coons and Weaverdyck, 1986), and in Europe (Haugen, 1985; Woods and Britton, 1985). These researchers have pointed to what the writer sees as the sociological connections to Alzheimer's Disease. For instance, some researchers suggest that catastrophic social situations may play a role in the onset of AD (Powell and Courtice, 1986). Other researchers ask to what extent cognitive decline is the result of a lack of meaningful social interaction, role loss, or loss of significant others (Haugen, 1985). Another study suggests that confusion or dependency may be the result of a combination of social isolation, sensory deprivation, immobility, muscle weakness, and visual and auditory deficits (Hellebrandt, 1978). Hence, there may be social dimensions to cognitive decline.

In order to manage the problem behaviors of persons with AD, traditional nursing homes emphasize the use of a psycho-medical model of "behavioral management." Behavioral management strategies usually involve the use of a combination of medications and various types of restraints for AD patients. The drugs most frequently selected to help with what are perceived as organically-based behaviors, like sleeplessness, agitation , and paranoia, are major tranquilizers like Haldol and Mellaril. It may be that these drugs are given not so much for the AD resident as for the benefit of the staff and/or family in their attempts to control the "negative" behaviors of the AD patient. In addition, by the time an AD patient reaches the nursing home he or she is in the later stages of the disease, and the once reasonably successful use of a vasodilator like Hydergine is no longer an option for behavior management. The AD residents' various problems with eating are controlled by physical restraints, drugs, or simply withdrawing patients from large cafeterias to eat alone in their rooms. These strategies may cause AD residents to continue to lose weight.

Traditional nursing homes, including some new versions of the same philosophy of care, called Acute or Intensive Care AD Wings, typically place AD residents in rooms with roommates without the disease who are thought to help orient the person with AD to reality. However, the AD patient tends to invade the privacy of a roommate. In addition, the roommate of a person with AD often suffers from lost or damaged property, decreased socialization, interrupted sleep, and the fear of physical harm from his or her roommate. Under the conditions in traditional nursing homes AD patients frequently wander up and down hallways leading to unlocked doors into other people's rooms or out into the street. Those patients who are not supervised closely enough may get injured or lost. The continuous hallway invites wandering by the person with AD because it gives no cues to stop and rest. Other typical "problem" behaviors of AD patients in these settings include: combative behavior, hallucinating, seizures, compulsively changing things around, repetitive movements, shifts in gait that make walking more difficult, frequent falling, changes in sleep patterns (they sleep more or less—usually less), shortened attention span; changes in speech, the decline in hygienic routines, and increased visual and motor problems which are heightened by typically poor lighting in hallways or rooms, or by glossy floors; then, in later stages, non-recognition of loved ones, incontinence, weight loss, and loss of speech or hearing. All of these behaviors are falsely believed to be the result only of an organic process of irreversible brain disease.

In order to maintain safety and to manage the AD resident's behaviors, the staff will spend most of the day walking with the patient as he wanders, medicating the patient, and tying the patient to a chair or bed during the day. At night the staff controls AD resident sundowning, which is wandering at night, by a combination of sleep medications, physical restraints, and raising bed railings to discourage the AD person from crawling out of bed. Frequently the results for AD residents of these traditional interventions are: (1) increased likelihood of falls or muscle atrophy due to the effects of being restrained or medicated; (2) decreased socialization due to exclusion from planned activities as a result of disruptive behavior; (3) family and friends' discomfort with the AD resident's being restrained or drugged; (4) increased likelihood of agitation, fear, and combative actions; and (5) increased likelihood of weight loss due to continual overstimulation. These chronic problems for the nursing home staff and the family suggest a need for change in the strategies for care of persons with AD.

LOW STIMULUS AD WINGS IN NURSING HOMES

A Call for Change. In 1973 Brody and Associates called for social and environmental interventions for people with organic brain disorders. They reported their research findings and stated that the existence of disabilities that are accessible to treatment interventions signifies that the diagnostic label of chronic brain syndrome should indicate treatment intervention. The pioneering work of Dorothy Coons (Coons, 1983; Coons and Weaverdyck, 1986) has called for therapeutic environments as treatment agents. Her studies of Wesley Hall (an AD Residential Unit) indicate the salience of grouping persons with similar skills in order to design a therapeutic milieu. She provided these elderly persons with opportunities to continue in normal social roles and social interaction even though they required some medical attention. Coons writes of the sociological nature of this process (1983:31):

> Social roles suggest appropriate behaviors and define society's expectations. If a treatment setting provides only the opportunity for the elderly person to assume the role of 'patient,' it states clearly that the individual is expected to be sick. On the other hand, if the setting offers a variety of opportunities to continue in normal social roles, for example, friend, home-maker, family member, and volunteer, the expectations are that the older person will continue to function in normal ways to the extent possible and thus deserve the respect attributed to 'normal' persons. The implication is that each individual still has a degree of wellness which staff recognize and value.

From a symbolic interaction perspective it follows that if the nursing home staff or the family expect the person with AD to act sick, or to act hopeless and demented, the patient may to some extent fulfill the role expectation. In addition, when practitioners and care-givers view the AD resident's behavior as solely the result of irreversible forces due to organic conditions, they will act as if the person's behavior is immutable. One article (Kapust, 1982) describes AD as an "ongoing funeral" for family members. Unfortunately, in some cases care-givers treat persons with AD as if they were already dead and buried, instead of perceiving them as *living* with a disability called Alzheimer's Disease. Hence, the pictures we have in our heads become self-fulfilling prophecies. Also, the persons with AD may act as they are expected to act. For example, we know that persons with AD frequently mirror the negative feelings of care-givers who have written them off as dead and either want to do everything for them or ignore them altogether. This damages the self esteem of the person with AD.

Segregation or Integration of AD Residents.   A survey of the clinical care staff (physicians, nurses, aides, physical and occupational therapists, and social workers) was given to ten skilled nursing units (Grossman, et al., 1986). Two major issues were addressed in this survey: 1) Could better care be provided to the residents if the units were segregated by behavior and function? and 2) Would the residents be more comfortable if they were so segregated? The survey provided the following information on these issues. Of the staff surveyed, 76 percent felt they could provide more direct care and perform better if the units were segregated according to level of care, and 83 percent felt the residents also would feel more comfortable if they were segregated by level of care (Grossman, et al., 1986). The author agrees with the clinical care staff surveyed.

The concept of the ''Low Stimulus AD Wing'' came from the author's experiences in working with the cognitively-impaired elderly, his travels to AD units in nursing homes around the country, the ideas of his sister-in-law, an R.N., concerning activities for the cognitively-impaired in the nursing home where she worked, and surveying what little research that has been done on AD wings or residential units (cf., Lawton, 1981; Hall, Kirschling and Todd, 1986; Coons, 1983; Coons and Weaverdyck, 1986). The author found in his research that AD wings around the country vary a great deal in their levels of care, care philosophy, and approaches to the environment. Therefore, the writer tried to gather qualitative data on what seemed to work and what seemed not to work in these units.

After doing the background research, the author developed a specially designed ''Low Stimulus AD Wing'' for residents of Affiliated Nursing Homes, Incorporated, who had AD and similar dementias. Affiliated approached the author to help resolve problems concerning a small number of residents (ten to fifteen) in a 100-bed home who had such acute memory deficits that they were unable to cope in the large, busy, noisy environment in which they lived. In addition, AD residents caused problems for other residents who were becoming increasingly impatient and frustrated by their constant rummaging through drawers, urinating in their closets or wastebaskets, or wandering in and out of their rooms. In addition, other residents feared the angry outbursts and combative behaviors of some AD residents.

Goals of the Unit.   The goals for the ''Low Stimulus Unit'' include: to develop individualized care plans by recognizing that each resident is living with dementia and is a unique person with needs, desires, and abilities; to select staff who have the skills and interpersonal abilities required to interact effectively with individuals with dementia; to educate all unit staff members about the normal aging process and the dementias; to encourage residents to behave in ways that promote safety, and to breakdown tasks so that they can work with their remaining assets; to provide information and support to staff and families in the form of group and individual counseling so that each caregiver can affirm the self-esteem and skills of the person with AD; and to integrate the community into the planning and continuation of the program for the unit.

Staffing. The staff for the unit is carefully selected by the Head Registered Nurse. Weekly training sessions are held to help staff members handle unusual behaviors that arise. Although during their training all staff members receive some education about the unit and AD, more intensive training is directed toward the AD resident aides, R.N., and administrator who daily work with the AD residents and families. The following personnel are assigned to the AD unit: a licensed staff nurse, two trained AD resident assistants, an Activities Director, and a Social Service Director.

The specific responsibilities of each of these people are clearly defined. The licensed nurse implements the individualized care plans, administers medications (as a last resort), initiates treatments, and provides other required nursing interventions. One trained resident assistant gives individual care to each resident. The other trained resident assistant monitors residents and insures that the environment and atmosphere remain therapeutic, calm, and safe. Both aides work under the direct supervision of a licensed nurse, who rotates in and out of the unit during the day. The Activity Director develops an activity care plan for each resident. The Social Service Director constructs a social care plan for each resident. These care plans are then communicated to each of the staff members and implemented daily. Finally, physical therapists may be called in to assist in the care.

Selection of Residents. The selection of residents for the AD wing normally requires the following criteria to be met: the resident (a) is ambulatory or wheelchair bound; (b) gives evidence of having organic brain syndrome of the Alzheimer's type or a related disorder; (c) does not require more than the minimal amount of medical care that can be administered by the limited number of staff members; and (d) can manage some self-care with staff assistance.

Pre-Admissions Assessment. Prior to the admission of the person with AD into the "Low Stimulus AD Unit," the R.N. and Social Service Director go to the home of the potential resident to conduct a pre-admission assessment and develop an optimal care plan to meet the resident's needs on admission. Pertinent health and psychosocial data are collected from: Title XIX, Medical/Social Information Forms; 90L, compiled by a physician; the physical assessment and social history given by a significant other that focuses on the resident's medical, nutritional, and psychosocial needs. Before going to the home of the potential resident, the author or staff prepares the families for some of the unorthodox practices in a non-traditional "Low Stimulus AD Wing."

Admission Procedure. The staff and family are educated to work with and cultivate the remaining skills of the AD resident from the pre-admission meeting with the family until the resident dies in the final stage of the disease. Staff and family reframe the resident's situation as "living with AD" rather than "dying from AD" and the person with AD is reframed as a "resident" instead of a "patient." By attending both the local Alzheimer's Disease and Related Disorders Association (ADRDA) Support Group meetings and the in-house support group meetings at the nursing home once a month, families of AD residents learn how to help the AD resident throughout the progression of the disease.

Life in Low Stimulus AD Wings.   According to the author's research, two sociological factors play a part in the actions of AD residents: the social milieu in which they live, and the social interactions between staff or family and the AD resident. The traditional nursing home is a setting that is bustling with activity. Many of the attendants are rushing around trying to deal with the patients' symptoms. The general feeling is not of a quiet, therapeutic environment. Contrary to traditional strategies for care, the low stimulus environmental approach places AD residents in a small, separate wing, apart from other residents. This approach also differs from what could be called "instant AD wings," which often had as many as 35 to 38 beds, and where overstimulation may have occurred in two ways: (1) overstimulation from too many staff members walking in and out of the residents' rooms; and (2) overstimulation caused by the large number of residents in the unit and the consequent noise and activity. Hence, the author recommends no more than 25 beds to a wing. This seems to reduce overall activity levels. To minimize disruptions and noise in a "Low Stimulus AD Wing," the central nursing station is moved outside the unit and the intercom is eliminated.

Specially trained staff function within the "Low Stimulus AD Wing." Social bonding, such as holding hands and sharing rooms, seems to help the residents. Roommate selection is important, and the R.N. carefully monitors roommate compatibilities. Large doors are used to close off the wing, keeping its atmosphere calm and undisturbed by outside noise. Staff members are trained to be therapeutic enablers, not custodial caretakers. The environment is modified because it has been found to have a profound effect on the moods and behaviors of persons with AD. For instance, the wing is closed off by a door because it was found that long halls, unlocked doors, and large, open spaces are overstimulating and noisy and encourage the AD resident to wander or endlessly pace. AD residents are encouraged to eat in small groups of three or four persons, like their families of origin, at U-shaped tables. In traditional nursing home settings, we found that the appetites of AD residents often decreased when they were overstimulated by eating in noisy, busy cafeterias, or understimulated by eating alone in their rooms.

Safety is a high priority for AD staff, and an inoffensive alarm system is used on both of the doors to the unit to keep the AD residents from wandering outside where they are at risk for accidents. High-backed chairs are placed in the hallway of the wing to encourage AD residents to stop and rest. Because physical restraints and lack of exercise are related to overall muscle atrophy and a decline in general health, the use of restraints is de-emphasized and, for most residents, totally eliminated.

Rummaging, that is, constantly going through belongings looking for something, is a common activity of AD residents. Using a symbolic interactionist's perspective, it was found that staff members can keep the AD residents from going through each other's things by acting differently (i.e., by distracting them or gently pulling an arm in another direction). Also, we place a personalized symbol or identification label on all items so that the AD resident often can recognize his or her own possessions. These symbols are preferably chosen by the resident. Some consideration of the resident's earlier special roles and capacities are considered as much as possible in labeling items. For instance, a pencil symbol on the door of a resident who once was an accountant may be something he can identify with. If this pencil symbol is chosen, then it also may be pinned on the resident's shirt and placed on his drawers and cupboards, as well as on bathroom doors to orient him to reality. In addition, doors, rooms, and hallways can be color-coded to orient confused residents. Also, rummaging appears to be reduced by interior furnishings selected to add texture and stimulate interest. Hence, the result of creating symbols and an environment especially for persons with AD is changed actions by AD residents.

Maintaining the resident's dignity is important. A little bulletin board with a picture and short biography of the AD resident, and pictures of his or her family, are placed on the door of each AD resident. This may orient the resident to his or her room and remind the staff and family that the resident is a person, not just a patient. Another approach is to decorate the residents' doors with personal mementos, as these symbols might be useful for some limited reminiscences and reality orientation. The door decorations can be made by the residents, their families, and the staff (Grossman, et al., 1986). The author found increased resident stimulation by designing different textured wall hangings with geometric figures for the hallway, rooms, or laps (for wheelchair bound persons) of residents, and found that the carpet pieces attracted residents' attention and helped them to occupy their time. As residents rest in chairs in the hallway, they are presented with "busy boxes" which are designed to be attached to each resident's geri-chair or table. These boxes contain 20 to 30 items of interest to the resident. The items, determined through the in-home assessment and testing in the AD wing, can be affixed either to a hard board or on the multiple (20 to 30) arms of a stick-like plastic doll which can be attached to a geri-table. The resident's activity items can be attached to the doll's arms so that they cannot be easily torn off or broken. The box, or board or doll, usually is given to the resident two or three times daily.

Families have to be helped to accept the idea of the staff allowing residents to wander in and out of each other's rooms without much restriction. It is believed that when the staff continually stops and restricts the AD resident from wandering, agitation frequently results. Therefore, in a low stimulus unit, residents are allowed to wander under the supervision of aides. In rare cases it may be necessary to install Dutch doors, which are cut in half with the top and bottom opening separately, to keep residents out of each other's possessions or cut down wandering.

Walls should be painted in non-glossy light off-pink, soft blue-gray, or soft yellow colors for calming effects, alternating the colors of the bedrooms to help orient AD residents to their rooms. Doors to bathrooms and other rooms are painted white to orient the AD resident to the rooms. Materials should be highly textured and in contrasting pastels, and should be sound-absorbent. The residents dislike sharp color contrasts in flooring, like strips which make it appear that there are different levels to step over or under, causing the fear of crossing them. High glare surfaces (like shiny, waxed floors), fluorescent lighting, and busy patterns should be eliminated, if possible, to prevent disorientation and falls. Home-like additions to rooms could include a tape player, imitation houseplants, a pet bird, and an aquarium. For AD residents who have always liked animals, pets may have a calming effect. Pets either can be kept in an enclosed outside wandering area used exclusively by AD residents, or there can be days when animals are brought to the nursing home for a "petting day." Music therapy is supplied on a regular basis with the use of taped, slow tempo, soft music developed specially for those with dementia. Sing-alongs sometimes work out well in a small activity room in the AD wing.

Staff training in specific areas of social interaction with AD residents is critically important. Figures B,C,D, and E address training for agitation, incontinence, mealtime procedure, and hygiene.

Therapies are sociologically significant and are extensive and varied in "Low Stimulus AD Wings." For example, regular, daily exercise is encouraged both indoors and outdoors and is tailored especially to the resident's previous behaviors (e.g., outdoor exercise if she was an "outdoors person"). As previously stated, complications from immobility often lead to other diseases or the premature deaths of AD residents, therefore, persons with AD. AD should be given as much exercise as possible (see Figure F).

STAFF DEVELOPMENT

Shortcuts are seldom taken where quality and excellence of care, as opposed to profit, is the prime motive of the nursing home. Therefore, the better nursing homes frequently use social gerontologists as AD wing consultants. Some sociologists are expertly-trained in understanding the group dynamics of the elderly, and studying the effects of environment on behavior. Affiliated Nursing Homes asked the author, a clinical sociologist and gerontologist, to develop an AD wing and to provide ongoing training for the staff. The author uses a plethora of pedagogical aids for staff education, such as: lectures, handouts, computer assistance, audio-visual aids, role-playing staff-resident social interaction, use of task breakdown with AD residents, personalized learning, keeping staff journals, and weekly staff meetings assessing AD resident assets.

Some clinical social gerontologists are skilled in communication techniques which can be employed with mentally disabled persons. Social interaction with any AD resident can be difficult, but good communication skills and positive staff actions often can prevent catastrophic behaviors. The author encourages the staff to use the communication techniques presented here with AD residents.

According to the author's research, that persons with AD often overreact to social situations is due not as much to organic processes as to negative staff or family actions. For instance, when asked to do something, the person with AD may respond in a huff and angrily say, "Do you think I'm stupid?" This behavior is sometimes called a "catastrophic" reaction. A few steps that can help prevent catastrophic behaviors are: take activities one step at a time, reassure the AD person after each completed step if the AD person is upset, remain calm and remove her or him from upsetting stimuli, and, avoid using restraints because these will only increase panic.

Operant Conditioning. Clinicians also can use reinforcement to encourage, increase, decrease, or cease the actions of advanced AD residents. Among target behaviors for reinforcement are self-care, verbal behavior, walking, eating, incontinence, purposeful activity, appropriate behavior, and sociability. (See Eisdorfer, et al., 1981 for a review of these studies.) Operant conditioning, from a symbolic interactionist perspective, is changing the care-giver's acts in order to change the AD resident's acts. The first strategy is to identify the behavior of the AD resident that needs to be changed, and to select an appropriate alternative behavior, which must be specific. To select a specific alternative to an AD resident's behavior, care-givers are required to analyze the resident's behavior by asking who, what, where, when, and how questions.

The second procedure is to identify and change the events or circumstances that immediately preceded the "problem behavior." Some circumstances that maintain problem behavior in AD residents are related to time, staff or family, location, and the social situation.

The third step of operant conditioning is identifying actions in the staff that reinforce the AD resident's negative acts. For example, consider the AD resident who screams when the resident assistant is out of the room. Typically, a staff member will run into the resident's room in response to the yelling, which then stops. In this way, the screaming is reinforced by the care-giver's actions.

The fourth step in operant conditioning is to identify the reinforcers, or rewards, that eliminate problem behaviors. Using the previous example, to eliminate or reduce the screaming it would be necessary to change the contingency for the care-giver's presence in the room. Thus, the resident assistant usually would come into the room when the AD resident was not yelling, and generally not come into the room when the AD resident was screaming for no reason. Thus the AD resident learns that screaming brings no one and calmness brings the staff into the room.

An excellent way to change actions is to reward the AD resident. There are no reinforcers that apply to all residents but in the most cases praise is best, while other reinforcers being are the provision of food and desired activities or objects. Each AD resident's pre-admission and ongoing assessment reveals idiosyncratic needs. AD residents respond poorly to criticism (e.g., the use of words like "that's bad," "nasty," and "no"), and often respond well to multiple reinforcers. It is important that the reinforcer be given immediately after the AD resident enacts the desired behavior. Also, it may be necessary to continue reinforcement indefinitely in order to maintain desired behaviors. For instance, consider Mr. X who sometimes shouts "NO!" when asked to put on his shirt. When Mr. X does put on his shirt by himself, the staff should praise him and pat him affectionately on the shoulder. Initially it may be necessary to cue the desired action by holding up or pointing to Mr. X's shirt. As soon as Mr. X puts on his shirt (target behavior), the staff need to praise him and pat him on the shoulder (reinforcement).

SUMMARY

Employing a symbolic interactionist perspective to train the staff and family of AD residents to change *their* negative actions creates a therapeutic environment for AD residents. Care-givers need ongoing education about the nature of the AD disability and how to cultivate remaining abilities in AD residents. The social environment also plays a big role in the life of an AD resident in a nursing home. The "Low Stimulus AD Wing," coupled with the quality education of staff and family, can create positive social change in the attitudes and behaviors of the care-givers as well as the AD resident. While more sociological research is needed on both AD environments and staff behaviors, the results of our studies indicate that AD residents who are placed in AD "Low Stimulus Wings" gain weight, are calmer, require less medication and restraint, and have fewer violent and aggressive behaviors than AD residents in traditional nursing home settings or persons with AD who remain in their own homes during the final two stages of AD. The writer encourages other gerontologists to develop meaningful research projects on different care strategies for AD residents in long-term care settings.

REFERENCES

Brody, E. M., C. Cole, and M. Moss. 1973. Individualizing therapy for the mentally impaired aged. *Social Casework* October: 453–61.

Coons, D. H. 1983. The therapeutic milieu. In W. Reichel, ed. *Clinical Aspects of Aging.* Baltimore, MD: Williams and Wilkins

Coons, D. H. and S. E. Weaverdyck. 1986. Wesley Hall: A residential unit for persons with Alzheimer's Disease and related disorders. In E. D. Paira, ed. *Therapeutic Interventions for the Person with Dementia.* New York: Haworth Press, 29–53.

Eisdorfer, C., D. Cohen, and C. Preston. 1981. Behavioral and psychological therapies for the older patient with cognitive impairment. In N. E. Miller and G. D. Cohen, eds. *Clinical Aspects of Alzheimer's Disease and Senile Dementia (Aging* Vol. 15.) New York: Raven Press, 209–24.

Grossman, H. D., et al. 1986. The milieu standard for care of dementia in a nursing home. *Journal of Gerontological Social Work* 9 (2): 73–87.

Gwyther, L. P. 1985. *Care of Alzheimer's Patients: A Manual for Nursing Home Staff.* Washington, DC: American Health Care Association.

Hall, G., M. V. Kirschling, and S. Todd. 1986. Sheltered freedom—an Alzheimer's unit in an ICF. *Geriatric Nursing* (May/June):132–37.

Haugen, P. K. 1985. Behavior of patients with dementia. *Danish Medical Bulletin* 32 (Supplement No. 1):62–65.

Hellebrandt, F. 1978. A comment: the senile demented in our midst. *The Gerontologist* 18 (1):67–70.

Heston, L. L. and J. A. White. 1983. *Dementia: A Practical Guide to Alzheimer's Disease and Related Illnesses.* New York: W. H. Freeman.

Kapust, L. R. 1982. Living with dementia: the on-going funeral. *Social Work in Health Care* (Summer) 7(4):79–91.

Lawton, M. P. 1981. Sensory deprivation and the effect of the environment on management of the patient with senile dementia. In N. Miller and G. Cohen, eds. *Clinical Aspects of Alzheimer's Disease and Senile Dementia.* New York: Raven Press.

Mace, N. L. and P. V. Rabins 1981. *The 36-hour day: A Family Guide to Caring for Persons with Alzheimer's Disease, Related Dementing Illnesses, and Memory Loss in Later Life.* Baltimore, MD: John Hopkins University Press.

Mead, G. H. 1934. *Mind, Self and Society.* Chicago: University of Chicago Press.

Powell, L. S. and K. Courtice. 1986. *Alzheimer's Disease: A Guide for Families.* Reading, MA: Addison-Wesley.

Robertson, I. 1987. *Sociology.* New York: Worth Publishers.

U. S. Department of Health and Human Services. 1984. *Alzheimer's Disease*. Washington, DC: U. S. Government Printing Office.

Woods, R. T. and P. G. Britton. 1985. *Clinical Psychology and the Elderly*. Rockville: Aspen Systems Corporation.

Zarit, S. H., N. K. Orr and J. M. Zarit. 1985. *The Hidden Victims of Alzheimer's Disease*. New York: New York University Press.

Figure A: Stages of Behavior in Alzheimer's Disease*

Stage 1:

Depression, mood swings, apathy, withdrawal
Difficulty focusing attention
Decreasing interest in environment and present affairs
Decreasing social courtesies
Uncertainty in actions
Short-term memory loss
Personality alterations (such as paranoia)
Distractibility

Stage 2:

Verbalization, stereotyping, inappropriate behavior
Hesitation in verbal response
Obvious deficits in memory
Disorientation to time and place
Complaints of neglect or suspiciousness
Forgetting appointments and significant events
Forgetting normal routines
Rummaging, pillaging, and hoarding
Catastrophic behavior

Stage 3 (Usual time of placement in a nursing home due to safety risks):

Disorientation to place and persons
Wandering
Sundowning
Deterioration in motor ability
Immodesty
Communications difficulties (repeating words or perseveration)
Compulsive acts of lip licking, chewing, tapping
Hyperorality
Mirror signs (not recognizing his or her own reflection)
Inability to read or write
Seizures (sometimes)
Delusions and/or hallucinations

Stage 4 (terminal stage):

Loss of all long term memory
Swallowing problems
Ataxia
Aphasia
Visual hallucinations
Extreme psychomotor retardation
Inability to communicate or to recognize family
Little or no response to stimuli
Susceptibility to infections
Marked weight loss
Becoming bedridden
Death

*None of these stages is mutually exclusive.

Figure B: Handling Agitated Residents

Check to see if resident needs to go to bathroom.
Check to see if resident is hungry.
Allow resident to rock in a rocking chair.
Take resident for a brisk walk.
Keep voice quiet and soothing.
Avoid use of chemical restraints.
Use 1–2 ounces of wine (if not medically contraindicated).
Avoid physical restraints unless resident is in danger of injuring self or others.
Ask family members to assist during these times.

Figure C: Modifications for Incontinence

Affix a sign or figure to the bathroom door.
Paint bathroom door a bright color.
Remove waste baskets from room.
Install toilet seat of a different color from the floor.
Install high toilet seat of a different color from the floor (to cue person to the toilet).
Install grab bars in bathroom.
Make sure bathroom is nearby and in sight.
Dress resident in clothes that are easy to remove.
Set up individual bathroom schedules.
Use night lights to the bathroom.
Set up a bathroom schedule during the day.
Do not scold the patient for incontinence.
Use in and out types catheters if they are needed.
Limit fluid intake after 8 p.m.
Take resident to the bathroom before bed.

Figure D: Mealtime Protocol

Use kidney- or U-shaped tables.
Offer one food at a time.
Feed residents in small groups of 3 or 4.
Keep the environment calm and quiet.
Occasionally, use soft music.
Use plastic bowls and glasses.
Use heavy silverware.
Use bright colors on the table to stimulate appetite.
Keep damp washcloths under dishes.
Keep a dish of finger foods available.
Remind resident to swallow.
Check the temperature of foods.
Monitor the dislikes and likes of AD residents.

Figure E: Hygiene

Follow the person's old established routine.
Place only 2–3 inches of water in the tub.
Refrain from arguing.
Gently tell AD resident, step-by-step which body part to wash.
Allow the person to do as much as possible for himself or herself.
Lay out the resident's clothes in the order they are to be put on.
Keep the resident's hair cut short.

Figure F: Exercise Program

Encourage daily exercise, preferably outside.
Alternate schedules of activity and rest.
Create predictable daily routines.
Include activities a few hours before bedtime.
Avoid keeping AD resident in bed during the day, except at designated resting periods.

Figure G: Communication Techniques with AD Residents

Face the resident with your body sideways to him or her.
Maintain a distance of 1–2 feet from the resident.
Hold eye contact.
Smile often.
Do not frown.
Make sure the resident has his or her hearing aid and glasses on.
Use a low-pitched, slow speaking voice.
Eliminate distracting background noises.
Use short, simple sentences.
Ask only one question at a time.
Repeat key words if the person does not understand.
Use many nonverbal cues.
Ask specific questions (e.g., "Does your stomach hurt?" rather than "How do you feel?").

25

Rituals and Ideology: The Case of the Funeral in Non-Religious Kibbutzim[1]

Devorah Kalekin-Fishman, and Avigdor Klingman

"A kibbutz is a particular type of socialist community . . . [whose] . . . founders were inspired by a vision . . . of a new society to be created," and they shared the belief that there were unlimited opportunities for shaping new institutions, as well as for developing a "new man" (Spiro, 1983: 2). Buber (1983) described the kibbutz as a "religious Gemeinschaft" because it embodied the sacred fulfillment of a humanist dream. As the kibbutz evolved from a revolutionary commune to an orderly society in which the guiding motivation is affect (Talmon-Garber, 1983), several life-cycle rituals were specially created and institutionalized. It no longer was accepted, for example, that a funeral was no more than an interment (Ben-Gurion, 1963; Rubin, 1979).[2] The development of relatively stable practices provides an opportunity to study a rare social phenomenon, the synthesis of ritual in an ideologically aware socio-cultural context that is consciously attempting to preserve its character while undergoing change (Gorni et al., 1987; Krausz, 1983; Lieblich, 1983).

This chapter will discuss the practices related to death, mourning, and bereavement that have developed in non-religious kibbutzim, and examine how the funeral reflects the central values of the kibbutz way of life. The analysis will focus on the formal acts, the ideological assumptions embedded in them, and their implications for social structure. On the basis of this analysis, the degree to which kibbutz practices are adequate to the immediate needs of mourners and the community will be discussed.

The Kibbutz as a Radical Movement

With a population of about 105,000 (Yadlin, 1987), the non-religious kibbutz movements are autonomous networks of relatively closed communities.[3] In them, the means of production are the property of all members. Work is divided according to ability, while profits are distributed according to need. The community controls methods of child-rearing and education, attuning them to the perceived needs of both adults and children at different stages of life (Rabin and Hazan, 1973). Policies are the province of "town meetings," and decisions are executed by committees on which all the members of the community are eventually likely to serve. The kibbutz movements exercise some wider political influence through their affiliation with political parties.

Barzel (1987) has summarized what he terms "the unique kibbutz ethos" in the following "constitutive principles:"

1. Organic and comprehensive equality;
2. Total common responsibility;
3. Organic belongingness and direct democracy;
4. Non-exploitation of the work of others and moderate habits of consumption;
5. No class distinctions based on the division of labor;
6. A missionary commitment, i.e., a commitment to the transformation of society as a whole (cf. also, Ben-Gurion, 1963; Lieblich, 1984; Spiro, 1983).

There are two questions about these constitutive principles that are of central concern: their relationship to the social structure, and their implications for the individual kibbutz member.

The ethos refers to a highly flexible, intimate, democratic social structure. Such an image is put in question by recent economic trends. Committed as it is to rationality, equality, and collectivism (Cohen, 1966; Krausz, 1983), the kibbutz is almost by definition a society in transition—a society that adapts to modernity easily. Researchers who monitor these trends have looked into the interaction of modernity and the social structure. Rosner and Shur contend that despite industrialization, kibbutz society is in a "position to successfully prevent the dangers . . . of monopolization of positions of authority, formation of a permanent elite and stratification" (1988:29). Findings from other studies, however, support the claim that "differentiation of status does exist" (Ben-Rafael, 1988:11). In Ben-Rafael's view, there are serious obstacles to mobility, because under conditions of modernity, groups with access to resources upon which the kibbutz is heavily dependent coalesce.

These issues have implications for understanding and evaluating the environment that the kibbutz has created for the "new man" and for fulfilling the needs of individual members.

In this chapter, we assume that the way of life of the kibbutz is expressed in significant rituals. These shed light on the practices shaped by kibbutz ideology and on the social relationships that the kibbutz fosters.

THE DEFINITION OF RITUAL AND ITS FUNCTIONS

Rituals are normative collective acts that accord transcendental and social significance to selected changes in the physical-biological sphere, as well as in the realm of personality (Parsons and Lidz, 1967). They are constituted by a prescription which is the discursive basis for the sacred, and by a concrete physical and psychological realization whose source is the social contract (Rappaport, 1979). They ". . . refer to postulated matters about society or ideology" (Moore and Myerhoff, 1977:22), and are specially suited for reaffirming the social ethos, providing a framework for communicating values, life-styles, and world views to participants (MacCannell, 1976).

A strategic point of departure for studying how rituals function is the ritual of the funeral. The interpretation of death, definition of bereavement, social location of the bereaved, behaviors that are appropriate for meeting death, and feelings evoked, are expressions of the transcendental meanings embedded in each society (Durkheim, 1965; Hertz, 1960). The effectiveness of funeral practices in assuaging the pains of mourning, however, has been said to be correlated with the degree to which they are consonant with the social structure that generates them (Palgi and Abramovitch, 1984).

On the basis of the analysis of the kibbutz as a social form, and of the social functions of ritual, our hypotheses were the following:

- The funeral ritual in the secular kibbutz accords significance to death and bereavement that is in keeping with the constitutive principles of the kibbutz ethos.
- The meanings embodied in the kibbutz funeral are compatible with the communal social structure.
- Thus, the funeral reinforces communal identity and serves to assuage the needs of individuals.

THE STUDY

In a preliminary study of the ways in which non-religious kibbutzim deal with death, mourning, and bereavement and of the implications of these practices, we sought answers to three central questions:

(1) What is the nature of the funeral in non-religious kibbutzim and how is it related to kibbutz ideology?
   (a) What are the funeral practices?
   (b) How are these practices implemented?

(c)   What criteria of value are cited as determining the selection of procedures?

(2)   How is the funeral related to the social structure of the kibbutz?

(a)   What roles are reinforced during bereavement?

(b)   How are societal processes (exchange and reciprocity) reflected or expressed in the funeral?

(3)   In what ways does the funeral confirm the viability of the kibbutz as an environment that meets the individual's needs?

METHODS

Methods for this study included analysis of documents, interviews with kibbutz members, and participant observation at kibbutz funerals. Substantive obstacles to the random collection of quantitative data were encountered. Documents were found to cluster unevenly about salient dates—periods of warfare, or days of crisis in a particular community. Furthermore, because it was necessary to consider the sensibilities and anxieties of the bereaved, we were constrained to non-random sampling in the interviews.

Sampling

Written materials.   The data studied include official guidelines distributed by the membership committees of each of the non-religious kibbutz movements until 1983. An early source of information was a compilation of practices introduced before the 60's (Ben-Gurion, 1963). Additional data used included guidelines compiled for internal use in ten kibbutzim until 1986. Documents dealing with the "way of the kibbutz" in death and bereavement since 1965, found in the central archives of the kibbutz movements, were sampled. These included pieces of writing from the newsletters of each movement for every year from 1970 to 1983. At least ten items were sampled from each of the more extended discussions that appeared in the newsletters during periods of intensive military action—in 1970, 1973, 1978, and 1982.

Interviews.   Interviews were conducted in kibbutzim in the northern and central regions of Israel, selected according to size (up to 300 members and over 300 members) and according to ideological orientation. Altogether, there were 42 interviewees in 32 kibbutzim; among them 15 general secretaries of kibbutzim nine of whom were women), and 27 bereaved (ten of whom were women). A third of those interviewed—four functionaries and ten of the bereaved members—were from the leftist Kibbutz Artzi Movement. The remainder were from the centrist United Kibbutz Movement.

Observations.   The researchers participated in four kibbutz funerals.

Procedures

The study was carried out in two stages. First, we collected the relevant documents—pamphlets, circulars, and newsletters, and summarized the funeral practices and the legitimating criteria cited. The level of agreement was 90 percent when two people analyzed 15 documents independently.

In the second stage of the study, three research assistants, who had been specially coached, interviewed members of kibbutzim with experience of bereavement, and officials who had at some time been responsible for funeral arrangements. The general secretary in each kibbutz facilitated our access to people and none of the people we asked to meet refused us.

Interviews, which lasted from 1.5 to 3.5 hours, were conducted in interviewees' homes during their free time. Respondents were asked to describe the official practices of the kibbutz in which they live, and reactions to the arrangements were probed.[4] Responses were analyzed and compared with the formal guidelines.

While we were collecting data we attended funerals in four different kibbutzim—one from the Kibbutz Artzi movement, and three in kibbutzim of the United Kibbutz Movement.

FINDINGS

The Nature of the Kibbutz Funeral

Practices Recommended[5]   In 1967, the year of the Six Day War, the Central Membership Committee of the Union of Kvutzot and Kibbutzim (part of the United Kibbutz Movement of today) for the first time published detailed recommendations for dealing with bereavement and mourning. In 1970, the Kibbutz Artzi published its first paper on the subject. Amendments published during the 70's were formulated by the central secretariats, circulated to kibbutzim, and discussed in weekly newsletters. These documents specified practices related to notifying members of the death, digging the grave, interring the body, and arranging for community mourning and appropriate commemoration of the deceased. Among the recommendations were the provision that gravestones be of "equal or similar" size, form, and content for all; that the kibbutz newsletter be dedicated to the life and work of a newly deceased member; that an archive of outstanding events of each member's life be maintained; and that "corners of commemoration" be set up in every kibbutz.

The guidelines recommend three days of public mourning for a deceased member or child, during which no films are shown, no music is played, and no public meetings are allowed. One day of public mourning is suitable for the parent of a kibbutz member; and no public mourning is cited for a person who was not officially connected with the kibbutz. It also was recommended that the community honor all its dead on a special day of commemoration.

The extensive correspondence in the newsletters relating to every detail that was communicated shows that the formal recommendations were highly pertinent to members' concerns.

Practices of Burial, Mourning and Bereavement Implemented. Interviewees' accounts shed light on the extent to which rituals were instigated as "automatic rather than thought out behavior" (Goody, 1977:32). All the interviewees were well informed about their community's customs and agreed that they follow a set pattern. The framework of the funeral was described in a similar way in the 32 kibbutzim sampled.

In Table 1, the acts, designated agencies, times, and localities prominent in the funeral are presented in the chronological order that was presented as "what is always done." Kibbutz secretaries and the local Committee of Mourning and Bereavement handle the details of the funeral. Local guidelines mention specific names and places. They are revised when there are changes in the distribution of tasks or when new buildings (a club-house, a library) make it necessary to change the placement of the coffin, or the path of the funeral procession. Each kibbutz makes its own rules for public mourning.[6.] To clarify the range of practices implemented, the stages of the funeral are described below in some detail.

Pre-Burial Practices

The kibbutz nurse, or the general secretary, is first notified of a death, and one or the other notifies members of the family. Then an announcement of the death and of the time of burial is placed on the central bulletin board which has been cleared of all other notices. The body is prepared for burial while in the hospital, brought to the kibbutz in a specially-prepared coffin, and laid on a platform in a central place. At the appointed time, before the funeral procession starts, the family is seated nearby and members approach to express their sympathy. At a funeral observed in one kibbutz, music that the deceased had been known to love was played during this time, and colleagues of the deceased eulogized him *before* the descent to the cemetery.

In most of the kibbutzim with which we had contact, preburial arrangements for transportation of the body and digging the grave were dealt with by members. In some Kibbutzim, there is a group of people who "specialize" in these tasks. In others, the person in charge of the work roster recruits a group when-

Table 1
Syntax of Funeral Practices.

Act	Agency	Time	Locality
Notice to family	Kibbutz nurse	Immediately	Home
Notice to kibbutz	Secretary	Same day	On bulletin board
Arranging for coffin, grave	Secretary	Immediately	Secretariat
Bringing body home	Driver on work roster	Same day	Hospital
Placing	Members of committee	Same day 1.5 hrs.	"Club" platform
Procession	Kin and others	Same day 0.5 hr	Car (riding) path (walking)
Prayers and words	Kin and friends	Same day 0.5 hr	Cemetery
Eulogy	Friend(s), secretary, colleagues	Same day 0.25 hr ea	Cemetery
Interment	Friends	Same day 0.25 hr	Cemetery
Return	Kin, colleagues, all	Same day 0.25 hr	Rooms
Commemoration	Kin and friends	7 days later	Cemetery
Commemoration	Kin and friends	1 year later	Dining hall

Kin = family of the deceased who are members of the kibbutz as well as those who are non-members
Friends = members of the kibbutz
Colleagues = people who have worked with the deceased outside the kibbutz community

ever there is a death in the community. In one kibbutz among those studied, arrangements are made through the regional government office of the Ministry of Religion, as in the non-kibbutz communities of the area.

The Funeral Procession

The procession usually is held in the afternoon so that all those who work (either in the kibbutz or outside it) can take part. Motor vehicles convey the coffin and the family to the cemetery, while the other participants go on foot to the area of the newly-dug grave. Recommended practice is to bury the dead in chronological order. But ten of the communities that we studied set aside family plots, and 31 of the 32 kibbutzim had a separate burial ground for soldiers. This was the location of military funerals.

We were told that attendance at funerals varied from 30 percent to almost 100 percent of the members. Rates of attendance were determined by members' evaluation of each case. "Everybody" attended the funerals of members who had been popular, or who had played an outstanding role in community life. The same was true of the funerals of people who had died "unnatural" deaths— funerals for soldiers or young people. By contrast, funerals of the old or those who had "withdrawn from kibbutz affairs," often were attended by no more than 30 to 50 percent of the members. Still fewer attended funerals of members' parents, or of transients.

The Interment

The nine kibbutzim in our study that belong to the Kibbutz Artzi movement observed complete silence at the interment except for a eulogy. In the 23 kibbutzim sampled from the United Kibbutz Movement, texts that were thought suitable—poems by contemporary writers, quotations from books loved by the deceased, sections of the writings of outstanding thinkers, or sections from the Bible—were read. Two kibbutzim incorporated traditional Jewish prayers in their service. We learned that kibbutzim generally arrange for a full-scale religious service at the interment if members of the family of the deceased request it. And a military burial is accompanied by a religious service unless the family objects and is willing to forego the honor. When the service is completed, participants lay flowers or stones on the mound, and remain in the cemetery until the family has left the burial ground.

Eulogies generally described the "way of life" of the deceased, the work he or she had done, and details of his or her contributions to the kibbutz. Speakers who knew the deceased well in childhood told about the family background and the "road to the kibbutz." There is an abundance of material on those who had been very active in kibbutz affairs, either on the local or the national level. Kibbutz officials complained, however, that it was sometimes hard to find someone to speak about the deceased. On the demise of an elderly kibbutz member who spent his or her life performing routine tasks, it was often found that "there is nothing to say." Then the duty was left to the kibbutz secretary—a situation considered shameful. One secretary reported that when this happened, she brought pressure to bear on peers of the deceased, even to the point of threatening them that if they refused to compose a eulogy, there might not be anyone to eulogize them when their time came!

Post-Burial Customs: Public Mourning

In practice, the days of public observance were variously counted from the day of the demise, the funeral, or, the day after. Only five of the kibbutzim that we studied observed the full three days. Most counted two days of mourning including the day of the interment. In practice, children under 18 and volunteers were not constrained to participate in collective mourning at all.

Post-Burial Customs: Private Mourning

The family returns to their apartment and the kibbutz kitchen provides them with food, as well as refreshments for those who make consolation visits. Behaviors are not prescribed for the family in any of the documents, nor was there a consensus about behavior among the interviewees. The family is in full charge of its own observance of mourning. They are consulted in regard to all the procedures for which alternative practices are available.

Criteria for Deciding on What Practices to Adopt. In the interviews, as in the newsletters, criteria cited for accepting or rejecting funeral practices were related to whether or not a proposed procedure was considered an "authentic expression" of the kibbutz and its ideological principles. Interviewees agreed that the funeral had to be carried off impeccably. This was the measure of its effectiveness. Beyond this, two ideological principles were foremost among the criteria that determined the nature of the funeral practices. These were "organic and comprehensive equality" and "total common responsibility."

There were several opinions about the best way to express the principle of equality. Some argued that each individual's life experience is unique and the most suitable way to mark uniqueness was by expressing feeling. Silence was considered the deepest expression. Others insisted that equality was best measured in numbers: rates of attendance at the interment, the length and detail of the eulogy, and the number of visitors that came to console the mourners. They argued for the participation of all the members of the kibbutz.

In the less "devoutly" secular communities, it was claimed that equality and feeling were embedded in tradition. The bereaved father of a soldier killed in battle insisted that there could be no consolation in a secular funeral. They argued for deriving the funeral agenda—immediate interment, commemorations on the 7th and the 30th days, as well as on the anniversary—from Jewish religious tradition.

"Total common responsibility" also was cited in connection with different kinds of behaviors. Those who argued that mourners needed privacy, felt that the leniency with which bereavement was defined was evidence of the common responsibility for their fate. Most of the mourners, however, claimed that they had difficulty in deciding how to spend the time during which they were "officially" in mourning. They felt that the community's responsibility should be signalled by active involvement.

The Funeral and its Relation to the Social Structure of the Kibbutz

In the funeral ritual, roles are inverted and reclassified (cf. Turner, 1977). This process includes a release "from structure into communitas" which is followed by a "return [that is] revitalized by the experience" (Turner, 1969:129). Findings about the relationship between the funeral and the social structure of the kibbutz demonstrate that this process is not easily available in the secular kibbutz.

Roles that are Reinforced in Bereavement. The content of the kibbutz category, "member," is radically altered for the dead and the bereaved.

Table 2 shows the ordinary, or natural, as well as the extraordinary distribution of significant roles among the living and the dead. Each of the roles of worker, consumer, collaborator, neighbor, and friend is associated with an array of qualities and orientations. The ultimate role—builder of the community, figure of reference—is assigned routinely to all the dead while it is an extraordinary distinction for the living.

Members of the kibbutz are called upon to deal with the event of death from a standpoint that is oriented to the collect and universal, but specific to the achievements of the deceased. Some affect is assumed, but not institutionalized. Those designated as mourners, however, are thrust out of this collective experience. The bereaved are separated from their work roles, and positioned in the status of passive consumers and beneficiaries—roles over-burdened with "rights" and, overtly, with no "duties" (Biddle, 1971). The mourner's orientation is by definition emotional, particular, diffuse, ascriptive, and oriented to self.

The Funeral's Relationship to Social Exchange and Reciprocity. Concomitantly, normal kibbutz social exchange and reciprocity are suspended. In the kibbutz, which is governed by communal property relationships, no member has an enforceable right to appropriate communal property or exclude another

Table 2
Allocation of Roles: Ordinary and Extraordinary

Orientation	ORDINARY	EXTRAORDINARY
	Living	**Dead**
Particular	Young	
Diffuse	Collaborating	
Ego	Serving the community	
	Consuming	
	Autonomous at leisure	
	Participating	
	Dying	**Living**
Universal	Old	
Specific	Ill	
Collective	No longer collaborating	
	Needs to be served	
	Isolated	
	Dead	**Alive**
Universal	Builder of the community	
Collective	Member of reference group	
	Bereaved	**Other members**
Universal	Consumer	
Specific	Beneficiary	
Collective	Affect	
	Other members	**Bereaved**
Particular	Producer	
Diffuse	Contributor	
Ego	Affective neutrality	

member from using it (Willer and Urban, 1984).[7] Instead, members of kibbutzim "exchange" energy and investments of time. They are expected to show reciprocity in providing services to the community as a whole. In the condition of bereavement, reciprocity and exchange are displaced to the realm of intangibles: empathy, attention, and time for socializing and communicating.

The degree to which these human resources are mobilized for a member in need turns out to depend on principles of stratification. According to data collected from the newsletters and in interviews, more of these resources are available for deceased members who were most popular and outstanding. It was claimed that the members who were identified with the routine jobs of the kibbutz were less likely to be allotted intangible resources.

Communal Intervention in Mourning: The Viability of the Kibbutz as an Environment that Fulfills Individual Needs. The bereaved family become key figures in a situation for which only a partial script is available. They are "on-stage" before and during the burial, but they are required to sit back, somewhat like an audience, and receive whatever acts of consolation may be forthcoming during the period of mourning. Yet they are responsible for defining that period and for giving it structure. The relationship of the role of mourner to that of kibbutz member is undefined, for bereavement reinforces the ties of kinship.

Bereaved interviewees stated, moreover, that they were constantly aware of being under observation, although kibbutz functionaries and many members were careful not to discuss the loss. They felt that they had to negotiate "an acceptable bereavement." "The kibbutz" expected the mourners to be "quiet and cultured," to behave with restraint at the funeral and on all occasions of commemoration. The implicit social demand to overcome sorrow and join in social activities again was expressed in the logic of context as: "it is not nice to cry" and "do not let your grief show" (Garfinkel, 1975).

Mourners generally accepted these rules as appropriate, but in return they expected that their needs would be intuited and met. Two aspects of the situation militated against achieving mutual understandings "intuitively." One aspect was the tension between the orientations of family and community. Talmon-Garber (1965) pointed out that the kibbutz had to defend itself against "the tendency to revert to a familistic division of labor." This is held in check by emphasizing collectivism and extending "organizational units of rationalization and specialization" (1983: 275). During the period of mourning, these mechanisms disappear. The gathering to regain inner strength (communitas) is experienced by close relatives, whether or not they belong to the kibbutz. Bereavement affected the normative intimacy of kibbutz members as significant others. The rhetoric of "our crops. . . . our kitchen. . . . our machines. . . . our sons and daughters . . . ." did not apply to grief. The mourner was thus confronted with contradictions that could not be dealt with on an individual basis without cost to the community. At this crossing of two forms of existence, the collective project of membership and friendship was defeated (see also, Maron, 1987). The image of the collective that was reinforced in the minds of the bereaved (as evidenced in the interviews) was bureaucratic, a hierarchical structure that exercised expertise and responded selectively to requests.

Another aspect of kibbutz practices that prevented intuitive understandings was the lack of symbolic acts that signalled the mourner's reaggregation into the collective. The decision to return to work is left to the mourners and there is no formalized public response to ease the transition.

DISCUSSION

From the analysis of materials related to death, mourning, and bereavement, it appears that the non-religious kibbutzim in this study have indeed developed a funeral ritual. Their practices are formalized, well-known, and performed "automatically" on the occasion of a death (Goody, 1977; Middleton, 1977). They include conventional sets of acts intended to be meaningful, referring "to postulated matters about society [and] ideology" (Moore and Myerhoff, 1977:22). It is therefore of interest to see what this ritual implies about the nature of the kibbutz as a society, and how this comprehensive picture relates to the needs of the individual.

The funeral created in the kibbutzim studied accords significance to this life-cycle crisis that is only partially in keeping with the constitutive principles of the kibbutz ethos as formulated by Barzel (1987). In contrast to the ideal of "comprehensive equality" for all deceased members of the kibbutz, funeral practices expose "a division of laborers" that is at least analogous to class distinctions. This is signalled in the inequalities between the funerals in the wake of routine deaths and of those in the wake of the non-routine deaths as cited from the interviews.

The kibbutz is a closely-knit network in which economic and political ties are congruent with friendship ties (Rubin, 1979). This is the basis for "direct democracy" and the "organic belongingness" of each individual. Mourners are the focus of communal concern, which is expressed in their release from the constraints of rational scheduling. This, however, does not ease the transitions. The care and consideration often cause anomie and a feeling of being marginal to the real events of kibbutz life. These feelings are intensified by the fact that throughout the period of bereavement, mourners violate principles of "non-exploitation of the work of others" and "irrational consumption."[8]

From the analysis of the funeral in non-religious kibbutzim, it is concluded that the kibbutz has not yet found the fusion of form and content in this ritual that meets the needs of the community and of the individual (see Rappaport, 1979). In many ways, the kibbutz funeral is a concrete, formal statement of farewell. But the variations in the prescribed funeral service, from complete silence to readings from literature, undermines its unifying impact. The individual experience of mourning, on the other hand, is bereft of structure and pre-scription. The benevolent "liberation" of the mourner from all obligations does not serve the need for stability in readjusting to a world without a loved one. And as we have seen, the benevolent interest that the kibbutz displays is inter-preted by the mourner as pressure to conform to unwritten rules.

Kibbutz rituals are the outcome of shifts in social structure and a conscious bid to secure the ideological basis of this form of society. By confronting kibbutz ideology with its ritual practice, some of the moral paradoxes to be dealt with have been uncovered. The needs of the mourners that are not met by kibbutz funeral and mourning practices are a force toward re-establishing the social contract of the kibbutz within the framework of traditional religion. This would be a complete negation of the basis for the formation of this society (Helman, 1987).

We recommend that kibbutzim re-examine the ritual of the funeral with a view to resolving some of the moral paradoxes. Even in the short run, trained ritual specialists "may help to promote responses by the bereaved that are inconsistent with anger and aggression" (Rosenblatt et al., 1972: 271) and alienation.

NOTES

1. We thank Ephraim Buchriss, Drorith Cohen, and Inbal Yagen for their help in conducting the field work.

2. Kibbutzim had sought to develop social practices that would reflect the secular, collectivist values so fundamental to the kibbutz way of life. Thus, Jewish religious holidays were not observed unless they coincided with celebrations of community events. None of the traditionally defined life stages was marked by ceremony or ritual. When baby boys were circumcized, for example, at the age of eight days as prescribed by the Jewish religion, the circumcision was performed by the kibbutz doctor in the name of hygiene. Instead of having marriage ceremonies, couples applied to the secretariat for a "family room." Funerals were no more than hasty interments (Bartolke et al., 1980; Krausz, 1983; Krook, 1968; Lieblich, 1984; Rubin, 1979; Talmon-Garber, 1965). Until the 1960's, every death that occurred was marked by practices improvised by each community (cf. Ben-Gurion, 1963; Rubin, 1982).

3. There are two non-religious kibbutz movements. The Kibbutz Artzi Movement represents kibbutzim with populations of 150 to about 400 members, destined, according to the ideology, to serve as the nucleus of a socialist society. The United Kibbutz Movement includes kibbutzim with 600 to 1000 members whose ideology is nationalist and expansionist. But it also represents smaller kibbutzim or "kvutzot" whose ideology is based on the perception of agriculture as a "religion," and the kibbutz as the embodiment of an ideal of brotherhood.

4. Interviewees were also asked to elaborate on their feelings in attending funerals, their reactions to various practices, and the degree to which the kibbutz succeeds in providing networks of support. For data and findings on support networks, see Kalekin-Fishman & Klingman, (forthcoming).

5. Material quoted here was culled from the weekly newsletters of 32 representative kibbutzim filed in the archives of the kibbutz movements at: Beth Hashita, Ef'al, Giv'at Haviva, and Hulda.

6. One interviewee described the implementation of the funeral in his kibbutz as follows: "We have a faded page that is passed on from one kibbutz secretary to the next. It begins with the instructions, 'Take the identification cared of the deceased and go to L.' This means: 'Go to the carpenter with evidence of the measurements of the deceased so that he will be able to prepare the coffin.' Further instructions tell the secretary how to arrange for the digging of the grave, how to mobilize the vehicles necessary for transporting the deceased and the family during the funeral, and so on."

7. Willer and Urban (1984) claim that there are varieties of exchange according to the types of

property rights involved. Where "exclusion, alienation, appropriation and reciprocity" are enforceable, the mutual ceding of property rights can be practiced.

8. This is exacerbated for kibbutz mourners who have lost a soldier. By law, parents, widows, and children have the right to rather high sums of money as compensation, in the form of monthly allotments for life. They are also entitled to purchase luxury goods at reduced prices. These arrangements, which were designed to ease the plight of the bereaved who have lost a source of support, perpetuate the kibbutz mourners' deviance. Interviewees in this position complained of the conflicts that regularly arise because the community may not approve of these privileges.

REFERENCES

Attir, M. O., B. Holzner, and Z. Suda. 1981. *Directions of Change: Modernization Theory, Research, and Realities* Boulder, CO: Westview.

Bartolke, K. 1980. Introduction: Motivations and challenges of an international symposium on the kibbutz. In K. Bartolke, T. Bergmann and L. Liegle, eds. *Integrated Cooperatives in the Industrial Society: The Example of the Kibbutz.* Assen: Van Gorcum.

Barzel, A. 1987. Ideals, principles and their embodiment in reality. In Y. Gorni, Y. Oved, and I. Paz., *Communal Life.* Efal: Yad Tabenkin and Transaction, 37–48.

Ben-Gurion, A. 1963. *Mourning.* Ha-Histadrut Ha-Klalit shel Ha-Ovdim, Ha-Merkaz Le-Hinuch ule-Tarbut (mimeographed pamphlet).

Ben-Rafael, E. 1988. The kibbutz as modern stratification. Tel Aviv University: mimeo.

Biddle, B. 1971. *Role Theory: Expectations, Identities, Behaviors.* New York: Academic Press.

Buber, M. 1983 [1949]. An experiment that did not fail. In E. Krausz, ed. *The Sociology of the Kibbutz.* New Brunswick and London: Transaction, 25–35.

Cohen, E. 1966. Progress and communality: Value dilemmas in the collective movement. *International Review of Community Development* 15–16: 3–18.

———1983. The structural transformation of the kibbutz. In E. Krausz, ed. *The Sociology of the Kibbutz.* New Brunswick and London: Transaction, 75–114.

D'Aquili, E. G., C. D. Laughlin, Jr. and J. McManus, eds. 1979. *The Spectrum of Ritual.* New York: Columbia University.

Durkheim, E. 1965 [1915]. *The Elementary Forms of the Religious Life.* New York: Macmillan.

Geertz, C. 1980. Blurred genres: The refiguration of social thought. *American Scholar* 49:165–79.

Gluckman, M. 1962. *Essays on the Ritual of Social Relations.* Manchester, England: University of Manchester.

Goody, J. 1977. Against 'Ritual': Loosely structured thoughts on a loosely defined topic. In S.F. Moore and B. G. Myerhoff, eds. *Secular Ritual.* Assen/Amsterday: Van Gorcum.

Gorni, Y., Y. Oved, and I. Paz, eds. 1987. *Communal Life.* Efal: Yad Tabenkin and Transaction.

Helman, A. 1987. The inclination to give up kibbutz values in favour of economic efficacy. In Y. Gorni, Y. Oved and I. Paz, eds. 1987. *Communal Life.* Efal: Yad Tabenkin and Transaction, 666–73.

Hertz, R. 1960. *Death and the Right Hand.* Aberdeen, Scotland: Pritchard, Cohen and West.

Krausz, E., ed. 1983. *The Sociology of the Kibbutz.* New Brunswick and London: Transaction.

Krook, D. 1968. Rationalism triumphant: An essay on the kibbutzim of Israel. In P. King and B. C. Parekh, eds. *Politics and Experience: Essays Presented to Michael Oakeshott.* Cambridge, England: Cambridge University.

Lieblich, A. 1984. *Kibbutz Makom* (in Hebrew). Jerusalem: Schocken.

Liebman, C. S. 1982. The rise of neo-traditionalism among Moderate religious circles in Israel (in Hebrew) *Megamoth* 27(3): 231–50.

MacCannell, D. 1976. *The Tourist: A New Theory of the Leisure Class.* New York: Schocken.

McLaren, P. 1986. *Schooling As A Ritual Performance*. London: Routledge and Kegan Paul.

Maron, S. 1987. Centrality of the kibbutz family. In Y. Gorni, Y. Oved and I. Paz, eds. *Communal Life*. Efal: Yad Tabenkin and Transaction, 627-35.

Moore, S. F. and B. G. Myerhoff. 1977. Introduction In S. F. Moore and B. G. Myerhoff, eds. *Secular Ritual*. Assen/Amsterdam: Van Gorcum, 3-24.

Moore, S. F. and B. G. Myerhoff, eds. 1977. *Secular Ritual*. Assen/Amsterdam: Van Gorcum.

Myerhoff, B. 1977. We don't wrap herring in a printed page: Fusion, fictions and continuity in secular ritual. In S. F. Moore and B. G. Myerhoff, eds. *Secular Ritual*. Assen/Amsterdam: Van Gorcum, 199-226.

Palgi, P. and H. Abramovitch. 1984. Death: A cross-cultural perspective. *Annual Review of Anthropology* 13: 385-466.

Parsons, T. and V. Lidz. 1967. Death in American society. In E. S. Shneidman, ed. *Essays in Self-Destruction*. New York: Science House, 133-70.

Rabin, A. I. and B. Hazan, eds. 1973. *Collective Education in the Kibbutz—From Infancy to Maturity*. New York: Springer.

Rappaport, R. A. 1979. *Ecology, Meaning, and Religion*. Richmond, CA: North Atlantic Books.

Rash, Y. 1986. Left, Right religion—The political aspect. In Y. Rash, ed. *Regard and Revere— Renew without Fear* (in Hebrew). Tel Aviv: Sifriat HaPoalim, 194-210.

Rosenblatt, P. C., D. A. Jackson, and R. P. Walsh. 1972. Coping with anger and aggression in mourning. *Omega* 3(4): 271-86.

Rosner, M. and Shur S. 1988. Structural Equality: The Case of the Kibbutz. Haifa: The Institute for Research and Study of the Kibbutz and the Cooperative Idea (mimeographed pamphlet), 35 pp.

Rubin, N. 1979. Social networks and mourning patterns. In A. Carmi and A. DeVries, eds. *The Dying Human*. Ramat Gan: Turtledove.

Shelach, I. 1972. Secular Rituals in Israel (in Hebrew) Unpublished Masters thesis. The Hebrew University of Jerusalem.

Talmon-Garber, Y. 1965. The family in a revolutionary movement: The case of the kibbutz in Israel. In M. Nimkoff, ed. *Comparative Family Systems*. New York: Houghton Mifflin.

Turner, T. S. 1977. Transformation, hierarchy and transcendence: A reformulation of Van Gennep's model of the structure of rites de passage. In S. F. Moore and B. G. Myerhoff, eds. *Secular Ritual*. Assen/Amsterdam: Van Gorcum, 53-70.

Tzaban, Y. 1986. Secular Jewish identity and its content. In Y. Rash, ed. *Regard and Revere— Renew without Fear* (in Hebrew). Tel Aviv: Sifriat Poalim, 97-130.

Turner, V. 1969. *The Ritual Process*. Chicago: Aldine.

Van Gennep, A. 1960 [1909]. *The Rites of Passage*. Chicago: University of Chicago.

Weiler, G. 1976. *Jewish Theocracy* (in Hebrew). Tel Aviv: Am Oved.

Willer, D. and Urban, M. 1984. Social exchange, property and the myth of reciprocity. Paper presented at the Conference of the American Sociological Association, San Antonio, Texas.

Yadlin, A. 1987. Political and Ideological Trends in the Kibbutz Movement in Israel. In Y. Gorni, Y. Oved and I. Paz, eds. *Communal Life*. Efal: Yad Tabenkin and Transaction, 81-97.